Private, Not Hidden

Private, Not Hidden

Smart Privacy for Normal People

Omar Valen

Mindful Pages

Published in 2026

ISBN: 9789376558667 (PB)
ISBN: 9789376556748 (eBook)

Published by

Mindful Pages
Imprint of Alpha Editions LLC
312 W. 2nd St #1834
Casper, WY 82601, USA

This book was developed using advanced writing tools to support the drafting and ideation process. All content has been thoughtfully curated, refined, and reviewed to ensure quality and relevance.

Content

Introduction

In January 2018, a map lit up with tiny points of heat, and somewhere in Helmand Province, Afghanistan, the desert did what deserts always do: it got into everything. Fine grit rasped against fabric, a dry wind hissed, and a runner's breath came loud inside his own head. The run felt private. The phone did not. When Strava's global "heatmap" became public and journalists began tracing the glowing lines, those anonymous-looking loops and out-and-backs started to resemble something else: the perimeter of a base, the rhythm of a routine, the predictable arc of a life lived in a place where predictability is a risk. It looked harmless. It was not. Privacy is a form of manners.

Most people do not live on military bases in Helmand, and the point is not to borrow someone else's danger for drama. The point is simpler, and more unsettling: the same mechanism that drew bright lines around remote compounds also draws lines around ordinary homes, schools, workplaces, clinics, and late-night detours that never make it into conversation. Phones keep receipts for behaviour, and modern services are built to collect them. Not in a melodramatic "someone is watching" way, but in a quietly procedural one, like a shop that counts footfall or a train station that tallies tickets. The information is not always read by a human. It is processed, categorised, and stored, ready for the day it becomes useful to someone.

This is the paradox that sits in everyone's pocket: a device that feels personal because it is intimate, yet behaves like a networked sensor because it is profitable. A phone knows where its owner sleeps not because it is nosy in a moral sense, but because location data makes maps smoother, adverts more expensive, fraud detection easier, "nearby" results snappier. It knows what was typed and deleted because predictive keyboards learn patterns, because messaging apps synchronise drafts across devices, because analytics teams chase the moment a user hesitates. It knows who argued with whom because contact lists link identities, because call logs and message metadata sketch social geometry with brutal efficiency. The miracle is not that this happens; the miracle is that people are expected to manage it through settings buried under cheerful icons and tick-boxes tapped years ago, often in a hurry, often to make a pop-up go away.

The modern data trail rarely arrives with malice. It grows the way mould grows: in the corners, in the damp, in places no one checks until the smell reaches the living room. A single "allow" is small, almost courteous. A loyalty card feels like a bargain. A log-in offers convenience, then silently becomes a passport. A photo uploaded for a family member's birthday becomes training data for facial recognition, a memory indexed and cross-referenced. The trail is made of breadcrumbs: tiny, ordinary crumbs that accumulate into a path someone else can follow if they have the patience, the tools, or the commercial incentive.

Consider a mundane purchase, the sort that never features in anyone's autobiography. A person buys a kettle online. The browser stores a handful of cookies; the retailer tags the visit; the payment processor confirms a transaction; a delivery firm receives a name, an address, and a parcel's journey. None of this is scandalous. Yet the same person later looks up descaling instructions, then replacement filters, then a repair video. A search engine links the queries; a video platform suggests related content; the phone's operating system notes that the user is, for a week, at home more than usual. If an advert follows them for kettle filters, it feels mildly irritating. If an insurance provider uses similar data to infer something about a household's habits, it is no longer an advert; it is a decision made elsewhere. If an abusive ex-partner gets hold of an old shared account and learns that a package is arriving on Tuesday, the data trail has become a safety issue, not a marketing one. Data leaves footprints. Some prints matter more.

The detail worth insisting on is that privacy is not the same as secrecy. Secrecy is a door slammed shut. Privacy is the ability to choose which doors are open, to whom, and for how long. It is the difference between giving a courier a delivery address and giving a random website permission to read a contacts list. It is the difference between letting a bank verify identity and letting a free game listen through a microphone. It is also the difference between what people imagine they are doing—sharing a piece of information for a single purpose—and what many services actually do, which is share that information across time, across devices, and across companies. The social bargain of the internet is rarely explained plainly: people trade a slice of their lives for convenience, then discover that the slice has been copied.

A second, checkable example shows how quickly "ordinary" can become "exposed". In September 2022, Uber disclosed that an attacker had accessed internal systems after persuading an employee to approve a login request, and the company's communications described a range of affected systems and tools. The story unfolded publicly because Uber is large and scrutinised, but the mechanism was painfully universal: a human being, interrupted and tired, clicked a prompt that felt routine. The detail here is not the brand; it is the pattern. Accounts are now the hinges of modern life. A single compromised email inbox can reset passwords for shopping, banking, social media, and cloud storage. A single sign-in can open calendars, addresses, photo libraries, and location histories. The cost is not only the money stolen in a moment; it is the time spent unravelling the mess, the embarrassment of messages sent by someone else in your name, the quiet dread that arrives when you realise how many doors are chained to one key.

It is tempting, when confronted with these examples, to reach for extremes. Some people fantasise about disappearing, as if privacy were a magic cloak. Others throw up their hands and declare the fight lost, as if the only options were total exposure or monastic retreat. Both reactions miss the practical middle: the small set of changes that reliably reduce risk without turning daily life into a technical hobby. Most of it is mundane. That is good news. The most effective privacy work rarely involves obscure tools; it involves maintenance, tidying, and an honest look at what is actually worth protecting.

The first step is mental, not technical. A useful privacy mindset does not begin with fear; it begins with control. It asks what should be shared, with whom, and under what conditions. It treats privacy like context, not like virtue. People already do this instinctively offline. A person might tell a neighbour their first name without offering a full address. They might share a phone number with a child's school but not with a pop-up stand at a shopping centre. Digital life erodes these instincts because it collapses contexts. A delivery app looks like a shop, a map looks like a diary, a photo library looks like a shoebox in a cupboard. Underneath, many of these services behave like record-keeping systems designed to remember indefinitely. If privacy is control, the task becomes less mystical: regain enough control to make the data trail proportionate to the life that creates it.

That is where threat modelling—an unpleasant phrase with a simple meaning—quietly earns its keep. Not everyone needs the same defences. A public-facing journalist, a teacher dealing with difficult families, a person leaving a coercive relationship, a teenager navigating social pressure: each has a different set of plausible risks. Even within one household, the risks differ by role and temperament. Some people fear scammers; others fear embarrassment; others fear a former partner with too much knowledge and too little restraint. The smart move is not to perform maximal privacy theatre, but to match effort to danger. Choose what matters. Measure what changes.

There is also an honest counter-example that needs saying. Privacy measures can create friction, and friction can produce harm. A person who disables all location services may lose a safety feature that helps them share their whereabouts on a late-night walk home. A family who locks down every account with complex verification may find themselves stranded when a phone is lost abroad and a bank needs confirmation quickly. A business that blocks all third-party cookies may break its own accessibility tools. Still, these are not arguments against privacy; they are arguments for proportion. The goal is not to build a bunker. The goal is to avoid leaving the front door wide open because locking it is mildly inconvenient.

The practical work begins with the devices that act as the primary sensors of modern life. Phones deserve attention first because they travel, they listen, they locate, they photograph, and they carry authentication codes for other accounts. A phone's privacy posture is shaped less by dramatic "spyware" stories than by boring settings: automatic updates, backups that prevent panic, lock screens that resist casual snooping, permissions that limit what apps can read. It is astonishing how many people accept a four-digit code chosen a decade ago, or leave notification previews visible on a lock screen that can be read by anyone standing nearby on a train. A small change there is not paranoia; it is basic physical etiquette for the digital age.

Computers, for all their decline in glamour, remain the workhorses of serious tasks: documents, taxes, school portals, job applications, medical letters, family finances. They also remain the favourite target for malicious downloads because they still run the software that people trust blindly. A laptop left unencrypted is a suitcase full of papers; a laptop with encryption enabled is a safe with a key. The difference matters when devices are lost in cafés, stolen from cars, or borrowed "just for a minute". Physical access is the oldest attack in the world. Technology does not abolish it; it just makes the loot easier to copy.

Accounts are the next layer, and here the modern world shows its oddest fracture: people accept that they must lock their front door, yet resist the idea of using a password manager because it sounds complicated. Meanwhile, attackers do not guess passwords the way films suggest. They do not stand in a dark room trying "password123" until it works. They purchase leaked credentials from prior breaches and test them at scale. They use automated tools to compare and crack. They exploit the fact that people reuse secrets across services because remembering is hard and life is busy. A password manager is not a luxury; it is a way of turning memory into a single strong secret instead of a brittle web of half-forgotten ones. Two-factor authentication, when set up sensibly, is not a burden; it is a second latch on a door that too many people assume is solid.

Then there is the web itself, that apparently weightless space where behaviour becomes measurable. Browsers are not neutral windows; they are instruments. They store histories, autofill forms, remember logins, sync tabs across devices, and quietly expose enough characteristics—fonts installed, screen size, device model—to allow "fingerprinting" even when cookies are blocked. Tracking is not only about adverts. It is also about profiling, pricing experiments, and the kind of invisible sorting that decides which offers appear, which news is prioritised, which content is suggested. Switching a few defaults, adding a small amount of friction to third-party tracking, and thinking of search as a form of disclosure can alter how much of a person's inner life becomes an external asset.

Cloud storage and photo libraries deserve their own seriousness because they hold what people cannot bear to lose. The cloud is not one place; it is a set of commercial promises. Some services synchronise, which means deletions travel too. Some back up, which means old versions persist. Some do both, with rules that are hard to parse in a moment of panic. Photos, in particular, invite a gentle kind of carelessness: faces, children's names, location tags, school uniforms, street signs reflected in windows, a birthday banner showing a full date of birth. None of this is shameful; it is human. Yet the same features that make photo libraries searchable—automatic tagging, geotagging, shared albums—also make them legible to someone who should not have access, especially when links are shared too broadly or old accounts are forgotten.

Messaging, email, and social platforms are where privacy stops being a personal preference and becomes a social negotiation. End-to-end encryption can protect message content from intermediaries, but metadata—the fact that two people spoke, when, and how often—can remain readable. Email is a marvel of resilience precisely because it is open, old, and widely compatible; it is also a privacy compromise baked into the protocol. Social profiles persist, and what felt harmless at twenty-two can look like a liability at thirty-five, not because the person has changed into someone else, but because context changes faster than the internet forgets. A single public post can become a data point in a stranger's model of who someone is and what they might buy, fear, or tolerate.

The home network is the quiet background to all of this, the domestic infrastructure that almost never receives the attention it deserves. Routers ship with default passwords for a reason: most buyers never change them. Smart televisions and printers now run the sort of software once confined to desktops, complete with microphones, cameras, address books, and automatic updates that may or may not arrive. "Smart" speakers move the boundary between private space and corporate server into the kitchen. Sometimes that is an acceptable trade. Sometimes it is an unexamined one. It is not romantic to talk about router firmware, but it is intellectually honest. Much of privacy is plumbing.

Families complicate matters further, because privacy is not an individual sport. Children learn what is normal by watching adults. A parent who posts a child's full name and school uniform for the sake of a proud moment is not wicked; they are operating under a set of social norms that have not caught up with the permanence of online indexing. Teenagers deserve a different approach again. They need tools, not sermons: how to adjust settings, how to block, how to report, how to recognise pressure disguised as affection, how to understand that screenshots are forever even when messages disappear. The aim is not surveillance of children; it is competence. It is also respect: a family can treat privacy as a shared value rather than a punishment.

Travel exposes how local privacy truly is. In airports and hotels, people surrender devices to charging stations and unknown networks with astonishing trust. Border crossings introduce another layer of uncertainty, not because every traveller will be searched, but because the possibility changes what counts as wise preparation. Cars, too, have become rolling data collectors, logging routes, syncing contacts, remembering destinations, and tying journeys to accounts. Location histories can be lifesavers in one context and liabilities in another. Deliberate sharing is the point. Default broadcasting is not.

Behind the screens and domestic decisions sits an industry most people never meet: data brokers. Their work is not always illegal; that is what makes it insidious. They buy, combine, and resell personal information, sometimes scraped, sometimes purchased, sometimes inferred. The products are not only adverts; they can be "audiences" sold to marketers, risk scores sold to insurers, address lists sold to anyone with a budget. Opt-outs exist in some jurisdictions, and they can help, but they are rarely a silver bullet. The more durable approach is to shrink the upstream supply: provide less unnecessary information, reduce the casual linking of identity across services, decline the loyalty scheme that offers pennies in exchange for a behavioural diary. Privacy work is often less about hiding and more about refusing to generate crumbs that never needed to exist.

And then there are breaches and scams, the moments when privacy stops feeling abstract and becomes urgent. Scammers rarely defeat technology; they defeat attention. They create urgency, impersonate authority, and exploit the human habit of politeness. A breach notification is not a moral judgement; it is a weather report. The question is not whether the storm was deserved, but what preparations exist: unique passwords, two-factor authentication, a habit of checking key accounts, a way of recovering access without improvising at three in the morning. Panic is optional when a plan exists. Even a small plan.

The through-line across all of this is not secrecy, and it is not rebellion against technology. It is agency. It is the decision to treat convenience as a choice rather than a destiny. It is the recognition that trust, in a digital context, is often a design feature that shifts responsibility onto the user while keeping the defaults lucrative for the company. A person who accepts every prompt is not stupid; they are busy. A person who has not "sorted their privacy out" is not lazy; they are living. The problem is not character; it is architecture. The systems are designed to make disclosure easy and restraint awkward. That is why restraint, when practised calmly and consistently, is powerful.

Two echoes from that January 2018 heatmap matter here. One is technical: small signals, aggregated, become patterns. A single run is personal. A hundred runs become a route. A thousand runs become infrastructure. The other is moral: what feels private in the moment may not remain private when the context shifts. People make decisions under one set of assumptions, then discover the assumptions were temporary. The breadcrumbs do not care. They wait. They can be followed years later by a new employer, a new partner, a bored teenager, an advertising algorithm, or a stranger with a grievance.

The question that remains, and that quietly governs every practical choice that follows, is not "How can someone become invisible?" It is sharper, and more humane: what is the smallest set of changes that would make a meaningful difference to risk, without demanding a new personality? There is always a trade-off—time, convenience, cost, social friction. Refusing to acknowledge that trade-off produces either martyrdom or denial. A better move is to name it, then choose deliberately. That choice is the beginning of privacy that is private, not hidden: less performative, more durable, and designed to survive contact with real life, where the crumbs are always there and the table is always being wiped.

Chapter 1
Everyday Privacy Mindset

In December 1890, in Boston, the air around a printing press would have carried a particular kind of smell: ink, metal, paper warmed by friction. Newspapers were getting faster, louder, more intimate, and a pair of lawyers—Samuel Warren and Louis Brandeis—looked at the new machinery of exposure and realised something old had changed. They called it "the right to be let alone", a phrase that still sounds slightly rebellious, as though solitude itself were a civil liberty. Their complaint was not that society had become wicked overnight. It was that technology had made intrusion cheap. When intrusion becomes cheap, it becomes normal. When it becomes normal, it becomes invisible.

That is the peculiar challenge of privacy now. The tools that gather information about ordinary people are not housed in smoky newsrooms but in pockets, routers, browsers, loyalty programmes, and polite little prompts that ask for "permission" in the way a bouncer asks whether you "mind" showing your ID. Most of the time, nobody feels invaded. The taps and swipes feel like errands. The data, though, accrues with the patience of dust. And dust has a talent for revealing footsteps.

The word "privacy" is often treated as a moral mood—something earnest people care about, something careless people do not. That framing is both unfair and strategically useless. Privacy is not a personality trait. It is the ability to control how information about a person moves: what is shared, with whom, for what purpose, and for how long. It is also the ability to notice when control has quietly slipped away. The world is full of people who love their friends and still close the bathroom door. That is not secrecy. It is context. It is dignity. It is a boundary with good manners.

A great deal of confusion begins with three words that get tossed into the same bucket: privacy, anonymity, security. They overlap, but they are not the same creature wearing different hats. Anonymity is about not being identified. It is the mask. Security is about preventing harm—loss, theft, tampering, impersonation. It is the lock. Privacy is about appropriate sharing and limitation. It is the set of rules that decide which doors exist in the first place, who gets keys, and whether the house keeps a detailed log of every visitor, every hour, every room entered. People chase the wrong goal when they treat privacy as invisibility. Most lives do not need invisibility. Most lives need fewer unnecessary records.

That distinction matters because the internet sells a particular kind of fantasy: that if a service is "free", you are only paying with attention, not with information. In reality, attention is simply one use-case for personal data; the more durable value is the profile that predicts behaviour. That profile does not require scandal. It does not require dark secrets. It requires consistency, which is exactly what everyday life provides. Where a person tends to be on weekday mornings. Which brands they habitually trust. How quickly they respond to a message. Whether they often travel alone. Which devices appear on the same network. The details do not need to be thrilling to be powerful. Most of the important details in a life are not thrilling.

A simple example exposes the shape of the bargain. A person gives an address to a delivery company. That is a sensible disclosure, bounded by purpose: bring the parcel to the right door. The same person, minutes later, is asked by a cheerful quiz site to "confirm your location to find your nearest match" or "allow contacts to see which friends are here". The request is framed as convenience, not as surveillance. Yet the disclosure is qualitatively different: location and contacts are not needed for the service to function in any basic way; they are valuable because they link identity to place and identity to people. A delivery address is a practical detail; a contacts list is a social map. Treating those as equivalent is how privacy becomes a series of accidents.

The hardest part for many people is not deciding what they believe in, but seeing the shape of the trail they already leave. Data rarely travels in a straight line from person to company. It travels through chains: sign-in providers, analytics services, advertising networks, payment processors, customer support tools, device manufacturers. A person can truthfully say, "I never told that company anything," and still be right only in the narrowest sense. They did not tell the company. Someone else did. Or something else did. Or the company inferred it from patterns it purchased.

Take one modest action and watch it grow legs. A person pops into a supermarket and scans a loyalty card because it knocks a pound off detergent. They pay with a card or a phone. They later receive an email receipt because paper feels wasteful. The following day they search for reviews of the same detergent because the scent is too strong; they click a result that happens to include trackers from an advertising firm. A week later they scroll past an advert for "sensitive skin" products and feel a faintly creepy sense of being known. Nothing supernatural occurred. A discount tied a purchase to an identity. A payment linked that identity to a bank or a wallet provider. An email address offered a durable handle that follows across services. A browser offered technical signals that are easier to connect than most people imagine. The crumbs were small. The path was clear.

It is tempting to react to that picture with indignation, and indignation has its uses. But indignation alone does not change settings, and it does not make decisions easier. The more useful response is curiosity mixed with discipline: what information is necessary for a service to do what it promises, and what information is simply *nice to have* from the company's point of view? The difference between those two categories—necessary versus extractive—sits beneath almost every practical choice. People do not need to become suspicious of everything. They need to become fluent in a particular kind of question: "What am I actually giving away here?"

This is where privacy becomes less like a political identity and more like domestic competence. Just as a person learns, over time, which cupboards attract moths and which foods go stale, they can learn which digital habits reliably create future problems. The trap is to imagine that privacy is one enormous decision, a grand stance taken once and then admired. In reality it is closer to housekeeping. A few routines, done occasionally, prevent disasters. A few habits, done automatically, lower risk without requiring constant vigilance. The point is not perfection. The point is reducing the number of ways a normal life can be turned into leverage against itself.

The most persistent myth about privacy is that it is mainly about "hackers". The word has become a cartoon villain, a hooded figure tapping into a bank. In practice, the everyday threats most people face are more banal and more social. A scammer persuading someone to approve a login. A stranger reading lock-screen notifications on a crowded train. A colleague who should not have access to private files, but does because a shared computer never had separate accounts. A landlord who "just happens" to know more than feels reasonable. A former partner who still has the password to a streaming account, which also happens to contain purchase history, addresses, and saved cards. None of these require elite technical skill. They require opportunity.

Thinking clearly about opportunity is the heart of threat modelling, a term that sounds like something done in a war room but really belongs at a kitchen table. It asks three questions in plain clothes: what could go wrong, who might care, and how bad would it be? The elegance of those questions is that they prevent two equal and opposite errors. One is catastrophising—treating every new app permission as a potential life-ruiner. The other is complacency—assuming that because something hasn't gone wrong yet, it never will. A nosy employer and a random scammer pose different kinds of risk. An abusive ex-partner is not the same as a brand that wants to sell shoes. A person with a public-facing job may reasonably worry about doxxing in a way that their neighbour does not. The aim is not to panic. The aim is to place risk in context and allocate effort accordingly.

Modern life encourages the opposite. The default privacy culture oscillates between shrugging and obsessing. Shrugging is easy because the problem feels huge, and huge problems invite resignation. Obsessing is seductive because it feels active, but it can become its own form of helplessness: endless tweaks, endless anxiety, a sense that safety depends on never making a mistake. The steadier option is to decide on a posture—an intentional level of privacy that fits the life being lived. Not a manifesto. A setting.

A posture recognises trade-offs that are real, not theoretical. Convenience matters. Cost matters. Time matters. Some protections are easy wins: they deliver a meaningful reduction in risk with little friction. Others are costly or socially awkward, and should be reserved for people who genuinely need them. The idea that everyone must behave like a dissident under surveillance is not only unrealistic; it is corrosive. It turns privacy into a performance and guarantees burnout. Yet the idea that only people with "something to hide" should care is equally poisonous. People close curtains at night. People lock bicycles. People do not leave their diaries open on café tables. These are not confessions of guilt. They are normal boundaries in a world where other people exist.

There is, however, a limitation worth admitting without theatrics. Some privacy losses are structural. A person can refuse a loyalty card and still appear in marketing databases because a retailer bought a list. A person can tighten browser settings and still be tracked through fingerprinting and server logs. A person can choose a more private messaging app and still leak metadata through who talks to whom and when. And sometimes privacy is not the highest value in the room. A family might choose location sharing for safety, accepting the risk of a location history because the benefit is tangible. A medical appointment system might require personal details because the alternative is worse care. Not every demand for data is cynical. Not every compromise is foolish. The point is to choose compromises deliberately rather than drifting into them.

The deeper reason this mindset matters is that privacy is not merely about exposure. It is about autonomy. When information about a person circulates freely, it can be used to shape their options without their awareness: which adverts appear, which prices are offered, which services are denied, which messages arrive at the most vulnerable moment. Even when the outcome is not dramatic, the habit of being measured changes behaviour. People speak differently when they suspect they are overheard. They search differently when they suspect their searches will be judged. They avoid topics, soften opinions, leave questions unasked. A society does not need overt censorship to become timid; it merely needs a culture where everything is recorded by default and forgetting becomes a luxury product.

This is why a practical privacy mindset needs a philosophical spine. The spine is not paranoia. It is the insistence that people deserve private space to think, to make mistakes, to change their minds, to experiment with identity, to grieve without performing, to learn without being profiled, to be inconsistent without being punished by permanent records. Technology that remembers everything has benefits—lost phones found, fraud detected, memories resurfaced. Technology that remembers everything also creates a world where past selves become liabilities. A mature approach holds both truths at once and refuses to treat "convenience" as an unanswerable argument.

Notice, too, that privacy is not only personal; it is relational. The information one person shares often reveals someone else. Uploading a contacts list does not only disclose the uploader's social world; it discloses everyone else's. Posting a child's school photo is not only a parenting choice; it is a child's data footprint before they can form a view. Saving a shared password is not only a memory aid; it is a potential weapon in a future conflict. A household does not need to become a surveillance state to take these dynamics seriously. It needs a shared language and a few shared boundaries.

A mindset, then, is the opposite of a checklist. It is the way of seeing that makes checklists meaningful. It teaches the reader to recognise when a request for data is proportional and when it is opportunistic. It teaches the reader to notice trails as they form, rather than only after something goes wrong. It teaches the reader to think about threats in terms of humans and incentives, not only in terms of villains and software. It teaches the reader to accept trade-offs without surrendering. Above all, it teaches the reader to stop confusing privacy with hiding—because hiding is exhausting, and most people do not need to hide. They need to be able to live normally without leaving unnecessary crumbs behind them.

By the end of this opening stretch of the journey, the reader should feel something rare in the privacy conversation: steadiness. Not the brittle confidence of someone who believes they have outsmarted the internet, and not the weary defeat of someone who has given up. Something more useful. A sense that privacy can be approached like any other adult skill: learn the principles, understand the moving parts, decide on a level that fits, and then make a few deliberate changes that hold under pressure. The next pages tighten the lens until the abstract becomes practical, and the practical becomes almost obvious—because once the trail is visible, it becomes surprisingly hard to keep walking as though it isn't there.

What Privacy Really Means

On 13 May 2014, in Luxembourg, the Court of Justice of the European Union handed down a decision that did something quietly radical to the modern internet. The case is usually shortened to *Google Spain v AEPD and Mario Costeja González*, but its human centre was a man who disliked what a search result made him look like. Years earlier, a newspaper notice about his financial troubles had been published legitimately; later, typing his name into Google produced that notice as if it were the headline of his life. The court ruled that, in certain circumstances, a search engine must remove links to information that is "inadequate, irrelevant or no longer relevant" when searched by a person's name. The paper record remained. The library stayed open. But the index changed.

That distinction is the scent of modern privacy: not the fantasy of erasing reality, but the practical power to shape how reality is retrieved. It is one thing for an old notice to exist in an archive; it is another for it to be the first thing a stranger learns. Privacy, in other words, is often about *access*, not existence. It is about the friction between a fact and the people who can easily reach it.

Control beats concealment every time.

That five-word truth irritates the popular imagination, which wants privacy to mean vanishing. Vanishing is dramatic. Control is unglamorous. Control involves deciding, repeatedly, what gets shared, with whom, and for what purpose. It involves tolerating the fact that some information must move in order for modern life to function—deliveries need addresses, employers need bank details, doctors need histories—while refusing the equally modern idea that everything should move simply because it can. Privacy is not the absence of data; it is the presence of boundaries. And boundaries, like doors, exist to be opened selectively.

This is where privacy parts company with two neighbouring concepts that are often muddled together: anonymity and security. Anonymity is about identity. It is the state of acting without being singled out as *you*. A masked protester aims for anonymity; so does a source sending a tip to a journalist. Security is about resilience against harm: preventing unauthorised access, preventing tampering, preventing impersonation, limiting damage when something goes wrong. A bank's fraud detection is security. A device encryption key is security. Privacy is something else. Privacy is the governance of information flow: what data is collected, what data is retained, what data is linked, what data is sold, and what data is exposed as a side-effect of convenience.

The difference matters because people often pursue the wrong objective. They will say they "want privacy" when what they actually want is security—protection from account takeover, blackmail, identity theft, stalking. Or they will say they "want privacy" when what they actually want is anonymity—freedom to read, search, and speak without their name attached. Those goals overlap, but confusing them produces poor decisions. Someone who wants security but chases anonymity may install complicated tools while leaving their email account protected by a reused password. Someone who wants privacy but focuses only on secrecy may avoid obvious disclosures while quietly allowing apps to harvest location data in the background.

A useful way to see the distinction is to watch how people behave offline, where the language is older and the instincts are clearer. When a courier knocks at the door, most people will confirm their address because that is the point of the exchange. The disclosure is bounded: one person, one parcel, one destination. If a stranger on the street asks for the same address "for reasons", most people decline. They do not decline because the address is a cosmic secret. They decline because the request is unbounded. The purpose is unclear. The audience is unknown. The future use is unpredictable. Privacy is the judgement that separates the bounded request from the unbounded one.

Digital systems are skilled at blurring that boundary. They invite disclosure in exchange for speed, personalisation, and relief from minor friction. A website asks to "use your location" to show "relevant" results. An app requests access to contacts to "find friends". A service offers "one-tap sign-in" and quietly turns a single account into a master key. The moment of consent is tiny—tap, allow, continue—but the consequences can be durable because data tends to persist, replicate, and recombine. Privacy, properly understood, is not a mood of suspicion; it is the habit of asking whether a disclosure is proportionate to a purpose.

The modern world is drenched in slogans about "trust". Trust, however, is not a sentiment; it is a decision with a structure. A person who hands over an address to a delivery company is trusting that the company will use it to deliver a parcel and not, say, publish it for sport. That trust has a shape: it is limited by the company's incentives, policies, legal obligations, and practical ability to misuse the information. When a person hands over an address to a random website, the structure changes. The incentives are opaque. The policies may be unreadable. The ability to resell, leak, or mishandle data may be high. The trust is no longer a neat exchange; it is a wager. Naming that difference is how privacy stops being moral theatre and becomes ordinary competence.

This is also where the popular obsession with "having nothing to hide" collapses under its own clumsiness. People close curtains not because they are criminals, but because they are human. People keep diaries, have private conversations, change their minds, make mistakes, worry about things they never act on, and sometimes simply want a room where they are not being measured. Privacy is the space in which a person can be unfinished. When systems treat all behaviour as a commodity, they shrink that space and then act surprised when people feel exposed without being able to point to a single dramatic violation.

A second checkable example shows how privacy harms can arise even when people feel they are behaving normally. In March 2018, reports about Cambridge Analytica and Facebook brought a messy ecosystem into public view, including how personal data gathered through an app could be used to build psychological profiles for political advertising. The story mattered not because everyone suddenly learned a new technical term, but because it illustrated a basic privacy failure: information given in one context being repurposed in another without meaningful consent. A person might have been taking a trivial quiz, expecting a trivial use. The implication was not trivial. A disclosure that felt like a game became a building block in a machinery of persuasion. That is privacy's core anxiety in its most realistic form: not that someone will learn a single embarrassing secret, but that small, mundane facts will be assembled into a leverageable model.

This assembly is why the idea of privacy as "secrecy" is both inaccurate and self-defeating. Secrecy suggests that the safest state is to reveal nothing. Most adult life makes that impossible. Rent agreements need bank details. Airlines need passport information. Schools need emergency contact lists. Refusing all disclosure is not privacy; it is dysfunction. The smarter aim is *selective disclosure* and *limited retention*: disclose what is necessary, resist what is opportunistic, and shorten the time a disclosure remains useful to anyone else. Privacy as control is a dial, not a switch. A dial allows calibration.

The dial matters because different situations call for different settings. A public-facing academic, a clinician, a journalist, a union organiser, a person leaving a relationship, a teenager navigating peer pressure: each faces different costs if information leaks or is misused. Even a person with an unremarkable life can face sharp, targeted harms—scams, harassment, account takeover—precisely because "ordinary" accounts are easy prey. Security protects against many of those harms, but privacy shapes how much information exists to be stolen or abused in the first place. If security is the lock, privacy is the decision not to leave the spare key under the plant pot and then announce it on social media.

One way to keep the concepts clean is to anchor them to visible actions. Privacy decisions show up as choices about collection and sharing: whether a fitness app records precise location; whether photos retain embedded location metadata; whether a service is allowed to read contacts; whether a browser accepts third-party tracking cookies; whether an account is tied to a real name.

Anonymity decisions show up as identity separation: using a pseudonym, keeping certain activities detached from a primary email address, avoiding unnecessary account creation, limiting cross-linking between profiles. Security decisions show up as defences: using unique passwords, enabling multi-factor authentication, keeping devices updated, encrypting storage, locking screens. People can care about all three. The danger is to treat one as a substitute for the others.

There is a quiet moral trap here as well. When privacy is framed as secrecy, it sounds antisocial: "What are you hiding?" When privacy is framed as control, it becomes recognisably civic: "Who gets to decide what is known, and in which context?" That framing has a long lineage. The legal philosopher Alan Westin argued in *Privacy and Freedom* (1967) that privacy is the claim of individuals to determine for themselves when, how, and to what extent information about them is communicated. Westin's language is old-fashioned in a useful way: it assumes privacy is normal, and that the question is degree. The implication is liberating for modern readers who have been trained to feel slightly guilty for wanting boundaries.

Still, control has limits, and pretending otherwise breeds disappointment. The most honest counter-example is that much of what is known about a person is created by other people. A friend posts a group photo. A landlord keeps records. An employer logs building access. A retailer retains purchase history for accounting. A government agency holds identity documents. A hospital stores medical data because it must. Even a person who is disciplined about their own disclosures can be exposed through the behaviour of others or through mandatory systems. Control is therefore partial. Privacy is rarely absolute. It is a negotiated space shaped by law, social norms, institutional habits, and the design choices of companies that profit from data.

Reconciling this limitation requires a slightly mature stance. If privacy is not total control, it is tempting to abandon the effort as futile. That reaction confuses "not perfect" with "not worth doing". Seatbelts do not make driving risk-free, yet nobody argues the sensible response is to remove them. A locked door does not guarantee a house will never be burgled, yet most people still lock their doors. Privacy measures work similarly: they reduce exposure, raise effort for would-be abusers, and limit the consequences when things go wrong. Partial control can still be powerful control, particularly when it targets the most unnecessary, most easily abused flows of information.

The dial metaphor helps here because it encourages precision instead of purity. A person might decide that sharing location with a partner during travel is worth the trade, while keeping long-term location history off. They might accept that a bank will analyse transactions for fraud, while refusing a supermarket's attempt to turn groceries into a behavioural profile via a loyalty card. They might keep a professional identity public, while separating it from a private email address used for personal life. Each decision is a dial turn: a reduction of unnecessary exposure, not a vow of invisibility.

It is worth noticing how often convenience is used as an argument against privacy, as though efficiency were a natural law rather than a preference. Efficiency is measurable: fewer clicks, faster checkouts, more personalised recommendations, quicker logins. Privacy costs can also be measurable: an extra login step, a slightly less tailored feed, the occasional need to re-enter details, a small amount of time to check settings. People should not be shamed for valuing convenience. But convenience should not be treated as automatically superior. It is a trade-off. The question is whether the convenience gained is proportional to the information surrendered and the future risk created.

Risk, too, benefits from being made visible. A useful risk question is not "Could this be abused?"—almost anything can be. The better question is "If this were abused, what would it enable?" Giving a delivery firm an address enables a parcel to arrive and, in a failure case, might expose a home address in a database leak. Giving a random website an address enables very little that is genuinely necessary, while potentially enabling spam, targeted scams, or data broking. Giving an app access to contacts enables social features and, in a failure case, exposes an entire social graph. The difference is the radius of harm. Privacy is, at heart, about limiting radius.

The right mental model is not that data is a secret diary, but that data is a set of keys. Some keys open one door once. Some keys open many doors for years. When a company asks for information, it is worth asking what door that information unlocks, and whether the door needs to be open at all. The "right to be forgotten" case in Luxembourg is revealing precisely because it did not delete the underlying story; it altered the key's power by changing the index. It reduced the ease with which the story could be used against someone in casual contexts. That is privacy as control over retrieval—control over which keys remain potent.

There is also a quieter, more personal implication that rarely appears in technical discussions: privacy is a condition for honest selfhood. People explore ideas in private before they risk them in public. They search questions they would not ask aloud. They test beliefs. They read about topics that feel embarrassing, tender, or politically fraught. If every exploratory action becomes a permanent entry in a profile, people adapt. They do not stop being curious; they become cautious. They gravitate towards safe questions, safe purchases, safe opinions. A society that treats private exploration as suspicious will slowly produce people who explore less. The harm is subtle. The cost arrives later.

The purpose of separating privacy from anonymity and security is to stop the mind skidding into extremes. Privacy is not a demand to live untraceably. Privacy is not a guarantee that nothing bad will ever happen. Privacy is not a declaration of moral purity. It is a set of choices about information flow, made with an awareness that data tends to spread, to persist, and to be repurposed. It is learning to recognise when a request is bounded and when it is unbounded. It is turning the dial to a setting that fits the life being lived, rather than accepting whatever setting someone else chose for their business model.

The forward tension that remains—useful, unavoidable, and worth holding onto—is this: which conveniences are worth the keys you hand over, and which are merely habits you have never examined? The next decision is rarely dramatic. It is often a small, everyday tap. The question is whether that tap is opening a door for a moment, or leaving it ajar for years.

How Data Trails Grow

In December 2019, in New York, *The New York Times* published an investigation by Stuart A. Thompson and Charlie Warzel that made an abstract problem suddenly tactile. They described how commercially available location data—bought from an ordinary source, not obtained through a warrant—could be used to follow people's movements with unnerving specificity, tracing visits to workplaces, homes, and sensitive locations. The story's power was not in a single scandal. It was in the banality of the method. Data did not need to be stolen. It was already for sale. The trail was not hidden. It was merely *elsewhere.*

The unsettling detail is how little is required to create such a trail. A few pings from a phone. A handful of app interactions. A couple of identifiers passed around like polite introductions at a crowded party. And then, slowly, the portrait sharpens. The receipt keeps its timestamp. That is the quiet logic of modern data: tiny records become durable evidence of life.

Most people imagine their digital footprint as a set of separate puddles: shopping here, messaging there, photos somewhere else. In practice, the puddles connect. The connection is not magic. It is accounting. It is the industrial habit of making records interoperable so that services can measure, optimise, detect fraud, personalise, attribute, and—when profitable—sell. The result is an information trail that grows the way a footpath grows across grass: each step looks insignificant, yet repetition makes a route that can be followed by strangers.

Start with the smallest action that feels like nothing. A person creates an account. In the moment, the account is a convenience: saved preferences, order history, faster checkout. Show: a login screen, an email address typed once, a password created in haste. Name: an identifier. Explain: the email address becomes a stable handle that links activity across time, and often across services if the same address is reused; even when the address is not shared directly, it can be hashed—turned into a mathematical fingerprint—and compared across datasets. Implication: what felt like a single relationship between a person and a service becomes a joinable record in a wider marketplace of profiles.

Identifiers rarely travel alone. There are device identifiers, advertising identifiers, cookie IDs, and account IDs. The names differ; the effect rhymes. Show: a free weather app runs, an advert loads, and a silent request leaves the phone to fetch content. Name: third-party tracking. Explain: the app often includes software development kits—SDKs—provided by analytics and advertising companies; those SDKs report back events ("app opened", "screen viewed", "purchase completed") alongside device signals, sometimes including approximate location, language settings, and a persistent advertising ID. Implication: a person's relationship with the weather becomes part of an advertising company's understanding of that person, even if the person never heard the company's name.

Location data is where the trail becomes almost unfair, because location is both intimate and routinely generated. Show: a phone checks for signal, Wi-Fi, Bluetooth beacons, and satellite positioning so maps can work and emergency services can locate callers. Name: location pings. Explain: even when a person is not actively navigating, apps and operating systems can request location in the background for "nearby" features, fraud prevention, local content, or analytics; the resulting coordinates may be precise or coarse, but repeated over days they outline patterns—home at night, work in the morning, regular stops, unusual detours. Implication: you do not need a diary to know a life; a repeated set of coordinates will do.

A person may reasonably object that they never granted some company their location. The objection can be true and irrelevant at the same time. Show: an app developer includes a third-party advertising SDK; the SDK receives data from many apps on many phones; a data broker aggregates and resells. Name: data brokerage. Explain: brokers combine datasets from app ecosystems, public records, and commercial purchases; they may not need a person to *give* them data directly because the data arrives as a by-product of other transactions, bundled into commercial feeds. Implication: control is lost not only through direct disclosure, but through indirect propagation—information leaking sideways from the services people do use to companies they never knowingly chose.

Loyalty cards are another small, domestic-looking mechanism that produces a surprisingly coherent trail. Show: a plastic card scanned at a till in exchange for a discount; a receipt printed with "points earned"; an email sent because paper is deemed wasteful. Name: purchase history. Explain: loyalty programmes tie transactions to an identity over long periods, turning groceries and household goods into behavioural records; combined with payment data, they can reveal household composition, dietary preferences, pregnancy, illness, travel patterns, and financial stress—not because anyone is spying in the cinematic sense, but because the data is structured for analysis. Implication: the discount is not merely financial; it is informational, and the "cost" is paid in the currency of inference.

Photos deepen the trail in a different way. They are not only records of events; they are records of people, places, and relationships. Show: a photo taken at a birthday party, uploaded automatically, and placed into an album with a familiar face suggested for tagging. Name: metadata and recognition. Explain: many cameras embed technical details in image files—time, device model, sometimes location—while cloud libraries may analyse images to group faces, identify objects, and make search effortless; shared albums replicate these images across accounts, and links can outlive the moment they were intended for. Implication: a picture is no longer a private memory by default; it is a structured data object that can be indexed, searched, and linked.

To see how these mechanisms braid together, follow a single purchase as it moves through modern systems. A person decides to buy noise-cancelling headphones—nothing exotic, just a sensible defence against open-plan offices and commuter trains. They click an advert or a search result. The browser loads a retailer's site. A cookie is set. The retailer's analytics script records the product page view and the time spent scrolling. A payment processor confirms the transaction. A courier receives the delivery address and estimated delivery window. The retailer's email service sends an order confirmation and later a review request. Each step is ordinary. Each step produces a record.

Now watch the records echo. The person opens a video platform to look up how to pair the headphones with a laptop. The platform recommends "best noise-cancelling comparisons". The person clicks. They visit a review site that uses affiliate links; the click is logged for commission attribution. The person later sees adverts for headphone stands and travel cases on other websites. This is not clairvoyance. It is linkage: cookies, device identifiers, and advertising IDs connecting browsing behaviour to ad targeting. The trail becomes legible enough to be monetised.

Add one more commonplace layer: a fitness tracker app on the phone, already installed. It continues to log steps, and the phone continues to generate location pings. The person starts commuting a new route because the headphones make walking more enjoyable. After a week, the route becomes regular. After a month, it becomes predictable. No single company needs the whole story. Several companies hold pieces. A broker can stitch. A scammer can guess. A curious colleague can infer. The trail has grown not through a single dramatic mistake, but through the ordinary alignment of convenience features.

This is where the language of "I never told them" breaks down. A person may never type their home address into a particular service, yet that service can still infer "home" if it sees a device at one location every night. A person may never disclose their employer, yet a service can infer "work" if it sees the same device at a particular building every weekday. A person may never state that they have children, yet purchase patterns, app usage, and photo tagging can imply it. Show: predictable routines. Name: inference. Explain: machine learning models do not require explicit confession; they thrive on repeated correlations, and modern data is thick with correlations because human life is repetitive. Implication: privacy risk is not only what you say; it is what your patterns reveal.

The legal and regulatory environment has tried to respond to this reality, sometimes effectively and sometimes clumsily. The European Union's General Data Protection Regulation (GDPR), enforced from May 2018, strengthened rights around access, deletion, and lawful bases for processing. That matters. It changes incentives. It also illustrates a limitation: rights on paper do not automatically produce simplicity in practice. Consent banners can become theatre. Privacy policies remain unreadable. Data flows can remain opaque even when technically "disclosed". Regulation can reduce some harms while leaving the basic economic logic intact: data remains valuable, and valuable things attract collection.

A second, sharper example shows how regulators describe the stakes when location data becomes a tradable commodity. In August 2022, the US Federal Trade Commission filed a complaint against Kochava, a data broker based in Idaho, alleging that the company sold geolocation data that could be linked to visits to sensitive locations such as places of worship and healthcare providers. The allegation matters because it places a formal name on what many people intuit: certain data types, when sold as a product, can become tools for stalking, discrimination, or intimidation. Show: a broker selling location feeds. Name: sensitive data. Explain: when a dataset includes persistent identifiers and fine-grained location over time, it can reveal where a person sleeps, where they seek care, what institutions they visit, and with whom they move; even without a name attached, repeated patterns can be re-identified. Implication: the trail is not merely a marketing artefact; it can be an instrument of harm.

And yet it would be dishonest to pretend the trail is always used malignly. There are credible counterexamples where data collection provides clear, socially valuable functions. Fraud detection is one. Payment networks monitor unusual transactions to flag theft. Mapping services use aggregated location signals to estimate traffic. Public health researchers sometimes use mobility data in aggregated form to study movement trends, with safeguards intended to reduce individual identifiability. Companies increasingly advertise "privacy-preserving" approaches—processing on device, minimising collection, aggregating results—because users and regulators demand it. These developments matter. They show that data can be handled with restraint.

But "can" is not "will". The reconciliation is simple and unsentimental: beneficial uses of data do not negate the risks of collection; they coexist with them. A system can detect fraud and still collect more than necessary. A service can provide traffic estimates and still retain fine-grained histories longer than users realise. A photo library can group faces for convenience and still create new exposure if sharing links leak. The question is never whether data has *any* legitimate purpose. The question is whether the trail is proportionate, bounded, and governed in ways that align with the person who generated it.

One reason trails grow so quickly is that modern organisations outsource parts of their digital plumbing. Show: a small business installs a marketing pixel to measure whether adverts work; a developer includes a crash-reporting tool to diagnose errors; a customer support chat widget records conversations. Name: instrumentation. Explain: these tools are often provided by third parties, and each tool introduces its own data flows—events, identifiers, device signals—creating multiple copies of similar information across systems. Implication: even well-intentioned organisations can create sprawling trails because measurement has become the default setting for digital services.

The "searchable" part of the trail is what turns accumulation into power. Data that exists but cannot be queried is inert. Data that can be queried becomes actionable. Show: an analyst runs a dashboard report and filters by region, device, or customer segment; an advertising platform builds "lookalike audiences" from known buyers; a broker offers queries by postcode. Name: indexing. Explain: databases are built to answer questions quickly; once a person's behaviour is stored in a structured form, it can be retrieved, compared, and used to make decisions at scale. Implication: the trail becomes a lever. Someone can pull it without ever meeting you.

This is why the earlier emphasis on bounded disclosure matters. Small actions are not dangerous because they are immoral, but because they are permanent enough to be combined. The trail grows through repetition and linkage. A single location ping is a speck. A thousand pings are a routine. A single purchase is a preference. A hundred purchases are a household profile. A single uploaded photo is a memory. Ten thousand photos, tagged and searchable, become a biographical archive. The receipts do not rot. They pile.

The motif worth holding, then, is not fear but accounting: what receipts are being generated, and who keeps the filing cabinet? People tend to focus on dramatic incidents—an exposed celebrity photo, a major breach, a public scandal—because dramas have clear villains. Data trails are rarely dramatic. They are quiet, administrative, and cumulative. Their harm is often indirect: a scammer who knows just enough to sound credible, a price that shifts because a profile suggests higher willingness to pay, a stranger who can infer routines, an employer who draws conclusions from online traces. It is difficult to get angry at accumulation. It is easy to ignore it. That is precisely why it works so well.

Understanding how trails grow does not require technical obsession. It requires seeing the system as a set of hand-offs. Each hand-off is a decision point: a login that becomes an identifier, a discount that becomes a history, a location request that becomes a routine, a photo sync that becomes an archive, a third-party tool that becomes a parallel dataset. Once those hand-offs are visible, the problem stops looking like an undifferentiated fog and starts looking like a series of controllable chokepoints. Not all chokepoints are equally important. Some are minor. Some are pivotal. The trail is not one thing; it is a chain.

The forward test, then, is uncomfortable in a productive way: when a service asks for a piece of information, is it receiving a single-use detail, or is it receiving a receipt that will be copied into a cabinet you will never see? The answer is rarely obvious in the moment. It becomes obvious later—when the adverts follow, when the links persist, when the "recommended for you" starts sounding like it knows you. The question is whether the trail remains a by-product of living, or becomes a product in its own right.

Simple Threat Modelling

On 19 March 2016, in Washington, D.C., John Podesta—then chair of Hillary Clinton's presidential campaign—received an email that looked like routine account security. It claimed someone had his password and urged him to change it. A staffer forwarded the message to internal IT, and a reply came back with a small but consequential mistake: the word "legitimate" was misspelt as "illegitimate". Podesta clicked. Within months, his emails were published by WikiLeaks, shaping headlines, narratives, and the emotional weather of an election. The lesson was not that elite hackers always win. The lesson was that the most expensive breaches often begin as ordinary decisions made at speed.

Risk is always about context.

That is the essence of threat modelling once the corporate sheen is stripped away. It is not a grand theory. It is a habit of attention. When people hear "threat model", they imagine diagrams, consultants, and a wall of monitors in a darkened room. Households do not need any of that. They need a way to ask three questions that do not care whether the target is a campaign chairman or a commuter with an overdraft: what could go wrong, who might care, and how bad would it be?

The first question—what could go wrong—sounds melodramatic until it is grounded in something visible. Show: a phone left unlocked on a table while someone pays at the counter; a laptop borrowed "for ten minutes" by a cousin; a message that appears to come from a manager asking for an urgent document; a shared streaming account that also stores delivery addresses. Name: exposure. Explain: modern systems are designed to remember and to reuse, so a momentary lapse can create durable access—an unlocked screen reveals notifications, a borrowed device reveals saved sessions, a rushed reply reveals personal information, a shared account becomes a gateway to more than entertainment. Implication: the threat is rarely cinematic; it is mundane, and that mundanity is what makes it plausible.

The second question—who might care—removes a great deal of wasted effort. "Hackers" are not a useful category because it hides the variety of motives and methods inside a single villain mask. A scammer wants money quickly and tends to prefer psychology over software. A nosy employer wants leverage or reassurance and tends to prefer visibility over sophistication. An abusive ex-partner wants control and often already knows enough to bypass the obvious barriers: birthdays, pet names, old passwords, shared devices, shared cloud accounts. A petty criminal wants resale value and may care less about your photos than your ability to unlock a banking app. Each actor has a different appetite for effort and a different tolerance for failure. Threat modelling begins by naming likely actors, not by fantasising about the most talented ones.

The third question—how bad would it be—keeps the exercise humane. Not every privacy compromise is a catastrophe. Some are irritations: more spam, more targeted adverts, mild embarrassment. Others are expensive: drained accounts, identity theft, lost wages from time spent restoring access. Others are existential in a quieter way: coercion, stalking, professional ruin, the sudden feeling that home is not a safe place. "Bad" needs to be measured in the currency of a real life—money, time, reputation, safety, dignity. Without that measurement, people either do too much, becoming anxious and brittle, or do too little, telling themselves nothing matters until it does.

A household threat model is, at heart, a map. Not a fortress. Maps show terrain and routes. They show where someone is most likely to slip, and where the consequences would be steepest. The terrain of modern life includes devices, accounts, and relationships. Devices because they contain access. Accounts because they connect everything else. Relationships because trust is the most exploited technology on Earth.

Begin with the assets worth protecting—not as a philosophical inventory, but as a practical one. Show: an email inbox that resets every password; a photo library containing children's faces and the inside of a home; a messaging history that includes confidential work conversations; a banking app tied to a debit card. Name: high-value targets. Explain: some assets function as "root access" in ordinary life; email is the classic example because password resets and verification links flow through it, and because it often stores years of receipts, correspondence, and identity clues. Financial accounts matter for obvious reasons. Messaging matters because impersonation can damage relationships and reputations quickly. Implication: protecting everything equally is inefficient; protecting a few pivotal assets well often reduces overall risk more than a thousand minor tweaks.

Once the assets are visible, the routes of attack become easier to see. Show: the same password used across a social account and an email account; a phone number used as a recovery method; a laptop that stays logged in for convenience; a browser that autofills card details. Name: dependency chains. Explain: modern systems are interlocked; one credential can open several doors, and one compromised device can harvest multiple sessions. Recovery methods—SMS codes, backup emails, security questions—are often weaker than the primary login, which means an attacker does not always need to break the strongest lock; they can look for the side door. Implication: the relevant question becomes "What would this compromise unlock next?" rather than "Is this one service important?"

This chain-thinking is where the "who might care" question becomes crisp. A scammer who buys leaked passwords is likely to test them at scale against email providers and bank logins because those yield fast payoff. A nosy employer is more likely to look for public traces—social profiles, posts, photos, professional platforms—because that requires no technical intrusion and carries less personal risk. An abusive ex-partner is more likely to exploit intimate knowledge and proximity: shared subscriptions, old devices, family plans, unrevoked access. Each actor chooses the cheapest route. Threat models that ignore cheap routes are fantasy literature.

A second, checkable example shows how cheaply "cheap routes" can work. In September 2022, Uber disclosed that an attacker gained access to internal systems after persuading an employee to approve a login request, a technique often described as "MFA fatigue" because it relies on repeated prompts until a tired person accepts. The attack was notable not because it relied on exotic malware, but because it turned a security feature—multi-factor authentication—into a lever. Show: repeated prompts and a single mistaken tap. Name: social engineering. Explain: humans are pattern-seeking and interruption-prone; a prompt that looks like yesterday's routine can be mistaken for legitimate, especially under pressure. Implication: the threat is not always a technical weakness; it is often the ordinary fragility of attention.

Household threat modelling benefits from stealing one idea from professional security without importing the bureaucracy: separate likelihood from impact. Likelihood is about how easy a threat is to attempt and how often it occurs in the wild. Impact is about the size of the damage if it succeeds. Show: spam messages are common; targeted stalking is less common but can be severe. Name: prioritisation. Explain: focusing only on unlikely disasters can lead to elaborate defences that neglect common, low-effort attacks, while focusing only on common annoyances can lead to complacency about rare but life-changing risks. Implication: a sensible approach tends to begin with high-likelihood, medium-impact threats (scams, account takeover attempts), while also addressing any low-likelihood, high-impact threats that match a person's circumstances (domestic abuse, doxxing, professional targeting).

This is where the word "household" matters. People share space, devices, passwords, subscriptions, and assumptions. A household is often the unit that creates privacy risk. Show: a family tablet that stays logged in to multiple accounts; a smart TV that remembers payment details; a shared email used for bills; a teenager borrowing a parent's phone to check something quickly. Name: shared surfaces. Explain: sharing increases convenience and reduces friction, but it also expands the number of hands that can accidentally reveal information or intentionally misuse it, and it complicates accountability—no one knows who changed a setting or clicked a link. Implication: in domestic environments, privacy failures are as likely to be relational as they are technical.

The word "abusive" cannot be treated as an exotic edge case. It is not. Many people have, at some point, had to navigate a relationship where boundaries were ignored and information was used as a tool. Digital systems can make that tool sharper because they preserve access long after the relationship changes. Show: an ex-partner still able to see shared photo albums, delivery addresses, calendar events, or location sharing that was once offered in good faith. Name: residual access. Explain: modern services are sticky by design; they keep sessions alive, offer convenient sharing, and bury revocation options because friction reduces engagement. Implication: the end of a relationship does not automatically end the data flow, and the danger is often not a stranger breaking in but a familiar person never fully locked out.

Nosy employers sit in a different moral category, but the mechanism is similar: information used beyond its rightful context. Show: an employer asking for social media passwords (a practice restricted or banned in some jurisdictions), or informally searching an employee's name and drawing conclusions from old posts. Name: context collapse. Explain: professional environments often reward certainty and punish ambiguity, which can turn incomplete information into decisive judgement; digital traces provide a false sense of completeness. Implication: the risk is not only technical compromise; it is interpretive harm—being assessed through partial data that feels authoritative because it is searchable.

Scammers occupy the purest form of opportunism. Their methods are repetitive because they work. Show: a text claiming a parcel is awaiting payment, a call pretending to be a bank, an email claiming an urgent invoice needs approval. Name: pretexting. Explain: scammers construct a plausible story that compresses time ("urgent"), invokes authority ("bank", "HMRC"), and discourages verification ("do not share this code"), relying on social norms of helpfulness and fear of missing a deadline. Implication: many privacy failures begin as compliance failures; people are not "hacked" so much as hurried into granting access.

At this point, a reasonable objection appears, and it deserves respect. If threats are everywhere, does threat modelling simply become a way of living nervously? The answer lies in acknowledging a limitation that is both practical and philosophical: uncertainty cannot be eliminated. Some threats remain unpredictable. Some harms come from systems outside personal control—breaches at companies, data sold by brokers, policy changes, law enforcement requests, and the general entropy of digital life. A person can tighten their defences and still be affected by an incident they did not cause. The implication is not futility. The implication is humility. Threat modelling is not a promise of invulnerability; it is a method for reducing avoidable risk and for avoiding the worst surprises.

Reconciling that limitation requires a shift in what counts as "success". Success is not "nothing bad ever happens". Success is "bad things are rarer, and less damaging when they happen". That is why the household version of threat modelling stays lightweight. It is closer to choosing smoke alarms and locks than to building a panic room. It aims to reduce the cheap wins available to opportunists and to ensure that the most important assets are not protected by the weakest habits.

A ten-minute risk picture, when done well, tends to contain a few concrete elements rather than a long catalogue of anxieties. It names the handful of accounts that function as master keys. It notes the devices that travel and the devices that stay at home. It identifies any relationships—professional, domestic, social—where information misuse would be particularly harmful. It acknowledges the most common channels through which scams arrive. It also notices the points where convenience creates hidden dependency: shared logins, persistent sessions, recovery methods that can be hijacked. The output is not a spreadsheet. It is a mental map with a few bold routes marked in pen.

The map metaphor matters because it changes how later decisions feel. Without a map, privacy actions become superstitions: install this, delete that, avoid the other. With a map, decisions become proportionate. A person can compare two choices in plain terms: which one reduces exposure on a route that is both likely and costly? Which one merely adds inconvenience without addressing a meaningful path? Threat modelling restores a sense of agency because it turns the problem from "everything is risky" into "these are the routes that matter most".

It also restores sanity to conversations about tools. Tools are not virtues. A password manager is not moral. Two-factor authentication is not a personality. Encrypted messaging is not a badge of honour. These things matter only insofar as they block plausible routes to plausible harms in a particular life. The same tool can be essential in one context and marginal in another. A person subject to harassment may prioritise controlling location traces and social visibility. A person managing research data may prioritise account security and device encryption. A household with children may prioritise boundaries around photos and shared devices. The map decides. The toolkit follows.

The thread that runs through all three questions—what could go wrong, who might care, how bad would it be—is not fear but proportion. It is the refusal to treat privacy as an abstract virtue divorced from lived stakes. It is the recognition that most risk enters through ordinary doors: tired clicks, reused passwords, casual sharing, forgotten access. It is also the recognition that not every door needs to be bricked up. People need to live. They need to communicate, travel, work, flirt, argue, recover, and change. Privacy that cannot survive normal life is not privacy; it is a hobby.

And so the forward test is less about vigilance than about honesty. When a privacy decision arises—and it will, because modern systems constantly request disclosures—does the choice reflect the real map of risk, or merely the loudest story in the news? Does it close a cheap route to a meaningful harm, or does it create performative friction while leaving the master keys jangling in plain sight? The next pages turn that question into something operational, but the tension remains deliberately alive: the safest system is the one a person can actually keep using when they are busy, tired, and human.

Choosing Your Privacy Level

On 3 October 2016, in Paris, Kim Kardashian was robbed in the early hours after returning to a private residence during Fashion Week. The headlines fixated on jewellery and celebrity, but the mechanics were depressingly ordinary: a person with a public profile, predictable movements, and a world that treats attention as currency. Fame did not cause the crime, yet visibility shaped the opportunity. What counts as "enough" privacy for a celebrity moving through a city at night is not what counts as "enough" privacy for a lecturer commuting to campus or a researcher handling sensitive interviews. The dial is not set once for humanity and forgotten. It is set for a life.

Choose the level that fits.

The temptation, when privacy becomes a topic, is to reach for absolutes. Either one performs maximal self-protection—every app suspect, every feature off, every decision slowed by scrutiny—or one shrugs and accepts that "everything is tracked anyway". Both positions are psychologically understandable. Both are strategically weak. A workable privacy life requires a third stance: intentional sufficiency. Not because minimalism is morally superior, but because a privacy posture that collapses under everyday pressure is not a posture at all; it is a weekend project that evaporates on Monday morning.

The most useful way to think about privacy levels is not as a ladder that everyone should climb, but as a set of postures—stable stances that match a person's circumstances, priorities, and appetite for friction. Show: a commuter paying for lunch with a phone, tapping through "allow" prompts, sharing a calendar invite, uploading photos automatically, and managing dozens of logins without a second thought. Name: default exposure. Explain: modern services are designed to make sharing effortless and to make restraint slightly awkward; the default posture is therefore whatever the interface quietly rewards. Implication: without an explicit choice, most people inherit a privacy level chosen by other people's incentives, not their own.

A posture becomes meaningful when it is anchored in trade-offs that can be felt, not merely admired. Convenience is felt as speed: fewer logins, fewer verification prompts, fewer decisions about sharing. Cost is felt as money and opportunity: paid services, upgraded devices, time spent maintaining habits. Time is felt as friction: the extra minute to find a setting, the extra step to approve a sign-in, the extra pause before posting. These are not abstractions. They show up in the day's tempo. A privacy level that demands constant attention will fail for busy people not because they lack virtue, but because attention is scarce.

Start, then, with the simplest posture: basic modern hygiene. This is the posture of people who do not face unusually targeted risks but want to reduce the cheap wins available to opportunists. Show: an email inbox that can reset other accounts, a phone carried everywhere, and a browser that remembers everything because it is helpful. Name: hinge accounts and hinge devices. Explain: certain assets are disproportionately powerful because they unlock others; a modest improvement to these few assets reduces the total attack surface more than scattered tinkering across minor apps. Implication: hygiene is efficient. It aims for the highest return per unit of effort.

The next posture is not "more paranoid". It is more segmented. It suits people whose work or public presence increases exposure: academics with visible research topics, clinicians, journalists, activists, managers dealing with sensitive HR issues, or anyone who attracts attention by virtue of role. Show: a public-facing professional whose name is easy to search, whose email address appears on websites, whose calendar contains meetings with identifiable names, and whose inbox holds attachments that could be embarrassing if leaked. Name: identity linkage. Explain: public profiles create natural hooks for attackers and for casual snooping; the risk often lies less in deep technical compromise than in simple association—linking a name to a location, a routine, a private interest, a set of contacts. Implication: segmentation reduces the blast radius of disclosure. It makes it harder for one compromised corner of life to contaminate everything else.

A third posture exists for people facing specific, human threats rather than general background risk: domestic coercion, stalking, persistent harassment, or a history of boundary violation by someone with proximity and knowledge. This is not a posture one adopts for aesthetic reasons. It is a posture shaped by the fact that the most dangerous actors are sometimes the ones who already know the answers to security questions, who have touched the devices, who can guess what "memorable" passwords might be. Show: a shared streaming account that also stores delivery addresses, a family plan that shares location, an old device left in a drawer still signed in. Name: residual access. Explain: modern sharing features are sticky by design, and relationships leave behind digital entanglements that persist long after trust has changed. Implication: higher-risk postures prioritise control over access paths that are uniquely domestic: shared accounts, shared devices, shared recovery methods, and shared visibility.

These postures are not moral categories. They are situational responses. The same person may move between them over a lifetime: a graduate student becomes a public researcher; a private individual becomes a local councillor; a calm household experiences a relationship rupture; a person moves to a new country with different laws and different risks. Privacy level is therefore less like a certificate earned and more like a stance adjusted when the terrain changes. The dial turns. Life turns it.

Two examples clarify why matching posture to circumstance matters. In July 2015, the extramarital dating site Ashley Madison suffered a breach and, in August 2015, data was published that exposed users' details. The incident became a cultural spectacle precisely because the impact was uneven: for some, it was humiliating gossip; for others, it meant professional risk, relationship collapse, or vulnerability to blackmail. The same technical event landed differently depending on personal context—public prominence, workplace norms, family dynamics, social environment. That is the point. The privacy question is not "Could this be exposed?" but "What would exposure *do* in this life?"

Return to Paris in October 2016 and the logic becomes starker. A famous person's location, routine, and visible possessions are not simply "personal data"; they are tactical information. For public figures, privacy is not only about dignity. It is sometimes about physical safety and predictable patterns. Many ordinary people do not face that particular risk. Some do. A mid-level civil servant working on sensitive issues may attract different attention than a celebrity, but attention nonetheless. A school teacher in a small town may not be famous, yet may still face risk from a disgruntled parent. The relevant variable is not celebrity; it is exposure combined with motive.

A credible limitation now needs to be faced honestly: increasing privacy level can also increase fragility. Show: an account protected by strong verification methods, a phone lost during travel, and a recovery process that takes days. Name: lockout risk. Explain: as systems add security and reduce convenient recovery pathways, the user's capacity to regain access becomes a crucial dependency; in a crisis, the absence of a recovery route can be more disruptive than the original compromise would have been. Implication: higher privacy levels can impose costs that are invisible until the worst moment. This is not an argument against tightening. It is an argument for choosing a posture that a person can sustain without creating new vulnerabilities through brittleness.

Reconciling that limitation brings the discussion back to proportion. The goal is not maximal hardness. The goal is resilience. A posture should reduce exposure while preserving the ability to function under stress: tiredness, travel, illness, relationship turmoil, work pressure. A privacy level that assumes perfect attention is fantasy. A privacy level that assumes perfect memory is cruel. Any posture worth adopting must make allowances for human error because humans are the only users most systems have.

That is why "basic hygiene" is not dismissive language. It is the foundation that supports every higher posture. Hygiene is the set of actions whose costs are low and whose benefits are broad, regardless of specific threat models. Show: reducing how much sensitive information is exposed through routine interactions—login flows, notifications, casual sharing. Name: baseline protections. Explain: opportunistic scams and account takeovers thrive on predictable weakness—reused credentials, unsecured devices, over-shared personal details; baseline protections raise the effort required for the most common attacks. Implication: hygiene buys time. It reduces the chance that an ordinary mistake becomes an expensive crisis.

Segmentation, the next posture, is about separating roles. Show: a person using the same email address for professional correspondence, newsletters, retail receipts, and social media; then a single breach floods the inbox with password reset attempts and targeted phishing. Name: role separation. Explain: when one identifier becomes a hub, it attracts both legitimate traffic and malicious exploitation; separating roles reduces how much one compromise enables and reduces how much unwanted attention can be funnelled through a single channel. Implication: segmentation reduces complexity later. It trades small upfront effort for a calmer future.

The high-risk posture, when needed, is about removing cheap leverage for a known or plausible actor. Show: an abusive ex-partner who knows the answers to "security questions", recognises the devices, and can manipulate social trust. Name: adversary proximity.

Explain: threats from close actors differ from threats from strangers because the attacker's information advantage is built-in; standard defences that assume a stranger can fail when the attacker already knows personal history and routines. Implication: high-risk postures prioritise controlling visibility and access that proximity makes easy—reducing discoverability, reducing shared account entanglement, reducing passive tracking. The objective is not invisibility; it is to deny the easiest forms of control.

The reason these postures matter is psychological as much as technical. People abandon privacy efforts when the work feels either endless or irrelevant. A posture gives a stopping point that is neither complacent nor obsessive. It permits a person to say: this is the level that matches my life right now. It also permits escalation without drama. If circumstances shift—new job, new visibility, new relationship dynamics—the dial can be turned deliberately rather than in a panic after something happens.

Notice how this approach changes the emotional flavour of privacy. Without postures, privacy feels like an accusation: "You should care more." With postures, privacy becomes a design problem: "Which costs are acceptable for which risks?" That question respects the reality that privacy competes with other values: ease, sociability, speed, even joy. People share photos because they love. They use maps because they want to arrive. They keep location services on because they do not want to feel lost. Privacy that treats these motivations as foolish will lose. Privacy that acknowledges them can win, because it can propose trade-offs that do not require a personality transplant.

There is also a subtle intellectual payoff: postures expose how much of privacy is really about *defaults*. Most people do not make hundreds of deliberate decisions about data; they follow the path of least resistance. Show: the pre-ticked box, the "continue with Google" button, the default "anyone with the link" sharing setting. Name: default bias. Explain: interface design shapes behaviour because it makes certain choices effortless and makes others cognitively costly; over time, effortless choices become habits and habits become identity—"I'm not a privacy person." Implication: choosing a posture is a way of resisting default bias. It is a commitment to make a small number of decisions once so that future behaviour changes without constant deliberation.

The quiet motif here is the dial, not because it is poetic, but because it is accurate. A dial implies gradation. It implies reversibility. It implies calibration against conditions. It also implies that the "highest" setting is not always right. A household might turn the dial towards convenience for a season—new baby, exhausting work project—then turn it back towards restraint when life steadies. A person might turn the dial up during travel, then down afterwards. The sophistication lies not in always maximising, but in matching settings to reality.

The unresolved tension at the end of this is deliberately practical: when privacy choices begin to demand time, money, or friction, which posture will govern the trade—hygiene, segmentation, or high-risk defence? The answer is not a declaration. It is a test. It is the next decision made under ordinary pressure, when convenience offers a shortcut and the dial is sitting right there, waiting to be turned.

Chapter 2
Hardening Your Phone

In May 2019, WhatsApp disclosed a vulnerability that allowed spyware to be installed on a phone through a call that did not even need to be answered. A ring. A vibration. A screen lighting up in a pocket. The mechanism was technical, but the experience was almost insultingly ordinary: the sort of ghost-call people ignore dozens of times a year. Later that year, in October 2019, WhatsApp sued NSO Group in the United States, in the Northern District of California, alleging the company's software had been used to target users through that weakness. Most people were not targets of that particular campaign. The point is not to borrow someone else's nightmare. The point is to notice how a device can be both intimate and exposed at the same time.

A phone is the most personal object most adults own. It is also the most socially entangled. It is camera, diary, wallet, map, office, and keyring. It is the authentication token for other systems that matter more than the phone itself. The strange trick of modern life is that the object treated with the most casual handling—left on café tables, handed to friends for a quick photo, brought into bedrooms, used half-asleep—is also the object that now carries the most consequential access. People often speak about "hacking" as if it were a rare skill applied to high-value targets. Yet much of what makes phones vulnerable is not exotic attack; it is ordinary neglect, compounded by design choices that reward convenience and bury restraint.

Hardening a phone is not about fear. It is about engineering. The aim is not to make the phone unuseable, joyless, or permanently suspicious of the world. The aim is to move it from "easy to exploit" to "annoying to exploit". That shift sounds modest, but it changes the economics of harm. Opportunists pick the cheapest route. Scammers choose the lowest friction. A nosy colleague relies on casual access. A thief counts on weak locks and generous notifications. Even sophisticated actors—when they exist—still prefer the path of least resistance, which is often the one created by outdated software and permissive defaults.

The first hard truth is that phones age faster than their owners' habits. People grow attached to their devices; the device grows obsolete anyway. Software updates arrive with an air of inconvenience, as if the phone were asking for a favour. In reality, updates are the closest thing the user has to a time machine. They patch known weaknesses. They close doors that are already mapped. The difference between a patched phone and an unpatched one is not abstract. It is the difference between a lock that has been improved and a lock whose flaws are written down in public. When a vulnerability is disclosed, it becomes, effectively, a recipe for anyone with motivation and a little skill. The phone does not become unsafe on the day the user ignores the update; it becomes unsafe on the day the rest of the world learns what the update was meant to fix.

Still, patching creates a practical anxiety that people rarely admit: the fear of losing things. Photos. Messages. Notes. The small scraps of life that have become precious precisely because they are mundane. That is why updates and backups are inseparable. A backup is not a moral gesture; it is an insurance policy against dread. Without it, people postpone security improvements because the risk of change feels higher than the risk of stasis. With it, they can accept the ordinary disruptions of software maintenance without the sense that their memories are perched on a single slab of glass. A hardened phone is not merely locked down; it is recoverable.

If updates are the maintenance of the building, the lock screen is the front door. This is where privacy stops being a philosophical preference and becomes a visible decision. It is also where people lie to themselves in surprisingly consistent ways. They believe a short PIN is "fine because nobody cares" or "fine because I'm careful". They forget that "careful" is not a permanent state. It vanishes when someone is rushing for a train, distracted at a bar, or exhausted at the end of a long day. A lock is not for the moments when attention is perfect. It is for the moments when attention fails.

Biometrics complicate this in a uniquely modern way because they feel like magic. A thumb. A glance. The door opens. The convenience is real, and in many lives the convenience becomes part of the security because it encourages locking that would otherwise be skipped. But biometrics also carry a philosophical weight that a passcode does not. A passcode is a secret that can be changed. A fingerprint is not. A face is not. A secret can be revoked; a body cannot be rotated like a password after a breach. This is not an argument to fear biometrics. It is an argument to treat them as what they are: a trade between speed and control, between comfort and reversibility. The wise approach is neither technophobic nor naive. It is deliberate.

Deliberateness matters most when the threat is not a stranger in a hoodie but a person close enough to exploit moments of proximity—someone who might pick up a phone when its owner is asleep, or someone who feels entitled to access because access once existed. Phones are designed to glide between hands. Relationships are messy. The lock screen is where messy realities meet hard access control. A hardened phone respects that reality. It does not pretend everyone lives in a tidy world of purely external threats.

Then there are apps, the true organs of modern phones. Operating systems are the skeleton; apps are the metabolism. Most people would never knowingly install "spyware", and they do not. They install games, scanners, photo editors, and cheerful utilities. The problem is not always that apps are malicious. It is that apps are curious, and curiosity is profitable. They ask for more than they need because extra data enables extra features, extra personalisation, extra targeting, extra measurement. Permissions are the polite language of this bargain: a small dialogue box that turns a complex data flow into a simple choice. Allow. Don't allow. Ask next time. It feels like control, and sometimes it is. Sometimes it is also a ritual that moves too quickly for meaningful judgement.

A concrete example exposes the pattern without melodrama: a flashlight app that requests access to location, microphone, and contacts. The flashlight itself is not suspicious; the request is. Why would a light need to know where a person is? Why would it need to listen? Why would it need a social graph? The questions are not rhetorical. They force a clarity that many app stores do not encourage. Some permissions genuinely support features—location for local weather, microphone for voice notes, contacts for messaging. But the burden of proof belongs to the app. A hardened phone treats permissions as a budget: spent when the return is obvious, saved when the return is vague.

The quiet genius of permissions hygiene is that it scales. It does not require a person to become an expert in every app's internal behaviour. It requires a repeatable way of sorting: what is necessary for function, what is optional for convenience, what is unrelated to purpose. The result is not purity. It is reduction. And reduction is one of the few reliable paths to privacy that does not depend on perfect vigilance.

Connections are the final layer because phones are, at heart, radios. They talk constantly: to towers, to Wi-Fi, to Bluetooth devices, to nearby services looking for a handshake. Most people experience this chatter as seamlessness. Headphones connect. Cars pair. Cafés offer a network name and a password scribbled on a chalkboard. The phone, always eager to be useful, reaches out. The risk here is not that every network is a trap. The risk is that connection is treated as neutral when it is really a context shift: different environments mean different exposure. A phone on a trusted home network behaves differently, in terms of who can observe traffic and which devices are nearby, than a phone on public Wi-Fi in an airport lounge. The same action—checking email, logging into an account—can be trivial in one context and unwise in another.

Public networks also reveal a more general truth: privacy is often about reducing unnecessary broadcasting. Phones announce themselves in small ways—looking for known networks, advertising their presence to Bluetooth devices, responding to prompts and pings. The details can be technical, but the principle is simple. A hardened phone is not silent; silence would be impractical. It is selectively chatty. It speaks when it must. It quiets when it can. That selectivity is a form of dignity, the digital equivalent of not shouting personal details across a crowded room.

There is an emotional dimension to all of this that deserves to be named. People often treat phone security as a kind of self-reproach, a guilty sense of being behind, of having failed to "keep up". That mood is counterproductive. Phone hardening works best when approached as routine maintenance rather than moral reform. The point is to remove the easy failures. The point is to stop handing out accidental access. The point is to keep the device's future self from becoming a liability—because the phone is not static; it evolves, it accumulates, it becomes more valuable to its owner and more interesting to other people over time.

A hardened phone also supports a deeper ambition of this book: living with technology on terms that remain human. The world does not need more people performing privacy as an identity, broadcasting their cleverness. It needs more people treating privacy as a practical craft: calm, repeatable, proportionate. Updates and backups are craft. Lock screens and biometrics are craft. Permissions are craft. Network habits are craft. None of this requires a bunker. It requires a willingness to take seriously the fact that the most personal object most people own is also one of the most networked.

The reward for doing this well is not a sense of invincibility. That would be childish. The reward is a quieter mind. When the phone is less fragile—less dependent on luck, less reliant on perfect attention—it becomes easier to use without the faint dread that one mistake will cascade into weeks of recovery. Hardening is, in that sense, a kind of mercy towards one's future self.

The next step is a practical tension rather than a tidy lesson: how much friction is worth adding to the most intimate device in your life in exchange for fewer accidental disclosures, fewer cheap routes to harm, and fewer moments of realising—too late—that the front door was never really shut?

Updating And Backups

On 12 May 2017, hospitals across England found themselves dragged into a kind of technological farce that stopped being funny within minutes. Computers in NHS trusts displayed a red ransom note; staff reverted to pen and paper; appointments were cancelled; phones rang with the particular edge of panic that comes when routine collapses. The malware was called WannaCry, and its spread was propelled by systems that had missed a critical security patch released by Microsoft in March 2017. The details of that week belong to desktop computers, not phones, yet the lesson lands squarely in the palm: modern failures rarely require genius. They require drift.

Updates are boring, and vital.

Phones feel different from computers because they are smoother, newer, and built to hide their machinery. They ask less. They nag in friendlier tones. They appear to take care of themselves. That is an illusion created by good design. Underneath, phones are small general-purpose computers with radios attached, running vast amounts of code—millions of lines, maintained by teams who discover, fix, and sometimes publicly disclose flaws at a pace no ordinary person can track. The only realistic way for most people to benefit from those fixes is for updates to happen without drama. When updates do not happen, the phone becomes a museum: a beautiful object preserved in a state that attackers and scammers understand better every month.

The reasons updates matter are not mystical. Show: a security bulletin describing a vulnerability, a patch released, and a period of time in which unpatched devices remain exposed. Name: the patch window. Explain: once a weakness is known—whether discovered by researchers, exploited in the wild, or quietly found in internal testing—the clock starts; patching closes the weakness for updated devices, but it also clarifies the weakness for everyone else, because the change in code often reveals what was wrong. Implication: delaying updates does not keep a phone stable; it keeps a phone readable to people who enjoy breaking things.

It is tempting to believe that phone vulnerabilities are too rare to worry about, or too sophisticated to be relevant to ordinary lives. Yet many successful compromises exploit the same human pattern: devices are valuable, people are busy, and software maintenance feels optional until it is not. Show: a phone that hasn't updated in a year, still happily sending messages and taking photos. Name: functional complacency. Explain: a device can appear "fine" while becoming progressively easier to compromise, because vulnerabilities do not announce themselves with visible symptoms; the phone does not slow down to warn that its security assumptions are rotting. Implication: waiting for a problem to appear is a poor security strategy, because the first visible sign can be account takeover, data exposure, or a costly reset performed under stress.

A checkable phone-specific example makes this concrete. In August 2016, the research group Citizen Lab at the University of Toronto published analysis of a sophisticated spyware tool later widely associated with NSO Group's Pegasus, and Apple released iOS 9.3.5 to patch vulnerabilities being used to infect iPhones. The people targeted were not random: journalists, activists, lawyers—lives where information is leverage. But the mechanism is the point. A phone did not become safer because its owner suddenly gained technical insight. It became safer because a patch landed. The implication is quietly democratic: a boring update can protect someone from a very un-boring attacker. The reverse is also true. A skipped update can make an ordinary phone vulnerable to an ordinary scam that relies on nothing more than an outdated component and a persuasive message.

Phones age quickly in a way that is partly technical and partly commercial. A handset can remain physically intact while its software support expires, and that expiry is the true moment of obsolescence. Show: a device that no longer receives major operating system updates, only occasional app updates, and the creeping appearance of compatibility warnings. Name: end-of-support. Explain: operating system vendors and manufacturers support devices for finite periods; once a device falls out of support, known vulnerabilities may remain unpatched because the vendor no longer ships fixes for that model. Implication: an unsupported phone is not merely "older"; it is structurally more exposed, regardless of how carefully its owner behaves.

This is where the phrase "too old to trust" becomes precise. It does not mean "too old to work". It means "too old to be confidently maintained". Trust, here, is operational: can the device still receive the repairs that the rest of the ecosystem assumes it has? Many apps and services build on the security features of modern operating systems—hardware-backed key storage, improved permission controls, tighter sandboxing, stronger encryption defaults. When a phone is frozen on an old operating system, it may lack not only patches but entire categories of defences. The implication is uncomfortable but clear: sentimentality about devices can become a security liability when it keeps a person locked into an unsupported platform.

Still, there is a credible limitation, and it deserves air rather than dismissal. Updates sometimes break things. They can introduce bugs, drain batteries, change interfaces, and disrupt workflows people depend on. Organisations with specialised apps sometimes delay updates because compatibility matters. Individuals may delay because they cannot risk a device behaving unpredictably during a work trip or an exam period. This is not irrational. It is risk management of a different kind: the risk of disruption versus the risk of exposure.

The reconciliation is to stop treating "update now" and "never update" as the only two temperaments available. A practical approach recognises that the highest-risk period is not "a short delay to avoid disruption"; it is indefinite postponement that turns into permanent staleness. Show: a person who postpones an update for a week, then forgets, then discovers three months later that several updates are queued. Name: drift. Explain: drift is what happens when maintenance is not attached to any routine; the device slowly diverges from the supported baseline until catching up feels daunting, and daunting tasks are postponed again. Implication: the real enemy is not the update; it is the absence of a maintenance rhythm that keeps updates small and survivable.

Backups exist to make that rhythm psychologically easy. A phone update is not frightening when the phone is disposable in the best sense: if it fails, life can be restored. Show: a person hesitating to enable a stronger passcode or to update the operating system because they fear losing photos and messages. Name: anxiety tax. Explain: fear of data loss acts as a tax on security decisions; people accept higher exposure because the alternative feels like risking the disappearance of their own history. Implication: a reliable backup is not merely about resilience after theft or accidents; it is the foundation that allows people to take sensible security steps without dread.

The word "backup" is often used loosely, and the looseness causes avoidable confusion. Many services offer synchronisation, which is excellent for convenience and continuity but not always the same as a true backup. Show: a photo deleted on one device and then disappearing everywhere because the library is synchronised. Name: propagation. Explain: sync is designed to keep data consistent across devices; deletion is therefore often treated as a command, not an accident, and it propagates. Implication: relying on sync alone can create the illusion of safety while leaving a person vulnerable to the most banal disaster: accidental deletion that obediently spreads.

A proper backup, by contrast, is an escape hatch: a stored state that does not immediately mirror every change. Even when people use cloud backups, the key features are cadence and recoverability—whether the backup occurs regularly without fuss, and whether it allows restoration after loss, theft, or failure. There is also a privacy dimension that deserves honesty. Backing up to a commercial cloud means trusting a provider with a copy of data, even if much of it is encrypted in transit and at rest. Some people are comfortable with that trade; others, because of profession or personal circumstances, are not. The important point is not to sanctify one choice. It is to understand what is being traded: reduced data-loss risk in exchange for storing a copy elsewhere.

A second checkable example shows why backup and update decisions must be considered together. In May 2019, WhatsApp disclosed a vulnerability that could be exploited to install spyware through crafted calls, and later that year WhatsApp filed suit against NSO Group in the United States, alleging abuse of the platform. Whatever one thinks of that litigation, the episode revealed a reality many people prefer not to hold in mind: certain attackers target phones precisely because phones are the keys to everything else. When a phone is compromised or lost, recovery is not merely about replacing hardware; it is about restoring access to accounts, identities, and records. Backups—of data and of the ability to restore—become part of the security posture, not an optional convenience.

That includes an often-overlooked aspect of "backup" that is less about photos and more about identity. Show: a person buys a new phone, restores from backup, and discovers that key logins require verification codes sent to the old device or an old number. Name: recovery dependency. Explain: modern services rely on multi-factor authentication and device-based approvals; losing the device without a planned recovery route can lock a person out of accounts even when they know their passwords. Implication: the practical value of backups includes the ability to recover *access*, not just content—a difference that only becomes visible in the worst moment.

All of this leads to a strangely liberating conclusion about efficiency. People often treat maintenance as a time thief, yet maintenance is what prevents time being stolen later. Compare the time cost of a routine update with the time cost of recovering a compromised account, replacing a device, proving identity to support teams, and re-securing everything under pressure. The first is a small, predictable inconvenience. The second is a sprawling, emotionally draining project that invades workdays and weekends. The trade is not subtle. The difficulty is that humans discount future pain. Phones exploit that human trait by making the deferral button easy.

A monthly rhythm counteracts that bias not by moralising but by reducing decision-making. The point is to remove the need to "decide" about updates every time the phone asks. Decision fatigue is real; it is also exploitable. A routine—brief, consistent, unglamorous—turns maintenance into something like checking a smoke alarm or renewing a travel card. One month, the check takes seconds because everything is already current. Another month, it takes longer because something is pending. The important thing is that the phone does not drift into staleness unnoticed.

The motif worth carrying through this, quietly, is the expiry date. Not because technology is food, but because the analogy captures the psychology. People do not need to be frightened of milk every time they open the fridge. They need a habit of noticing when something is past its safe window. Software has a safe window too. Updates refresh that window. End-of-support closes it. Backups, meanwhile, are the spare pantry: the reassurance that even if something spoils, the household will eat.

There is also a final, uncomfortable truth: the cost of good maintenance is paid in small inconveniences, while the cost of neglect is paid in concentrated misery. That asymmetry is why so many intelligent, time-conscious people still postpone updates. They are not ignorant. They are responding rationally to the incentives presented in the moment. A phone that works today feels like proof that it will work tomorrow. But security is not about today's behaviour; it is about tomorrow's exploit.

The forward test is therefore not technical. It is behavioural. When the next update appears—when the phone offers a postponement button and the day feels too full—does the choice treat the update as optional comfort, or as routine maintenance that keeps the device within its safety window? The answer determines whether the phone remains a reliable companion, or slowly becomes a beautifully engineered liability waiting for the first bad week.

Lock Screen And Biometrics

In February 2016, in the wake of the San Bernardino shootings in California, Apple found itself arguing in public with the FBI about a single iPhone. The Bureau wanted Apple to create software that would help bypass the device's passcode protections; Apple refused, warning that such a tool would not stay "just this once". The legal filings, press statements, and televised commentary turned a familiar domestic action—typing a code into a glass rectangle—into a question of state power. Later that year the US Department of Justice withdrew its request after the FBI accessed the phone with third-party assistance. The phone remained one phone. The point became universal: the lock screen is not a nicety. It is an access boundary.

Locks fail when we forget.

Most people do not expect their phone to become the centre of a constitutional dispute, yet the underlying issue touches ordinary life daily. A phone is carried into bedrooms and meetings, into trains and hospitals, into arguments and reconciliations. It stores messages that were never meant for an audience, photos that were meant for a handful of people, and authentication that can open other accounts that matter more than the phone itself. The lock screen is therefore not a single door but a front door with several rooms behind it. Choosing how that door opens—PIN, password, fingerprint, face—means choosing what sorts of access you are most willing to trade convenience for, and what sorts of access you need to resist.

Start with the simplest truth: a lock screen defends against the most common attacker, who is not a cinematic genius but a human being in the same physical space. Show: a phone left on a café table while someone collects a coffee; a colleague picking it up to "move it out of the way"; a friend scrolling through notifications because they light up like sweets. Name: opportunistic access. Explain: physical proximity collapses many technical defences because the device is already present, already trusted by itself, already logged in to accounts; an attacker does not need to "hack" a cloud service if the unlocked device can be used as a key. Implication: the lock screen is not mainly about stopping distant adversaries; it is about stopping casual, high-probability invasions that occur in ordinary environments.

A four-digit PIN is the classic compromise between ease and resistance. It feels private because it is not written down, and familiar because it resembles the codes used for bank cards and door entry systems. Yet its mathematics are blunt. Show: someone watching from behind on a crowded train as a thumb taps four numbers in a consistent rhythm. Name: small keyspace. Explain: a four-digit PIN has 10,000 possible combinations; that sounds large until you remember that human beings do not choose combinations evenly, that some sequences are common, and that shoulder-surfing reduces the problem to one observed performance rather than 10,000 guesses. Implication: a short PIN is less a lock than a speed bump, particularly in environments where other eyes exist.

Longer passcodes and passwords expand the keyspace dramatically and change the nature of attack. Show: a phone that demands a longer code after a restart or after a certain time, and the small moment of irritation as the user types it carefully. Name: memorised secret. Explain: a longer passcode is not merely "more characters"; it shifts the attacker's options, making casual observation harder and brute-force guessing less feasible, especially when devices enforce delays or wipe after repeated failures. Implication: a longer secret tends to protect against opportunists and petty thieves in a way a short PIN cannot, even if it costs a few seconds a day.

Biometrics—fingerprints and face recognition—arrived as a promise to dissolve that cost. Apple introduced Touch ID with the iPhone 5s in September 2013, and Face ID with the iPhone X in September 2017 in Cupertino, framing them as both convenience and security. The pitch was seductive because it aligned with human laziness in a flattering way: you could be safer without trying harder. That pitch is not entirely marketing. Biometrics can make locking a phone feel frictionless, which means more people actually lock. Show: a person who would never tolerate typing a long passcode dozens of times a day but will happily glance at a screen. Name: compliance advantage. Explain: security mechanisms succeed when people use them consistently; a mechanism that is theoretically strong but practically ignored produces the illusion of safety without the benefit. Implication: biometrics can improve real-world protection precisely because they remove the temptation to leave the door open.

Yet biometrics change the meaning of the lock. A passcode is something you know. A fingerprint is something you are. A face is something you carry through every public space. Show: a person unlocking a phone without thinking, in sunlight, in a queue, with others inches away, the act almost invisible. Name: embodied credential. Explain: embodied credentials are convenient because they cannot be forgotten, but they are also less easily revoked; if a passcode is compromised, it can be changed immediately, while a fingerprint or face cannot be swapped out in the way a password can. Implication: biometrics shift risk from "I might forget" to "I might be compelled, copied, or misused", and that shift matters more in some lives than others.

This is where the earlier idea of threat modelling stops being abstract and becomes the right tool. The correct question is not "Are biometrics good?" but "Good against whom?" Show: the opportunistic thief who wants a quick sale, the curious partner who wants access, the employer who is too interested, the border agent who has time and authority, the scammer who can't get near the device but can pressure remotely. Name: attacker model. Explain: different attackers have different capabilities; a thief might not have time to manipulate a sleeping face or coax a finger to a sensor, while a coercive domestic actor might. A law enforcement officer might have authority to seize a device and hold it, while a café opportunist does not. Implication: the lock choice should be matched to plausible pressure, not to generic fear.

Coercion is an unpleasant word, but it belongs here because it changes the calculus. Biometrics can be activated without the owner choosing to cooperate, in ways that are easier than extracting a memorised secret from someone who refuses to speak. Show: a phone brought close to a face, or a finger placed on a sensor, with the owner present but not consenting in the meaningful sense. Name: compulsion risk. Explain: an embodied credential can be used with the body itself; a memorised secret requires a decision to disclose, even under pressure. Implication: in environments where coercion is plausible—domestic control, certain professional risks, certain encounters with authority—a strong passcode can offer a different kind of protection than a fingerprint or face unlock.

Law adds another layer of uncertainty without offering a universal answer. Different jurisdictions treat compelled disclosure differently, and case law has evolved unevenly. In the United States, for example, courts have grappled with whether compelling a biometric unlock is more like taking a fingerprint (often considered non-testimonial) than compelling a person to reveal a memorised passcode (sometimes argued to be testimonial under the Fifth Amendment). The legal landscape is complex and not consistent across states and cases. The implication is not that biometrics are "unsafe" in some definitive way. The implication is that biometrics can alter the kinds of pressure a person is vulnerable to, and those pressures include legal ones that vary by place and circumstance.

A second checkable example illustrates how "front door" choices intersect with the realities of forensic access. In 2020, the FBI publicly acknowledged in court filings connected to the Pensacola naval air station shooting in Florida that it had been unable to access the contents of two iPhones used by the attacker, and it pressed

Apple for assistance. Apple stated it had provided iCloud data it possessed but could not unlock the devices without undermining its security model. The dispute, like the San Bernardino one, became a public proxy fight about encryption and access. Whatever one's politics, the technical lesson is clear: modern phone security is built around the idea that the passcode protects the cryptographic keys that protect everything else. When the passcode is strong and the device enforces it properly, access becomes genuinely difficult.

That is also the most important limitation to admit: biometrics are not a standalone lock; they sit on top of the passcode. Phones require the passcode at certain moments—after a restart, after a period of inactivity, after repeated failed biometric attempts, sometimes after changes to biometric settings. The passcode is the bedrock credential. Biometrics are a shortcut layered on top, like a smart latch on a solid door. Show: the sudden demand for the passcode after a reboot, or after a face unlock fails in low light. Name: fallback control. Explain: the device uses the passcode to gate access to encryption keys and to confirm identity when biometric confidence is low. Implication: anyone who treats biometrics as replacing the passcode is missing the real architecture; the strength of the foundation still matters.

Security is also not simply about stopping an attacker from opening the phone; it is about controlling what can be seen without opening it. Lock screens leak. Show: notifications displaying message previews, one-time codes, calendar details, and names of contacts while the phone remains technically "locked". Name: surface exposure. Explain: even when the device is locked, the lock screen can act like a noticeboard, broadcasting snippets that are enough to infer relationships, routines, and sometimes access tokens. Implication: a "locked" phone can still be talkative, and talkative locks are a contradiction in terms.

Convenience, meanwhile, has its own ethics. People work, travel, parent, and care for relatives with phones in hand. Friction has a cost, sometimes a real one: missing a train because an authentication prompt appears at the wrong moment, fumbling a passcode while carrying bags, struggling to unlock a phone with wet hands in the rain. These are not excuses; they are facts. The best lock is not the one that wins in theory. It is the one that remains in place on a bad day. Show: a person who disables the lock because it is annoying, then forgets to re-enable it. Name: abandonment risk. Explain: an overly demanding security set-up can cause users to bypass it, creating a bigger vulnerability than a slightly weaker but consistently used method. Implication: convenience is not the enemy; it is a constraint that any realistic security posture must respect.

This is where biometrics can be not merely acceptable but actively beneficial for many people: they can raise everyday security by increasing consistent locking. A fingerprint sensor can make a device harder to access for casual snoopers because it eliminates the "I'll just leave it unlocked for a minute" habit. Face unlock can reduce shoulder-surfing risk because it removes the visible tapping of digits in public. The limitation is that biometrics introduce different failure modes—false rejects, occasional spoofing attempts, potential compulsion—that matter more in some contexts than others. A thoughtful posture chooses which failure modes are most tolerable.

Spoofing deserves a brief, unsensational mention because it is both real and often overstated. Researchers and security firms have periodically demonstrated ways to bypass certain biometric systems under controlled conditions, sometimes using masks, high-quality prints, or 3D models. Some demonstrations are persuasive; others are more theatrical than practical. The key point is not whether a particular device can be fooled in a laboratory. It is whether an attacker who wants access to *your* phone has the time, resources, and proximity to attempt such a trick. For most opportunists, stealing a phone and hoping it is poorly protected is cheaper. For certain targeted actors, more effort can be rational. The implication returns to threat modelling: the question is always "Who might care?" and "How much effort would they pay?"

The front door metaphor remains useful because it keeps the conversation grounded. A front door does not need to resist a siege in most neighbourhoods. It needs to resist the common risks: a curious passer-by, a petty thief, a moment of human forgetfulness. Some households do need stronger doors because their risk profile is different. Phones are the same. People with public visibility, with adversarial relationships, or with particular legal exposure may rationally prefer a posture in which the passcode is the primary gate and biometrics are used cautiously, if at all. Others may rationally choose biometrics because the everyday benefit—consistent locking—outweighs the less likely coercion scenario. Both can be intelligent choices. The stupidity lies in choosing by default.

The final piece of honesty is that there is no lock that replaces judgement. A person can have the strongest passcode in the world and still hand their phone unlocked to someone they trust too quickly. A person can use biometrics and still expose themselves through lock-screen previews. The lock is necessary, not sufficient. It is, however, one of the few defences that is always present, always relevant, and always under the owner's control. It sits at the threshold between the public world and the private device, and thresholds are where most mistakes become expensive.

The forward test is simple enough to feel uncomfortable: when the front door of the phone is designed for speed, who benefits more—its owner, or anyone who can get close enough to try it?

App Permissions Hygiene

In December 2013, in Washington, D.C., the US Federal Trade Commission announced a settlement with Goldenshores Technologies over a flashlight app called "Brightest Flashlight Free". The allegation was not that the app failed to shine a light. It was that it collected and shared precise location information without telling users properly, including with advertising networks. A torch in the hand became a beacon in the data stream. Nothing about the interface looked sinister. The controversy lived in the gap between what the app *appeared* to need and what it quietly took.

Small doors swing wide.

That is the central problem with app permissions. They are presented as a moment—Allow or Don't Allow—yet they behave like a relationship: once granted, they can persist across months, operating in the background while the phone sits in a pocket, on a bedside table, in a meeting. People do not experience permissions as surveillance; they experience them as friction. They tap to remove the friction and move on. The result is not one dramatic privacy failure but a gradual widening of access across dozens of apps, each holding a slightly larger slice of life than it strictly requires.

Permissions are the grammar of modern phones. They are supposed to translate an app's needs into a set of bounded capabilities: location, camera, microphone, contacts, photos, Bluetooth, calendar, motion sensors. In theory, this is beautifully civilised. In practice, the translation is often muddy, and the incentives are skewed. Many app developers would like more data than they need because additional data makes user profiling easier, ad targeting richer, retention experiments more precise, and "personalisation" more profitable. Even when a developer's intentions are benign, third-party software embedded inside apps—analytics and advertising kits—may hunger for signals that have nothing to do with the app's surface purpose. A permission granted to a silly utility can feed a serious machinery.

The most useful way to approach permissions is neither paranoid nor trusting. It is *proportional.* Show: a map app requesting location while navigating; a banking app requesting camera access to scan a cheque; a voice recorder requesting microphone access. Name: purpose alignment. Explain: when the permission directly enables the core function the user has chosen, the request is bounded and intelligible; the user is trading a capability for a clear benefit. Implication: saying yes can be entirely reasonable, because the disclosure is tethered to an obvious purpose.

Now invert the example, because inversion is where clarity arrives. Show: a flashlight app requesting location, microphone, and contacts. Name: purpose drift. Explain: the torch function does not logically require any of these; the requests are therefore likely to serve secondary goals—analytics, advertising, social features no one asked for, or data collection "just in case". Implication: the burden of justification shifts. The request is no longer a fair exchange; it is a grab bag.

This is not about assuming all developers are villains. It is about recognising that the permission system is a marketplace: apps compete for attention and revenue, and data is a commodity that can be converted into both. The FTC's Goldenshores settlement matters precisely because it was mundane. The app category was trivial. The users were ordinary. The data collection was invisible. The outcome, at minimum, was unwanted sharing; at maximum, it demonstrated how easily people can be tracked through apps that appear innocent.

A second checkable example makes the point from another angle. In February 2012, the social networking app Path faced public backlash after it was discovered to be uploading users' address books to its servers without clear consent; the company apologised and changed the behaviour. That episode was not a story about one obscure start-up being uniquely reckless. It was a story about how tempting contact lists are. Contacts are not just names and numbers. They are a social graph. They reveal relationships, communities, professional networks, family structure, and often the private nicknames people use for one another. A permission to access contacts is therefore not a small concession; it is an export of social reality.

In both cases—location harvesting by a flashlight app and address-book uploading by a social app—the pattern is the same. Show: the phone offers a capability that feels like a technical detail; the user grants it to remove friction; the app uses the capability to collect data with a value far beyond the immediate feature. Name: asymmetric value. Explain: the user receives a small convenience (a torch, a friend-finder), while the app receives a stream of data that can be retained, analysed, and monetised; the exchange is lopsided because the user experiences the benefit immediately and the costs later, if at all. Implication: the permission prompt is not merely a technical pop-up. It is a contract offered in the language of convenience.

Modern operating systems have tried—sometimes clumsily, sometimes well—to rebalance that contract. Apple's App Tracking Transparency prompt, introduced with iOS 14.5 in April 2021, forced many apps to ask whether they could track a user across other companies' apps and websites. Android, beginning with Android 10 and Android 11 (2019–2020), expanded controls such as "only while in use" location access and one-time permissions for sensitive capabilities like camera and microphone. These features did not eliminate tracking. They did change the default bargaining position by giving users more granular refusal options. The implication is quietly important: privacy is not only a matter of individual discipline; it is also shaped by how systems make refusal easy or hard.

Still, software design cannot substitute for judgement, because the real problem is not that permissions exist. The problem is that people accumulate them. Show: a phone that has been in use for three years, with dozens of apps installed for one-off tasks—scanning a form, editing a video, checking a flight—many of which were never deleted, many of which retain whatever permissions were granted in haste. Name: permission debt. Explain: each app is a potential channel for data, and each granted permission increases the app's ability to observe or infer; over time, the phone becomes less a curated tool and more a junk drawer of semi-trusted software. Implication: privacy risk becomes a property of *quantity* as much as of any single bad actor.

This is why permissions hygiene matters more than heroic one-time configurations. Hygiene is an ongoing practice of pruning and narrowing. It is also a way of aligning the phone's behaviour with the life that owns it. A person who rarely uses the microphone outside calls does not need half a dozen utilities to have persistent microphone access. A person who never shares their contact list with apps does not need "friend-finder" features embedded in shopping, games, and lifestyle tools. A person who only occasionally needs precise location does not need constant background location collection. The principle is simple: grant the narrowest access that plausibly supports the chosen function.

The phrase "plausibly supports" matters because the line is not always clean. Some permissions are bundled in ways that frustrate common sense. An app might request Bluetooth access to connect to headphones, but Bluetooth scanning can also be used for proximity tracking. A fitness app might request motion sensors to count steps, and those sensors can, in some research contexts, be used to infer patterns of behaviour. A camera app might request access to photos in order to save edits, and "access to photos" might mean access to an entire library unless the operating system provides finer controls. The implication is not that every request hides a plot.

It is that capabilities are multipurpose, and multipurpose tools deserve careful allocation.

An honest approach also distinguishes between access granted "while using the app" and access granted "always", because the difference is behavioural. Show: a weather app that updates only when opened versus a weather app that pings location in the background all day to provide hyper-local forecasts and targeted ads. Name: background authority. Explain: background access turns an app from a tool you summon into a sensor that runs when you are not thinking about it; the phone becomes chatty on the app's behalf, not only on yours. Implication: background permissions are where privacy quietly erodes, because the collection happens without the moment of conscious use that might prompt second thoughts.

The same logic applies to photos. People treat photo libraries like drawers of printed pictures. Apps treat them like datasets. Show: an app asking for photo access "to upload a profile picture" when, in reality, it could accomplish the task with access to a single chosen image. Name: overbroad scope. Explain: broad photo access can expose not only images but embedded metadata, screenshots, documents photographed for convenience, children's photos, and the incidental background details of domestic life. Implication: a permission that looks like "let me pick a picture" can, depending on platform and settings, become "let me see your archive".

A permissions audit, done properly, is less a technical procedure than a series of small judgements anchored to visible questions. What does this app do for me now—not what did it do once? Which permissions are essential to that function? Which are optional, and what is the price of refusing them? Does the app need access constantly, or only during active use? These questions translate lofty notions like "control" and "risk" into concrete decisions: keep or delete, allow or deny, precise or approximate, always or while using.

The difference between iOS and Android is largely one of interface and terminology rather than underlying logic. Both platforms now offer ways to review what an app can access and to change that access after the fact. Both also increasingly surface "recent access" signals—microphone or camera indicators, logs of when location was used—because the designers have accepted a truth many users already sensed: trust improves when behaviour is visible. Yet visibility can create its own illusion of safety. An indicator light tells you the microphone was used. It does not tell you whether the audio was stored, how it was processed, or which third parties received related metadata. The implication is that transparency helps, but it does not replace the underlying discipline of narrowing access.

The credible counter-example deserves to be stated plainly: sometimes broad permissions are genuinely useful and not sinister. Messaging apps often need contacts to make friend-finding simple. Video conferencing apps need microphone and camera, and "while using" is meaningless when "using" is the whole point. Navigation apps need precise location, and they need it continuously during a journey. Some accessibility features rely on deeper system access to function at all. A blanket refusal posture can produce a phone that is technically private and practically frustrating. That frustration often ends in abandonment: people either grant everything in a burst of irritation or delete privacy-minded choices because they "made things break". The reconciliation is proportion: grant when the permission is aligned with purpose, narrow when it is not, and treat "always" permissions as exceptional.

A subtle, recurring image helps keep the judgement steady: the keyring. Permissions are keys. Keys are not inherently dangerous. A house can't function without keys. The problem arises when keys are handed out casually, forgotten, duplicated, and never reclaimed. A person who would never give a spare key to a stranger for no reason will often give an app the equivalent of a spare key to their microphone or contacts because the request appears as a one-second prompt, not as a physical key exchange. Seeing permissions as keys restores the right emotional weight without tipping into panic.

This keyring view also clarifies why deleting apps is often the cleanest privacy move. Revoking permissions narrows access, but the app remains installed, potentially collecting whatever it still can, consuming attention through notifications, and waiting to be granted something else later. Show: an app installed for a holiday two years ago, still sending alerts and still holding whatever access it was granted at the time. Name: stale software. Explain: software that is not actively used provides little benefit while retaining the capacity to misbehave, be breached, or simply leak data through routine analytics. Implication: removal is a form of privacy optimisation because it reduces both collection and maintenance burden.

There is also a wider institutional implication that matters to thoughtful professionals and researchers. App permissions are not just a consumer issue; they shape workplace data exposure. A phone with overly permissive apps becomes a porous boundary between personal life and professional life—calendar entries, contact lists, documents, and meeting locations can be inferred or harvested in ways that create reputational and operational risk. This does not require espionage. It requires ordinary tracking. When an app knows who you talk to and where you go, it can sketch patterns that overlap with work. The keyring in your pocket can open more than your own doors.

None of this requires perfection. It requires a repeatable habit of review that prevents permission debt from compounding. The point is not to interrogate every single prompt as if it were a moral referendum. The point is to treat access requests as decisions with consequences, especially when they involve location, contacts, microphone, camera, photos, and background activity. Those are high-leverage keys. Hand them out rarely. Hand them out with purpose.

The forward test is deliberately awkward because it mirrors real life: the next time a trivial app asks for a powerful permission, will you treat the prompt as a minor nuisance to be dismissed, or as a key exchange that deserves a moment's audit—what door does this open, and who benefits from it staying open after the task is done?

Safer Mobile Connections

In October 2010, in San Diego, a developer named Eric Butler released a small Firefox extension called Firesheep and turned an old truth about public Wi-Fi into a mainstream embarrassment. On an open network in a café or hotel lobby, the extension could capture the session cookies of users browsing certain popular websites and let the operator log in as them with a click. The technical details were less important than the cultural moment: the attack was not exotic, and it did not require a basement full of hardware. It required proximity, a shared network, and a world that still treated unencrypted web traffic as acceptable. A laptop became a fishing rod. A login became a floating token.

The air was always crowded. People simply didn't notice. The air remembers your device.

That line is not mysticism. It is physics with paperwork. Phones are radios that pretend to be notebooks. They negotiate connections constantly—Wi-Fi, mobile data, Bluetooth, sometimes near-field communication—each one a different compromise between convenience, speed, battery life, and privacy. If a phone is the most intimate object most adults own, the network is the most public space it visits. Every time the device reaches into the air for connectivity, it makes announcements: what networks it can see, what networks it trusts, sometimes what devices it wants to pair with, and always, at minimum, enough information to be routed through someone else's infrastructure.

The aim of safer mobile connections is not to treat every network as hostile or to turn daily life into a siege mentality. It is to reduce unnecessary broadcasting and to choose the least exposed path for the most sensitive actions. That language—"sensitive actions"—matters, because this is not about abstract purity. It is about matching behaviour to threat models that are actually plausible. A person checking train times is not taking the same risk as a person logging into a bank, approving a work document, or resetting an email password. The same network can be low-stakes for one task and foolish for another.

Begin with public Wi-Fi, because it is the most familiar theatre of worry and the place where many people either overreact or drift into complacency. Show: an airport lounge, a network named "Free_WiFi", a captive portal that asks for an email address, and a phone that auto-joins because it has seen something similar before. Name: shared medium. Explain: on many public networks, traffic passes through infrastructure controlled by someone else, and other users share the same local environment; that makes it easier for attackers to attempt interception, impersonation, or manipulation, especially when devices are careless about trusting what they see. Implication: public Wi-Fi is not automatically dangerous, but it is automatically *less controlled* than a private network or a personal hotspot.

Firesheep worked as well as it did because, in 2010, too much of the web travelled without encryption, and too many services relied on cookies that could be stolen from the air. A credible limitation must be acknowledged: the web has improved. HTTPS is now the norm for most major services, and modern browsers actively warn when sites are not encrypted. That shift has reduced the simplest forms of "sniffing" that made Firesheep famous. If someone is only imagining the internet of 2010, they will imagine more danger than usually exists. The reconciliation is that "reduced" is not "removed". Encryption protects content in transit, but it does not magically erase risk. Public Wi-Fi still creates opportunities for malicious hotspots, for tricking devices into joining lookalike networks, for tampering with unencrypted connections, and for harvesting metadata—what services a device contacts and when—through the network operator's position.

The most important concept to name here is trust anchoring. Show: a phone sees two networks with similar names—"HotelGuest" and "Hotel_Guest"—and chooses one, or remembers the wrong one from a previous trip. Name: network identity. Explain: Wi-Fi network names (SSIDs) are not proof of ownership; anyone can create a network called "CafeWiFi", and devices are inclined to connect to familiar names because familiarity reduces friction. Implication: the risk is not only that someone will read what you send; it is that someone can impersonate the network you believe you are using, and then position themselves between you and the internet.

That positioning is the essence of a man-in-the-middle scenario: an attacker interposes themselves in the communication path. It sounds theatrical. In practice it can be dull. A malicious hotspot offers better signal and a tempting name; the phone joins; a captive portal asks for a login; the user complies because they are tired and the flight is delayed. This is not a plot. It is a routine made slightly predatory. The "who might care" in such scenarios is rarely a state agency. It is more often a scammer who wants credentials, or a petty criminal seeking access to accounts that can be monetised.

Mobile networks—4G and 5G—often feel safer simply because they are not shared in the same casual way as public Wi-Fi. Show: a phone switching to mobile data without ceremony, a small "5G" icon appearing, and everything continuing smoothly. Name: carrier mediation. Explain: mobile traffic passes through a telecom operator's infrastructure; the local "shared medium" problem is reduced, and certain classes of casual interception are harder for nearby strangers. Implication: for many everyday purposes, mobile data is often a simpler, calmer choice than unknown Wi-Fi, particularly when the task involves logging into important accounts.

Yet it would be naïve to treat mobile networks as private sanctuaries. Carriers have visibility by design. They route traffic, manage authentication to the network, and retain records for billing, capacity planning, and sometimes legal compliance. Even when content is encrypted end-to-end by apps, metadata often remains visible: which services are contacted, at what times, from which approximate locations. There are also specialised threats—such as IMSI catchers, sometimes discussed in connection with "Stingray" devices—that can impersonate mobile towers to force phones to connect and reveal identifiers. Mentioning this is not an invitation to paranoia; it is a reminder that "not Wi-Fi" does not equal "invisible". The implication is that network choice is about reducing exposure, not achieving purity.

Bluetooth is the third radio that people forget because it is marketed as intimacy: headphones, watches, cars, fitness trackers. Show: a commuter's earbuds connecting automatically, a car pairing as soon as the door closes, a smartwatch pinging quietly all day. Name: proximity radio. Explain: Bluetooth is designed for short-range communication, which makes it feel safe; but "short-range" still includes everyone in the same train carriage, café, or conference hall, and Bluetooth stacks have had vulnerabilities over the years that allow tracking or, in rare cases, more direct compromise. Implication: leaving Bluetooth enabled permanently can increase the device's "broadcast surface" even when nothing is actively being used.

A named, checkable example underlines that Bluetooth risk is not hypothetical. In September 2017, the security firm Armis disclosed a set of vulnerabilities they branded "BlueBorne", affecting Bluetooth implementations across multiple platforms and potentially allowing attacks without pairing in certain circumstances. The press coverage was understandably alarmed; the technical reality was more nuanced, involving device versions and patch status. But the lesson belongs in a chapter on safer connections: radios are complex, and vulnerabilities do not politely wait for the user to be ready. Patches matter. Radios left on unnecessarily increase the value of a vulnerability when it appears.

This brings the discussion back to the chapter's wider through-line: make the phone chatty only when you truly need it. That is a behavioural stance, not a technical obsession. A chatty phone looks for known Wi-Fi networks as it moves through the city. It announces itself to Bluetooth devices. It auto-joins networks because it prefers continuity. It hands over traffic to whatever route seems easiest. A quieter phone still connects, still functions, still serves, but it does less unprompted socialising with the air. It is slightly less eager to strike up conversations in public.

The word "VPN" arrives here as the usual talisman, and it deserves careful handling. VPNs—virtual private networks—create an encrypted tunnel between a device and a VPN provider, which can be useful on untrusted networks because it reduces the ability of local observers (including the Wi-Fi operator) to see and tamper with traffic. That is the promise. The implication is straightforward: a VPN can shift trust from the café's network to the VPN provider. It does not remove trust. It relocates it.

This is where many discussions become dishonest. A VPN is not a magic cloak. It does not make a person anonymous. It does not prevent tracking by the websites and apps a person uses, which can still identify users through logins, device fingerprints, and behavioural patterns. It does not stop a phone from being recognised by the mobile network. It does not fix weak passwords.

What it can do, in the right circumstances, is reduce exposure to local network threats and make certain types of interception harder. The trade is that the VPN provider becomes a new point of visibility, and the user must decide whether that provider is more trustworthy than the local network. That decision is a posture choice, not a universal commandment.

To keep the evaluation grounded, pair "risk" with visible decisions. If a person is in a hotel in an unfamiliar country and needs to access work email, the local network is an unknown variable, and the cost of compromise may be high; adding encryption through a VPN may be a sensible move, provided the VPN provider is reputable and the phone is otherwise maintained. If a person is scrolling news headlines at a café, the risk profile is different, and the added complexity may offer little real benefit if most traffic is already HTTPS. The same tool shifts from helpful to ornamental depending on the task and the environment. That is not ambiguity. That is reality.

Hotspots—the simple act of using a phone's mobile data to provide internet to another device—sit in a sweet spot for many people because they reduce reliance on unknown Wi-Fi without requiring new services or providers. The phone becomes a private gateway, and the traffic goes through the mobile network rather than a shared café router. The trade-off is often cost and battery. A hotspot can drain power quickly, and some data plans make heavy use expensive. Again, this is not a moral question. It is an allocation question: is the cost worth the reduction in exposure for the task at hand?

The most subtle and underrated aspect of safer connections is not the choice of network but the management of *automatic behaviour.* Phones are designed to anticipate. Anticipation is a convenience feature. It is also a privacy risk when it causes the device to join networks without conscious intent. Auto-joining a network is a form of commitment made on a person's behalf. The danger is not simply that the network is malicious; it is that the phone's pattern of remembered networks becomes a record of where it has been and what it considers familiar. This is where the "quiet phone" motif becomes practical: a phone that asks before joining unknown networks, and that does not cling to every Wi-Fi name it has ever met, carries less ambient exposure into new places.

Bluetooth has a similar "automaticity" problem. Pairing devices is meant to feel effortless, and for many daily uses—headphones, watches—that effortlessness is welcome. Yet Bluetooth also offers a channel for passive tracking through device identifiers and behavioural patterns, and it can be exploited in crowded spaces when vulnerabilities appear. The calmer approach is not to treat Bluetooth as inherently dangerous, but to treat "always on, always discoverable" as an unnecessary default for many people. A radio that is not needed does not have to be broadcasting. That is not paranoia. It is thrift.

A second limitation must be admitted to keep the piece honest: turning off radios can break things in ways that matter. Navigation becomes less accurate when Wi-Fi scanning is disabled in some systems. Wearables lose functionality. Car hands-free systems become irritating. People with accessibility needs may rely on Bluetooth devices that must reconnect seamlessly. The reconciliation returns to the book's central temperament: choose the smallest set of changes that lower risk without making life brittle. The goal is not to wage war on connectivity. The goal is to stop offering connectivity to every passer-by by default.

What emerges, if the reader holds these ideas together, is a network posture that feels almost old-fashioned: treat public networks as public spaces, treat unknown networks as unknown, treat automatic joining as an invitation you did not necessarily mean to send, and treat encryption as a tool that shifts trust rather than abolishing it. This posture does not require memorising technical details about protocols. It requires noticing when the phone is speaking on your behalf.

The forward test is a simple one, and it is deliberately uncomfortable because it reveals habit: when the device offers an easy connection in a public place, is the convenience worth the phone becoming chatty—announcing itself, trusting infrastructure it does not control, and leaving a trail of network relationships behind—just to avoid a small pause to choose a quieter path?

Chapter 3
Securing Laptops And Desktops

On 22 July 2010, in Washington, D.C., a small USB stick made a mockery of the idea that digital security is mainly about distant villains in distant places. The device was later described in public reporting as a simple-looking thumb drive, and the outcome was extraordinary: malware jumped an air-gapped network and became what the world came to call Stuxnet, a piece of code designed to sabotage Iran's nuclear programme. That episode is famous precisely because it was exceptional. Yet it also reveals something embarrassingly ordinary: computers are vulnerable not only when connected, but when trusted. They break at the point where convenience meets assumption.

A laptop is a suitcase of keys.

Phones are intimate; laptops are expansive. A phone captures daily life in fragments—messages, locations, photos—while a computer tends to hold the long form: contracts, tax records, research notes, medical letters, drafts, spreadsheets, correspondence stretching back years. Computers are where people do serious work, and seriousness has a way of accumulating. The directory called "Documents" becomes a personal archive with no curator. The downloads folder becomes a fossil record of decisions made in haste. The desktop becomes a landscape of shortcuts whose names are meaningful only to the person who placed them there in a moment of urgency. If the phone is a pocket diary, the laptop is a filing cabinet with wheels, often carried into cafés and conferences and left, briefly, unattended.

That physical reality makes computer security slightly different in flavour from phone security. Phones are designed to be carried and locked; computers are designed to be sat down and used for long stretches, sometimes with multiple people taking turns, sometimes with the same user drifting between tasks without pausing to lock the screen. They are also designed for flexibility, which is another word for complexity. Complexity is not wicked. It is simply harder to manage. The result is that the most common breaches on personal computers are not sophisticated feats of cryptography. They are a single bad click, a forgotten user account, a postponed update, a laptop left open in a hotel lobby, a device stolen from a car boot. It is the same pattern again: ordinary actions becoming expensive because the machine behind them is powerful.

The first place where power turns into vulnerability is the question of accounts—who can log in, and with what level of authority. Many households treat a computer like a shared appliance, akin to a kettle or a television. It sits in a common space. Everyone uses it. Passwords are an inconvenience. A single account becomes "the family account", and the password, if there is one, is taped to the side of the monitor like a private joke. This is understandable. It is also structurally risky. When one account has full administrative rights, every action performed under that account has the power to install software, change system settings, and access everyone's data. It is the digital equivalent of giving every house guest a master key and hoping nobody misplaces it.

The case for separate accounts is not moralistic; it is mechanical. Separate accounts limit the spread of mistakes. They confine browsing histories, saved logins, and personal files to the people who created them. They also allow the daily work of the computer to happen under a standard user profile rather than an administrator one, so that installing new software or altering critical settings requires an intentional step rather than being the default mode of existence. This is not bureaucracy for its own sake. It is a way of making it harder for a single slip—opening the wrong attachment, installing the wrong "PDF converter"—to become a machine-wide infection.

Updates return as the second, relentless theme, because the most professional-looking computer can still be undermined by software maintenance deferred in the name of productivity. People postpone updates because they fear disruption: a deadline, a lecture, a presentation, a child's homework due in the morning. That fear is rational. It is also exploitable. Attackers do not need to invent new weaknesses when there are known weaknesses sitting in unpatched systems. The irony is that postponing updates to protect productivity often results in the worst productivity loss of all: a compromised system, a forced rebuild, lost work, days spent resetting passwords and restoring files. Security is what makes productivity durable.

Then there is the one threat that feels almost too simple to mention until it happens: theft. A laptop is portable. That is its point. Portability makes it useful and makes it stealable. When a computer is stolen, the questions people ask themselves are rarely technical. They are painfully concrete. Who can read my emails? Can they see my photos? What about my banking? What about the folder with scanned passports? A person can be highly disciplined about passwords and still be exposed if the device's storage is readable once removed from the machine or accessed through a recovery environment. This is where disk encryption stops being an abstract security feature and becomes a kind of promise: even if the hardware is taken, the contents remain sealed.

Encryption is often spoken about as if it were a wizard's spell, but its everyday meaning is wonderfully plain. It turns stored data into something that cannot be understood without the right key. It does not stop theft. It does not prevent a computer being wiped and sold. It does not protect a device that is already logged in and left open. What it does, when correctly enabled, is make the stolen laptop far less useful as a source of personal information. It changes the economics of loss. A stolen laptop becomes a hardware problem rather than a life problem.

Yet encryption comes with its own psychological challenge: the fear of locking oneself out. Recovery keys sound like the kind of thing responsible people keep track of and real people misplace. That tension—between sealing the suitcase and keeping a spare key—runs through this chapter because it is the central human challenge of security. Good security is not meant to punish the owner. It is meant to frustrate everyone else. The art lies in storing recovery mechanisms sensibly so that protection does not become panic.

Downloads are the next quiet hazard, not because people are foolish but because computers are designed to make opening things easy. Malware almost never arrives labelled as such. It arrives as a document that looks urgent, an invoice that looks plausible, a delivery notice that arrives at the exact moment a person is waiting for something. It arrives as "free software" that offers a shortcut around a paid tool, or as a browser extension that promises to organise life and quietly expands its permissions until it can see everything. This is where threat modelling becomes painfully relevant, because the actor is often not a genius but a scammer who understands timing, authority, and the human tendency to comply quickly with anything that appears official.

The most important thing about downloads is that they exploit the gap between appearance and reality. A file icon looks trustworthy because it resembles the files people use every day. A message sounds official because it borrows the language of officialdom. A link looks familiar because it uses a brand name in the first half of the address. Computers are obedient machines; they do not have intuition. They do what the user asks, including when the user has been tricked into asking for the wrong thing. The real defence here is not an endless array of additional tools; it is a small set of habits that restore friction at the moments where friction prevents regret.

Finally, the chapter returns to the oldest and least glamorous threat: physical access. Most breaches do not require remote wizardry when a device is left unlocked in a café, or when a screen is visible to the person sitting behind you on a train, or when a laptop is borrowed and the borrower is curious. Physical access turns security into manners: lock the screen when stepping away, even briefly. Choose where to work. Notice who can see. Treat a laptop like a wallet, not like a magazine. Calm awareness matters because modern work is increasingly mobile, and mobility means working in spaces designed for comfort rather than confidentiality.

If the phone chapter was about the device that follows you everywhere, this chapter is about the device that often contains the most consequential record of your life. The laptop's danger is not that it is mysterious; it is that it is familiar. People trust their own machines the way they trust their own kitchens. They do not expect a threat to arrive through something as ordinary as a USB stick, a "PDF", a shared user account, a forgotten update. That trust is precisely what must be gently, respectfully retrained—not into suspicion, but into a kind of literacy about how computers fail.

The payoff is not paranoia. It is containment. A well-secured computer turns mistakes into small incidents rather than cascading disasters. It turns theft into inconvenience rather than exposure. It turns shared households into less chaotic webs of access. It turns work into something that can be done in public spaces without constantly feeling like one is performing vulnerability.

The next page tightens the focus to a question that sounds almost domestic and yet carries the weight of everything that follows: who, exactly, can open your suitcase of keys—and what happens if the answer is "more people than you think"?

Accounts And Updates

In May 1975, in Cambridge, Massachusetts, Jerome H. Saltzer and Michael D. Schroeder published "The Protection of Information in Computer Systems" in the *Proceedings of the IEEE*. The paper is remembered for many ideas, but one of them has aged with unnerving grace: the principle of least privilege. Give each process, each user, each action only the access it needs, and no more. It sounds like a tidy technical preference. It is, in practice, the difference between a spill and a flood.

Admin rights are not ordinary.

Most household computers are configured as if they were. A single account, created on the first day, accumulates everything: family photos, tax PDFs, saved passwords, browser bookmarks, work documents, children's school logins, the odd scanned passport. Over time, that account becomes a master key, carried around casually because it is convenient. The computer appears to work perfectly—until the day one careless click inherits the authority to change everything.

Accounts are not a mere UI detail. They are the way a computer decides who is allowed to do what, and that question sits beneath every other security measure. Show: a child downloads a "free game" and clicks through installation prompts without reading them. Name: privilege. Explain: if the child is using an account with administrative rights, the installer can change system settings, add background services, alter browser behaviour, and embed itself deeply; if the child is using a standard account, the same installer faces friction and limitation. Implication: the same click produces wildly different outcomes depending on who is effectively "holding the keys" at that moment.

A computer with tidy accounts behaves like a house with separate keys: the front door key that most people use daily, and the master key that is kept deliberately and used rarely. A computer with chaotic accounts behaves like a house where the master key hangs on a hook by the entrance with "HELP YOURSELF" written above it in cheerful handwriting. The harm is not guaranteed. The vulnerability is structural. It invites the worst sort of failure: the kind that arrives through perfectly normal behaviour.

The most common household pattern is familiar. A family buys a laptop. It is set up quickly, often under time pressure. The first user becomes the "main" user, which in many systems also means the administrator by default. Later, other people use the same profile because it is already logged in and already has the bookmarks, the apps, the saved Wi-Fi, the stored passwords. Show: "just use mine", said in the tone of a small kindness. Name: shared identity. Explain: shared identity collapses accountability and boundary; it mixes browsing histories, merges password stores, and makes it difficult to tell which changes were intentional, accidental, or malicious. Implication: the computer becomes a communal brain with no membrane, which is wonderfully convenient until it becomes expensive.

Separate accounts are often dismissed as fussy because they sound like office procedure. In reality they are domestic common sense. Show: one person's work email sitting open in a browser while another person opens a social media tab; a calendar of confidential appointments visible to anyone who wakes the screen. Name: lateral visibility. Explain: when multiple people share one profile, the system cannot distinguish "my data" from "your data"; it therefore shows everything to whoever is present. Implication: privacy leaks become interpersonal, not merely technical—information drifts across relationships without anyone choosing it.

The second part of the accounts story is more subtle: the difference between a standard user and an administrator. Most people assume "administrator" is a status symbol, the account that owns the machine. In truth, administrator is a capability—permission to install, to configure, to override. It is the ability to make deep changes that persist after the browser is closed and the laptop lid is shut. Show: a pop-up that requests permission to install "a required update" for a video player, framed as routine. Name: elevation. Explain: many systems require an explicit step to "elevate" privileges for certain actions; if the user is already an administrator, elevation becomes a speed bump rather than a locked door. Implication: running daily life as an administrator turns the computer into an always-open workshop where anything that asks nicely can pick up the tools.

Least privilege, the old 1975 idea, remains one of the few security principles that can be explained without mystique and applied without heroics. It does not demand perfect judgement. It assumes judgement will fail occasionally, because it belongs to real life. When it fails, it aims to confine the damage. A standard account is a containment strategy. It keeps ordinary browsing and ordinary downloads from automatically acquiring the power to change the system itself.

This containment is not theoretical. It shows up in the difference between a nuisance and a disaster. Show: an adware installer that tries to add a background service, replace a browser homepage, and install a "helper" extension. Name: persistence. Explain: persistence mechanisms often require system-level changes—services, startup items, scheduled tasks—that are easier to create when the user context has elevated privileges. Implication: removing the same unwanted software can range from a quick uninstall to a complex clean-up depending on what privilege it gained at birth.

If accounts are about *who* is allowed to do what, updates are about *when* the machine is repaired. Update culture reveals a peculiar human weakness: people can understand the importance of maintenance in almost every physical domain—cars, boilers, roofs—yet treat software maintenance as optional because the machine still turns on. Computers exploit that weakness by failing silently. A system can be vulnerable and appear fine. It can, for weeks, give no sign that it is behind.

May 2017 made the cost of this silence vivid. The WannaCry ransomware attack hit organisations worldwide and caused significant disruption to parts of the UK's National Health Service; many reports tied the impact to unpatched systems and delayed updates following Microsoft's March 2017 security patch. The details are messy, as large incidents always are, but the pattern is crisp. Show: a vulnerability publicly known and patched, followed by systems that remained unpatched and therefore exploitable. Name: the patch gap. Explain: once fixes are released, attackers can study what was fixed and target those who did not apply it; the act of patching is both repair and disclosure. Implication: postponing updates does not preserve stability; it extends exposure during the period when exposure is easiest to exploit.

A home computer is not an NHS trust. The stakes differ. The mechanism does not. A postponed update is a small decision that carries forward. It compounds. It creates what might be called vulnerability debt: the longer the delay, the more patches stack up, and the harder it feels to catch up. Catch-up then becomes a project, and projects are postponed again. The machine drifts away from the supported baseline until the owner is living in a museum of known flaws.

Automatic updates exist to prevent this drift. They are an attempt to replace willpower with routine, and in security, routine is often the more reliable tool. Show: a laptop that installs updates overnight while the lid is closed, then quietly restarts and returns to work. Name: maintenance automation. Explain: automation reduces dependence on attention and time; it narrows the patch gap by making repair the default rather than a choice that must be renewed each week. Implication: for many people, enabling automatic updates is less about being "good at security" and more about removing a recurring cognitive burden from an already busy life.

Here, an honest limitation must be treated as part of the design rather than an inconvenience to be waved away. Updates can break things. The example that forced this truth into the mainstream, even for people who never read security news, was 19 July 2024, when a faulty update to CrowdStrike's Falcon sensor caused widespread Windows crashes and disrupted organisations across the world. The incident did not mean updates are bad. It meant update pipelines are fallible, and automatic change can carry risk. The implication is not "never update". The implication is that update strategy should reflect context: a household machine used for everyday tasks has different tolerance for disruption than a production system in a hospital or an industrial plant, and the right balance between speed and caution will differ.

Reconciling these truths requires maturity rather than absolutism. The question is not whether updates are safe or unsafe in the abstract. The question is whether the risk of disruption is greater than the risk of remaining exposed to known weaknesses. For most ordinary personal computers, the risk of permanent staleness is the heavier weight. A short delay—waiting a day or two when a major update is freshly released and early bug reports are still emerging—can be rational, particularly for people who rely on specialised software. Indefinite postponement is not rational. It is drift disguised as prudence.

A tidy household account structure makes this trade-off easier because it reduces the blast radius of the most common disasters. Consider again the family computer, but this time compare two versions of it. In the chaotic version, there is one account—"Family"—which is an administrator. Everyone uses it. The browser remembers everything. Kids install games. Adults download forms. Grandparents click "OK" to prompts because they do not want to be a bother. In this environment, a single malicious attachment or a deceptive installer inherits maximum authority and maximum access: every file, every saved credential, every connected cloud account. The computer is one big room with no doors.

In the tidy version, each person has their own account for daily use, and the administrative account exists as a separate key brought out when needed. The child who installs a game does so under their own profile, with limited ability to make system-level changes. The adult's work documents are not casually visible. The saved passwords are not pooled. When something goes wrong—and eventually something will—the failure is more likely to be contained to one user context rather than infecting the entire household's digital life. The difference is not a moral improvement. It is an architectural one.

That architecture also supports better updating behaviour. When people share one account, updates become everyone's problem and therefore no one's responsibility. When accounts are separated, the system's maintenance can be more predictable: the machine updates itself, and individual users are less likely to disable protections for convenience because they feel the consequences personally. Accountability becomes clearer. Clarity is a security feature.

There is a further, often overlooked advantage: standard accounts make certain types of deception more obvious. A well-crafted malicious installer that suddenly requests administrative permission introduces a moment of friction that can serve as a cognitive alarm. The user is forced to notice, however briefly, that the action is not ordinary. Show: an unexpected prompt asking for an admin password while the user is simply trying to view a "delivery invoice". Name: interruption. Explain: interruptions can be annoying, but they also puncture autopilot; they create a moment in which the user can compare the request to the task and ask whether it fits. Implication: the system's insistence on elevation can turn an invisible risk into a visible decision point.

The same principle applies to forgotten users and old accounts, which are the digital equivalent of spare keys left with people who no longer visit. Households accumulate these gradually: a guest account created for a friend, a child's account abandoned after they get a new laptop, a "temporary" profile created for a project. Each dormant account is a potential access path, especially if it has weak authentication or retained administrative rights. The computer remembers what the household forgets. That is why tidiness matters. Security is, in part, a form of cleaning.

None of this requires a person to become technically intense. It requires adopting the most boring and therefore most powerful stance in security: reduce the number of master keys in circulation, and keep the machine repaired as a matter of routine. The rest of the chapter builds from that stance into other forms of containment—

encryption, download habits, physical awareness—but accounts and updates are the first locks on the first doors.

The forward test is almost embarrassingly simple, which is why it works: when the computer asks for an administrative password, does it feel like a normal part of maintenance, or like a nuisance to be eliminated by making every account a master key? The answer is not a preference. It is a posture. And it determines whether the next bad click becomes a small mess in one room, or smoke through the entire house.

Disk Encryption Basics

In May 2006, in Washington, D.C., the US Department of Veterans Affairs announced that a laptop and external drive had been stolen from an employee's home, potentially exposing personal information on millions of veterans. The figure most often repeated—26.5 million—came from the VA's own statement at the time (Department of Veterans Affairs, 2006). It was a blunt lesson in modern vulnerability: the most sensitive data can leave an office in a shoulder bag, and the most consequential breach can involve no clever code at all, only a missing object and a quiet, irreversible copy.

A stolen laptop is not a puzzle. It is a question: what can the thief *read?* Most people instinctively picture their files as being "inside" the computer, as though the casing were a safe. It isn't. A laptop is a container, not a guarantee. The part that matters is the storage drive, and the drive does not care who owns it. If the drive's contents are readable, they are readable to whoever holds the hardware long enough—whether that person is a petty criminal hoping for quick resale, a curious neighbour, or a more patient actor with time and tools.

Encryption is the simplest, least theatrical answer to that question. Think of it as sealing your data into an envelope that only opens with the right key. With no key, the contents are still there, but they are noise: scrambled characters without meaning. The power of disk encryption is not that it makes theft impossible. It is that it makes theft less *useful.* A laptop can be sold. Its parts can be stripped. But the private history—documents, photos, saved browser sessions, cached emails—does not have to become part of the haul.

Seal the envelope. Keep the key.

That five-word sentence contains both the benefit and the anxiety. Encryption protects by making data unreadable without authorisation. It also introduces the human fear of losing access oneself. That fear is why encryption is sometimes delayed by intelligent people who would never leave their front door open. They are not irrational. They are responding to a real trade-off: stronger protection versus the risk of self-lockout. The trick is to understand what encryption does, what it does not do, and how modern systems are designed to make the key manageable if you treat it with the seriousness of a spare house key rather than the casualness of a sticky note.

Start with the clearest scenario: a laptop is powered off, stolen, and taken elsewhere. Show: a commuter steps away from a café table, returns to find only an empty space and a cold coffee cup. Name: offline access. Explain: when a device is off, the attacker can remove the drive or boot the machine from external media and attempt to read the contents directly; without encryption, much of the filesystem can be copied with surprising ease. Implication: a password that protects the login screen does not necessarily protect the data on the drive if the attacker bypasses the operating system entirely.

This is the first conceptual correction most people need. A login password is an access control mechanism inside a running system. Disk encryption is a storage protection mechanism that remains relevant even when the system is not running under your control. When people say, "My laptop has a password, so it's fine," they are often describing the wrong layer of defence. A well-configured login password makes casual snooping harder. Encryption is what prevents someone from turning the drive into a harvestable archive.

Modern operating systems have made encryption more approachable by building it in rather than treating it as an exotic add-on. On macOS, Apple's FileVault has long offered full-disk encryption, and on Windows, Microsoft's BitLocker (and on some devices, "Device Encryption") provides a similar capability. The names matter less than the structure: both systems aim to encrypt the drive using keys protected by hardware features where available, and both create a recovery mechanism that can restore access if something changes—hardware replacement, firmware update, or a forgotten credential.

The recovery mechanism is where most panic is born, and it is best understood before it is needed. Show: a laptop update triggers a recovery screen asking for a long key the user has never typed before; the user's stomach drops. Name: recovery key. Explain: the recovery key exists because encryption keys are valuable and fragile; systems anticipate that legitimate users will sometimes be locked out by changes in hardware, security settings, or authentication, and they provide a controlled alternative route back in. Implication: encryption is only as usable as its recovery plan, and the recovery plan is only as good as where that key is stored.

It is here that people discover the difference between "my data is safe" and "my data is safe *and accessible*". Storing a recovery key in the wrong place can be worse than not having one, because it breeds false confidence. If the key lives only on the encrypted device, it vanishes when the device vanishes. If it lives in an email account that the laptop can access automatically, it may be accessible to anyone who gets into that email. If it lives in a photograph stored in the same cloud account that is logged in everywhere, it may be easier to reach than intended. The recovery key is a spare key. Spare keys are meant to be separate.

A second named example shows what encryption changes in practice. In 2013, the journalist Glenn Greenwald wrote that David Miranda, travelling through Heathrow Airport in London in August 2013, was detained under Schedule 7 of the UK Terrorism Act 2000 and had electronic devices seized, including storage devices. The political arguments around that event are long and complex, and the circumstances were highly unusual. The point here is narrower and mechanical: when devices are seized or accessed by authorities, the practical difference between encrypted and unencrypted storage can determine whether the contents are immediately readable or require additional legal, technical, or procedural steps. That is not a guarantee of protection in every jurisdiction or scenario. It is a reminder that encryption shifts the default from "readable" to "locked", and that shift can matter not only to criminals, but to journalists, researchers, lawyers, and ordinary people carrying sensitive work.

This example also surfaces an important limitation that should be stated plainly: encryption is not a forcefield. If a laptop is open and logged in when it is stolen, encryption may not help in the moment because the keys are already in use. Show: a device left awake, lid open, screen unlocked for convenience. Name: live access. Explain: encryption protects data at rest, but once the user has unlocked the drive, the operating system can read and write data normally; someone who gains access while the system is running may be able to access files through the same authorised context. Implication: encryption must be paired with basic habits—screen locking and shutdown or sleep behaviour—if the goal is to protect against opportunistic physical access.

A second limitation is equally important: encryption does not protect against malware that runs under your account. If malicious software is already operating with your permissions, it can often read whatever you can read, because the system must decrypt files for you to use them. Encryption is therefore not a substitute for updates, sensible account privilege, or caution with downloads. It is a containment measure for a particular failure mode: loss of the device or loss of the drive. If you want a single sentence to keep your expectations sane, it is this: encryption protects against theft of hardware, not theft of access.

With expectations calibrated, the practical question becomes: how does a person know whether encryption is already enabled? Here, a quiet reality helps: many modern devices ship with encryption enabled by default when certain conditions are met—such as signing in with a modern account, using supported hardware, or enabling particular security settings. People sometimes already have the envelope sealed without realising it. That can be good news, provided they also know where the spare key lives.

On Windows, checking encryption typically involves looking at BitLocker settings or device encryption status, often surfaced in system settings or control panel tools. On macOS, FileVault status is available in system preferences or settings under security and privacy. The existence of these controls is itself a clue to modern design: encryption is no longer a niche practice for specialists; it is part of mainstream device hygiene. The friction is not technical impossibility. The friction is attention—finding the setting and verifying what it says.

Turning encryption on safely is less about clicking a button and more about managing the conditions that make the encryption meaningful. The system needs a reliable method of unlocking—usually tied to the user's login credential—and it needs a recovery plan. On many systems, enabling encryption will prompt you to record or store a recovery key, sometimes offering a few storage choices: saving to a cloud account, printing, storing to a file. The correct choice depends on one's privacy posture. A person comfortable with a cloud account as a recovery channel may accept it because it is convenient and reduces lockout risk. A person with higher sensitivity—public-facing work, research involving vulnerable participants, or any context where account compromise would be catastrophic—may prefer a recovery method that does not rely on an online account being intact.

Convenience is not a sin. It is a constraint. The goal is to choose a recovery plan that does not collapse under predictable human failure: lost paper, forgotten passwords, changed email addresses, account lockouts. The right plan is the one that survives real life. That is why many serious security failures happen not through technical weakness but through administrative chaos—keys stored in places no one remembers, passwords known only to someone who moves away, recovery options left to default assumptions that later become false.

A good recovery plan also respects the obvious but often neglected principle of separation. If the recovery key is stored, it should be stored where it can be reached even when the laptop is gone, and where it is not casually accessible to whoever might steal the laptop. This is not a puzzle. It is a balancing act. A printed key stored securely at home may work for some. A key stored in a well-protected password manager may work for others, particularly if the manager is accessible from another device. A key stored in a cloud account may be acceptable where the account itself is strongly protected and where the risk of lockout is more damaging than the risk of that account being accessed by someone else. What matters is that the key is treated like a spare: protected, separate, and retrievable.

The envelope metaphor returns here because it captures the practical shape of the problem. If you seal your life into an envelope and then tape the key to the outside, you have performed security as theatre. If you seal the envelope and drop the key into the ocean, you have performed security as self-harm. Sensible encryption is neither. It is the boring middle: the seal holds against strangers, and the key remains available to you.

For professionals and researchers, disk encryption is also a matter of ethics, not merely self-protection. A laptop is often a container for other people's data—emails from students, interviews with participants, drafts shared in confidence, legal correspondence, medical scheduling, HR files. When such data leaks, the harm is distributed. Encryption reduces the chance that a theft becomes a breach affecting others. It is one of the few privacy measures that protects not just the owner but anyone whose information has been entrusted to the machine.

There is one more subtle point about encryption that is worth naming because it shapes how people think about "safety". Encryption is not just a feature you turn on; it is a state your device inhabits. Once enabled, the device's security posture changes. Certain types of repair become more complex. Certain kinds of forensic access become harder. Recovery becomes more dependent on credentials and keys. This is why a person should treat encryption as a deliberate commitment, not as a casual toggle. Commitment does not mean drama. It means you know where the key is, you know what "locked" means, and you accept that the small daily inconvenience is a trade for a large reduction in catastrophic loss.

This subchapter cannot offer a guarantee, because guarantees do not exist in real security. Drives can be mishandled. Passwords can be stolen. Devices can be left unlocked. Keys can be found if stored carelessly. What encryption offers is not certainty but a strong default: if the laptop disappears, your files do not immediately become someone else's reading material. That is a meaningful shift in a world where theft is common, travel is routine, and the contents of a hard drive are often more valuable than the hardware.

The forward test is therefore not "Is encryption good?" It is sharper and more personal: if your laptop vanished tonight—left on a train, stolen from a café, taken from a car—would your first fear be the price of replacement, or the thought of someone opening your envelope and reading your life?

Handling Downloads Safely

In May 2000, in Manila, a computer worm later dubbed "ILOVEYOU" raced around the world by email, arriving as a love letter with an attachment and leaving offices scrambling to disconnect networks and rebuild machines. The message was simple, the trick embarrassingly human: curiosity, flattery, urgency, a file that looked like a note rather than a weapon. The episode is now an artefact of internet history, yet its core mechanism remains modern. Malware did not announce itself as malware. It arrived as something people wanted to open.

Trust is a file format.

That sentence sounds glib until one watches how a malicious download succeeds. It succeeds when the user's brain categorises an object as familiar and low-risk: a PDF, a Word document, a delivery label, a "scan", an invoice, a "driver update", a free utility. The attacker's craft is not primarily technical brilliance; it is packaging. The payload is wrapped in something that matches the recipient's daily life. That is why the most useful security skill around downloads is not memorising threats. It is learning to read the wrapping.

Consider how a fake delivery notice tends to work, because it is almost too ordinary to notice. A person is expecting a parcel. They receive an email with a subject line that sounds plausibly logistical, sometimes with a real courier's name and branding borrowed from the web. The message offers a small drama—delivery failed, address incomplete, fee required—and a single clear action to make the problem go away. There is usually an attachment, "label.pdf" or "invoice.doc", or a link that promises tracking information. The timing feels right. The emotional tone is practical. The user clicks not because they are reckless, but because the message matches a legitimate pattern they have experienced before.

Show: a document opens and prompts the user to "enable content" to view it properly. Name: consent laundering. Explain: modern operating systems and office suites often place suspicious files into safer modes—limited view, warnings, blocked macros—yet attackers design prompts that frame these safety features as obstacles rather than protection; the user is asked to override their own defences in the name of clarity. Implication: the most critical step is frequently not the click itself, but the moment the user is persuaded to grant extra capability to a file that has not earned it.

This is where the word "download" can mislead. People think of downloads as intentional acquisitions, like bringing a book home. Many threats arrive through what looks like reading rather than acquiring: "open this document", "view this receipt", "see this scan". The computer, however, must still *execute* code to render documents and run installers, and execution is where the risk lives. Show: a "PDF" that is actually an executable file disguised by a double extension, or a document that triggers a vulnerable component in a reader. Name: masquerade. Explain: computers identify files partly by extension and partly by internal structure; attackers exploit the fact that humans read filenames as language, not as system metadata, and that some systems hide extensions by default, smoothing away the user's chance to notice the mismatch. Implication: the social layer—how the file is named and presented—often matters as much as the technical layer.

A first anchor for sensible judgement is provenance: where, exactly, did this thing come from? Not "from the internet" in general, but from which organisation, which address, which path. Show: an email that appears to come from a colleague but uses a subtly altered domain; a link that begins with a familiar brand name but routes through an unrelated site; a download offered on a forum rather than the vendor's own page. Name: the postmark. Explain: in physical mail, the postmark and return address help establish origin; in digital life, the equivalent is the sender's real address, the domain behind a link, and whether the file is arriving through an expected channel. Implication: when origin is ambiguous, the safest interpretation is not "it must be fine" but "it is unproven", which is a different category entirely.

This framing also clarifies why "free software" is such a fertile disguise. Many people have had the experience of searching for a tool—video converter, PDF merger, driver updater—and finding dozens of near-identical sites offering downloads wrapped in aggressive adverts. Some of those tools are merely annoying. Some are actively hostile. The user is not being foolish when they want a quick solution. They are being placed in a market where the incentive is to bundle extra software, harvest data, or push subscriptions through dark patterns. Show: an installer that offers "recommended" add-ons and buries the decline option in faint text. Name: bundling. Explain: legitimate businesses sometimes bundle for revenue; malicious actors bundle for access; the user experience can look similar, especially when the installer is polished. Implication: the risk is not only that the main program is bad, but that the installer is an ecosystem of opportunistic extras.

A second checkable example shows how even reputable-seeming downloads can be compromised at the source. In September 2017, Avast reported that a popular utility, CCleaner, had been distributed with malicious code embedded in official versions available for download in August and September 2017. It was a supply-chain compromise: users who trusted the brand and fetched the software through normal channels could still end up installing something tainted. Avast's public analysis described the incident as affecting millions of downloads (Avast, 2017). The point is not to frighten people away from software. It is to puncture a comforting myth: "If it's popular and looks professional, it can't be dangerous." Popularity is not a security guarantee; it is sometimes an attractive target.

Show: a legitimate download page, a familiar logo, a normal installation process. Name: upstream compromise. Explain: when attackers manage to tamper with a vendor's distribution pipeline—build systems, update servers, code signing keys—the trust that users place in that vendor is weaponised; the user is no longer choosing between "safe" and "sketchy" based on the site's appearance, because the site itself is part of the compromise. Implication: download safety is not only about personal caution; it is also about layered defences that assume trust can be breached.

That last sentence matters because it points towards a more adult relationship with "safety". People often hope for a single perfect test—one thing to check that will guarantee a file is safe. The world does not offer that. What it offers is a set of friction points and guardrails, many of which already exist on modern machines. Windows has mechanisms such as SmartScreen warnings and "Mark of the Web" metadata that can cause downloaded files to be treated with suspicion. macOS uses Gatekeeper and notarisation to warn about unrecognised developers and prevent certain classes of silent execution. Office applications have long offered "Protected View" to open files from the internet in a more constrained mode. Browsers run in sandboxes, and built-in antivirus tools scan files and behaviours. These are not perfect, but they are meaningful because they move the system away from blind trust.

The danger is that users treat these guardrails as nuisances to be dismissed. Show: a warning appears; the user clicks through because they are busy; the file runs. Name: friction removal. Explain: safety systems rely on the user honouring their interruptions; attackers, in turn, design their lures to make those interruptions feel illegitimate—"your computer blocked this by mistake", "enable editing to view", "your security settings are outdated". Implication: the success of built-in protections is partly cultural; it depends on whether people treat warnings as signals or as background noise.

A credible limitation belongs here, because overconfidence in built-in defences can be just as harmful as ignoring them. Not all malicious files are caught immediately. Attackers use encryption, compression, and novelty to evade scanning. They buy or steal code-signing certificates to make malware appear "legitimate" to systems that rely on signing as a signal. They compromise trusted accounts so that malicious documents arrive from real colleagues. They embed the lure into cloud sharing links rather than attachments, because links feel safer. The reconciliation is not despair. It is realism: built-in protections reduce risk; they do not eliminate it. The remaining gap is filled by human judgement about origin, necessity, and timing.

Timing, in particular, is where scams win. A fake delivery notice succeeds when the recipient is expecting a parcel. A fake invoice succeeds when the recipient is paying suppliers. A fake "share" notification succeeds when the recipient uses collaborative documents at work. Show: a message arrives at 4:55 p.m. on a Friday, when attention is thin and the desire to clear the inbox is strong. Name: urgency engineering. Explain: urgency narrows cognition; it makes the quick path feel like the responsible one, and it discourages verification because verification costs time. Implication: suspicious timing is not just an emotional cue; it is a technical risk factor, because it predicts lower scrutiny.

Once provenance and timing are in view, a third axis becomes decisive: necessity. Does the task truly require this file from this source right now? Show: a "delivery label" arrives, but the courier's official tracking page can be reached by typing the known address directly rather than clicking the link in the email. Name: alternative path. Explain: many tasks have a safer route that does not rely on the untrusted object; going through known channels—official websites, established apps, direct contact—reduces exposure to lures. Implication: download risk often collapses when the file is no longer treated as the only gateway to the outcome.

This is not an invitation to paranoia about every attachment. It is an invitation to notice the postmark. When a colleague shares a document through a known workplace platform, during an expected project, and the file behaves normally, the risk profile differs markedly from a surprise "urgent invoice" from an unfamiliar address asking for immediate action. Context is a security signal. Attackers try to counterfeit context; the user's job is to compare the counterfeit to what is expected.

The "family computer" version of this problem is where the consequences spread. A fake delivery notice lands in one inbox, one person opens it, and now the machine—shared, logged in, trusted—becomes a platform for further compromise. Show: the same computer holds multiple saved logins, a shared password manager in the browser, a session to a cloud drive, and perhaps access to school portals or bank statements. Name: cascade. Explain: once malicious code runs under a user context, it can search for credentials, capture keystrokes, hijack browser sessions, and spread to contacts via email or messaging; the initial lure does not need to succeed perfectly, it needs only to open a foothold. Implication: download safety is not only self-protection; it is household containment, because one person's click can become everyone's problem.

It is also worth noticing that "downloads" now include browser extensions and add-ons, which can be more dangerous than a one-off file because they persist and observe. An extension can see what a user types, which pages they visit, and sometimes what they purchase. This makes extensions attractive to both outright criminals and to companies with an aggressive appetite for data. The postmark matters here too: where did the extension come from, who maintains it, and what permissions does it ask for? An extension that requests broad access to "read and change data on all websites" is asking for the keys to the whole house.

For time-conscious professionals and students, the central promise of this section is not constant vigilance. It is a repeatable mental model that makes most bad downloads feel slightly wrong before they become disastrous. The model is simple enough to hold under pressure: check the postmark, check the timing, check the necessity. Notice when the file asks for extra powers—macro enabling, installer permissions, security bypasses—that do not fit the task. Treat unexpected friction as information rather than insult. Allow the machine's guardrails to do their job.

The motif returns because it is quietly practical. A postmark is not proof that a letter is kind, but it helps you decide whether you should open it at the kitchen table or outdoors, carefully, with a little scepticism. Downloads deserve the same respect. Many are harmless. Some are poisonous. Most are wrapped to look ordinary.

The forward test, then, is not whether a person can become perfectly discerning. It is whether, at the next moment of inbox pressure—when a file arrives with the emotional tone of urgency and the promise of quick relief—they pause long enough to ask: does this postmark match the life it claims to come from, or is it merely wearing the right costume?

Physical Access Precautions

In June 2015, in a hotel room in Bali, David Petraeus—former CIA Director—admitted in a US federal court to unauthorised removal and retention of classified information and to sharing it with his biographer, Paula Broadwell. The case drew attention for its personalities and politics, but its mechanics were strikingly low-tech: sensitive material stored and handled in ways that relied on discretion rather than robust controls, with the resulting exposure traced not to a remote hacker but to proximity, access, and ordinary human behaviour. The scandal was not a parable about laptops in cafés. It was a reminder that some of the most consequential breaches do not begin with code. They begin with *possession.*

A screen is a window.

People spend enormous energy imagining remote threats while ignoring the simplest fact of all: if someone can touch your device, they can often learn something useful from it, even without "breaking in" in the dramatic sense. They can glance at notifications. They can photograph a screen. They can shoulder-surf a passcode. They can plug in a USB device. They can open a lid that was left half-closed and wake the machine back into a logged-in session. Physical access is not the only problem in privacy, but it is the one that blends most easily into everyday life because it arrives disguised as normal social interaction: the colleague who borrows a laptop "for a second", the stranger who asks to make a quick call, the friend who takes a photo and swipes into your gallery without malice.

The goal here is not to cultivate suspicion of other people. It is to cultivate respect for how quickly a private machine becomes a public artefact when its owner treats it like furniture. The physical world has always demanded certain habits—locking doors, keeping wallets close, not leaving a passport on a café table—yet digital tools have disrupted those habits by being both valuable and deceptively casual. A laptop looks like a notebook. It is, in fact, a portable archive with an illuminated cover.

Start with the simplest breach: the unlocked screen. Show: a laptop open on a table in a café, a person stands to collect a drink, and the machine remains awake, email visible, a document half-drafted. Name: ambient exposure. Explain: an unlocked device is an invitation; anyone nearby can read, photograph, copy, or send messages while the owner is absent, and the owner may never know; even a short absence can be enough for a malicious or merely curious person. Implication: many "breaches" are nothing more than moments of unattended openness, and those moments are common because people underestimate how fast they happen.

Automatic screen locking is the quiet antidote. It is not a high-tech defence. It is the computer equivalent of a door that swings closed on a hinge rather than requiring you to remember to pull it. Show: a laptop that locks itself after a brief idle period, forcing a login to resume. Name: default closure. Explain: when closure is automatic, it does not depend on the user's attention or mood; it turns a brief lapse—answering a question, buying a coffee—into a harmless interruption rather than a full exposure. Implication: automation is a privacy tool because it reduces dependence on perfect behaviour.

Locking is also a social tool. It removes awkwardness. When a machine locks itself, it does not accuse anyone in the room; it simply behaves as if privacy is normal. That matters in shared spaces where actively locking in front of others can feel performative or distrustful. A laptop that quietly locks is a laptop that preserves boundaries without making a scene.

There is a reason, too, to distinguish between "sleep" and "shutdown", because physical access risk does not stop at the lock screen. Show: a laptop in sleep mode tucked into a bag, then later opened and instantly awake, still logged in. Name: session persistence. Explain: sleep preserves the session for speed; the machine's state is maintained, and if the lock requirements are weak or absent, the device can be reopened into a live environment; shutdown, by contrast, forces a clean re-authentication path and can strengthen the protection of encrypted drives by ensuring keys are not kept in memory. Implication: the choice between sleep and shutdown is not only about battery and convenience; it changes the conditions under which a stolen or borrowed laptop becomes immediately useful to someone else.

A credible limitation needs acknowledging before the piece becomes sanctimonious. People do not always have the option to shut down. They work across short interruptions. They rely on quick wake for meetings and travel. They may have accessibility needs that make repeated logins burdensome. The reconciliation is not to insist on one behaviour. It is to treat "awake and unlocked" as a special state that should not be left behind casually, and to treat "sleep" as something that should still demand a password quickly. The key is to narrow the time window during which physical access equals digital access.

Shoulder-surfing is the next form of low-tech breach, and it thrives on social politeness. Show: a commuter typing a password on a train while someone stands behind, eyes drifting naturally to the bright screen; a person entering a PIN at a conference table; a student unlocking a laptop in a library. Name: observation attack. Explain: many credentials are entered in public, and humans are excellent at noticing patterns, especially when they have nothing else to do; repeated observation can reveal not only the digits but also the rhythm and hand movements that make guessing easier. Implication: "strong" credentials can be weakened by the circumstances in which they are entered, which is why physical context matters as much as technical strength.

Privacy screens address this problem in the most literal sense. They narrow the viewing angle so that the screen becomes a window only to the person directly in front. They are not glamorous. They do not prevent all observation. They do not help if someone is behind you rather than beside you. But they reduce casual side glances in open-plan offices and public transport, where "over the shoulder" is often more like "from the side". Their value is highest for people who regularly work in public or handle confidential material, and lowest for those who seldom do. That is not a judgement. It is a posture choice.

There is also a subtler form of shoulder-surfing that arrives through reflections. Show: a glossy laptop screen reflecting a document's headings in a window; a phone screen mirrored faintly on a dark tabletop; a password entry visible in the sheen of a train carriage wall. Name: optical leakage. Explain: modern materials are reflective, and in bright environments the screen's content can be legible at angles the user does not notice; this is not espionage, it is physics. Implication: a person can be careful about who stands nearby and still leak information through the environment, especially in travel spaces designed with glass and polished metal.

Borrowed devices create a different kind of risk because they are wrapped in trust. The request sounds harmless: "Can I just use your laptop for a second to print this?" "Can I check my email quickly?" "Can I plug in my phone to charge?" People often agree because refusing feels rude. Show: a device handed over unlocked, because unlocking it and then hovering feels awkward. Name: social access. Explain: social norms pressure people to grant temporary access in ways that circumvent technical boundaries; the borrower may be innocent, but the borrower's account may not be, and a device left unlocked may expose more than intended. Implication: physical privacy is often negotiated through manners, not through settings, which makes it harder to manage without feeling antisocial.

Here again, automatic behaviours help. A device that locks quickly when idle reduces the need for the owner to hover. Separate accounts reduce the amount a borrower can accidentally see. A standard user environment reduces what can be installed casually. These are not "computer" measures; they are social measures that allow the owner to be generous without being careless. A boundary that is built into the device is easier to maintain without awkwardness.

USB and peripheral attacks feel old-fashioned, which is precisely why they work. Stuxnet's history, and later public examples such as the "BadUSB" research presented in 2014 by Karsten Nohl and Jakob Lell at Black Hat in Las Vegas, have shown that devices that look like harmless peripherals can behave as something else entirely. The ordinary user sees a thumb drive. The computer sees a device that can present itself as a keyboard, typing commands at machine speed. Show: a USB stick found in a car park and plugged in out of curiosity, or a "free" promotional drive handed out at a conference. Name: deceptive hardware. Explain: certain devices can impersonate trusted peripherals and execute actions without the user's understanding because operating systems are designed to trust keyboards and mice; the attack is physical, immediate, and bypasses many remote defences. Implication: physical access risk includes what can be connected to a laptop, not only who can look at the screen.

A credible limitation must be included to keep this grounded: most people will never be targeted with a custom malicious USB device. True. But the broader point stands: plugging unknown hardware into a computer is not a neutral act. It is granting access at the level of the machine's body. In privacy terms, it is letting a stranger touch the wiring behind the walls.

Travel magnifies all of these risks because travel places people in shared spaces with different norms and different levels of trust. Airports, hotels, conferences, trains: environments where devices are used in public, left briefly unattended, and plugged in at random outlets. Travel also changes the ratio of consequence to convenience. A laptop stolen at home is disruptive. A laptop stolen while travelling can be incapacitating, because the person is away from backup devices, away from familiar recovery routes, and often under time pressure. The device is not only a tool; it is the trip.

This is why travelling with "all of life" on one laptop is a quiet form of fragility. Many people carry more than they need because the storage is there and because it is comforting to have everything available. Yet availability is exposure. The more a person carries, the more there is to lose, and the harder it is to quantify the damage. Show: a laptop used for work and personal life, carrying tax documents, family photos, client files, research data, and saved logins. Name: concentration risk. Explain: concentrating everything onto a single portable device increases the payoff for theft and increases the personal cost of loss, because compromise becomes entangled with identity and memory, not merely hardware. Implication: a lighter travel data footprint is not asceticism; it is resilience.

A second named, checkable example helps anchor why physical control still matters even when encryption exists. In 2015, the UK Information Commissioner's Office fined several organisations over the years for data losses involving unencrypted laptops or improperly secured devices, reflecting a regulatory understanding that device loss is a predictable, preventable privacy event. The specific cases vary, but the consistent theme is that organisations are expected to anticipate physical loss and mitigate it. The implication for individuals is not "become a compliance officer". It is that device loss is normal enough to be built into policy, which means it is normal enough to be built into personal habit.

The motif of the window returns because it captures the heart of the matter without hysteria. Screens are windows. They invite looking. Computers are portable rooms with lit windows. Physical access precautions are simply ways of drawing the curtains at the right moments and ensuring the door latches when you step away. They do not require constant suspicion. They require a calm respect for the fact that public space is public.

There is also a deeper philosophical point that belongs here, because privacy is not only about adversaries. It is about preserving a zone in which thought can be unfinished. Many people do their most delicate work on laptops in public places precisely because they need to. They draft difficult emails, research personal matters, edit writing that will later represent them in public. The exposure of that process—someone reading over a shoulder, a colleague glimpsing a draft, a stranger snapping a photo—can change what a person is willing to think. Physical precautions protect not only data, but the freedom to think in draft.

The forward test is therefore behavioural rather than technical: when you stand up from your laptop in a public space, even for ten seconds, do you treat the screen as a private window that needs closing, or as a harmless object that will politely remain yours simply because you intend it to?

Chapter 4
Passwords And Two Factor

On 7 May 2021, in Florida, a phone call reached Colonial Pipeline, and within hours the company shut down a major fuel pipeline supplying the US East Coast. The disruption spilled into daily life: queues at petrol stations, anxious headlines, a sudden reminder that modern systems can be brittle. In the days that followed, reporting and official statements pointed to a familiar entry point—a compromised password on a VPN account, with no multi-factor authentication in place. The story was large, geopolitical, industrial. The opening was small: one credential that worked where it should not have worked, for someone who should not have had it.

Passwords are tiny keys.

They open enormous doors. They are also treated with astonishing casualness, partly because they are invisible. A front door key has weight. A password feels like a thought. It can be typed on autopilot while stirring pasta, while half-reading a message, while rushing to join a meeting. It is easy to believe that something so slight cannot be the weakest link in a system of global finance and cloud infrastructure. And yet, for most ordinary people, passwords remain the number-one point of failure not because attackers are brilliant, but because passwords are asked to do an impossible job: they are expected to be unique, strong, memorable, and constantly used across dozens of services, while humans remain distracted, tired, and fundamentally pattern-loving.

This is the chapter where the book's calmness must earn its keep. There is a special genre of password advice that makes people feel scolded and then abandons them to the same habits. "Use strong passwords," it says, as if strength were a mood. "Don't reuse," it says, as if everyone has an effortless memory palace. The truth is more interesting and more forgiving: password failure is largely a systems problem. When a system demands a hundred secrets from a finite mind, the mind responds by recycling, simplifying, and inventing clever little patterns. The patterns feel ingenious because they work for memory. They fail because attackers understand patterns too.

A useful way to see the problem is to imagine a keyring that keeps multiplying. Each new app and service hands you a new key, and each key looks the same: a string of characters. At first, you keep them distinct. Then the keyring grows. Then you start cutting corners. Then you begin to believe that adding an exclamation mark at the end is a meaningful upgrade, that swapping "a" for "@" is a cunning disguise, that capitalising the first letter is a private trick. Those moves were clever in the 1990s. They are now part of the attacker's first guess.

What makes this chapter matter is that it turns password talk into something concrete. Password cracking is often imagined as a person trying guesses one by one, like a thief jiggling locks in the dark. That image is quaint. Modern password attacks are industrial. When breaches occur—and they do, routinely—attackers harvest password databases and test them at scale. They use dictionaries of common words, lists of leaked passwords, and "rules" that mimic exactly the substitutions people think are creative. They do not need to know you personally to guess the sort of patterns humans prefer. They only need to know humans.

There is an emotional cost to this knowledge. People feel exposed, and then they feel tired. If attackers can automate guessing, what is the point? The point is that not all doors are equally easy, and not all keys are equally predictable. The way out of password despair is not heroic complexity. It is changing the system so that you, the human, are not the one manually carrying dozens of secrets in your head. That is where password managers enter—less as a gadget and more as a form of cognitive relief.

Password managers have an image problem. They sound like the sort of tool used by the kind of person who labels cables and owns a small screwdriver set. Many intelligent, busy people avoid them not because they are indifferent to privacy, but because they assume managers will be fiddly, risky, or time-consuming. There is also the fear of putting all keys in one place. That fear is not irrational. It is simply incomplete. A password manager does concentrate power. It also concentrates *control*. It replaces an unsafe, scattered system—reused passwords across sites, memorised patterns, passwords stored in browsers haphazardly—with a deliberate vault protected by one strong credential. It turns chaos into an object that can be defended.

The shift here is philosophical as much as practical. It asks the reader to accept that memory is not the right security mechanism for modern life. That is not a personal failing. It is a mismatch between human cognition and digital scale. When the scale changes, the tool must change. A password manager is a tool for scale. It does for credentials what a calendar does for appointments: it makes reliable recall possible without turning your mind into a fragile storage device.

Then comes the second door: two-factor authentication, often shortened to 2FA or MFA. Two-factor is one of the few security ideas that remains powerful even when explained plainly. It works because it changes what a password means. Without two-factor, a password is often enough. With two-factor, a password becomes one ingredient among at least two. That is not because passwords are worthless, but because passwords are stealable—through phishing, through breaches, through malware, through careless reuse. Two-factor makes stolen passwords less decisive.

Yet two-factor also has its own texture of trade-offs, and this is where sensible writing must resist sermonising. Different methods exist for a reason. SMS codes are widespread and convenient, but they can be vulnerable to certain forms of interception and account takeover, including SIM-swap scams. App-based codes are generally stronger, but they require managing an app and its migration between devices. Hardware keys can be extremely robust, but they cost money and require a habit of carrying a small object that most people will, at least once, forget. The point is not to worship one method. The point is to choose a method that matches both threat model and temperament, because a defence that people abandon is not a defence.

There is also a softer failure mode: lockout. People hear "two-factor" and imagine protection. They do not imagine a lost phone, a changed number, a broken device on a work trip, and the sudden realisation that the second factor has become a barrier to their own life. This is not an argument against two-factor. It is an argument for treating recovery as part of the security system rather than an afterthought. Good security is meant to frustrate attackers. It is not meant to punish the owner.

The chapter's final theme—shared accounts—sounds almost too domestic to belong beside pipeline disruptions and industrial hacking. It belongs precisely because households are where many people's privacy actually fails. Shared streaming logins, shared shopping accounts, shared utility portals, shared passwords scribbled on a fridge—these are not merely convenient hacks. They are a web of access that persists through relationship changes, house moves, teenagers growing up, flatmates rotating, families blending. The moment a shared account is compromised, the compromise is communal. And even without compromise, shared access blurs boundaries: purchase histories reveal more than people intend, stored payment details become available to the wrong person, and "just for a week" becomes "for years".

There is a quiet dignity in doing this part well. It is not about suspicion; it is about clarity. Households function better when access is intentional. Intentional access reduces awkwardness later. It also reduces harm when circumstances change in ways no one wants to imagine at the outset.

What ties all of this together is a shift in how one relates to identity online. A password is not merely a string. It is the assertion "I am me" presented to a system that cannot see faces or hear voices. Two-factor adds "and I also have this". Password managers change "I must remember everything" into "I must protect one well". Shared accounts ask "who counts as 'we'?" and, more sharply, "when does 'we' become 'not we'?" These are human questions disguised as settings.

The modern relevance is obvious without being melodramatic. Data breaches are routine. Phishing is industrial. Scams borrow the language of legitimate business. Work and home identities blur on the same devices. Yet the deeper relevance is timeless. It is the old problem of keys and trust, transposed into a world where the locks are invisible and the doors open onto bank accounts, medical portals, tax records, intimate conversations, and professional reputations.

The next pages do not promise that passwords will become fun. They promise something better: a way to stop being at war with memory, a way to make a stolen password less decisive, and a way to untangle the small domestic compromises that quietly turn into large exposures. The tension that remains—because it cannot be eliminated—is this: how many seconds of friction are you willing to pay, consistently, to ensure that your most important doors do not open for someone else simply because they found a tiny key?

Why Passwords Fail

On 1 October 2012, in California, security journalist Brian Krebs reported that the business network LinkedIn had confirmed a breach in which hashed passwords were stolen; in the years that followed, millions of those credentials circulated, were cracked, and were used as raw material for further attacks. The detail that matters is not the glamour of a "big breach". It is what happens afterwards. Stolen passwords do not stay politely within the walls of the company that lost them. They become a travelling library, copied, traded, tested elsewhere. A password is meant to be a private key. In a breach, it becomes a public specimen.

Passwords are memory made brittle.

That brittleness is not a character flaw. It is an engineering mismatch. Passwords ask a human mind to behave like a cryptographic system: generate secrets with high randomness, store them perfectly, retrieve them reliably, never reuse them, and do all this while under time pressure and distraction. Humans are superb at meaning. They are terrible at randomness. When passwords fail, they fail in predictable ways because humans solve problems in predictable ways.

Show: a person creates a password by taking a familiar word, adding a capital letter, swapping a letter for a symbol, and appending a number. Name: the cleverness trap. Explain: the user experiences the password as creative because it is customised and memorable; attackers experience it as routine because the substitutions and patterns are common, widely documented, and baked into cracking tools. Implication: "clever" passwords protect against guessing by a single person in a hurry, but not against automated guessing informed by how people actually behave.

To understand this, it helps to glimpse how password attacks work without getting lost in technical theatre. Most modern password compromise falls into two broad routes. One is theft: a user is tricked into typing their password into a convincing fake site, or malware captures it, or a breach exposes it. The other is guessing: an attacker attempts to determine the password without having seen it. Guessing is where people imagine a hooded figure trying "password1" in a dark room. In practice, guessing is statistical. Attackers do not guess like humans. They guess like machines that have studied humans.

When a company stores passwords properly, it does not store them in plain text. It stores a transformed version, typically a cryptographic hash. A hash is like a one-way blender: the password goes in, a fixed-length digest comes out, and reversing it is meant to be infeasible. When it works, the company itself cannot read your password, only verify that the password you type produces the same digest. This is a good design. But two things complicate it. First, not all systems are well-designed, and some store passwords in dangerously weak forms. Second, even well-designed storage can be attacked if passwords are weak, because attackers can guess passwords, hash each guess, and compare the result to the stolen digests. That is how "cracking" often happens: not by reversing the hash, but by finding an input that produces the same output.

Show: an attacker obtains a database of hashed passwords from a breach. Name: offline attack. Explain: once the attacker has the hashes, they can attempt guesses without interacting with the target service; there is no lockout mechanism, no rate limiting, no warning to the user; the attacker can run millions or billions of guesses locally, depending on resources. Implication: a password that survives online login limits may still be easy to crack offline, which is why storage practices and password strength interact.

This is where "salting" enters as a necessary concept, because it explains why some breaches are worse than others. A salt is random data added to each password before hashing, so that the same password produces different hashes for different users. Salting thwarts precomputed lookup tables and makes bulk cracking harder. When salts are absent or poorly handled, attackers can use rainbow tables—precomputed hash-to-password mappings—to crack large numbers of passwords quickly. The core implication is simple: systems can make cracking harder, but if a password is common, it will still fall sooner or later because attackers prioritise common guesses.

The human side of this is depressing in a way that is almost tender: people want passwords to be meaningful. They use names, pets, football teams, favourite cities, birthdays. They add numbers that correspond to years. They capitalise the first letter because the interface demands it. They add an exclamation mark because it feels emphatic. These habits are not stupid. They are the mind's attempt to store a secret in a system that refuses to accommodate human memory properly. The attacker's advantage is that the mind's habits are shared.

Show: a password like "Spring2024!" or a familiar word plus a year. Name: pattern density. Explain: patterns compress memory for humans, which makes them attractive; attackers exploit that compression by generating candidate passwords from dictionaries and applying common "mangling" rules—capitalise first letter, substitute "a" with "@", append "1" or a year, add punctuation. Implication: the more your password resembles a sentence in your own life, the more it resembles a sentence in everyone else's life too.

The number-one reason passwords fail, however, is not weakness in any one password. It is reuse. Reuse turns one breach into many compromises. A password that is "good enough" on a low-value site becomes catastrophic when reused on email or banking. Show: a person signs up for a forum, a small retailer, or an old app, using the same password they use elsewhere, because it is easy. Name:

credential stuffing. Explain: attackers take stolen username/password pairs from one breach and test them automatically across many services; the work is mechanical, cheap, and effective precisely because humans reuse. Implication: a breach you never heard about can still open doors in your life because you lent the same key to multiple locks.

Credential stuffing is a perfect example of how attackers think in terms of economics. They do not need to crack your password if they can borrow it from another company's failure. They do not need to target you personally if they can target thousands of people and profit from the fraction who reused credentials. This is why personal feelings—"nobody would target me"—miss the point. Most password attacks are not personal. They are industrial, and they thrive on the predictable overlap of human habits.

To keep the analysis grounded, two checkable examples help. The LinkedIn breach is one. Another is the 2019 revelation that millions of Canvas student accounts were compromised through credential stuffing, as reported by KrebsOnSecurity in August 2019, with school systems discovering that reused passwords from earlier breaches were being used to access education platforms. The details differ by case, but the pattern is consistent: attackers use previously leaked credentials because it is cheaper than guessing from scratch. The implication is not that education platforms are uniquely vulnerable; it is that any service becomes vulnerable when it accepts a password that exists elsewhere in the leaked credential ecosystem.

There is a further problem that complicates the usual advice: people do not only reuse passwords. They reuse *structures*. Show: a user has one base password and then alters it slightly per site—adding the site name, changing the number at the end, varying the punctuation. Name: schema reuse. Explain: schema reuse feels like a compromise: unique passwords without the pain; but schemas are learnable. If an attacker obtains one password, they can often infer the pattern and generate plausible variants for other sites. Implication: even "unique-ish" passwords can be vulnerable when uniqueness is achieved through predictable transforms.

Modern cracking tools are built to exploit schema reuse. They do not only try "password" and "Password1!"; they try "Password1!" and "Password2!", "P@ssw0rd!", "Password2023!", "Password2024!", and site-specific variants if the attacker knows the target. This is not because attackers are individually clever. It is because attackers can code human predictability into software, and then let the software work at scale.

At this point, it is tempting to declare passwords hopeless. They are not. They are merely insufficient on their own, and fragile when used in the way human beings naturally use them. The correct conclusion is not despair. It is a shift in method. Good password security is not a matter of personal virtue; it is a matter of changing the system by which passwords are generated, stored, and used.

A credible limitation must also be admitted, because it keeps the argument honest. Some password failures are not the user's fault at all. Services sometimes store passwords poorly, misconfigure security, or suffer breaches that expose data no matter how conscientious users are. Users can be harmed by the negligence of organisations they do not control. Even the best password cannot prevent a company from mishandling it. The reconciliation is that while individuals cannot control corporate security, they can control whether the same password is used elsewhere, and they can add layers—such as two-factor authentication—that reduce the impact of credential theft. The goal shifts from "prevent all compromise" to "reduce the blast radius when compromise happens", which is a more realistic definition of success.

The most practically important concept in this subchapter is the difference between a password that must be *remembered* and a password that must be *used*. Humans do well with a small number of high-quality secrets. They do badly with dozens. When a system asks for dozens, it creates conditions for reuse and patterns. This is why advice that insists on memorising a unique, complex password for every account is not merely difficult; it is structurally doomed for most people. A security strategy that depends on rare discipline will fail at population scale. Attackers know this. They build their methods around it.

Return to the metaphor of keys, because it remains truer than the language of "accounts". If you had to carry a hundred physical keys, you would either label them, store them carefully, or use a keyring system designed for the job. You would not carve near-identical keys and hope no one noticed. Passwords are keys made of memory. When they are treated as memory, they become brittle. When they are treated as keys that deserve a proper key-management method, the entire problem changes shape.

The forward test, then, is not whether you can invent a "strong" password in a burst of willpower. It is whether you will keep trusting the same brittle method—reuse and clever patterns—now that you know attackers have already built machines to read that cleverness as predictability.

Using Password Managers

In June 2017, in Gaithersburg, Maryland, the US National Institute of Standards and Technology published Special Publication 800-63B, part of its Digital Identity Guidelines, and quietly reversed a decade of unhelpful password folklore. The document did not romanticise human memory. It treated it as the unreliable mechanism it is. Among its practical acknowledgements was something that would once have sounded like heresy in corporate security culture: people benefit from password managers, and systems should stop sabotaging them by, for example, blocking copy-and-paste. A government standard-setter, of all institutions, effectively admitted that the "just remember better" approach had failed.

Memory is not a vault.

A password manager is what you reach for when you accept that sentence without self-reproach. It is not a magic object; it is an organisational solution to an organisational problem. The modern person is asked to maintain dozens—often hundreds—of logins across banks, email providers, schools, workplaces, travel sites, utilities, medical portals, retailers, subscriptions, and odd services created for one-off needs. The brute fact is that a finite mind cannot produce infinite unique secrets at high quality while also doing the rest of life. The mind responds by reusing, patterning, and simplifying. Attackers respond by automating against reuse, patterns, and simplification. Password managers interrupt that loop by changing who does the remembering.

Show: a person sits at a laptop, types the same familiar password into a forum, then into an airline site, then into email, because it is quick and it works. Name: key reuse. Explain: the same key opening multiple locks creates a single point of failure; a breach in one place becomes access elsewhere through credential stuffing. Implication: the weakness is not the individual's intention but the structure of the system they are forced to operate—too many locks, one memorable key.

Password managers do one job extraordinarily well: they generate, store, and fill unique passwords for each site or service, behind one strong master credential. That description sounds like "putting all eggs in one basket", and it is, in a sense. But it also changes the basket. The current situation for most people is not "many baskets", it is "eggs scattered across the kitchen floor": reused passwords in memory, half-saved logins in browsers, old credentials in notes apps, a few in emails, some written down, some guessed, some forgotten. A manager concentrates this chaos into a single container designed to be defended.

The container is usually called a vault, and the metaphor is useful as long as it is not taken literally. A vault is not invincible. A vault is a controlled space with a strong door and a known method of access. Password managers use encryption so that the stored data is transformed into something unreadable without the master secret. Many managers use a "zero-knowledge" design, meaning the provider does not hold the master key and cannot simply read the contents. The detail that matters for ordinary users is not cryptographic elegance but outcome: if the vault is properly protected, stealing it is not the same as opening it.

Show: a password manager generates a long, random password for a new account and saves it automatically. Name: randomness outsourcing. Explain: randomness is hard for humans and easy for machines; the manager can create passwords that do not resemble words, birthdays, or patterns, and can do so consistently without fatigue. Implication: the attacker's favourite advantage—predictability—shrinks, because the passwords stop looking like human artefacts.

This is where many people feel an unexpected emotional relief. Password managers are often described as "more secure", which is true in many contexts, but the more immediate benefit is that they are calmer. The user no longer performs the small daily anxiety of guessing which password variant fits which site, nor the shame of clicking "forgot password" yet again, nor the slow dread of knowing they are reusing credentials but not seeing an alternative. A manager turns password work into a system rather than a performance. It reduces the cognitive load of identity in a world that demands identity checks constantly.

The phrase "password manager" covers two categories that behave differently: built-in managers and standalone managers. Built-in managers live inside an ecosystem: a browser's password store, or an operating system's keychain. They tend to be frictionless because they are already present, and frictionlessness matters because tools only help when they are used. Standalone managers are dedicated applications, often with browser extensions and phone apps, designed primarily around credential storage and generation across platforms.

Show: a person uses Safari and an iPhone, and the system offers to save passwords, fill them, and sync them across devices through a built-in keychain. Name: ecosystem convenience. Explain: built-in managers reduce setup work and often integrate tightly with device security features; for people who live within one ecosystem, they can provide strong, low-effort improvement over reuse and guesswork. Implication: security can be raised through convenience, not only through discipline.

Now compare that to a person who uses Windows at work, macOS at home, and Android on the move, or who routinely switches browsers. Standalone managers earn their place in such lives because they travel. Show: a researcher logs into a journal portal on one machine, a grant site on another, and email on a phone, and the credentials must follow. Name: cross-platform continuity. Explain: when identity is spread across devices and environments, a manager that synchronises securely across them reduces the urge to simplify passwords for the sake of recall. Implication: portability protects security by reducing the pressure to compromise.

Neither category is automatically "better". The sensible question is how the tool fits the reader's actual habits. A beautifully configured manager that is awkward to use will be abandoned. A merely good manager that is used consistently will transform a person's risk profile. The most honest measure of a password manager is behavioural: does it make unique passwords easier than reuse?

Two named examples clarify how mainstream this shift has become, and why it is not a hobbyist's obsession. The first is NIST's June 2017 guidance, which treated password managers as normal and urged systems not to block their use. The second is the way major consumer ecosystems have made password management an expected default rather than a niche add-on. Apple's iCloud Keychain, for example, became an increasingly prominent part of the user experience across macOS and iOS, and the company introduced system-level support for passkeys in 2022, explicitly aiming to reduce reliance on traditional passwords. Google has similarly folded password management into Chrome and Android. The implication is not that every built-in manager is perfect. It is that the industry itself has conceded that password sprawl is a structural problem and that tooling, not scolding, is the realistic response.

A credible counter-example must be faced head-on, because any mature discussion of managers has to acknowledge the obvious anxiety: what happens when the manager itself is breached? In August 2022, LastPass disclosed a security incident, and later, in December 2022, it reported that attackers had accessed customer vault data and other information taken from its cloud storage environment. The company's public updates described how vault content was encrypted but could be subject to offline cracking attempts depending on users' master password strength and configuration. This is precisely the nightmare people imagine when they say "single point of failure".

The reconciliation is not to wave away the risk. It is to compare it to the baseline risk most people already live with. The baseline is not "many independent secrets safely memorised". The baseline is reuse, schema reuse, scattered storage, and ad hoc recovery methods—an ecosystem of small failures waiting for a breach elsewhere to turn them into account takeovers. A manager concentrates risk, yes. It also concentrates defence. It makes it possible to protect one vault well rather than pretending to protect a hundred passwords in the mind with equal quality.

Show: a person's reused password appears in a leaked database and is tested automatically against email and banking. Name: distributed fragility. Explain: reuse creates many weak points because the same secret is exposed to the security practices of every service it touches; the user's safety becomes hostage to the least competent site they ever joined. Implication: the "many baskets" model is often an illusion; it is one egg copied into many baskets, and the most cracked basket defines the outcome.

The more precise way to think about this is not "one point of failure" but "one point of control". With a manager, the decisive security question becomes the strength of the master credential and the integrity of the devices that can unlock it. That is a smaller, more manageable surface area than dozens of independent passwords, many of which are mediocre by necessity. It also aligns with how security actually works: defending a few high-leverage points (email, primary accounts, credential stores) is more efficient than trying to defend everything equally.

This brings us back to the recurring motif of the keyring, because it captures the practical shape of the change. Without a manager, you are effectively carrying loose keys in your pockets, dropping duplicates everywhere, and hoping no one notices. With a manager, you put the keys on a ring and keep the ring somewhere you can protect. You still have to protect it. But at least you know what you are protecting.

The staged adoption that people fear—"I'll have to migrate everything at once"—is usually unnecessary and, psychologically, counterproductive. A manager becomes useful long before it becomes complete. A common pattern is to begin with the accounts whose compromise would be most disruptive: email, banking, and any account that can reset other accounts. Those are the keys that open other keys. From there, people gradually add logins as they encounter them naturally. The manager grows with use rather than requiring a weekend of obsessive tidying.

It is worth pausing on why this staged approach works so well. Show: a person signs into an account they use rarely and is prompted to reset a forgotten password; the manager is available at that moment to generate and store a new one. Name: opportunistic consolidation. Explain: password moments already occur—resets, new sign-ups, device changes—so integrating the manager at those moments piggybacks on existing friction rather than creating new projects. Implication: security improvements become part of life's rhythm rather than an overhaul that demands perfect motivation.

There is also a professional advantage here that deserves explicit mention for researchers and time-conscious professionals: password managers reduce the risk of "shadow IT" workarounds. When passwords are difficult, people improvise—reusing across work and personal life, saving credentials in plain text, sharing logins through insecure channels. A manager makes the secure behaviour the easy behaviour, which is the only kind that scales in busy environments. It also makes audits of one's own digital life possible: you can see what accounts exist, which passwords are old, and which sites are no longer used. The manager becomes an index of identity rather than a heap of half-forgotten secrets.

No serious discussion should pretend there is no cost. Managers introduce dependence on a tool, on a master credential, and on recovery mechanisms. They can also be misused: people may store everything but protect the vault with a weak master password, or may leave the vault unlocked on shared devices, or may ignore the risk of phishing prompts that mimic the manager's interface. These are real failure modes. They are not arguments against managers. They are arguments for treating the vault as a critical asset rather than a convenience feature, and for aligning the tool with the broader hardening discussed earlier—device updates, locks, and sensible account posture.

The quiet irony is that password managers are often adopted for security and then kept for comfort. Once a person experiences the absence of password juggling, they rarely want to go back. That is a form of success more durable than fear, because fear fades. Comfort persists. If privacy is to become a way of living rather than a project, the tools must reward normal use.

The keyring returns one last time because it frames the unresolved tension that remains even after adoption. A keyring makes it easy to carry many keys. It also makes the ring itself precious. The question the reader is left holding is not whether a password manager is "worth it" in some abstract sense. It is whether they are willing to stop scattering keys across memory and mishaps, and instead commit to defending one well-made ring—knowing that the ring, like any valuable object, must be kept close.

Setting Up Two Factor

In August 2019, in San Francisco, Twitter's chief executive Jack Dorsey briefly lost control of his own account after attackers hijacked his phone number and used it to post messages from his profile. The incident was not a breach of some exotic cryptographic vault. It was a reminder that identity online is often routed through the oldest infrastructure we still trust: the telephone network. A password can be stolen in silence; a phone number can be stolen by paperwork. The result, in that case, was public embarrassment. In other lives, the same mechanism can become financial loss, reputational harm, or a private archive opened by strangers.

The strange modern bargain is this: we have taught passwords to stand guard at doors they cannot reliably defend. Two-factor authentication exists because the industry has finally admitted the limits of memory as a security technology. It does not abolish passwords, but it refuses to let them be the only lock. The second factor is the second latch, the extra click that changes an attacker's day from quick profit to tedious effort. The second latch really matters.

The most useful way to understand two-factor is to start with the attacker's economics. Show: a stolen password is tested automatically against many sites, and a few work because humans reuse. Name: credential stuffing. Explain: the attacker is not trying to prove brilliance; they are trying to find any door that opens cheaply, at scale, without conversation. Implication: anything that turns "one stolen password" into "still not enough" breaks the business model. Two-factor does exactly that by requiring a second ingredient that is not usually stored in the same breach database.

It is tempting to frame two-factor as an upgrade, like a better lock. It is more precise to call it a change in identity proof. A password is "something you know". A second factor is commonly "something you have" (a phone, an authenticator app, a hardware key) or, less often in consumer contexts, "something you are" (biometrics). When a system asks for two factors, it asks for two kinds of proof. The attacker may steal one. They are less likely to steal both at once.

This does not mean two-factor is invincible. It means it moves the fight. Show: an attacker who has phished a password now discovers they also need a code or a device approval. Name: friction shift. Explain: the attacker's easiest wins vanish, and they must either compromise a second channel, coerce the user, or move on to a softer target. Implication: most account takeovers are prevented not by perfect security but by raising the effort beyond what opportunists are willing to spend.

Where two-factor gets confusing for normal people is that it comes in multiple forms, and those forms are not equal. The differences are not merely technical. They are about which weak link you are most likely to face: weak passwords, weak networks, weak phone accounts, weak patience under pressure. A sensible comparison begins with the oldest and most widespread method: SMS codes.

SMS-based two-factor sends a one-time code by text message. It is popular because it requires no new app and fits the mental model of "prove you have the phone". For many people it is meaningfully better than a password alone, because it blocks the simplest kind of remote takeover: a stolen password used from afar. And yet it leans on a fragile foundation. The telephone network was not designed as a high-assurance identity system. Phone numbers can be reassigned. SIMs can be swapped. Support agents can be manipulated. The weakness is not that SMS codes are "bad"; the weakness is that the channel can be hijacked by an attacker who is willing to do paperwork and social engineering.

A checkable example illustrates this fragility without melodrama. In April 2018, Reddit disclosed that it had suffered a security incident after attackers intercepted SMS-based two-factor codes sent to employees and then accessed internal systems, including a database backup. Reddit's headquarters is in San Francisco; the breach was explained publicly as involving the compromise of a small number of employee accounts protected by SMS two-factor. The point is not to scold Reddit, or to pretend that app-based factors would have prevented everything. It is to notice the lesson: if the second factor travels through a channel an attacker can redirect, the second latch can sometimes be picked by rerouting the bell.

App-based codes—often called authenticator apps—solve part of this problem by removing the telephone network from the loop. They typically generate time-based one-time passwords (TOTP) on the device itself. The codes change regularly and are derived from a secret stored in the app. No text message needs to arrive. There is nothing to intercept in transit. Show: a login prompt asks for a six-digit code; the user opens an app and reads it. Name: local generation. Explain: because the code is generated on the device, an attacker cannot steal it by hijacking SMS delivery; they would need access to the device or to the secret seed that generates the codes. Implication: app-based codes often reduce exposure to SIM swap attacks and carrier-level mishaps.

App-based codes have their own failure mode, and it is painfully ordinary: device loss and migration. People change phones. Phones break. Phones get stolen. If the authenticator app is not backed up or transferred properly, the second factor can become a lock on the outside of your own door. This is why many people fear two-factor: not because they dislike security, but because they have tasted account recovery and found it slow, humiliating, and uncertain. The trade-off is real. The system offers stronger protection and, in exchange, asks you to care about the continuity of the device that generates proof.

Push-based authentication, where an app sends a prompt—Approve or Deny—tries to soften that friction by making the second factor effortless. Tap a button, log in. For many people, it is the first kind of two-factor that feels humane. It also introduces a psychological vulnerability: approval fatigue. Show: a user receives repeated prompts while busy, assumes they are glitches, and taps "Approve" to make the noise stop. Name: consent exhaustion. Explain: attackers who have the password can bombard a target with push prompts until the target makes a mistake, especially if the prompts are timed at moments of distraction. Implication: the second latch becomes less a lock and more a test of attention, which is exactly what busy humans are worst at sustaining.

This vulnerability is not hypothetical. In September 2022, Uber disclosed that an attacker had gained access after obtaining a contractor's credentials and repeatedly sending multi-factor prompts until one was accepted—an example often discussed as "MFA fatigue". The details included social engineering and messaging, not just button-tapping, but the pattern remains instructive: a second factor that depends on a user noticing and resisting a barrage can be abused by making the barrage itself the weapon. The reconciliation is not to reject push methods entirely. It is to prefer implementations that add clarity—number matching, contextual information about the login attempt, and rate limits—so the prompt becomes a deliberate decision rather than a reflex.

Hardware security keys, often based on standards such as FIDO U2F and WebAuthn, shift the landscape again. They are small physical devices that perform cryptographic authentication and are difficult to phish because they verify the identity of the site they are talking to. Show: a login page asks the user to touch a key or insert it; the key responds only to the genuine service. Name: phishing resistance. Explain: unlike a code that can be typed into a fake site, a properly used hardware key is bound to the legitimate domain; the attacker cannot simply trick the user into handing over a reusable secret. Implication: hardware keys can be exceptionally strong against the most common modern attack—convincing imitation—because they refuse to authenticate to the wrong door.

The limitation here is not primarily technical. It is behavioural and economic. Hardware keys cost money. They are physical. They can be forgotten, lost, or left at home. They demand a slightly different kind of routine: carrying a key for digital doors as well as physical ones. For some people—journalists, public-facing figures, researchers dealing with sensitive populations, anyone whose accounts would be attractive targets—that routine is a fair price. For others, it is an aspirational ideal that will not survive real life. A security measure that lives in a drawer is not a security measure.

If this begins to sound like a menu of compromises, that is because it is. Two-factor is not one thing. It is a family of second latches, each one vulnerable in a different way. The question "Which is best?" is less helpful than "Which failure mode can you tolerate?" SMS is vulnerable to phone account hijack. Authenticator codes are vulnerable to poor migration and device loss. Push prompts are vulnerable to fatigue and persuasion. Hardware keys are vulnerable to being misplaced and to simple inconvenience. The right choice is the one that raises the barrier for the threats you actually face without creating a brittle system you will abandon.

Where two-factor matters most is also less mysterious than people think. It matters most on accounts that can reset other accounts. Email is the obvious example because so many services use email as the recovery channel: "Forgot password?" becomes "Open your inbox." If an attacker controls email, they control the process by which other doors are re-keyed. Primary cloud accounts matter for the same reason, because they hold documents, photos, and sometimes backups and device-management tools. Banking and payment platforms matter because money moves quickly once access is obtained. Messaging accounts matter because they can be used to impersonate you convincingly to people who trust you. These are not moral categories. They are leverage points.

A modest, human concession belongs here: two-factor can be annoying. It adds steps. It creates moments where you cannot log in because the second factor is not available—no signal, dead battery, lost device. And yet the annoyance is the mechanism. The point is to make access slightly more expensive, so that cheap attacks fail. The second latch is meant to be felt.

Avoiding lockout is the part that deserves the most respect, because lockout is what turns "security" into resentment. The most common lockout stories begin with good intentions and end with panic: a phone replaced, an authenticator app forgotten, an old number abandoned, recovery codes never saved, a hardware key lost. Those stories are not evidence that two-factor is misguided. They are evidence that recovery is part of authentication, not an afterthought. A system is only usable when it can be restored.

Many services acknowledge this by offering recovery codes—single-use backups that can unlock an account if the second factor is unavailable. Recovery codes are the spare key under the plant pot, except you choose where the plant pot is. Some platforms allow multiple second factors—an authenticator app plus a hardware key, for example—so the loss of one does not strand the owner. Some allow trusted devices that remain logged in. Some offer account recovery processes that can be rigorous, slow, and, depending on the provider, of varying reliability. The implication is not that every account can be made perfectly recoverable. It is that a person should treat recovery materials like assets with weight: they should exist, and they should be stored deliberately rather than left to hope.

This is also where the earlier themes of device hardening quietly re-enter. If the second factor lives on your phone, your phone becomes more valuable. It is no longer merely a personal object; it is part of your identity infrastructure. A locked phone, kept updated, with restrained permissions and sensible backups, becomes not just privacy hygiene but account resilience. Two-factor does not sit apart from the rest of your security posture. It is braided into it.

The second latch metaphor holds because it keeps the point grounded. A single latch on a door is better than none. A second latch is better when you expect pressure. But a second latch also demands that you know where the keys are, and that you can find them when you are tired, travelling, or shaken. If you cannot, the latch becomes a trap. The goal is a second latch that frustrates strangers and still yields to you.

The forward test is not whether two-factor is "worth it". It is sharper: if someone already has your password—lifted from an old breach you never heard about, guessed through your clever pattern, or coaxed from you by a convincing email—what, exactly, stands between that person and your most important account?

Handling Shared Accounts

In December 2019, in London, the financial app Monzo published a blog post warning customers about a pattern it was seeing with "shared accounts" that were not actually designed to be shared: couples and households logging into one person's banking app from multiple phones, sometimes with the same passcode, sometimes with credentials passed around as if they were the Wi-Fi password. Monzo's point was not romantic. It was operational. When identity is shared, responsibility blurs, and when responsibility blurs, fraud becomes harder to detect, disputes become harder to resolve, and harm becomes easier to inflict. A bank was, in effect, saying: even love needs boundaries.

Shared logins feel domestic.

They are also a security architecture. Most people do not experience them that way because the sharing usually begins as a kindness. Someone pays for a streaming service and offers it to the household. Someone keeps the utility account in their name because the bill needs paying and the company only asked for one person. Someone starts a shared shopping account to save delivery addresses and subscriptions. The practical benefit is immediate: fewer payments, fewer passwords, fewer admin tasks. The cost is delayed and therefore invisible: merged histories, blurred consent, and a single credential that can quietly outlive the relationship it was meant to serve.

A shared account is not just "two people using the same login". It is a decision about whose identity is bound to a service and whose access is contingent. Show: one person's email address is the account identifier; the password is known by both; the payment method belongs to one; the device approvals go to the other. Name: asymmetric ownership. Explain: most consumer services are built around a single account owner with optional viewers, profiles, or secondary users; when households share a single owner login, they create a structure where one person has ultimate control and the other is effectively a guest without formal rights. Implication: shared logins often smuggle power dynamics into ordinary life, even in households that feel equal, and those dynamics matter most when circumstances change.

Change is the theme the sharing impulse ignores. People share accounts assuming continuity: the household will remain the household. Sometimes it does. Sometimes it does not. House moves happen. Relationships end. Flatmates rotate. Children grow up and leave home. When that happens, a shared login can become a stubborn thread that keeps access alive long after it should have been severed. The awkwardness is obvious. The potential for harm is less discussed, and therefore more dangerous.

Show: a couple separates; one person remains on the shared shopping account; the other can still see purchase history and delivery addresses months later. Name: residual access. Explain: services often persist sessions on devices, and people rarely review "logged in devices" or active sessions; access can therefore continue without a fresh login or a deliberate decision. Implication: "we broke up" does not automatically mean "access ended", which turns emotional separation into an information leak.

This is not an abstract risk. Accounts reveal intimate patterns: what medicines someone orders, what books they buy, what children's items appear, which addresses are used, what time deliveries occur. A streaming account reveals taste, routine, even the texture of evenings. A shared calendar reveals movements. A shared photo library reveals a life. The point is not to dramatise every domestic compromise. The point is to notice that shared accounts are not neutral—they are records of the household, and records persist.

The simplest improvement begins with a design principle that consumer services increasingly support: separate identities with shared access. Show: a streaming service offers profiles; a household plan offers separate logins; a family library allows sharing without sharing credentials. Name: delegated access. Explain: delegated access allows a household to share benefits—content, subscriptions, storage—without sharing the account owner's password and without merging all activity into one history. Implication: sharing can be made safer by aligning with how the service is designed to represent multiple people, rather than hacking around the design with a single shared credential.

The reason delegated access matters is that it restores accountability and boundaries. A profile can be deleted without deleting the entire account. A user can be removed without changing the owner's identity. Separate logins allow two-factor authentication to be meaningful, because each person can maintain their own second factor rather than trying to share one phone number. It also reduces the temptation to send passwords through messages or to store them in easy-to-find places. Delegation is not merely neatness. It is containment.

Still, reality is messy. Not all services offer family plans or separate logins. Some utility providers remain anchored in the idea of a "named account holder". Some older services allow only one login and one email. In those cases, households improvise, and improvisation is where both awkwardness and risk breed. The right response is not shame. It is a more deliberate improvisation—sharing that acknowledges its own fragility.

One way to make this tangible is to treat shared accounts as a house key lent to someone. A house key carries an implied contract: the key is used for agreed purposes, and it is returned when the person no longer lives there. Digital sharing often lacks that return moment. People hand out passwords with the breezy tone of "here you go", and then never revisit the decision. The key remains in circulation. The lock remains unchanged. Everyone forgets. Until something happens.

Keys should be returned.

That five-word sentence is not a moral instruction; it is a diagnostic for whether a household has any exit plan at all. Most do not. And yet exit planning is what turns sharing into something that does not haunt people later. An exit plan can be as simple as knowing which accounts are shared, which person is the owner, and what will happen if someone leaves the household, even temporarily.

To keep the discussion anchored in checkable reality, consider how some organisations have begun to formalise the end of shared access. In the UK, domestic abuse services and police guidance have increasingly highlighted "tech abuse" as a vector for coercive control, including the misuse of shared accounts, shared location services, and access to devices. The details vary by guidance and year, but the underlying recognition is consistent: residual digital access can be weaponised. This is not said to turn every household into a crime scene. It is said because a privacy book that ignores the worst-case use of shared accounts would be irresponsible. When a relationship becomes unsafe, shared logins can become a tool of surveillance and intimidation, precisely because they were established under the assumption of trust.

Show: someone uses a shared Apple ID or Google account to view location history or read synced messages. Name: account entanglement. Explain: ecosystem accounts—those that sync messages, photos, backups, and device management—are not like streaming accounts; they are identity anchors that can grant access to whole device histories. Implication: some accounts are too central to be shared casually, because sharing them is not sharing a service; it is merging identities at the infrastructure level.

This is where the earlier sections on threat modelling become quietly relevant. For some households, sharing a streaming password is a minor convenience with tolerable risk. Sharing a primary device ecosystem account is a different category entirely. Sharing the login that controls the email inbox used for account recovery is another. Sharing a bank login is often explicitly against a provider's terms and can complicate fraud protection. The point is not to memorise rules. The point is to distinguish "shared entertainment" from "shared identity".

A second checkable example helps illustrate how platforms have adapted to the messy reality of sharing. Apple introduced "Family Sharing" in 2014, allowing families to share purchases and subscriptions without sharing an Apple ID password. Google offers family groups with shared purchases and parental controls. Netflix, Spotify, and others have long offered multi-profile experiences. These features are not acts of benevolence; they are product responses to how people live. Their existence is evidence that services can separate ownership from access when they choose to. The implication is that when a service offers such separation, using it is often the least risky way to share because it reduces password circulation and supports individual boundaries.

Where services do not offer separation, the household has to supply it through habit. Habit, in this context, means two things: limiting what is shared, and being explicit about what sharing implies. Show: a household shares one shopping account with saved payment details, and the password is known by multiple people. Name: financial spillover. Explain: payment methods, order histories, and addresses are not "extras"; they are the sensitive core of the account; access to them allows mistakes and mischief, and it also creates privacy exposure through visibility into purchases. Implication: if such accounts must be shared, the household should at least recognise that the account contains both money and memory.

There is also a quieter harm: shared accounts can erode individuality. A person's recommendations, watch history, saved items, and search logs become a negotiated space. This sounds trivial until you remember that these services increasingly use personalisation to shape what people see and buy. Shared accounts can therefore distort choices, hide patterns, and confuse "who did what" when something goes wrong. Confusion is not only annoying. It is a weakness. When a household cannot tell whether a purchase was made intentionally, or whether an email alert was triggered by one person or another, it becomes easier for an attacker to hide in the noise.

The most difficult moment for shared accounts is not the start. It is the ending. Relationship changes are where residual access becomes a moral and practical problem. Show: a person moves out but keeps access "for now" because it feels petty to revoke it; months pass; the access becomes normal; then a new partner appears and the old access becomes uncomfortable, or worse. Name: deferred revocation. Explain: people postpone revocation to avoid conflict; postponement turns temporary access into semi-permanent entitlement; the eventual revocation then feels like betrayal rather than housekeeping. Implication: early clarity is kinder than late confrontation, and it is safer for everyone.

House moves create a different twist: accounts tied to addresses, such as utilities and deliveries, can leak location and routine if not updated. A shared account used for deliveries can continue to suggest old addresses. A smart home account can retain access to devices left behind or sold. A broadband account can remain linked to the old property. These are not dramatic hacks. They are administrative leftovers. Yet they can expose precisely the kind of information people most want private: where they live, when they are home, and who else shares the space.

A modest concession is needed here, because not all sharing is bad, and not all households should aspire to individualised digital life. Some people share accounts because it reduces financial strain. Some share because it reduces cognitive overhead. Some share because it expresses intimacy and trust. Still, trust is not the same as permanence, and intimacy is not the same as secure design. The reconciliation is to share intentionally rather than by drift: use separate profiles and delegated access where available, avoid sharing identity-anchor accounts, and treat the end of access as a normal part of the sharing lifecycle rather than an insult.

The motif of keys returns because it keeps the reader oriented towards the human truth: the problem is not that keys exist. The problem is that keys are handed out without keeping track. A household that can tell you, without rummaging through memory, which accounts are shared and who owns them is a household that has already reduced a surprising amount of risk.

The forward test is not whether your household can achieve perfect account hygiene. It is whether, if someone left tomorrow—by choice, by necessity, or by circumstance—you would be able to say with confidence which digital keys they would still be carrying, and whether those keys would open only the doors you intended.

Chapter 5
Browsers, Search, And DNS

On 24 May 2018, in Brussels, the European Union's General Data Protection Regulation came into force, and the internet briefly performed an awkward little dance. Banners appeared everywhere, asking about cookies in tones ranging from apologetic to coercive. News sites broke. Pop-ups multiplied. People clicked "Accept" with the reflex of someone swatting flies. The moment was meant to be about consent. It accidentally revealed something else: most adults had been living inside an invisible tracking system for years, and the first time it became visible it looked like paperwork.

Browsers are confession booths.

They record what you ask for, what you hesitate over, what you compare, what you almost buy, what you search at midnight when you cannot sleep. They also record it in forms that are not simply "history", but a layered, technical memory: cookies that persist, autofill fields that quietly accumulate, saved logins, cached pages, and the more modern, slipperier signs—fingerprints built from fonts, screen size, installed extensions, and timing quirks. A browser is where modern life is mediated, but it is also where modern life is observed. That is the chapter's central tension: the browser is your window to the world, and the world looks back through it.

Start with a scene most people recognise, because familiarity is what makes tracking feel uncanny when it becomes visible. Someone searches for a pair of shoes. They click through a few retailers, linger on one brand, abandon the basket because the price feels wrong, then return to their day. Later, adverts for the same shoes appear while reading the news, while checking the weather, while scrolling a recipe site. The experience is not merely "advertising". It is the sensation of being followed. And it raises the question that matters more than any individual ad: how did unrelated sites come to share the same understanding of you?

That question has more than one answer, and they stack. Cookies are the oldest and most straightforward: small pieces of data stored in the browser that allow a site to recognise a returning visitor. Some cookies are essential, like those that keep you logged in. Others exist primarily to track. Then there is third-party tracking, where a page loads resources—scripts, pixels, adverts—from other domains, and those domains set or read their own identifiers. The result is that the browser becomes a courier, carrying little markers between places you never knowingly introduced to each other. Tracking stops being one website knowing you and becomes an industry watching you through shared infrastructure.

What makes this chapter worth a full treatment is that the mechanics of tracking have changed, and the cultural conversation has not caught up. Many people still think of tracking as "cookies" in the simplistic sense. Yet as browsers and regulators put pressure on third-party cookies, tracking systems evolved. Fingerprinting is one of the most important evolutions. A fingerprint is not a single identifier stored in one place; it is a probabilistic portrait assembled from many small details—device characteristics, browser features, time zones, language settings, graphics rendering behaviour. It is harder to see and harder to control. It also reveals a deeper truth: even when you delete cookies, you may still be recognisable.

This recognition is the chapter's first major payoff. It does not demand that the reader become paranoid. It demands that the reader stop mistaking visibility for control. You can see cookies in settings. You cannot easily see a fingerprint being built. You can clear history. You cannot clear the fact that your device renders a particular font in a particular way. Once you understand that, the fussy toggles begin to look less like pedantry and more like a form of boundary-setting: ways of reducing the amount of information your browser volunteers to strangers.

From there, the chapter turns to choice—not ideological choice, not the kind of browser tribalism that turns people into unpaid brand ambassadors, but practical choice. Browsers are not equal in their defaults. Some block more trackers out of the box. Some make it easier to compartmentalise activity so that work, shopping, and personal browsing do not all bleed into one profile. Some allow fine-grained control over extensions, which matter because extensions can be both powerful defences and powerful leaks. Some update reliably, and updates matter because browsers are among the most attacked pieces of software on any device. The question is not "Which browser is best?" The question is "Which browser makes the safer behaviour the easier behaviour for the life you actually live?"

That is where the idea of using more than one browser becomes surprisingly liberating. Many people assume they must choose a single browser as a lifestyle. In practice, using one browser as the everyday workhorse and another as a "clean" tool for sensitive tasks is often the simplest form of compartmentalisation. You do not need to vanish. You need to stop smearing the same trail across every corner of your online life. A clean browser does not make you anonymous; it makes your browsing less entangled. It is a modest intervention with outsized psychological relief: fewer weirdly personalised adverts, fewer uncanny recommendations, fewer occasions where a work task bleeds into a personal feed.

Search brings the same problem into sharper focus because search is where intent is revealed. A browser visit can be accidental. A search query is deliberate. Search engines sit at the intersection of curiosity and commerce, and their incentives matter. Mainstream search is often funded by advertising, which rewards profiling and personalisation. Privacy-focused search engines tend to promise less logging, less personalisation, and fewer behavioural profiles, but they may trade off some convenience features. The choice is not purely technical. It is philosophical. Do you want your searches to become part of a long-term portrait used to predict and shape your behaviour, or do you want them to be treated more like ephemeral questions asked of a library catalogue?

There is also a practical dimension that people underestimate: defaults. Search is not just a website you visit; it is the engine behind your browser's address bar, your phone's assistant prompts, and sometimes your operating system's internal search. Changing the default search engine can be more consequential than people realise, because it changes what happens in moments of laziness, and laziness is where most data is generated. The reader does not need to become puritanical about search. They need to recognise that the search box is one of the highest-leverage places to shape data flow with minimal effort.

Then, just when the reader thinks the chapter is about what happens on screens, DNS arrives like plumbing. DNS—the Domain Name System—is the mechanism that translates a human-readable domain name into the numerical addresses computers use to route traffic. People rarely think about it because, when it works, it disappears. Yet DNS queries reveal where you are trying to go, even when the content of your connection is encrypted. They can be logged by whoever provides your DNS resolver, and they can be manipulated by attackers or misconfigured systems. DNS is the phone book of the internet, and like any phone book it can be used to learn a great deal about your interests, your routines, and your vulnerabilities.

The modern relevance of DNS is that the industry has been shifting towards encrypted DNS protocols—DNS over HTTPS and DNS over TLS—designed to protect DNS queries from being read or altered by local network observers. That shift does not magically make you invisible; it changes which parties can see what. It can also allow you to choose resolvers that promise not to log, or that offer basic filtering against known malicious domains. This is where the book's ethos of small, high-impact changes becomes tangible again. You do not have to rebuild your home network. You can make one quiet adjustment that reduces some tracking and blocks some obvious nasties at the network level.

A credible limitation belongs here too, because DNS discussions are prone to overclaim. DNS changes will not stop first-party tracking by the sites you choose to use. They will not defeat fingerprinting. They will not block everything, and overzealous filtering can break legitimate services. Encrypted DNS also concentrates trust: if you route DNS through a particular provider, you are trusting that provider with your browsing destinations, even if they promise not to log. The reconciliation is the same as with VPNs and password managers: privacy tools often shift trust rather than abolish it. The aim is to choose where trust sits, instead of leaving it to defaults you never examined.

Threaded through all of this is a subtle motif: the browser as a kind of passport. Each time you visit a site, your browser presents a set of credentials—some explicit, like cookies, and some implicit, like device characteristics. Sites and networks stamp that passport, sometimes with your consent, often without your awareness. The stamps accumulate into a travel history of the mind. You cannot stop the passport existing if you want to use the web, but you can choose how many stamps you collect, how legible they are, and whether you carry the same passport into every context of your life.

This chapter therefore is not a call to abandon the web. It is a call to stop treating the browser as a neutral pane of glass. It is an instrument. It measures and transmits. It can be tuned. When tuned well, it becomes less talkative, less sticky, less eager to introduce strangers to your habits.

The momentum at the end of this introduction comes from a question that is both mundane and decisive: when you type a query, click a link, or open a new tab, who else is allowed to learn from that action—your chosen service, your browser vendor, your ISP, an advertising network you have never heard of, a data broker you will never meet? The next pages make that question answerable in practice, not by chasing purity, but by choosing a browser posture you can actually live with.

How Browsers Track You

In May 2010, in San Francisco, the Electronic Frontier Foundation launched a public experiment called Panopticlick and invited ordinary people to visit a webpage and see how distinctive their browsers looked from the outside. The experience was unnervingly simple. A visitor loaded a page, waited a moment, and received a verdict about uniqueness based on details the visitor had never consciously "shared": fonts, plugins, screen characteristics, and other small signals that seemed too trivial to matter. Panopticlick was not a breach. It was a mirror. It showed, with unusual clarity, that a browser can be recognised without asking for a name.

Your browser carries a passport.

Most people learn the word "tracking" through a mild irritation: the advert that follows them. The first time it happens, it feels almost personal. You browse for shoes at lunchtime, close the tab, return to emails, and later—on a news site, a recipe page, a weather forecast—the same shoes appear, or their close cousins, as if the internet has been eavesdropping. The feeling is not abstract. It is intimate. The question that follows is always the same: how did these unrelated places coordinate?

Begin with the most visible mechanism, because visibility is how people build intuition. Show: a retailer remembers what is in a basket when you click away and return later. Name: a cookie. Explain: a cookie is a small piece of data stored by the browser on behalf of a website, often used to maintain sessions, preferences, and shopping carts; it allows a site to recognise a returning browser and link actions across visits. Implication: cookies are not inherently sinister, but they make continuity possible, and continuity is the raw material of tracking.

Now widen the scene to the modern web as it actually loads. A single shopping page rarely consists solely of the shop's own code. It pulls images from content delivery networks, fonts from third parties, analytics scripts, customer chat widgets, fraud detection tools, payment integrations, and, crucially, advertising and measurement tags. The browser fetches these components as part of rendering the page. Each fetch is a relationship. Many of those relationships are invisible to the user because they sit behind the surface of the site, like plumbing behind a wall.

Show: a page loads, and the browser silently requests resources from multiple domains, not just the one in the address bar. Name: third-party tracking. Explain: when third-party services are embedded across many sites, they can set or read identifiers (often via cookies or similar storage) and correlate browsing across those sites; the third party becomes a common observer, present in many places. Implication: tracking is not merely "a shop watching you"; it is an infrastructure that allows strangers to observe your movement between shops, newspapers, and forums.

This is where the shoe advert begins to make sense. A shopper visits a retailer, views a product page, and leaves without buying. A third-party advertising script on that page notes the visit and associates it with an identifier stored in the browser. Later, when the shopper visits a news site that uses the same advertising network, the news site's ad space is filled through that network, which recognises the identifier and selects an advert based on the earlier product interest. The shopper experiences a ghostly coincidence. The system experiences a simple lookup.

The passport metaphor matters because tracking is less about a single badge than about accumulated stamps. A cookie is one stamp. A login is a heavy stamp. Autofill is a quiet stamp. Cached data is a stamp. Each one makes the browser more recognisable, more continuous, more legible across time.

Cookies, however, are no longer the whole story, partly because browsers and regulators have squeezed them. In June 2017, at Apple's Worldwide Developers Conference in San Jose, Apple announced Intelligent Tracking Prevention for Safari, explicitly aimed at curbing cross-site tracking. That announcement matters as a cultural marker: a major browser vendor publicly named the problem and changed default behaviour. But the internet rarely abandons a profitable method without trying to rebuild it in a new shape. When cross-site cookies become harder to use, tracking shifts towards other signals and other storage.

Show: a browser blocks or limits third-party cookies, yet tracking still seems to persist. Name: alternative identifiers. Explain: websites and advertising systems can use other storage mechanisms and techniques—such as localStorage, cache-based identifiers, link decoration, and server-side tracking tied to logged-in accounts—to maintain continuity even when classic cookie tracking is restricted. Implication: controlling cookies helps, but it does not end tracking, because the goal is continuity and the web offers many ways to create it.

One of the most misunderstood pieces of this puzzle is the difference between "first-party" and "third-party" in practice. A "first-party cookie" sounds friendly because it is set by the site you are visiting. Yet first-party does not necessarily mean benign; a first-party cookie can still be used for profiling within that site's domain, and a large platform can treat large portions of the web as its "first party" through embedded services, sign-in buttons, and shared infrastructure. Meanwhile, a "third party" can appear as a first party through technical manoeuvres that place it under the visited site's domain. The labels help, but they are not moral categories. They are technical descriptions that tracking systems learn to bend.

Tracking also gains power through linkage: when a browser's activity is tied to an account identity. Show: a person remains signed in to a large platform in one tab while browsing elsewhere. Name: authenticated correlation. Explain: when a user is logged in, activity can be linked to an account through embedded scripts, pixel loads, or in-app browsers; the browser's "passport" can be stapled to a name, an email address, a payment method, or a phone number. Implication: logging in does not merely grant convenience; it can turn anonymous browsing into personally attributable behaviour in contexts the user may not expect.

The shoe advert is only the most polite symptom. The deeper consequence is that browsing becomes a behavioural dataset: interests inferred from reading patterns, politics inferred from clicks, health concerns inferred from searches, financial status inferred from products compared, relationship status inferred from gifts researched. None of these inferences needs to be perfectly accurate to be commercially useful. Probabilistic portraits are enough. This is why tracking is often described as "profiling": not the dramatic profiling of crime fiction, but the quiet statistical sorting of people into categories that predict what they might buy, fear, or support.

At this point, the obvious question is why the browser helps at all. The answer is mundane: browsers are designed to make the web fast, personalised, and functional. Caching improves speed by storing copies of resources. Autofill reduces friction by remembering addresses and cards. History allows you to return to a page you half-read. Cookies keep you signed in. The same features that make browsing smooth also make it trackable. The web's convenience features are, by their nature, memory features. Memory can serve you. Memory can also serve others.

Show: a browser offers to save your address and card details and then fills them quickly on a checkout page. Name: convenience memory. Explain: autofill data is stored locally, sometimes synced through a cloud account, and designed to be retrieved instantly; it can be exposed through device access, malicious scripts exploiting vulnerabilities, or careless sharing of devices. Implication: the browser is not merely a viewer; it is a storage layer, and storage layers become part of privacy risk even when no "tracking company" is involved.

Now we reach fingerprinting, the technique Panopticlick made famous in public imagination. Fingerprinting is tracking without a single durable token like a cookie. Instead, it is recognition built from a constellation of attributes: browser version, operating system, language settings, time zone, screen resolution, installed fonts, rendering quirks, and other signals that can be observed through standard web capabilities. The browser becomes recognisable because it behaves in a slightly particular way, the way a voice can be recognisable without stating a name.

Show: two people visit the same site, and the site can probabilistically tell their browsers apart even after cookies are cleared. Name: fingerprinting. Explain: fingerprinting combines many small signals into a composite identifier; while any one signal may be shared by many users, the combination can become distinctive, and it can remain stable across sessions. Implication: the "clear cookies and you're fine" mental model is incomplete, because recognition can be rebuilt from the browser's own characteristics.

Here a counter-example is necessary, because the story is not one-directional doom. Fingerprinting is harder to do well than people assume. It can be brittle. Browsers change. Devices update. Users install and remove extensions. Some privacy features deliberately reduce uniqueness by making browsers look more alike, or by limiting access to high-entropy signals. Tracking is a contest, not a completed conquest. And yet the contest itself is revealing: when browsers attempt to reduce one avenue of tracking, the industry tests another. That behaviour tells you where the incentives sit.

What makes tracking particularly slippery is that it is often stitched together through intermediaries you never see. Advertising does not simply involve a site choosing an advert. It often involves an auction-like process where information about the page and the visitor is shared with multiple parties to decide which advert to show. Those parties may include exchanges, demand-side platforms, measurement providers, and data brokers. The user sees a banner. Behind the banner is a market.

Show: a browser loads a page, and within milliseconds an advert appears, seemingly chosen instantly. Name: real-time ad selection. Explain: advertising infrastructure can transmit contextual data (the page) and behavioural data (the browser's identifiers and inferred interests) to multiple actors to select an advert; even when the content is innocuous, the metadata can be revealing. Implication: "just an advert" can involve data sharing far beyond the site you chose to read, which complicates any simple idea of consent.

The passport metaphor returns because it captures the feeling of involuntary disclosure. A passport is shown at borders. You do not negotiate every stamp. You accept a system in which movement implies inspection. Browsing increasingly resembles that: moving between sites implies being inspected by a set of parties whose names you will never learn, whose policies you will never read, and whose data retention you will never directly control.

This is why browser protections often feel fussy. They interrupt flows that have been optimised for frictionless extraction. Blocking third-party scripts can break parts of pages. Clearing site data can log you out. Limiting cross-site tracking can make certain "personalised" features less responsive. These frictions are not proof that protections are misguided. They are proof that the web has been engineered around persistent recognition, and persistent recognition becomes visible only when it fails.

Another subtle point deserves attention: not all tracking is about advertising. Some tracking is about fraud prevention, bot detection, security, and performance. A retailer wants to spot stolen card patterns. A bank wants to detect unusual sign-ins. A publisher wants to know whether its site is being scraped. These aims can be legitimate. They can also be overbroad. The same techniques that catch fraud can build profiles. The same scripts that measure performance can record behavioural fingerprints. The implication is not that every measurement is malicious. It is that "legitimate purpose" and "maximal collection" are not the same, and systems often slide from one to the other because data is easy to keep once collected.

So how does one reconcile the need for a functioning, personalised web with the desire not to be perpetually profiled? The first step is conceptual rather than technical: stop imagining tracking as a single thing you either "have" or "don't have". Tracking is layered. Some layers are chosen: logging in, saving a card, syncing history. Some layers are inherited: third-party scripts embedded by the sites you visit. Some layers are emergent: fingerprints built from your device's characteristics. Once you see layers, you can see leverage. The browser becomes a place where small constraints change what others can learn.

The second step is to understand the difference between being tracked and being harmed. Tracking is not always immediately harmful. It becomes harmful when it enables discrimination, manipulation, unwanted exposure, or the aggregation of intimate patterns into dossiers that outlive context. The shoe advert is merely a visible sign that the dossier exists. A dossier is valuable even when no advert is shown. It can be sold, combined, and used in ways the original browser session never implied.

And yet, a final limitation should be admitted with some humility: you cannot browse the modern web without leaving traces. The goal is not to erase all trace, which is a fantasy that tends to produce either despair or performative complexity. The goal is to reduce unnecessary trace and to make the remaining trace less linkable across contexts. That is what makes the "fussy" toggles worth understanding: they are not decorations. They are boundary tools.

The forward test is deliberately simple, because the web's complexity can otherwise paralyse: when you open a new tab and begin to browse, is your browser's passport being stamped only by the place you intended to visit, or by a crowd you never invited to the border?

Choosing Privacy Browsers

In June 2017, in San Jose, Apple used its Worldwide Developers Conference to announce Intelligent Tracking Prevention for Safari, an explicit attempt to curb the advertising machinery that had grown fat on cross-site recognition. The announcement landed with a peculiar mixture of applause and outrage, which is often how you can tell a design decision has touched money. Apple framed it as a privacy upgrade. Advertisers framed it as sabotage. Ordinary users mostly noticed, if they noticed at all, that some websites began to behave differently—logins that expired sooner, shopping carts that forgot, adverts that seemed less eerily accurate.

Browsers are not neutral. They are political economy rendered as software. The same application that opens a library catalogue also negotiates, on your behalf, which third parties may observe you, how long identifiers persist, whether a site can stitch your visits together, and how quickly the programme patches its own weaknesses. Privacy in browsing is less about heroic effort than about choosing a passport that is harder to counterfeit and less eager to collect stamps from strangers.

Defaults do most of it.

That one sentence is the uncomfortable heart of browser choice. Most people do not spend their evenings tuning settings, and they should not have to. The practical question is therefore not "Which browser is perfect?" but "Which browser's defaults and guardrails align with the life that will actually be lived?" A browser can be technically excellent and still fail you if it invites you—through convenience, through nagging prompts, through sync temptation—to carry the same passport into every context and then hand it over at every border.

Begin with what browsers are up against. Modern websites are composites. A single page often calls out to dozens of other domains: analytics, content delivery networks, ad exchanges, embedded videos, social widgets, fraud detection services. Each call is an opportunity for observation. Some browsers, by default, attempt to limit that observation by blocking known trackers or partitioning the storage they rely on. Others leave the web's status quo mostly intact, prioritising compatibility and performance. Show: a news page loads cleanly in one browser but triggers a flurry of third-party requests and tracking scripts in another. Name: tracking protection. Explain: tracking protection is a set of rules—sometimes curated lists, sometimes behavioural heuristics—that prevents the browser from loading or fully enabling known tracking resources. Implication: a browser's privacy posture is partly visible in what it refuses to load, and those refusals determine how much of your browsing becomes legible to outsiders.

A second layer is subtler and, for many readers, more consequential: separation. If a browser treats "storage" as one big pot, then cookies, site data, and logins can leak context across activities. Shopping bleeds into work. Work bleeds into personal reading. A single sign-in in one tab can influence what happens elsewhere. Some browsers have begun to treat storage as something that can be partitioned—by site, by context, sometimes by tab container—so that one identity does not automatically contaminate another. Show: a user signs into a social platform for one task and later finds other sites making assumptions, offering "helpful" integrations, or preloading content based on that identity. Name: context collapse. Explain: when identities share the same storage space, they can be correlated across sites through embedded scripts and shared identifiers; compartmentalising storage makes correlation harder. Implication: privacy is often less about blocking everything and more about preventing unrelated parts of life from being stitched into a single narrative.

Mozilla's work on containers is a useful, checkable illustration of this idea entering mainstream tooling. In 2017, Mozilla released the Firefox Multi-Account Containers extension, allowing users to separate browsing contexts—work, shopping, social—within the same browser window. It was a product decision that made a philosophical claim: people are not one identity online; they are a set of roles, and software should respect that. Containers do not make anyone anonymous. They do something more achievable: they reduce accidental linkage. The advert still appears. The profile becomes less coherent. The passport collects fewer cross-context stamps.

This is where browser "fanboyism" becomes a distraction. The right question is not whether you feel loyal to a brand. The right question is whether the tool offers mechanisms that match your risk and your temperament. Some people will happily run one browser for everything, if that browser has strong tracking protection and sensible partitioning. Others will find the simplest, least cognitively expensive strategy is to use two browsers: one as the everyday workhorse, logged in, synced, personalised; another as a cleaner space for sensitive tasks, used sparingly, with minimal extensions and limited history. Show: a person researching a medical condition, a job change, or a difficult personal matter prefers not to feed that curiosity into the same profile that drives adverts and recommendations elsewhere. Name: role separation. Explain: using a separate browser creates a practical boundary; it reduces the chance that sensitive browsing becomes entangled with routine browsing through shared cookies, autofill, and account logins. Implication: privacy can be achieved through architecture—separate spaces—rather than through constant vigilance.

Extensions complicate this picture because they can be both the best and worst thing about browsers. A good extension can block trackers, enforce secure connections, and reduce the amount of data sites can extract. A bad extension can observe everything you do. Extensions can read pages, capture keystrokes, modify content, inject scripts, and exfiltrate browsing data. The difference between "helpful" and "predatory" is not always obvious from a slick description. Show: a free coupon extension promises savings and quietly requests permission to "read and change data on all websites". Name: privileged add-on. Explain: extensions often run with broad permissions; if the extension is malicious, compromised, or simply over-intrusive, it can become a surveillance layer with access far beyond any single website. Implication: browser choice is inseparable from extension governance—what you install, what you allow, and whether the browser makes that governance visible and manageable.

There is also an industry-level example of how extension ecosystems shape privacy, and it is worth naming because it demonstrates that browser "privacy" is not only settings; it is policy. In January 2019, Google announced Manifest V3 for Chrome extensions, a platform change that would alter how extensions can intercept and modify network requests. The debate that followed was noisy, but the underlying point was simple: browser vendors set the rules of the extension world, and those rules can constrain or empower privacy tools. Whatever one thinks of the details, the implication is solid: when you pick a browser, you are also picking a governance regime for the add-ons that can most directly influence your privacy.

Updates are the least glamorous feature and the most non-negotiable. A browser is a complex programme that ingests untrusted content constantly. It parses images, scripts, fonts, videos, and documents delivered from countless sites. Vulnerabilities in that parsing surface regularly, and attackers love browsers because a browser is a bridge between the wild internet and your private machine. Show: a browser prompts for an update, the user postpones, and the machine continues to process the same untrusted web content with known weaknesses. Name: the patch window. Explain: once a vulnerability is patched, the existence of the patch can reveal what was broken; attackers can target those who have not updated. Implication: a browser that updates promptly, reliably, and without drama is a privacy tool because it reduces the chance that someone else can take control of the window you stare through.

Here, a credible limitation should be stated plainly, because browser privacy discussions often drift into myth. A "privacy browser" does not grant invisibility. Fingerprinting exists. Logged-in accounts exist. Network observers exist. A determined tracker can often recognise a device across sessions, especially when the user behaves consistently and signs into the same platforms. Even the best browser cannot make a user's choices—what they click, what they search, where they log in—disappear from the services they choose to use. The reconciliation is not to abandon the effort. It is to aim for reductions in linkability and collection, not total erasure. A browser can make surveillance harder, noisier, and less comprehensive, even if it cannot abolish it.

This framing also prevents a common mistake: treating browser choice as a referendum on morality. Some browsers are built by companies whose business models depend heavily on advertising. Some are funded by different structures. Some prioritise compatibility and speed because that is what keeps users. None of this automatically makes a browser "evil" or "pure". It does, however, shape incentives. Show: a browser vendor profits when browsing becomes more measurable and adverts become more targetable. Name: incentive alignment. Explain: incentives influence product defaults, the aggressiveness of anti-tracking features, and how much friction is imposed on tracking infrastructure. Implication: privacy browsers are not just technical artefacts; they are business choices embodied in software design.

At this point, the reader may wonder whether it is sensible to choose a browser solely on privacy grounds. It is sensible to include privacy as a primary criterion, but it is rarely sensible to ignore everything else. If a browser breaks too many websites, a user will abandon it. If it feels slow or unfamiliar, it will not become daily habit. If it does not sync bookmarks across devices in the way a user needs, workarounds will reintroduce risk elsewhere. The right browser is the one that makes privacy sustainable—something you do by default, not something you perform when you remember.

This is why the "one main browser plus an optional clean browser" strategy is so powerful. It is not a nerdy indulgence; it is a humane compromise. The main browser carries the messy necessities of modern life: logins, work tools, shopping, forms, saved addresses. It is tuned to be less talkative—tracking protection on, extension set minimal and trusted, updates automatic. The clean browser is treated like a fresh notebook: used for tasks where you would rather not leave ink everywhere, and kept deliberately boring. The point is not to live in the clean browser. The point is to have it available so that sensitive browsing does not have to fight its way through a decade of accumulated cookies and personalisation.

The passport motif matters here because it clarifies a subtle psychological trap. Many people assume that once they pick a "privacy browser", the problem is solved. In reality, the browser is a passport that can still be stamped heavily if you carry it into every border crossing with the same identity attached. Logging into a major platform, syncing everything, granting dozens of extensions broad permissions—these choices can turn any browser into a chatty, recognisable document. Conversely, a mainstream browser with good defaults and disciplined extension use can be significantly quieter than its reputation suggests. The passport can be managed. The trick is to stop handing it out as if it were a loyalty card.

Two further features are worth understanding in this light: private browsing modes and profile separation. Private browsing, despite its marketing aura, is usually best understood as "local non-retention" rather than "invisibility". It tends to prevent the browser from saving history, cookies, and site data after the session ends, but it does not hide you from the websites you visit, your employer's network, or your internet provider. It can, however, reduce the persistence of certain identifiers on your own machine. Profiles, meanwhile, create separate browser spaces with different histories, cookies, and sometimes different extension sets. For many people, profiles are the gentlest version of compartmentalisation because they fit the familiar idea of "work" and "personal" without demanding multiple applications.

None of these features is a silver bullet. Their power is cumulative. Tracking protection reduces what third parties can load. Containers or partitioning reduce cross-context correlation. Extension controls reduce privileged surveillance inside the browser. Updates reduce exploitability. Profiles or a clean browser reduce the smear of identity across contexts. Each step is modest. Together they change the character of your browsing: less sticky, less predictable, less profitable to observe.

The remaining tension—the one that makes this chapter worth reading rather than skimming—is a choice that cannot be avoided by any setting. Do you want your browser to behave like a helpful but discreet assistant, or like an enthusiastic intern who narrates your every move to whoever is standing nearby? The difference is not only technical. It is the difference between a life in which your curiosity stays mostly yours, and a life in which your curiosity becomes a commodity by default.

Search And Tracking Choices

On 4 December 2009, in Mountain View, Google announced that it would use web search history to personalise results for all users, including people who were not signed in. The practical outcome was subtle at first: two people could type the same query and see different answers, shaped by what they had clicked before. The cultural outcome was larger. Search stopped being a shared map and became, in part, a mirror—one that reflected you back to yourself whether you had asked for that intimacy or not.

Search is a private question.

It rarely feels like one. A search box sits there, blank and polite, inviting you to ask anything: how to fix a leak, whether a job is hiring, what a strange symptom might mean, how much a train ticket costs, what a politician said last week, how to leave a relationship safely, how to grieve. The act is quick. The afterlife is longer. Most people experience search as a moment. Many search engines experience it as a record.

The simplest way to think about this is to imagine each query leaving a receipt. Not a dramatic dossier, not a spy novel folder, just a small receipt: time, words typed, device details, location hints, and what you clicked next. One receipt is nothing. A month of receipts is a pattern. A year of receipts is a portrait.

Show: someone searches for "flights to Lisbon", then "Lisbon hotels near Alfama", then "carry-on luggage size", then "best travel insurance". Name: intent trail. Explain: search queries are not random; they encode plans, fears, purchases, and curiosities, and the sequence of queries reveals more than any single one. Implication: logging is valuable because it turns fleeting intent into analysable behaviour, which can be used to personalise results, target advertising, and infer categories about a person's life.

Mainstream search engines are often excellent at relevance because they are excellent at data. They learn from billions of queries, clicks, and outcomes, and they use that learning to rank results in ways that feel uncannily helpful. The trade is not mysterious. Personalisation can reduce friction: fewer irrelevant pages, quicker answers, results that reflect your language, region, and habits. Yet personalisation is not only convenience. It is also a mechanism for long-term tracking, because "better results" are frequently purchased with memory.

Show: you search for "jaguar". Name: ambiguity resolution. Explain: a search engine can guess whether you mean the animal or the car brand by looking at past queries, location signals, and browsing behaviour; it uses memory to disambiguate. Implication: the same memory that reduces confusion also increases traceability, because it links your present question to your past self.

Here is where privacy-focused search engines make their claim. They argue, in essence, that search can function without building a long-lived profile. Some avoid storing identifiable query logs. Some minimise personalisation. Some rely on contextual signals in the moment (language and coarse location) rather than on historical identity. Advertising may still exist, but it can be based on the query itself rather than on a behavioural profile. The promise is not magic. It is restraint.

DuckDuckGo is the most widely known example of this approach, founded in 2008 in the United States and marketed explicitly around not tracking users. Startpage, based in the Netherlands, has long positioned itself around privacy while delivering results sourced from larger engines. Brave Search, launched in 2021, is part of a broader attempt to build privacy tooling into mainstream browsing habits. These names matter not because one must treat them as saints, but because they demonstrate a spectrum: search can be built with different incentives and different defaults.

The first comparison worth making is logging. Show: a person searches for a topic they would not want attached to their name—perhaps a legal dispute, perhaps a personal crisis, perhaps a sensitive health concern. Name: query retention. Explain: retention policies vary; some services store query logs for defined periods, some link them to accounts, some use them to train ranking and advertising systems, and some claim to avoid storing identifiable logs altogether. Implication: the privacy question is not merely "Do they show ads?"

but "Do they keep receipts, and can those receipts be linked back to you?"

The second comparison is personalisation. Mainstream engines often personalise aggressively when you are signed in, and may still personalise when you are not, using browser identifiers and device signals. Privacy-focused engines generally provide results that are more "generic" in the sense that they are less shaped by your personal history. That can be a relief. It can also be a frustration.

Show: you search for "best laptop for data analysis", then for "best laptop for university", then for "best laptop for video editing". Name: filter bubble pressure. Explain: personalisation can narrow what you see over time, reinforcing past clicks; generic results can widen the field but may require more judgement and refinement. Implication: privacy often arrives with a small tax: you may need to steer your own search more actively instead of letting the engine steer you.

A credible limitation belongs here, and it should be stated without euphemism. Privacy-focused search is not the same as anonymity. Even a search engine that avoids storing identifiable logs can still see your IP address when you connect, can still be compelled by law in its jurisdiction, and can still be influenced by the infrastructure it relies on. Many privacy-focused engines source results from larger providers, which can shape what is available and how it is ranked. The reconciliation is the book's recurring theme: the aim is not purity. It is reducing unnecessary collection and linkability. Fewer receipts kept, fewer receipts stapled to a name, fewer receipts available to be combined.

Now consider advertising, because advertising is where people's intuitions tend to harden into slogans. The relevant distinction is behavioural advertising versus contextual advertising. Behavioural advertising uses your past actions across time and sites to predict what you might buy. Contextual advertising uses the immediate context—what you are searching for right now—to decide which ad is relevant.

Show: you search for “noise-cancelling headphones”, and you see ads for headphones. Name: contextual relevance. Explain: these ads can be served without knowing who you are; the query itself provides enough context. Implication: advertising does not automatically require surveillance, but surveillance makes advertising more precise and therefore more lucrative.

The difference becomes clearer with an everyday example that involves no exotic topics. Suppose one person searches for “running shoes” because they are training for a race. Suppose another searches for “running shoes” because they have been recommended a specific brand by a friend. A highly personalised engine might connect that query to a profile—past fitness searches, smartwatch use, location patterns around gyms—and feed the result page with an ecosystem of fitness marketing. A less personalised engine might simply show strong general results and a few context-driven ads. Neither is “wrong” in a purely functional sense. But one builds a private portrait as a side-effect, and the other tries to operate without it.

The third comparison, often overlooked, is integration. Mainstream search engines are rarely only search engines. They are part of a broader identity platform: email, maps, video, documents, cloud storage, advertising networks, and analytics tools embedded across the web. When search is integrated into such a platform, the receipts become easier to link. A signed-in account becomes a binding agent.

Show: a person stays signed in to a major platform for email and calendar, then uses the same platform for search. Name: account linkage. Explain: when services share a single identity layer, data from one service can inform another—search can inform ads in video, location can inform local results, browsing can inform recommendations. Implication: the convenience of an integrated suite often increases the ease of correlation, making the profile more coherent and harder to escape.

This is why changing search can feel like swimming against a current. Search is not just a homepage. It is a default embedded into browsers, phones, and habits. Many people intend to switch and then find themselves back where they started because the address bar still points to the old engine, because their phone’s assistant uses a particular backend, because a work machine is configured by policy. The realistic approach is to treat switching as a gradient rather than a dramatic conversion.

Defaults determine drift.

That sentence describes why this matters. People do not make most searches by visiting a search engine's website. They type into a browser bar, they tap a widget, they ask a phone a question, they highlight text and search from a menu. Changing the default search engine therefore has outsized effect because it changes the behaviour that happens when nobody is paying attention.

On desktop browsers, the default search engine is usually a setting buried under "Search" or "Address bar", alongside choices for privacy, suggestions, and autofill. On phones, the story depends on the browser and the operating system. Safari and Chrome have their own default search settings; alternative browsers often allow choosing a default within their own preferences. Some systems let you change the default browser application as well, which indirectly changes where search queries are routed. The practical takeaway is not a checklist. It is the idea that "switching search" means changing the place your device sends your reflexive questions, not merely bookmarking a different site.

The quiet motif of receipts returns here because it clarifies why partial switches can still matter. Even if you continue to use a mainstream engine for certain tasks—because it is simply better at a niche query, because it integrates with work tools, because it handles local results more effectively—you can route other searches through a more privacy-respecting engine and therefore reduce the volume of receipts being collected in one place. This is not ideological inconsistency. It is intelligent segmentation.

Show: you use one engine for map-heavy local searches and another for general research queries. Name: channel separation. Explain: different search tasks produce different kinds of data; local searches often reveal location and routine, while research queries reveal intellectual interests and projects. Implication: separating channels reduces the chance that one provider holds the whole portrait.

A further nuance that deserves attention is query suggestion and autocomplete. When you type into a search bar, suggestions may be fetched from the provider as you type. That can create extra receipts—partial queries, fragments, the early shape of your thought. Some browsers allow disabling search suggestions or limiting what is sent. The point is not to treat autocomplete as sinister. It is to recognise it as another point where convenience and disclosure are traded.

There is also the phenomenon of "search in the app". Many people encounter search not through a browser at all but through apps: shopping apps, social networks, video platforms. Those searches are often deeply logged and tightly tied to identity because the app already knows who you are. Switching your web search engine does not touch that world. The reconciliation is simple: focus on what you can control without pretending it solves everything. Web search remains one of the highest-leverage controls because it is so frequent and so revealing, but it is not the only place questions are asked.

If all of this sounds like a negotiation, that is because it is. Search sits at the edge between your interior life and public infrastructure. You ask. Systems answer. Systems also record. The decision is not whether to use search—modern life makes that unrealistic—but whether to let a single provider keep every receipt, link them to an identity, and feed them back into an advertising and recommendation machine that shapes what you see next.

The forward test is therefore intimate rather than technical: when you type your next private question into a search box, are you comfortable with who keeps the receipt—and with how long they might keep it?

Safer DNS And Filtering

In March 2018, in the United States, the Federal Bureau of Investigation took the unusual step of warning the public about "DNSChanger" and other forms of malicious interference with the machinery that translates web names into network addresses. The warning was not about an exotic zero-day or a cinematic hack. It was about a quiet sabotage: if an attacker can control where your computer thinks a domain name points, they can reroute you to impostor sites, inject adverts, or watch where you try to go. The web feels like a map of names. Underneath, it runs on look-ups.

DNS is your device asking, "Where is this?"

When you type a web address—news site, bank, school portal—your device does not inherently know where to find it. It asks a resolver, a service that answers with the numerical address to contact. This translation happens constantly and quickly, usually without you noticing. Because you do not notice it, you rarely choose it. Your router or your internet provider often decides. And because DNS queries are about destinations, they can reveal a great deal about your life: what you read, what you buy, what you search, when you wake, what your children watch, where your work habits pull you.

The phone book metaphor is almost too tidy, yet it remains useful. A phone book does not record the content of a call. It does reveal who you are trying to reach. DNS behaves similarly. Even when your web traffic is encrypted, your device often still needs to resolve names, and those look-ups can be observed and logged by whoever runs the resolver, or by anyone positioned to monitor the network path. Show: a household uses a mainstream internet connection; web pages load normally; behind the scenes, the router sends DNS queries to the ISP's resolver by default. Name: default resolution. Explain: many networks rely on the ISP's DNS resolver because it is configured automatically; the resolver can see the domains your devices request and may retain logs for performance, security, or commercial reasons. Implication: much of your browsing footprint is visible at the level of destinations even before any website begins tracking you.

DNS is also a security boundary, because it can be attacked. If an attacker can change your DNS settings, they can direct you to counterfeit services without changing what you type. You type "bank.co.uk" and land on something that looks right but is wrong. This is why some attacks target routers, not because routers contain your photos, but because routers decide where everyone in the home gets sent. The router is a traffic controller. It is also a point of trust that most people never inspect after the day the broadband technician left.

Show: a home router's DNS settings are altered, and every device in the house begins resolving certain domains through the attacker's server. Name: DNS hijacking. Explain: DNS hijacking changes the translation layer; it can enable redirection, ad injection, and selective interception; it is powerful because it operates beneath the browser interface people rely on for cues. Implication: DNS is not merely a privacy question; it is an integrity question about whether the destinations you reach are the ones you intended.

This is the moment where "safer DNS" becomes meaningful. The phrase can sound like a niche obsession, but the underlying move is straightforward: choose a resolver you trust more than the default, and protect DNS queries from casual interception on the local network. Two broad techniques matter here. One is selecting a resolver with privacy-respecting policies—limited logging, clear retention practices, and a reputation for resisting commercial exploitation. The other is using encrypted DNS protocols so that queries are not sent as plain text for anyone on the same network to read.

Encrypted DNS is a recent enough development that it still feels like plumbing being retrofitted while the building is occupied. Two protocols dominate the conversation: DNS over TLS (DoT) and DNS over HTTPS (DoH). DoT sends DNS queries through an encrypted channel designed specifically for DNS. DoH sends DNS queries through HTTPS, the same protocol used for secure web traffic, which can make it easier to deploy because it blends into ordinary web traffic. In both cases, the basic effect is the same: someone watching the local Wi-Fi cannot easily read the DNS queries in transit.

Show: a traveller uses public Wi-Fi in a hotel lobby; their laptop connects; web traffic is largely encrypted; DNS queries, however, can still be visible if not protected. Name: destination leakage. Explain: without encrypted DNS, network observers can see which domains a device resolves even if they cannot see the content of the pages; encrypted DNS reduces that leakage on the local network.

Implication: "secure browsing" is not only about HTTPS; it is also about protecting the look-ups that precede it.

A checkable, concrete example helps anchor that this is not speculative. In October 2018, Cloudflare launched its public DNS resolver at 1.1.1.1, marketing it explicitly on privacy and speed, and later supported encrypted DNS protocols. Google has long operated Public DNS at 8.8.8.8, and supports encrypted DNS as well. Quad9, launched in 2017, has positioned itself around security-focused filtering, blocking known malicious domains, with operations anchored in Switzerland. These services differ in governance, logging policies, and filtering aims. The point is not to crown a winner. It is to recognise that DNS is a choice, not a law of nature.

Filtering is the second part of the promise, and it is where DNS becomes quietly powerful for ordinary households. DNS filtering works by refusing to resolve certain domains, usually because they are known to host malware, phishing, or aggressive tracking infrastructure. When a device tries to reach such a domain, the resolver returns a non-answer or directs to a benign sinkhole. No connection occurs. The page element fails to load. The malicious site does not open. A filtering resolver does not inspect the content of your traffic. It changes whether your device can find the address of a known bad destination.

Show: a phishing email contains a link to a domain used for credential theft; a user clicks; the browser attempts to load; the DNS resolver blocks the domain. Name: pre-connection blocking. Explain: because DNS resolution happens before the browser can fetch a page, blocking at the resolver can prevent connections to known malicious domains across all devices on a network. Implication: DNS filtering can reduce risk in a low-maintenance way, especially for households where not everyone has the same level of vigilance.

The quiet virtue of DNS filtering is its scope. A browser extension protects the browser where it is installed. DNS filtering can protect everything on the network that uses that resolver: phones, laptops, tablets, smart TVs, and the odd devices that have poor security posture and rarely update. This matters because home networks are filled with forgotten computers. A DNS filter can block some of the worst destinations those devices might attempt to contact, without requiring per-device tool installation.

Yet this is where a credible limitation must be made explicit. DNS filtering is not perfect. It is a coarse tool. It cannot block a malicious page served from a legitimate domain. It cannot stop first-party tracking by the sites you choose to use. It cannot prevent a compromised account from being abused. It can also create false positives, breaking legitimate services that share infrastructure with domains on block lists. The reconciliation is to treat DNS filtering like a smoke detector, not like a locked vault. It reduces certain categories of harm and does so with low friction. It does not replace cautious behaviour or other defences.

There is also a subtle privacy trade-off inside the phrase "privacy-respecting resolver". You are moving trust. If you stop using your ISP's resolver and start using a third-party resolver, you may reduce one party's visibility but increase another's. Encrypted DNS reduces the ability of local observers to see queries, but it can concentrate query visibility in the resolver provider, because your device now sends more DNS traffic to that provider directly. The question becomes: who should hold the phone book of your destinations?

This is not a purely technical question. It is a governance question. A resolver provider may promise not to log. It may publish transparency reports. It may be subject to certain jurisdictions. It may be audited. Or it may simply claim virtue without evidence. The sensible stance is not to assume any provider is angelic. It is to choose a provider whose incentives and public commitments are more aligned with your goals than the default, and to recognise that the goal is reduction rather than elimination of data exposure.

To bring this back to household reality, consider the home router. The router is the simplest place to change DNS because it sits upstream: it can tell every device which resolver to use through DHCP, the mechanism by which devices receive network settings automatically. Change the resolver at the router, and every device that joins the network inherits the choice. That is the promise of low maintenance: set it once, benefit everywhere. The router becomes not only a Wi-Fi box but a policy device, deciding how the household resolves names.

On individual devices, changing DNS can be more precise, especially for phones that roam between networks. A phone that uses an encrypted DNS setting can keep that behaviour on public Wi-Fi, where it matters most for destination leakage. Some operating systems now offer system-level controls for encrypted DNS. Some browsers also offer their own DoH settings, creating a layered approach: even if the network is misconfigured, the browser's DNS look-ups for web traffic can be protected. The underlying idea is that DNS can be defended at multiple layers: router, operating system, browser. Defence is not a single toggle. It is a set of sensible defaults that reduce exposure across contexts.

A small narrative example keeps the "so what" tangible. Show: a family's teenager clicks a "free game" link from a chat message; the site tries to load a domain known for malware distribution; the household's DNS filter blocks it; the page fails with an error that looks like a network hiccup. Name: accidental interception. Explain: many dangerous clicks are not deliberate; they are curious, bored, or hurried; a network-level block can catch some of these moments without demanding perfect judgement from everyone in the home. Implication: DNS filtering is a household defence because it compensates for the fact that households contain multiple threat models at once.

Notice what this does to the broader theme of the book. It takes privacy out of the realm of personal virtue and puts it into the realm of environment design. You do not ask everyone to be an expert. You design the network so that certain traps are harder to fall into. That is what "smart privacy for normal people" looks like at the infrastructure layer: modest changes with broad effect.

The phone book motif returns because it keeps the reader oriented. DNS is where you ask for directions. You can ask the nearest stranger (the default resolver). You can ask someone you trust more. You can whisper the question rather than shouting it across the café. You can refuse directions to known bad neighbourhoods. None of these choices makes you invisible. They make your movements less broadcast and your chances of stumbling into obvious danger smaller.

The forward test is therefore not technical at all. When your household's devices ask, many times a day, "Where is this site?", who do you want answering—and who else are you comfortable letting overhear the question?

Chapter 6
Cloud Storage And Photos

On 1 September 2014, in the United States, Apple confirmed that attackers had obtained private photographs from iCloud accounts and that some of the images had been posted publicly. The episode became a tabloid spectacle, but the mechanics were painfully ordinary: access to an account, access to a cloud library, access to a person's private life. It was not a story about cameras hidden in bedrooms. It was a story about a modern habit—automatic upload—turning the most intimate material into something that could be reached from anywhere once the door was opened.

Cloud is not a place.

It is a promise: your files will be there when you need them, on whatever device is nearest, even after a phone is lost, even after a laptop dies, even after a hard drive makes its final, unromantic click. For most people the promise has kept. Cloud services have rescued dissertations, family albums, tax forms, medical letters, house deeds, passports, job contracts, and the small, irreplaceable fragments of daily life. The trouble is that the promise contains a second clause most users barely read: *your files will also be there when someone else can reach them.*

The cloud is a mirror with a long memory. It reflects not only what you chose to save but what your devices saved on your behalf: screenshots, message attachments, scans of documents, voice notes, and the accidental miscellany that accumulates when storage becomes invisible. It reflects your relationships in shared folders and group albums. It reflects your movements in location-tagged photos. It reflects your identity in copies of passports, bank statements, visa letters, and the administrative debris of modern life. If you want to know what a person values, you no longer need to search their house. You can look at the folder called "Important".

This chapter sits at a hinge in the book's arc, because it deals with privacy where it becomes emotional. Browsers and DNS involve traces and metadata; cloud storage and photos involve memory and family. People tolerate astonishing levels of risk in this domain because the benefit is so tangible. A photo saved automatically feels like a gift to your future self. A document synced across devices feels like competence. A shared album feels like connection. What makes the cloud difficult is that the same features that produce comfort—sync, sharing, searchability—also produce exposure.

Begin with an everyday scene, because that is where the cloud's power hides. Someone takes a photograph of their child at the kitchen table, flour on the fingers, the light slanting across a face that will change too fast. The photo appears on a partner's phone moments later. It appears on a laptop at work later that afternoon. It appears in a "Memories" montage a year later. All of that feels miraculous. It is also a data pipeline: a moment captured, uploaded, processed, tagged, indexed, and made retrievable from multiple devices. The miracle is not only storage. It is distribution.

Cloud storage is often marketed as "backup", but the distinction between backup and sync is one of the most important conceptual clarifications a normal person can make. Sync means the cloud mirrors what your device has now, and mirrors changes quickly. Delete a file in one place and it may vanish in others. Backup means a copy is kept even when the original changes or disappears, ideally with versions and recovery options. Most consumer cloud services blend these concepts, and that blending is precisely where people get hurt: they assume "it's backed up" when in fact it is merely synchronised. Then they delete something, or a device is compromised, or a folder is cleaned up, and the loss propagates.

This matters for privacy as well as resilience. If sync mirrors everything automatically, then the cloud becomes an ever-expanding archive that contains far more than you would deliberately upload if each file required a conscious decision. When you stop noticing what is being uploaded, you stop controlling what exists in the archive. The archive is where breaches become consequential, because it holds not one piece of information but an interlocking set: IDs, addresses, financial documents, family photographs, private correspondence, and the raw material for impersonation and coercion.

This chapter's first task is therefore inventory—not in the spirit of paperwork, but in the spirit of regaining authorship. Which services hold what? Which accounts are tied to which email addresses? Which devices are feeding those accounts? Which folders are synced by default? Where are your photographs actually stored? What happens when you delete a file, and how long does it linger in "recently deleted" or in version history? These questions sound administrative. They are, in fact, about power: who holds the copy, who can access it, and who can erase it.

The money question matters too, because it explains why cloud services behave the way they do. Some are paid subscriptions. Some are bundled with devices. Some are free at the point of use and monetised through data or through conversion to paid tiers. Even when a company does not "sell your files", it may still analyse them for features: search, deduplication, face grouping, content recognition, and safety scanning. That analysis can be benign, helpful, or intrusive depending on design choices and transparency. The reader does not need a conspiracy theory. They need to understand that cloud storage is not a charity. It is an industry with incentives, and incentives shape defaults.

Then come photos, the most emotionally loaded data most people store. Photos are not just images; they are social objects. They contain faces, places, and time. They reveal relationships. They reveal routines. They reveal children before they can consent. Modern photo libraries are no longer simple albums; they are searchable databases. A person can type a name, a place, or a thing—"beach", "birthday", "passport"—and the system retrieves memories by algorithm. Facial recognition and location tagging are what make this magic possible. They are also what make the archive more sensitive than people realise.

An example family album clarifies the stakes without melodrama. Imagine a shared album set up for grandparents: birthday photos, first day of school, holiday moments. The album feels private because it is "just family". Yet link-sharing settings can be surprisingly permissive. "Anyone with the link" can mean exactly that, and links leak through forwarded messages, old emails, or a friend accidentally copying the wrong thread. Even without a leak, the album can be accessible on devices left logged in, on tablets used by visitors, on old phones in drawers. The private becomes merely unpublicised. That is a dangerous middle state: people behave as if it is private while the system treats it as broadly accessible.

This chapter also confronts a form of risk that is uniquely cloud-shaped: sharing that persists. Cloud sharing is designed to be effortless and therefore is designed to be durable. A shared link can remain live for years. A folder shared with an old colleague can remain accessible after jobs change. A document sent "just for now" can be downloaded, duplicated, and reshared. The convenience is real. So is the permanence.

The topic of link sharing reveals how small interface choices change the shape of exposure. "Public" means indexable and discoverable. "Anyone with the link" means unlisted but accessible. "Specific people" means access tied to authenticated accounts. Each option trades convenience for control. People often choose the easiest option in the moment and then forget the window they have left open. The result is not always catastrophe. But it is an open window into a room that contains more than you remember.

The chapter's final movement—leaving services gracefully—addresses the long tail of digital life. Most adults have a graveyard of accounts: old cloud drives from previous employers, free storage tied to an ancient email address, photo services used for a holiday a decade ago, collaboration tools for projects that ended and were never cleaned up. These accounts are not merely clutter. They are dormant repositories of personal data, sometimes with weak passwords, often with outdated recovery details, and occasionally with forgotten sharing links still active. Dormant accounts are attractive because they are neglected. Neglect is a security posture.

Yet the act of leaving is emotionally and practically difficult. People fear deleting something they will later need. They fear losing access. They fear the work of exporting, sorting, and migrating. They also overestimate how "deleted" deletion is. Many services retain data for a period. Backups exist. Cached copies exist. Legal and operational constraints may mean that complete erasure is not immediate. The honest stance is that deletion reduces exposure but does not necessarily produce instantaneous disappearance. That honesty matters because it prevents magical thinking, and magical thinking is what makes people either complacent or panicked.

A credible limitation should be woven in here too: the cloud is not merely a risk. For many people it is a safety tool. Automatic backups protect against theft and device failure. Shared albums maintain family connection across distance. Cloud collaboration enables modern work. A person fleeing an unsafe home may rely on the cloud to keep documents accessible. A researcher may rely on cloud versioning to prevent loss. The reconciliation is not to reject the cloud. It is to use it with intention: to know what is being stored, to know what is being shared, and to know what can be recovered.

Threaded through the chapter is a quiet motif: the cloud as a house with many doors. You may lock the front door—your password, your two-factor—and still forget the side door—an old sharing link, a device left logged in, a folder shared with "anyone with the link". You may lock the doors and still leave the curtains open through metadata—faces grouped, locations tagged, names embedded. Privacy here is not about sealing the house. It is about knowing which doors exist and which ones you actually use.

The reader should reach the end of this introduction with a particular kind of appetite: not for more fear, but for more clarity. Because the cloud is where modern life stores its evidence. It holds the documents that prove who you are, the photographs that prove who you love, and the small records that prove where you have been. The pages ahead make that evidence less casually exposed, not by demanding perfection, but by making a set of quiet decisions visible enough to be chosen.

The forward question is deliberately practical and emotionally sharp: if someone else could open your cloud account tomorrow—by a guessed password, a forgotten device, a leaked link, or a moment of carelessness—what would they learn about you in the first five minutes, and which door would they use to get in?

What Lives In Cloud

In February 2017, in the United States, the Pentagon's Defence Digital Service posted a short, blunt note titled "Top Ten Cloud Security Mistakes". It was not written as poetry. It did not need to be. The document read like a field report from a place where small configuration choices had repeatedly turned into large exposures: storage left open to the public internet, access keys scattered, audit logs ignored. A government team was, in effect, saying the same thing ordinary people discover in their own quieter way: cloud storage is powerful precisely because it is easy, and ease is where mistakes hide. Your files do not float in the sky. They sit in somebody's filing system.

A cloud account is a shadow filing cabinet.

That cabinet grows without asking permission. A scan of a passport for a rental car. A PDF of a payslip for a mortgage broker. A photograph of a prescription label to remember later. A spreadsheet of household budgets. A folder of old tax returns. A voice memo from a grief-heavy evening you never intended to share. The modern cloud does not merely store documents you consciously upload. It absorbs fragments produced by your devices and apps: message attachments, screenshots, "recent files", automatic camera uploads, and the little exports created when a service says, brightly, "Save a copy to your drive".

It is worth naming the emotional trick here. Cloud storage presents itself as absence of worry. You stop thinking about hard drives failing because the cloud is "there". You stop thinking about the single laptop being stolen because your files are "synced". You stop thinking about the disaster of losing family photographs because they are "backed up". The problem is that three different words—*sync*, *backup*, and *archive*—are routinely used as if they are interchangeable. They are not. Confusing them is how people lose data and how they unknowingly keep far more data than they meant to keep.

Show: a person edits a document on a laptop and, minutes later, sees the same edits on their phone. Name: sync. Explain: syncing services keep multiple devices consistent by propagating changes; they are designed to make "the current state" the same everywhere, which means deletions and mistakes can propagate too. Implication: sync is brilliant for continuity, but it is not automatically protection against loss, because it often preserves sameness rather than history.

Backup is different in intent. A backup exists to survive your mistakes and your bad luck. It keeps copies that are not instantly overwritten by your latest action. A true backup tends to keep versions, or at least retains deleted items for a meaningful period, and it is designed around recovery. Many consumer cloud tools offer some version history and "recently deleted" features, but the presence of these features does not erase the core logic of sync. A synced folder can still empty itself everywhere with one careless drag to the bin. Version history may or may not be enabled. Retention windows may be short. Services differ. Users rarely check.

Show: a person deletes a folder on a phone to "clear space" and later discovers it vanished from the laptop as well. Name: mirrored deletion. Explain: when a service treats devices as mirrors, deletion is a synchronised action; it is not local housekeeping but a command to the system. Implication: understanding the sync model is a privacy issue too, because it determines what exists where, how long it persists, and how easily it can be retrieved by someone who gains access.

An archive is a third thing again: a long-lived repository kept for memory, compliance, or sentiment rather than convenience. Many people accidentally create archives because cloud storage makes accumulation effortless. A folder called "Old" becomes a decade. An email attachment saved "just in case" becomes a personal dossier. A device's automatic uploads turn a daily camera roll into a searchable history of movement, relationships, and possessions.

This is why the first serious privacy move in the cloud is not a setting. It is an inventory. "What lives in cloud" sounds philosophical until you ask it plainly: which companies currently hold copies of your documents, photos, and account recovery materials? Most people cannot answer without hunting. That hunting is not shameful. It is the predictable result of a decade of services quietly offering "Save to…" at every turn.

The inventory becomes clearer when you think of cloud storage as a set of overlapping cabinets rather than a single one. There is the cabinet you deliberately chose—perhaps a drive service you use for work. There is the cabinet that arrived with your phone—an ecosystem account that offers seamless syncing. There are cabinets created by apps—notes, messaging, scanners, password tools, PDF editors—each with its own sync layer. Then there are cabinets created by employers and schools, where your work and research may sit under an account you do not fully control. The cabinets overlap, and overlaps are where assumptions break.

Show: a person believes their "documents" live in one place, yet the same document exists as an email attachment, a chat upload, a shared drive copy, and a scanned PDF in a notes app. Name: duplication drift. Explain: cloud systems encourage copying because sharing and convenience often work by duplication; files proliferate across services and contexts. Implication: privacy is harder than people think not because they are careless, but because the modern workflow produces multiple copies by default.

Two named, checkable examples help anchor what is otherwise an invisible phenomenon. The first is the iCloud photo leak publicised in September 2014, which demonstrated how automatic upload can turn private material into remotely accessible material once account access is compromised. The second is the sequence of misconfigured cloud storage exposures that have repeatedly surfaced in public reporting—such as the July 2017 exposure of a large dataset tied to the Republican National Committee's marketing vendor, stored in an openly accessible Amazon S3 bucket and reported by UpGuard. Different politics, same lesson: cloud storage is as private as its configuration and as safe as its access controls.

These examples do not exist to frighten. They exist to correct a common mental error: the belief that "cloud" is a neutral background service, like electricity. It is not. Cloud storage is an agreement between you and a provider about access, retention, and control. Agreements have terms. Terms have consequences.

Money sits inside those terms. Not every cloud provider makes money the same way, but every provider must make money somehow. Some sell subscriptions directly. Some bundle storage into devices and use it to strengthen brand loyalty. Some offer "free tiers" that act as funnels into paid plans. Some sit inside advertising-funded ecosystems where user data, in aggregate, helps refine targeting and prediction. Even when a company does not "sell your files", it may still process them to deliver features: search, previews, duplicate detection, spam prevention, safety scanning, and machine-learning-based organisation. Those features can be genuinely helpful. They can also expand what the system knows about your content.

Show: a photo service groups faces automatically, offering "people" albums. Name: content indexing. Explain: indexing requires analysis; the system extracts patterns and metadata from your files so it can retrieve and organise them; this may be done on-device, on servers, or in a hybrid model depending on the provider. Implication: the cloud cabinet is not a dumb box; it can be an active system that learns from what you store, which changes the privacy conversation from "who can access the file" to "what can be inferred from the file".

A modest concession belongs here. The cloud can be safer than the alternative. A laptop can be stolen. A hard drive can fail. A house can flood or burn. A paid, well-run cloud service may provide redundancy, encryption at rest, and security teams that most individuals cannot replicate. The cloud is not automatically reckless. The reconciliation is that the cloud's safety depends on two things at once: the provider's competence and the user's account security and sharing habits. A strong provider cannot protect you from a weak password. A careful user cannot fully compensate for a negligent provider. Both matter.

This is where deletion becomes complicated, and where the book's calmness is most needed. People often imagine deletion as a clean action: press delete, and the file disappears. Cloud services complicate this. Many maintain "recently deleted" areas as a safety net. Many keep versions of files. Many have backups. Some may retain copies for legal, operational, or technical reasons, at least temporarily. Deletion therefore often means "no longer visible in the account" rather than "erased from existence instantly".

Show: a user deletes a document and later finds it in a "bin" with a restoration window. Name: soft deletion. Explain: soft deletion is designed for recovery; it prevents accidental loss; it also means a file can persist for a period even after you believe it is gone. Implication: privacy decisions that rely on deletion must account for retention windows and hidden copies, because "deleted" may mean "waiting".

This is neither a scandal nor a conspiracy. It is an engineering trade-off. Systems that allow recovery are systems that keep copies. Copies create resilience. Copies also create persistence. The user's task is not to demand the impossible. It is to understand the shape of persistence well enough to make deliberate choices about what should exist in the cabinet at all.

The shadow filing cabinet motif matters because it highlights a quiet shift in what counts as "important". In paper life, you decided what went into a filing cabinet because filing took effort. In cloud life, effort has been removed. Therefore selection has been removed. Many people now store not only what is important, but what is momentary. That is why inventory is transformative: it reintroduces selection.

A short exercise—more like a lens than a worksheet—can be done in a few minutes of honest attention. Picture your digital life as rooms in a house: identity documents, finance, work, family photos, health, correspondence, and the miscellany drawer of screenshots and receipts. Now ask, for each room, which cloud cabinet holds the copies. You do not need perfect answers. You need enough clarity to notice surprises: a scan app that uploads automatically; a chat service that stores attachments indefinitely; an old employer drive still holding personal work; a photo library shared with a relative years ago. The purpose of the exercise is not completeness. It is orientation.

Show: a person realises their "tax folder" exists in two drives and a mailbox, and that one copy is shared with an accountant whose access was never revoked. Name: access creep. Explain: sharing is often granted for a moment and then forgotten; over time, access rights persist beyond their purpose. Implication: mapping the cabinet reveals not only where files are, but who else might be able to reach them.

This mapping also clarifies a subtle point about privacy and time. The cloud makes the past extremely portable. A youthful CV, an old address, an outdated passport scan, a breakup-era diary entry—these can all remain one password away. People often think of privacy as protection against strangers in the present. Cloud storage forces you to consider protection against your own forgotten past, preserved by defaults.

A final limitation should be faced with intellectual honesty: you cannot fully solve cloud privacy at the level of personal behaviour alone. Large platforms shape what is possible through interface design and business incentives. Sharing options are often ambiguous by design because friction reduces growth. "Anyone with the link" exists because it is easy. Sync is default because it sells devices and subscriptions. The individual can still do something meaningful, but the individual is working within constraints set elsewhere. Recognising that prevents both self-blame and magical thinking.

The chapter's deeper through-line is therefore not "avoid the cloud". It is "know your cabinets". Know which ones exist, which ones matter, which ones are actively feeding new material into themselves, and which ones have become dusty attics of old data. Once you see your cloud footprint as a set of cabinets with doors, you stop behaving as if a single password is the only lock. You begin to notice side doors: shared folders, logged-in devices, old integrations, copies in messaging apps, and recovery emails that point to accounts you barely remember.

The forward test at the end of this section is deliberately simple and slightly uncomfortable: if you had to name, without searching, the three cloud services most likely to contain your most sensitive documents, could you—and would you be confident about who else has a key to each cabinet?

Managing Photo Libraries

In October 2020, in the United States, the Federal Trade Commission reached a settlement with Everalbum, the company behind the photo app Ever, after alleging that the firm had used customers' photos to develop facial recognition technology and had failed to honour promises about deletion. The settlement required the company to delete models and algorithms derived from users' photos and to delete the photos and videos of users who had deactivated accounts. A regulator was, in effect, forced to spell out something most people assume without thinking: a photograph is not merely an image; it is data that can be repurposed, learned from, and retained in forms that outlast the visible file.

A photo is a time capsule.

It holds the obvious—faces, rooms, celebrations—and the incidental: a street name in the background, a child's school logo on a jumper, a passport left on a table, a prescription bottle on a kitchen counter. It holds where you were, when you were there, and often who you were with. Modern photo libraries do not treat photographs as static keepsakes. They treat them as a searchable database of life. That searchability is what makes them delightful. It is also what makes them sensitive.

The shift happened quietly. One day you had a camera roll. The next you had "Memories". The device suggested an album called "Beach trips", then "Dogs", then "Alice", as if it had been watching your life with the patience of an archivist. It has. The technology that groups faces, recognises scenes, and maps images to locations is a form of *indexing*: extracting structure from raw pictures so they can be found later. Indexing is why you can type "receipt" and find the photo you took for expenses. It is also why a photo library can become a dossier if accessed by the wrong person or shared too widely.

Show: you search your photo app for "passport" and it returns a crisp shot you took in a hurry at an airport check-in. Name: semantic search. Explain: modern photo systems use machine learning to classify images by objects and text; they build an internal index so that images can be retrieved by concept, not only by date. Implication: convenience increases the value of the library to you and to anyone else who can reach it, because it turns a chaotic archive into an organised one.

The first privacy question with photos is not "Do I take pictures?" It is "Where do they go by default?" Most phones now offer automatic upload to a cloud library. The pitch is irresistible: never lose a photo again. It works. The cost is that your library becomes accessible from anywhere your account is accessible, and the account becomes a single point of entry into years of memory. If you care about privacy, the correct emotional stance is neither fear nor defiance; it is respect. Treat the photo library as sensitive storage, not as a casual feed.

Organisation is the next lever. People assume organisation is a neatness hobby. In photo libraries it is a security feature because it affects what is surfaced, what is shared accidentally, and what is discoverable by someone browsing quickly. A library with everything in one infinite camera roll invites rummaging. A library with albums and sensible separation reduces accidental exposure. The goal is not to become a curator. The goal is to reduce the number of times you have to scroll past something you would rather not explain.

Show: a person hands their phone to someone to show one picture and ends up anxiously watching the other person's thumb. Name: incidental disclosure. Explain: unstructured camera rolls make it easy to swipe into unrelated images; anxiety is a sign that the library contains material you do not want to reveal casually. Implication: creating separations—albums, favourites, hidden folders where supported—reduces the risk of accidental exposure in ordinary social moments.

Tags and metadata are where many people are surprised. A photograph often carries embedded information in its file header, commonly called EXIF data. This can include the date and time, camera model, and, if enabled, precise GPS coordinates. That location data can be astonishingly specific: not merely "London" but the exact building. When photos are shared, this metadata may or may not be stripped depending on the platform and method. A photo sent through a messaging app might lose location data; a photo shared as a file attachment might retain it. A photo uploaded to a social network might be processed and stripped, but the platform itself may still learn the location through other means. The key is not to memorise which service does what. It is to understand that a photo can carry a hidden address.

Show: a child's photo is shared with relatives; the background looks harmless; the file's metadata reveals the family home coordinates. Name: location leakage. Explain: geotagging embeds location in the file; if the tag remains when the file is shared, a recipient or a third party can extract the location even if it is not visible in the image. Implication: location tags turn photos into maps, which is wonderful for personal memory and risky for privacy when sharing is loose.

Facial recognition adds a second, even more intimate layer. When a photo service groups faces, it is building a biometric index. Some systems perform this processing on-device; others process in the cloud. Either way, the practical effect is the same: it becomes possible to retrieve all photos of a person quickly. For a parent, this feels like magic. For privacy, it is a decision: do you want your child's face to be a search term inside a commercial system, and if so, under what controls?

This is where the Everalbum case matters as a checkable signpost. It demonstrates a simple truth: companies can be tempted to repurpose photos, and regulators sometimes intervene only after the fact. Even when major providers make stronger privacy claims and offer more robust security, the direction of travel in the industry has been towards more analysis, not less, because analysis enables features users love. The mature response is to choose where analysis happens (on-device where possible), to limit sharing of analysed libraries, and to treat face tagging as optional rather than inevitable.

A credible limitation belongs here too. Facial grouping can be genuinely useful for accessibility and memory. It helps people find images of loved ones. It can assist those with cognitive challenges. It can reduce the labour of sorting. Rejecting it on principle may be unrealistic for many. The reconciliation is to distinguish between the feature and its expansion. You can use facial grouping locally while being stricter about sharing links and account access. You can accept the convenience while refusing to turn the library into a broadcast channel.

The sharpest privacy errors with photos occur at the boundary between private library and shared album. Shared albums are seductive because they feel intimate: "just family", "just the team", "just the nursery group". They also tend to be implemented with sharing models that prioritise ease. "Anyone with the link" is common. Links can be forwarded. Links can be copied into the wrong chat. Links can remain active long after the moment has passed. A shared album can become an unmonitored window.

Consider an example that is emotionally familiar and technically instructive. A parent creates a shared album for grandparents. The album contains weekly photos: first steps, school uniforms, birthdays, a child asleep on the sofa after a long day. The parent shares a link in a family group chat. One grandparent forwards the message to a friend—innocently, to brag, to share joy. The friend now has the link. The friend's phone is backed up to their own cloud. The link appears in message history. The album has not been "hacked". It has been shared. The parent experiences the result as a breach anyway, because the boundary was social, not technical.

Show: the parent reviews the shared album settings and discovers it allows anyone with the link to view, and that the link has no expiry. Name: unbounded sharing. Explain: link-based access is durable and hard to audit; control depends on secrecy of the link, which is fragile once it enters social circulation. Implication: the safest sharing model is not the one that relies on everyone's discretion forever, but the one that limits who can access and for how long.

The "for how long" part is crucial because photos have a long half-life. A photo of a child is not merely sensitive today. It remains sensitive in ten years, when that child has their own social identity, their own boundaries, their own risks. Parents and relatives often share with good intentions. Intentions do not grant consent. Children grow up inside archives they did not choose. This is one of the most ethically charged aspects of modern privacy: adults build a child's digital footprint before the child can speak.

This is not a call for puritanical silence. It is a call for proportion. Some moments belong in the family album and not in the open web. Some details—school logos, street signs, uniforms, routines—can be avoided or cropped without losing the memory. Some sharing can be shifted from broad social platforms to smaller, controlled channels. The point is to keep the memory while reducing the broadcast.

Backing up photos adds another layer of complexity, because photos are often the most painful data to lose and therefore the most aggressively duplicated. People may have photos in a phone library, synced to a cloud account, duplicated to a partner's account, backed up to a laptop, and copied again to an external drive. Redundancy is good for resilience. It is also a multiplication of exposure. Each copy is another door. Each door has its own password, its own recovery channel, its own forgotten settings.

Show: a person changes phones and realises their photos exist in three cloud services and two old devices still logged in. Name: copy sprawl. Explain: photo backups proliferate because people fear loss; sprawl makes it harder to control access and harder to know what "delete" means. Implication: privacy depends not only on securing one account but on understanding how many copies exist and which ones are still reachable.

This is why deliberate consolidation can be a privacy move as well as a tidiness move. Fewer copies, better protected, can be safer than many copies scattered across accounts with forgotten passwords. The earlier chapters' principles apply directly: strong account security, two-factor, device locks, and sensible sharing controls. A photo library deserves the same seriousness as email. It is, in many lives, more intimate than email.

At this point it is useful to name a small behavioural metric, because abstraction is the enemy of action. One can measure "photo exposure" not by counting images but by counting doors: how many accounts can access your main library; how many devices are signed in; how many shared albums exist; how many links are still active; how many people have access through their own accounts. Each door is a risk surface. Reducing doors is often easier than policing content.

The time capsule motif returns because it captures what is at stake. Photos preserve time. They also preserve context. A time capsule is meant to be opened by the intended audience at the intended moment. If a time capsule is left on a public bench, the object has not changed, but the meaning has. Managing photo libraries is, ultimately, about putting the time capsule somewhere appropriate: accessible to you, shareable with care, not casually available to strangers or to future versions of social platforms with different incentives.

A final limitation should be admitted with some humility: no system can guarantee that a shared photo remains private once it leaves your control. A recipient can save it. A screenshot can be taken. A phone can be compromised. The goal is therefore not to achieve perfect control over every image after sharing. The goal is to reduce unnecessary sharing, to make accidental broad exposure less likely, and to avoid building a child's life into a public archive by default.

The forward test at the end of this section is intentionally human rather than technical: when you share a family album, are you designing for the best behaviour of everyone involved—or for the behaviour that will actually happen when someone forwards a link, loses a phone, changes an account, or forgets that a window was left open?

Sharing Links Safely

In June 2020, in San Francisco, the video-conferencing company Zoom announced that it had removed an option that had allowed meeting hosts to generate links which did not require passwords by default, after a wave of "Zoombombing" incidents had turned private calls into public spectacles. The detail mattered because it was not a story about sophisticated cryptography being broken. It was about links. A join link functioned like an open door in a corridor full of people who forward things without thinking. When the door was left open, strangers walked in.

Links are tiny keys.

They fit in messages, calendars, and casual emails. They cross devices, time zones, and social contexts without friction. That is why cloud sharing feels like magic: a file becomes reachable with a single click. It is also why cloud sharing can become quietly reckless. A link does not carry the tone you intended when you sent it. It does not remember that you meant "just for today". It does not know the difference between a colleague and a group chat. It is a key that can be copied perfectly, indefinitely, and without the original owner noticing.

The first step in sharing safely is to understand what link types actually mean in practice, not in marketing language. Cloud services tend to offer variations on three models. The first is public publishing: a link that is meant to be discoverable, sometimes indexable by search engines, often intended for public distribution. The second is link-based access: "anyone with the link" can view or edit, and the primary control is the obscurity of the URL. The third is identity-based access: specific people are granted access through accounts, and the service checks who they are before showing the file.

Show: a user clicks "Share" and sees options that sound like degrees of friendliness—"Public", "Anyone with the link", "Only people invited". Name: access model. Explain: access models define who must be authenticated and what the link itself represents; a public link represents publication, a link-based share represents possession of a URL as permission, and an identity-based share represents an access control list tied to known accounts. Implication: choosing an access model is choosing what counts as "authorised", and each choice has predictable failure modes.

The failure mode of public publishing is obvious. If a file is public, it is public, even if only ten people ever look at it. The failure mode of "anyone with the link" is more subtle because it feels private. Many people interpret it as a locked door with a hidden keyhole. In reality it is closer to an unlabelled door in a busy building: it is not on the main signage, but anyone who is handed the key can open it, and keys are handed around more often than we admit.

A useful way to keep this grounded is to follow a single document as it travels. Imagine a PDF containing a mortgage application: bank statements, addresses, payslips, perhaps a scan of a passport. The document is uploaded to a cloud drive and shared with a broker. The broker asks for it quickly, so the sender chooses "anyone with the link" because it works in one click. The link is pasted into an email. The email is later forwarded to an assistant. The assistant's inbox is synced to a phone. The phone is later recycled without a full wipe. Nothing dramatic happens. And yet the exposure footprint has widened: the link lives in multiple inboxes, on multiple devices, in search indexes within those mail clients, and in the cloud provider's access logs.

Show: a link is forwarded, copied into a different channel, and then sits in message history for months. Name: link persistence. Explain: most sharing accidents are not theft; they are durability; people do not revoke links because they forget they exist, and platforms preserve messages by design. Implication: the risk of link-based sharing grows with time, not because the link "gets weaker", but because the number of places it can leak from multiplies.

Identity-based sharing has a different failure mode: friction. It requires the recipient to have the right account, to sign in, to handle permission prompts, sometimes to juggle work and personal identities. People avoid it because it can feel slow. That slowness is a feature. It forces an explicit boundary: the file is for a particular person, not for "whoever ends up holding this URL".

Still, there are cases where link-based sharing is the only realistic option—working with someone outside your organisation, dealing with a service provider who refuses to create an account, sharing with relatives who struggle with logins. The point is not to ban it. The point is to treat it as a tool that needs extra safeguards, the way you might treat handing someone a spare key rather than letting them into a managed building with a fob.

This is where expiry dates and passwords come in. Many cloud services offer the ability to set an expiry on a link or to require a password. These are not glamorous features, and they are often hidden behind "Advanced settings" precisely because they add friction. Friction is the price of boundaries. An expiry date turns a link into a temporary key: useful for a short window, then dead. A password turns a link into two factors: possession of the URL and knowledge of a separate secret.

Show: a document is shared for a single transaction—an accountant needs it, a solicitor needs it, a contractor needs proof of address. Name: time-bounded access. Explain: time-bounded access constrains the period during which an accidental leak matters; after expiry, the link no longer functions. Implication: when access is temporary by purpose, making the link temporary by design reduces long-tail exposure.

A five-word sentence belongs here, because brevity can puncture complacency: Links outlive your intentions.

That is why the most reliable pattern in safe sharing is to match the access control to the sensitivity of the content and the expected lifetime of use. A holiday photo shared with friends for a week is not the same as a folder containing identity documents. A draft report for a project is not the same as a spreadsheet of employee salaries. People often share all of these with the same setting because the interface offers a single default and because urgency feels like a justification. Urgency is not a security model.

Two checkable examples demonstrate the stakes without drifting into melodrama. The first is the Zoom case: an open join link without a password became a route for disruption because links travel socially. The second is the long-running series of incidents involving misconfigured cloud storage, particularly Amazon S3 buckets left publicly accessible, which have been reported repeatedly over the past decade. Many of those incidents were not caused by attackers breaking encryption. They were caused by someone exposing a resource and not noticing, or by assuming obscurity was enough. The mechanism differs—misconfiguration versus share link—but the lesson rhymes: the easiest-to-share state is often the easiest-to-expose state.

Now for a limitation, stated honestly. Password-protecting a link is only as good as how the password is transmitted. If you send the link and the password in the same email, you have created theatre, not protection. If you send the password in a different channel, you improve matters, but you still rely on the recipient's handling. Expiry dates can also create operational problems if the recipient genuinely needs longer access; the temptation then is to extend the expiry repeatedly, turning a "temporary" key into a permanent one by increments. The reconciliation is to treat these features as risk-reduction tools rather than as moral absolutes: they meaningfully reduce exposure when used deliberately, and they are worth the slight friction when the content is sensitive.

Permissions—view, comment, edit—are another quiet lever. Many sharing accidents happen because people give edit access when they meant view access. Edit access can allow the recipient to change, delete, or reshuffle files, and in some systems it can allow the recipient to share onward. The permission is not just about collaboration; it is about control of the cabinet. Show: someone shares a folder to "let a friend take a copy" and later finds the folder structure altered or files missing. Name: delegated authority. Explain: edit permissions delegate power over the resource; in sync-based systems, changes propagate; accidental deletions can ripple. Implication: the least-permission principle applies to ordinary life: give the minimum access that achieves the goal, because the goal is usually narrower than the platform makes it feel.

The motif of keys also helps clarify the difference between sharing a file and sharing a folder. A single file link is a key to one drawer. A folder link can be a key to a room. People often share a folder for convenience—"everything is in here"—without noticing that the folder may contain more than intended: older drafts, unrelated documents, hidden metadata, and subfolders created by automatic app behaviour. Sharing a folder is often the moment where "I meant to send you one thing" becomes "I accidentally invited you into my filing system".

A family album example shows how this plays out outside professional contexts. A parent creates a shared folder called "Kids", intending to share only holiday pictures with grandparents. The folder contains holiday pictures, but also includes screenshots of school emails, photos of the child's school uniform, and a snap of a letter with the home address visible. The parent shares the folder link to avoid picking individual photos. The grandparents access it on a tablet that multiple visitors use. The visitors browse out of curiosity. No malice is required for exposure. Only proximity.

Show: content that seems harmless in isolation becomes sensitive in aggregate. Name: aggregation risk. Explain: photos and documents accumulate context—locations, routines, relationships—and shared collections expose patterns, not just moments. Implication: sharing a collection should be treated as sharing a portrait, because it reveals more than any single image.

There is also the problem of public indexing. Some cloud links are designed to be unlisted and are not meant to be indexed by search engines. Yet if a link is posted on a public webpage or a forum, it can be crawled. Some services allow turning off indexing for shared links; others rely on robots.txt conventions and "security by obscurity". The practical reality is that once a link appears in a public place, you should assume it can be found. That is not pessimism. It is an accurate model of how the web works.

The deeper question behind all this is a human one: who is the intended audience, and how stable is that audience over time? Sharing with a named collaborator is stable because it is tied to identity. Sharing with "anyone with the link" is unstable because the audience can expand without a deliberate act. The audience becomes "anyone who ends up with this key", which is not a group you can picture or consent to. The more sensitive the file, the more you should prefer an audience you can name.

This is where low-maintenance safety becomes possible. The aim is not to turn everyone into a permissions accountant. The aim is to establish a default that fits normal life: use identity-based sharing when possible; use link-based sharing when necessary; when using links, prefer time limits and separate-channel secrets for sensitive material; review old links occasionally because keys get lost in drawers. A system that makes it easy to see active shares and to revoke them without drama is not a luxury feature. It is a privacy feature.

The unresolved tension at the end of this section is not technical. It is social. Every act of sharing is a decision about trust, but the platform translates that trust into a mechanism that may not match what you meant. The forward test is therefore sharp and clarifying: when you share the next cloud link, are you granting access to a person—or are you minting a key that could open your door for anyone who happens to pick it up later?

Leaving Services Gracefully

In June 2011, in the United States, the FBI announced "Operation Ghost Click", a case in which malware had altered DNS settings on infected machines and quietly diverted users to advertising sites, generating millions in fraudulent revenue. The detail that matters here is not the specific scheme but the ecosystem it exploited: neglected systems. In many of these stories, the vulnerable surface is not a brand-new device. It is the forgotten one. The account nobody checks. The router nobody updates. The cloud drive created for a short-term project and then abandoned like a storage unit whose key is still hanging in a drawer.

Old accounts are sleeping doors.

Most people have more of them than they suspect. A university cloud account still holding lecture notes and scans of ID. A former employer's collaboration drive where personal documents were stored during a frantic move. A "temporary" file-sharing service used for a wedding photo upload. A second photo library created when switching phones. A backup account opened during a crisis and never closed. These are not merely clutter. They are repositories of personal data under security settings that were chosen in a moment and then left to age, quietly, for years.

A modern adult's privacy risk is often less about what they actively do and more about what they left behind.

Show: a person cannot remember which email address they used for an old storage account, yet the account still exists and still contains files. Name: account drift. Explain: as people change jobs, devices, and inboxes, accounts proliferate; credentials and recovery options become stale; access becomes harder for the rightful owner and easier for anyone who can exploit neglected recovery paths. Implication: abandoned accounts tend to be both more exposed and more difficult to manage, precisely because they have been forgotten.

"Leaving gracefully" sounds like etiquette, but it is really an engineering problem: how to retire a service without losing data you might later need, without leaving links and shares dangling, and without creating a new mess in the process. Many people avoid the task because they fear two outcomes at once: regret ("What if I need that file?") and hassle ("This will take hours"). The chapter's promise is that a staged departure can be calm. Not perfect. Calm.

The first stage is to treat departure as a mapping exercise, not an immediate purge. Cloud services are not all equal in what they hold. A photo library may contain the most emotional material. A drive folder may contain the most legally or professionally sensitive material. A note app may contain the most revealing thoughts. The aim is to identify which accounts matter, which are low-value, and which are dangerous precisely because you have no idea what is inside.

Show: a person logs into an old drive account and discovers scans of a passport and a folder of financial documents from a house purchase. Name: high-value residue. Explain: people store sensitive documents in the cloud during major life events, then forget they ever uploaded them; those residues persist. Implication: the most important abandoned accounts are not always the biggest; they are the ones holding identity keys and intimate records.

A second stage is to understand what "export" means in practice. When a service says you can export your data, it may mean different things. Sometimes it means downloading original files in a sensible structure. Sometimes it means receiving an archive with metadata in formats that require additional tools to interpret. Sometimes it means exporting only what you uploaded, not what the service generated (tags, albums, comments). For photos, export can be particularly tricky: will you receive full-resolution originals or compressed versions? Will the export preserve dates and locations? Will it include edits? A graceful exit begins with clarity about what you can actually take with you.

A named example helps here because it shows that export is a real, institutionalised concept. Google's Takeout service, launched in 2011, was explicitly built to allow users to download copies of their data from Google services. Whatever one thinks of Google's broader incentives, the existence of Takeout is a checkable sign that "portability" is part of the modern data conversation. Similar export tools exist across other ecosystems. The point is not to memorise brand names. It is to remember that leaving is not only closing; it is extracting.

Show: a user requests an export and receives a multi-gigabyte archive with folders, JSON files, and timestamps. Name: portability format. Explain: providers export in ways that suit machines and legal requirements, not always human usability; the export may be complete but still difficult to re-import elsewhere. Implication: a graceful exit requires patience with format friction, and it encourages taking a staged approach rather than assuming one click will create a perfect migration.

The third stage is to check sharing settings, because sharing is the silent way old accounts continue to leak. A cloud drive might contain a folder shared to "anyone with the link" years ago. A photo album might still be shared with an ex-colleague. A document might be embedded on a public webpage. The owner may no longer remember the share exists. The service, however, remembers perfectly. This is why leaving must include an audit of active shares, not just a download of files.

Show: an old folder is still accessible to a collaborator who changed companies long ago. Name: residual access. Explain: access permissions granted for convenience can persist indefinitely unless revoked; collaborators may retain access long after the relationship ends. Implication: old accounts are not only about what you stored; they are about who you accidentally invited and never uninvited.

A second checkable example illustrates how this can scale beyond individuals. Public reporting over the last decade has repeatedly exposed data breaches caused not by sophisticated intrusion but by misconfigured cloud storage—publicly accessible buckets, open shares, permissive access keys. Many of these incidents were discovered by security researchers who simply searched for accessible resources. The lesson is not that everyone is hunting for your files. The lesson is that exposed resources can be found, and abandoned resources are more likely to be exposed.

Now comes the most psychologically fraught part: deletion. People often treat deletion as the moral endpoint—press delete and the sin is forgiven. Cloud deletion is rarely that clean. Services may keep "recently deleted" items for a window. They may retain backups. They may retain some data for compliance, fraud prevention, or technical reasons. They may de-identify rather than erase. They may delete content but retain logs. They may delete your visible files but keep derived data—thumbnails, indexes, machine learning models—unless compelled otherwise, as in the Everalbum settlement in October 2020.

Show: an account is closed, yet the provider's policy states that some information may be retained for a period. Name: retention reality. Explain: retention is part of operational resilience and legal compliance; it limits what deletion can mean immediately, even if the user's access is removed. Implication: the primary value of deletion is reducing future exposure by removing access and stopping further collection, not achieving instantaneous metaphysical disappearance.

A credible limitation is necessary here too: you cannot fully verify what a provider retains internally. You can read policies. You can observe what disappears from your account. You can request deletion where laws provide for it. You can measure whether links still work. You cannot stand inside the provider's backup system. The reconciliation is to focus on the outcomes you can control: remove access, revoke shares, change recovery details, delete visible content, and stop future uploads. Perfection is not available. Reduction is.

This is where a calm, staged strategy becomes not merely convenient but rational. Most people procrastinate because they imagine the task as a single exhausting project. A staged approach reframes it as a sequence of reversible steps. You begin by securing the account: ensure you can log in, confirm recovery options, and set strong authentication so that you—not a stranger—control the transition. You then inventory and export what matters. You audit shares and revoke them. You reduce content gradually, starting with the most sensitive. You then close or minimise the account in a way that matches its importance.

You do not have to do it all today.

That five-word sentence is not indulgence. It is an antidote to the all-or-nothing thinking that produces indefinite procrastination. Privacy work fails when it becomes a purity ritual. It succeeds when it becomes a habit of completion.

A key practical insight is that "closing" and "minimising" are different endpoints. Some accounts can be closed entirely because they have no continuing purpose. Others are attached to devices, app ecosystems, or legal records and cannot be sensibly deleted without collateral damage. In those cases, minimising is the more realistic goal: remove unnecessary files, reduce sharing, tighten access, and limit what is synced going forward. Leaving gracefully does not always mean leaving completely. It means leaving the reckless version behind.

Show: a person cannot delete an ecosystem account without losing access to purchased apps or device services, but can remove old documents and disable automatic uploads. Name: partial exit. Explain: some accounts are infrastructural; they are tied to the device and to ongoing use; the user's best move is to reduce data stored and to reduce exposure rather than to pursue total deletion. Implication: the right endpoint is the one that reduces risk without breaking life.

The motif of doors returns because it makes the logic tangible. An abandoned account is a door you no longer walk through but which may still be unlocked. It may still have spare keys taped under the mat in the form of old recovery emails, outdated phone numbers, or trusted-device sessions on hardware you forgot. Leaving gracefully is, in essence, locking doors you are no longer using and retrieving the valuables before you do.

There is also a social dimension often missed. Old accounts are entwined with old relationships: collaborators, former partners, family members who were granted access. Ending access can feel emotionally charged, as if one is declaring a rupture. Yet access is not affection. Access is a mechanism. Mechanisms should match reality. If a relationship has changed, access should change too. That is not hostility. It is maintenance.

A final subtlety: exporting data is itself a moment of risk. Large archives are easy to misplace. They may end up on an unsecured laptop. They may be uploaded to another service carelessly. They may be emailed to oneself. The exit process can create new copies in new places. A graceful exit therefore includes deliberateness about where exported data lives, how it is stored, and whether it is necessary to keep everything. Some data is valuable precisely because you do not keep it indefinitely.

The forward test at the end of this section is meant to be uncomfortable in a useful way, because discomfort is often a signal of neglected reality: if you lost access to your oldest cloud account tomorrow—forgotten password, expired recovery email, provider shutdown—would you mostly lose nostalgia, or would you lose keys to your life, and how many doors would remain open in an account you no longer even remember walking through?

Chapter 7
Messaging, Email, And Social

On 3 June 2013, in The Guardian's London newsroom, journalists began publishing disclosures supplied by Edward Snowden about the scale of modern surveillance. The headlines travelled fast, but the more enduring shift was quieter: people started to look at ordinary communication—emails, messages, contact lists, social graphs—as infrastructure rather than intimacy. A private conversation was no longer just a moment between two minds. It was also a set of records moving through systems designed to copy, store, and analyse at scale. Somewhere between the hum of the newsroom printers and the glow of monitors in a late-night office, the twenty-first century's most uncomfortable truth became harder to ignore: communication tools are not only channels. They are archives.

Messages have afterlives.

Most people still behave as if they do not. We send a quick note, we react with an emoji, we forward a photograph, we write a long email at midnight and feel lighter for having written it. The mind treats these acts as speech—fleeting, contextual, bounded by trust. The machines treat them as data—structured, searchable, and, by default, persistent. The mismatch is where privacy problems breed: not because people are foolish, but because human communication evolved for rooms and faces, while digital communication evolved for storage and routing.

This chapter is about the everyday places where that mismatch shows up. It begins with chat apps, because chat is now the default mode of modern life: family logistics, work coordination, friendships, romance, parent groups, school clubs, healthcare appointments, deliveries, banking alerts. The interface looks like conversation. Under the surface, chat apps vary dramatically in what they protect and what they expose. Some encrypt messages end-to-end by default, meaning the service cannot easily read the content in transit or at rest. Some encrypt in ways that still leave copies accessible to the provider. Some protect content but leak metadata—who spoke to whom, when, and how often—which can be as revealing as the words themselves. Most people are not choosing between "secure" and "insecure". They are choosing between different kinds of visibility.

Then comes email, the stubborn elder of digital communication. Email is still where important things arrive: contracts, receipts, travel details, legal notices, job offers, academic correspondence, administrative paperwork. It is also a protocol designed for an earlier era, when the idea that a message would traverse multiple servers across the world and remain searchable decades later was not a daily assumption. Email can be encrypted, but it is rarely used that way in normal life, and pretending otherwise produces bad decisions. The sensible posture is not cynicism. It is clarity about what email does well and what it cannot reasonably promise.

Social networks sit alongside both chat and email but operate by a different logic. Social is not primarily a channel between two people; it is a broadcast system with incentives. It rewards posting, reacting, tagging, remembering. It turns life into a feed and then offers "memories" back as if the platform were a kindly relative. Yet the platform is also a database that outlives context. Old posts do not fade the way spoken remarks fade. They persist, searchable and screenshot-able, long after present-day you has changed. Social networks therefore create a kind of time-travel problem: your past self keeps speaking in public unless you intervene.

A quiet motif threads through the whole chapter: the envelope. Digital communication often looks like an envelope—sealed, personal, intended for a recipient—but many systems treat it more like a postcard, legible to intermediaries even if the address is correct. End-to-end encryption is the technology that tries to restore the envelope: content sealed so that only the sender and recipient can read it. Metadata, however, remains stamped on the outside: addresses, postmarks, routes. Social platforms do something stranger still: they invite you to write your postcards in public and then encourage you to forget that they remain pinned to a wall.

The chapter's purpose is not to make the reader distrust their friends or fear their devices. The goal is to restore proportion and agency. People do not need to abandon messaging or retreat from social life.

They need to understand which tools behave like envelopes and which behave like postcards, and to learn how to choose channels that match the sensitivity of what is being said.

Consider a simple, modern scene. A friend texts, "Can you send me your new address?" The request is ordinary. The information is not trivial. An address is a key to identity: it links to credit records, to deliveries, to family routines, to safety. If you send it in a chat app that stores messages in the cloud, syncs them across devices, and allows account recovery through an old email address, you have not merely told your friend. You have written it into a system that may be searchable later, by you, by your friend, by whoever inherits or compromises an account. If you send it in an end-to-end encrypted chat with disappearing messages enabled, the information still exists, but it is less likely to become a permanent record. The choice is not moral. It is architectural.

This is why the chapter avoids the usual evangelism: "Everyone must use one blessed app." That is not how humans work. Communication is networked; you cannot unilaterally change what your whole community uses. The practical, humane approach is to become bilingual. Keep the tools that keep you socially connected, but learn to tighten settings and to reserve a more private channel for higher-sensitivity exchanges. Most people already do this intuitively in the physical world: they speak differently in a crowded café than they do in a quiet kitchen. The digital world needs the same contextual intelligence, not a crusade.

The middle of the chapter will therefore do something slightly unfashionable: it will treat convenience with respect rather than contempt. Convenience is not a vice; it is the condition of ordinary life. People with families, jobs, and deadlines will not maintain privacy systems that demand constant vigilance. A privacy practice that relies on being perfect will collapse at the first busy week. The tools and habits that matter are the ones that survive stress: settings you can set once, defaults that reduce exposure automatically, and a handful of "high-sensitivity" moves that you can deploy when needed without announcing them.

From there, we move into email's limits, which are as much cultural as technical. Email encourages people to treat the inbox as a filing cabinet: search, archive, forward, attach. That is useful. It also means that email becomes a record that expands over time, often containing copies of passports, invoices, medical letters, confidential negotiations, and the small details that can be weaponised in scams. Email providers may scan content for spam detection and security; some may process content to offer "smart features". Employers may have access to work email. Recipients may forward messages. None of this requires malicious intent. It is simply how the medium functions. Knowing this allows one to choose when email is perfectly fine—administrative coordination, receipts, newsletters—and when another channel is wiser.

Social profiles then bring us to reputation and consent, which are not merely privacy themes but ethical ones. The question is not whether one should exist on social media. The question is whether the version of you that exists there is accurate, limited, and chosen. Many people's profiles are not chosen; they are accreted. Years of photos, tags, likes, old jokes, old arguments, old affiliations, old addresses, old workplace details—each small, each seemingly harmless. Together they form a portrait that can be used by marketers, employers, scammers, estranged relatives, or simply strangers with too much time. Tidying is therefore not vanity. It is boundary maintenance.

The chapter closes its conceptual loop with sharing. Social networks and group chats create a "default yes" culture: post it, share it, tag it, forward it. But families are not merely collections of individuals; they are entangled reputations. Posting a child's photo is not only about the child's cuteness. It is about the child's future autonomy. Posting a friend's story is not only about your excitement. It is about their consent. The mature form of privacy is often the mature form of love: treating other people's information as borrowed, not owned.

A modest concession belongs in this introduction because any honest reader will feel it. And yet, much of modern connection depends on these very systems. Grandparents see grandchildren through shared albums. Long-distance friendships survive through voice notes and memes. Support groups exist because people can find one another online. Work gets done because teams can message quickly. Privacy cannot be pursued as if connection were optional. The task is to make connection less extractive and less permanent where permanence is unnecessary.

This chapter's promise, then, is not secrecy. It is precision. It offers a way to think about communication that respects how people actually live: to understand what different apps protect, to accept email's role without pretending it is a vault, to tidy the public portrait without trying to vanish, and to share with boundaries that protect not only the self but the people you care about. The payoff is a calmer relationship with the tools that carry your voice.

The forward tension is the one that sits beneath every tap of "send": when you communicate, are you merely speaking to a person, or are you also feeding an archive—and if it is an archive, who else might someday read the envelope you thought you sealed?

Choosing Chat Apps

On 14 January 2021, in Washington, D.C., prosecutors filed a sentencing memorandum in *United States v. Enrique Tarrio* that described, among other evidence, messages from encrypted chats—material recovered not by cracking cryptography in flight, but by reaching the devices and accounts where conversations had landed. The wider lesson was not about one defendant. It was about a comforting myth: that the word *encrypted* ends the story. Encryption can protect a message as it travels. It does not automatically protect the message once it has arrived, been backed up, been forwarded, been screenshotted, or been left on a logged-in laptop in a shared flat.

Most messages are postcards.

They look like sealed envelopes because the interface is intimate: the typing dots, the read receipts, the little bubble that holds a joke or a confession. Yet the underlying system often behaves like a postcard network: copies made, metadata stamped, histories synchronised, backups generated, notifications displayed on lock screens, message previews cached, search indexes built. Choosing a chat app is therefore not choosing "privacy" in a moral sense. It is choosing which parts of your conversation become legible to whom, and at what distance.

The first term worth holding steady is end-to-end encryption. End-to-end encryption (often abbreviated to E2EE) means that the message content is encrypted on the sender's device and can only be decrypted on the recipient's device. The service in the middle routes the message but cannot easily read it, because it does not hold the keys that would unlock the content. That is the envelope. It is a powerful guarantee—when it is actually applied, when it is correctly implemented, when keys are verified, and when the app's design does not quietly create alternative copies that are not end-to-end encrypted.

Show: two people send sensitive information—a health update, an address, a financial document—through a chat app that advertises encryption. Name: content confidentiality. Explain: if E2EE is active, the provider should not be able to read the content of messages in transit or at rest on its servers; the message is opaque to intermediaries. Implication: E2EE reduces the risk from server-side breaches and from casual provider access, but it does not erase other exposures.

Those other exposures live under the word metadata. Metadata is information about the message rather than the message itself: who communicated with whom, when, from which device, for how long, how often, sometimes where. Metadata is the outside of the envelope: addresses and postmarks. It can reveal relationship networks, routines, and moments of stress. If content is the diary, metadata is the calendar.

Show: a person messages a lawyer late at night, then an employer in the morning, then a family member repeatedly over the next week. Name: behavioural signature. Explain: even without reading the words, timing and frequency patterns can suggest life events; social graphs can be inferred from contact patterns. Implication: a chat app may protect content while still exposing a rich portrait of behaviour, especially if it collects and retains metadata aggressively.

Here is the uncomfortable truth that many "secure messaging" arguments avoid: most ordinary people are not threatened primarily by state surveillance or by elite hackers with zero-day exploits. They are threatened by closer, more prosaic things: a stolen phone; a colleague glancing at a notification; a partner with access to shared devices; a scammer who tricks someone into handing over a verification code; a cloud backup that quietly stores unencrypted message histories; a group chat where someone forwards a screenshot into the wrong social orbit. A chat app's cryptography matters, but so do its defaults around backups, device access, notifications, and identity recovery.

The most practical way to evaluate chat apps is to ask three questions that correspond to three places a message can leak: in transit, at rest, and through the user interface. In transit, E2EE is the main control. At rest, backups and device storage determine whether messages live in one place or many. In the interface, previews, notifications, and forwarding controls determine how easily a message escapes the intended audience. This triad is not a technical flourish. It is the lived reality of how messages move through modern life.

Now for names, because vague talk of "secure apps" is pointless without examples. Signal, operated by the Signal Foundation, has long been associated with strong privacy posture and default end-to-end encryption. WhatsApp, owned by Meta, rolled out end-to-end encryption by default for personal messages in 2016, using the Signal Protocol, which is a checkable milestone that shifted mainstream expectations. iMessage, Apple's messaging service, provides end-to-end encryption for iMessage content between Apple devices, but its broader privacy properties depend on settings, device security, and the role of Apple IDs. Telegram offers end-to-end encryption only in "Secret Chats" rather than by default for all chats, which is a design decision with predictable consequences: most people will use defaults.

These are not endorsements. They are examples of different design philosophies. Some platforms choose default privacy even at the cost of friction. Some choose compatibility and growth even if that means privacy is optional or uneven. The user's task is not to find perfection. It is to stop being surprised by trade-offs.

Show: someone assumes all chats in an app are end-to-end encrypted because the app is known as "secure". Name: encryption ambiguity. Explain: some apps encrypt some chats some of the time; group chats may differ from one-to-one; cloud backups may reintroduce provider access; "secret" modes may exist but remain unused. Implication: privacy claims must be mapped to defaults, because humans live in defaults.

Defaults matter because chat is social. You cannot make your entire community adopt a niche platform by force of will. The realistic strategy is to become context-sensitive: use the tools that keep you connected for low-sensitivity conversation, and keep a more private channel available for higher-sensitivity topics. Many people already do this in the physical world: they do not discuss salary negotiations in a crowded pub. Digital life needs the same instinct translated into tools.

Use different channels.

That six-syllable sentence is not snobbery. It is a humane compromise between idealism and reality. It respects that people value convenience and community, and it still allows for pockets of greater privacy when the moment demands it.

The next step is to understand what "tightening settings" actually means without turning life into a settings safari. Most chat privacy gains come from a few high-leverage controls: whether backups are end-to-end encrypted; whether messages sync to multiple devices; whether notifications show content on lock screens; whether the app supports disappearing messages and whether you use them for certain contexts; whether contact discovery uploads your address book to the provider; whether read receipts and "last seen" leak patterns you would rather not broadcast; whether the app supports strong account recovery without relying on easily hijacked channels.

Backups deserve special attention because they are the classic way an envelope becomes a postcard. A chat app may deliver end-to-end encrypted messages perfectly, and then a cloud backup may store the message history in a way the cloud provider can access, or in a way that is vulnerable if the cloud account is compromised. The message's security is then bounded not by the chat app but by the cloud account.

Show: a phone is replaced; the user restores from a cloud backup; chat history reappears seamlessly. Name: convenience restoration. Explain: seamless restoration often requires that data be stored in a retrievable format; depending on the system, that format may be accessible to the backup provider or vulnerable to account takeover. Implication: a "secure chat" can be undermined by an insecure backup path, which is why backup settings matter as much as encryption settings.

A limitation should be acknowledged here, because it is easy to become doctrinaire. Backups also protect people. They help recover after theft. They preserve important evidence. They preserve grief messages that matter. Turning backups off entirely may be unrealistic or undesirable. The reconciliation is not to preach abstinence from backups. It is to treat backup security as part of chat security: a strong cloud account, careful recovery options, and—where supported—encrypted backups.

Group chats introduce another predictable weakness: the human node. Even if every message is encrypted end-to-end, any participant can copy, forward, or screenshot. Group chats are social spaces, not vaults. Their privacy is bounded by the least careful participant and by the social norms of the group. This is not cynicism; it is a recognition that privacy is partly a property of people.

Show: someone shares a private update in a group, and it later appears in another chat as a screenshot. Name: social exfiltration. Explain: cryptography does not prevent a participant from re-sharing; technical safeguards cannot override human agency once someone has read a message. Implication: group privacy depends on norms and boundaries, not only on app choice.

This is where the envelope motif becomes ethically useful. When you hand someone an envelope, you are trusting them not to photocopy the letter inside and post it on a noticeboard. Most people honour that trust. Some do not. The risk increases as the audience grows and as contexts blur. A group of eight friends is not a group of eighty colleagues. A parent group chat is not a confidential counselling session. The app can help, but it cannot supply judgement.

Metadata controls are often less visible to users, but they shape exposure in ways that matter for everyday life. Some services collect minimal metadata as a design principle. Others collect substantial metadata because it supports product features, analytics, growth, and advertising. The content may be sealed, but the pattern of your communication can still be monetised or requested.

Show: a messaging service offers "people you may know" suggestions and cross-platform friend discovery. Name: graph inference. Explain: friend suggestions often rely on contact lists, mutual contacts, shared networks, and behavioural patterns; these require metadata collection and analysis. Implication: convenience features can be built on the same metadata that makes your social life legible to platforms.

This is why "privacy" and "security" should not be treated as synonyms. A system can be secure against outsiders while still being intrusive from the inside. It can prevent criminals from reading your messages while still building a rich model of your relationships for its own purposes. That is not necessarily malicious. It is an incentive structure. Your job is to know which kind of risk you are managing.

A second checkable example helps keep this grounded in reality rather than ideology. In 2016, WhatsApp's rollout of default end-to-end encryption brought strong content protection to a vast user base. It also raised the importance of metadata debates, because even with encrypted content, WhatsApp could still see who messaged whom and when, and it remained part of a broader business whose revenue depends on data and engagement. The lesson is not "therefore don't use it". The lesson is "content protection is one axis; data about communication is another".

When switching apps is unrealistic, tightening what you already use becomes the mature move. The most effective tightening often concerns what appears outside the conversation itself: notification previews, lock-screen display, and device syncing. A message that is perfectly encrypted can still pop up on a lock screen in a taxi queue. It can still be mirrored on a laptop that a colleague borrows for a moment. It can still be visible through a smart watch on a meeting table. The interface is a leak surface.

Show: a phone lights up with a message preview while it sits face-up during a conversation. Name: ambient disclosure. Explain: notification previews turn private content into public text in shared spaces; the leak is not digital interception but social proximity. Implication: controlling previews can reduce real-world exposure more reliably than chasing theoretical adversaries.

All of this points to a pragmatic decision architecture. Instead of asking "Which app is best?", ask: for which conversations do you need an envelope, and for which conversations is a postcard acceptable? An envelope channel should default to end-to-end encryption, minimise metadata where possible, and avoid leaky backups. A postcard channel can be a mainstream app used for logistics and memes, where the stakes are low and the social benefit is high. The boundary is not moral purity. It is proportion.

The closing tension is the one that will guide everything that follows in the chapter. Communication is where privacy becomes relational: your choices affect other people, and other people's choices affect you. You can choose the strongest envelope in the world, and still watch the words appear on someone else's lock screen. You can keep a private channel ready, and still feel the pull of the group chat where life happens. The forward test is therefore sharp and personal: when the next message arrives that carries something you would not want repeated—a new address, a private worry, a family detail—will you reach for the app that keeps you socially comfortable, or the one that treats the envelope as real?

Email Privacy Limits

On 2 August 2013, in San Francisco, a federal judge approved a settlement between Google and users in a case challenging the company's scanning of emails for advertising purposes. The mechanics were not arcane. Gmail had been analysing message content to target adverts; the plaintiffs argued that this violated privacy expectations; the settlement, and later product changes, reflected a growing public discomfort with the idea that "mail" could be read by the post office. Whatever one's view of that particular dispute, it captured a more durable truth: email is an industrial system. It is optimised for delivery, storage, and search, not for secrecy.

Email is not an envelope.

It looks like one because it inherits the language of letters: inbox, sent mail, attachments, forwarding. Yet the underlying protocols were designed in an era when networks were smaller, trust assumptions were different, and the idea of universal encryption was not a default expectation. Email is closer to a postcard routed through many sorting offices, with copies often kept at each stop. Modern improvements—transport encryption, spam filtering, malware scanning—make email safer than it once was. They do not turn it into a private vault.

This matters because email has become the spine of digital identity. Password resets arrive by email. Banking alerts arrive by email. Job offers arrive by email. Receipts, contracts, travel itineraries, tenancy agreements, tax statements—email is where modern life deposits evidence. When people treat email as private by default, they put sensitive information into a system that was not built to keep it secret. When they treat email as hopelessly insecure, they refuse to use a system that remains essential. The right posture is neither innocence nor despair. It is realistic boundaries.

Show: a person sends a scanned passport to a letting agent by email because it feels normal and quick. Name: high-value payload. Explain: email is often used to transmit identity documents because it is universal; the message then exists in multiple mailboxes, on multiple devices, often indefinitely. Implication: what feels like a one-to-one exchange can become a long-lived, multi-party archive of sensitive material.

To see why, it helps to notice what happens when you press "send". Your message typically passes through your email provider's servers, then through the recipient's provider, and may pass through intermediate relays depending on configuration. Each hop is a machine that handles and often stores data. Even when the connection between servers is encrypted in transit, the providers can usually access the message content because they need to store it in a readable form for users to retrieve later. That readable form powers features: search, spam detection, virus scanning, and, in some services historically, advertising personalisation.

Show: you search your inbox for "contract" and instantly retrieve an attachment from six years ago. Name: server-side indexing. Explain: fast search and retrieval typically require the provider to index message content and attachments; indexing is a form of analysis. Implication: the convenience that makes email indispensable is built on the provider having deep access to your mail store.

Email privacy therefore has layers. One layer is transport security: the connection between your device and your provider, and between providers, is often encrypted using TLS. That protects against casual interception in transit. Another layer is storage access: your provider stores your mail and can, in most designs, access it. A third layer is endpoint access: the recipient's device, your device, and any synced devices all contain copies or caches. A fourth layer is forwarding and retention: recipients may forward messages, organisations may retain them for compliance, and your own mailbox becomes a personal archive. None of these layers require malice. They are simply the architecture.

Metadata adds its own exposure. Even if email content were magically sealed, the headers reveal who emailed whom, when, and often from where. Subject lines are particularly treacherous because they are often transmitted and stored in ways that are more visible than the body, and users place sensitive information in them because they feel like labels. "Mum's diagnosis", "Debt repayment plan", "Job offer details", "Legal dispute" — a subject line can be a confession.

Subject lines shout.

That five-word sentence is not drama. It is a reminder that email's most visible field is often the one people treat casually.

Now for a counter-example, because email is not a technological fossil incapable of improvement. End-to-end encryption for email exists. PGP (Pretty Good Privacy) and its open standard variants have been used for decades. S/MIME exists in corporate contexts. Some modern providers offer encrypted mailboxes and stronger privacy claims. Used correctly between two parties who both understand the tooling, end-to-end encrypted email can provide strong content confidentiality. The limitation is adoption and usability. Key management is fiddly. Interoperability is imperfect. Many people cannot persuade their solicitor, employer, school, or bank to change their email tooling. The reconciliation is that while encrypted email is possible, it is not the default condition of most people's lives, and planning as if it were default leads to mistakes.

Show: a researcher uses PGP to exchange sensitive drafts with a collaborator; content remains unreadable to the provider. Name: end-to-end email encryption. Explain: encryption keys live with users; providers see ciphertext; the system can work well when both parties commit to correct use. Implication: email can be made private in specific contexts, but the social and technical overhead makes it an edge case for everyday administration.

So when is email fine? It is fine when the content is administrative, low-sensitivity, or already broadly accessible: receipts, meeting arrangements, newsletters, routine work correspondence, confirmations. It is fine when the primary risk is not "someone reads this" but "I need a record". Email excels as recorded communication. It creates a paper trail. It allows search. It supports attachments. It is, in essence, a filing system with delivery built in.

When is email a poor fit? It is a poor fit when the content is exceptionally sensitive, when you would not want it preserved indefinitely, when it involves information that can be used for identity fraud, coercion, or reputational harm, or when it concerns someone else's privacy in a way you should not casually archive. People often feel this instinctively. They start to type something into an email and pause. That pause is usually wisdom.

Show: someone drafts an email containing personal details—address, date of birth, a scan, a private family situation—and hesitates before sending. Name: friction signal. Explain: discomfort often indicates a mismatch between the sensitivity of the content and the durability of the channel; email turns the moment into a record. Implication: treat the pause as a diagnostic tool, not as anxiety to suppress.

The provider's visibility is only one part of the picture. Workplace and institutional access is another. If you use a work email address, your employer may have access to mailboxes, backups, and logs, sometimes by policy, sometimes by technical necessity. Universities often have similar arrangements. Even personal email is not purely personal if it is logged in on devices you do not fully control—shared family computers, old laptops, tablets. Email's convenience is the reason it spreads.

Then there is the simplest form of access: account takeover. Email accounts are prime targets because controlling email often means controlling everything else through password resets. This is why the book spends so much time earlier on passwords and two-factor: email is the hub. If your email is compromised, the attacker does not need to read your messages to harm you; they can use your inbox as a control panel for other accounts.

Show: a password reset email arrives for a service you did not request. Name: account pivot. Explain: attackers often attempt to compromise email because it enables resets of other accounts; email is the key that opens other doors. Implication: email privacy is not only about message secrecy; it is about maintaining control of identity infrastructure.

Given these realities, the most productive changes around email are often behavioural and organisational rather than technological. One such change is separating the roles email plays in your life. Many people use one address for everything: banking, work applications, newsletters, shopping, logins, family correspondence. This creates a single, highly valuable inbox that accumulates both sensitive messages and low-value noise. Noise is not merely annoying. It is risk: it makes it easier to miss important warnings, and it increases the number of services that know your primary identity address.

Show: a person's inbox is flooded with promotional mail, making it harder to spot a security alert from a bank or a provider. Name: signal dilution. Explain: mixing high-value and low-value mail reduces attention and increases error; attackers exploit overloaded attention. Implication: separating channels is a privacy and security move because it preserves attention for what matters.

Email aliases are one of the quiet tools that make this separation realistic without demanding multiple full accounts. Many providers allow aliases or plus-addressing (adding "+something" to the local part of an address) so that you can create distinct addresses that still deliver to one inbox. Some services offer "hide my email" style relay addresses that forward mail to your real inbox while keeping your actual address private from the recipient. The exact mechanics vary, and one should not assume universal support, but the underlying principle is stable: give different contexts different identifiers so that one leak does not expose everything.

Show: a user signs up for a low-value newsletter with a relay address rather than their primary address. Name: identifier compartmentalisation. Explain: compartmentalising identifiers limits linkability across services; it reduces the fallout of breaches and reduces the spread of your primary address. Implication: privacy can be improved without radical tool changes by being deliberate about which address is used where.

Separating newsletters from primary correspondence is another surprisingly high-leverage change. Newsletters are not inherently bad; they often carry useful information. The issue is that subscription mail tends to be the vector for tracking pixels, aggressive marketing, and data brokerage, and it increases the number of entities that can reach your inbox reliably. Using a dedicated address or alias for subscriptions reduces cross-contamination. It also makes it easier to change one channel without disrupting core identity functions.

Then there is content discipline: watching what personal data you send. Email invites people to paste everything into a message because it feels like a safe container. It is not. A good heuristic is to treat email as a system you would be comfortable having copied and forwarded, because often it will be. That does not mean writing everything as if it were public. It means noticing which details create disproportionate risk if archived: full dates of birth, scans of documents, account numbers, full addresses, and intimate third-party information.

A limitation is necessary here too. Some institutions still demand documents by email because their processes are outdated or because they rely on email as the lowest common denominator. Refusing to comply may not be possible without real cost. The reconciliation is to be intentional about the record you create. If you must send sensitive documents, be aware that you are creating copies in multiple systems. That awareness should push you to prefer the least expansive disclosure that satisfies the request, to prefer purpose-specific channels where offered (secure portals), and to remember that "sent once" is rarely "stored once".

The motif of the envelope returns at the end because it helps keep the concept anchored. Email feels like sealed correspondence. It functions more like routed, stored communication with many clerks handling it along the way—some human, many automated. You can make it safer. You cannot make it behave like a whisper between two people without changing the medium entirely.

The forward test is a single decision that arrives more often than people admit: the next time you are about to email something you would not want sitting in four inboxes, two backups, and a decade of search history, will you treat email as the familiar envelope it resembles—or as the durable postcard system it actually is?

Tidying Social Profiles

On 10 April 2018, in Washington, D.C., Mark Zuckerberg sat under harsh lights before the United States Senate and answered questions about Facebook's handling of personal data. The room had that faint, over-conditioned scent of carpet and electronics, the kind that clings to committee hearings and airport gates alike. What made the moment memorable was not only the politics. It was the sudden public recognition that a social profile is not a scrapbook. It is an interface to a database, and databases have a habit of outliving moods, friendships, and eras.

Your past is searchable now.

That single fact changes the moral weather of the internet. A social platform encourages the user to speak in the register of the present—jokes, irritation, solidarity, flirtation, grief—while storing the artefacts in a way that belongs to the future: indexed, retrievable, cross-referenced. The platform wants spontaneity. The database wants permanence. Tidying a social profile is the act of reconciling those two desires inside one life.

Many people resist the idea because it sounds vain, like rearranging a living room before guests arrive. But social profiles are not only about aesthetics or reputation. They are about exposure: what strangers can infer, what colleagues can scrape, what scammers can stitch together, what an old acquaintance can find at 2 a.m., what an algorithm can recommend back to you with a chirpy "memory" prompt. A profile is a public-facing identity document with footnotes you wrote at different ages.

Show: someone googles your name and sees a decade-old photo, tagged by a friend, from a night you barely remember. Name: secondary publication. Explain: social platforms encourage tagging and resharing, which means other people can publish material about you into your profile ecosystem; it becomes part of your searchable presence even if you did not upload it. Implication: managing a profile is not only curating what you posted; it is controlling what has been attached to you by others.

A useful motif here is the attic. Most people treat their profile like a living room—current, tidy, representative. In reality it behaves like an attic—boxes stacked over years, half-labelled, full of objects you once needed and then forgot. The attic is not inherently shameful. It is human. The problem arises when the attic becomes publicly accessible, and visitors begin to treat your old boxes as if they were your current furniture.

One reason profiles become attics is that social platforms reward accumulation. The architecture is designed to minimise friction: one click to post, one click to share, one click to accept a friend request. The rewards are immediate: attention, affirmation, belonging. The costs are delayed and therefore psychologically discounted. That delay is why the "tidy later" plan fails so often. Later rarely arrives on its own.

Show: you join a new job, a new course, a new community, and realise your profile is now part of first impressions. Name: context collapse. Explain: social platforms blend audiences—friends, colleagues, relatives, strangers—into one channel; content created for one audience becomes visible to another. Implication: profile tidying is not about hiding; it is about restoring audience boundaries that the platform eroded by default.

A named, checkable example captures how quickly context can collapse into consequence. On 20 December 2013, Justine Sacco boarded a flight from London to Cape Town and posted a tweet that triggered global outrage while she was in the air. By the time she landed, the tweet had travelled farther than she had, and her employer had become part of the story. Whatever one thinks of the public reaction, the mechanics are instructive: a short message, intended as a throwaway remark, became a permanent artefact, amplified by a platform whose core function is distribution. The lesson is not "never joke". It is that a platform optimised for virality is a poor place to assume ephemerality.

Show: an old post resurfaces when someone searches, screenshots, or shares it into a new context. Name: resurfacing. Explain: social content does not "sink" reliably; search, recommendations, and human grievance can drag old material back into view. Implication: the risk of an old post is not proportional to how often you think about it; it is proportional to how easily it can be found and reframed.

The heart of tidying is therefore not self-censorship. It is three forms of control: control of visibility, control of association, and control of discoverability. Visibility is who can see your content and your profile details. Association is what other people can attach to you through tags, mentions, and posts on your timeline. Discoverability is how easily someone can find you through search engines, platform search, and friend networks.

Start with visibility because it is the most direct expression of privacy settings. Many people set privacy once, years ago, and never revisit it while platforms evolve. Defaults shift. Features expand. New options appear. A profile that was "friends only" in one era can become surprisingly porous in another because of changes in tagging, searchable friend lists, public reactions, or "about" fields displayed to strangers. Even the distinction between "public" and "private" can be muddied by previews, shared posts, or profile pictures that remain public by design.

Show: you change one privacy setting and discover it affects only future posts, leaving old posts unchanged. Name: temporal mismatch. Explain: platforms often separate settings for new content from settings for existing archives; users assume one switch covers everything, but history persists under older rules. Implication: tidying requires attention to the archive, not just the present tense.

Association is where many people feel blindsided. A friend tags you in a photo. A colleague mentions you in a post. A relative shares an old memory and tags your name. These actions can make content visible to people you do not know. They can also make content appear in search results associated with your name. The platform often treats tagging as a friendly gesture; privacy treats it as an index entry.

Show: a tag links your name to a photo that reveals a location, a relationship, or a routine. Name: identity binding. Explain: tagging binds an identity to content in a machine-readable way; it makes the content easier to retrieve, recommend, and scrape. Implication: controlling tag review and tag visibility is often more important than obsessing over your own posts, because it governs what others can attach to you.

Discoverability is subtler and, for that reason, often neglected. Some platforms allow your profile to be indexed by search engines. Some allow people to find you by phone number or email address. Some make your friend list visible by default, which turns a profile into a map of relationships. Even when you have little public content, discoverability settings can make you easy to locate and easy to triangulate: a name plus a city plus a workplace plus a visible friend list is enough to narrow identity rapidly.

Show: a scammer finds a target through a visible friend list and then impersonates a friend in messages. Name: social triangulation. Explain: visible connections enable attackers to craft plausible pretexts; they do not need your private messages if they can observe your network. Implication: limiting relationship visibility reduces a common pathway for persuasion-based attacks.

At this point a credible counter-example is necessary, because tidying can be misunderstood as an attempt to erase history. Erasure is rarely possible. Screenshots exist. Other people's devices store copies. Search engines cache pages. Archiving services and private collectors may have preserved material. The internet is not a single place you can clean with one wipe. Some attempts to purge can even draw attention—a phenomenon often called the Streisand effect, after a 2003 legal dispute involving Barbra Streisand and an aerial photograph that became more widely seen because of the attempt to suppress it. The limitation is real: you cannot guarantee complete disappearance.

And yet, limitation is not futility. You can still meaningfully reduce exposure by controlling what is readily visible, by reducing what platforms recommend, by narrowing what search engines index, by limiting how strangers can contact or locate you, and by curbing the most sensitive parts of the attic. The reconciliation is to aim for *control and proportion*, not perfect erasure. A locked attic is not the same as an empty attic, but it changes who can wander through your boxes.

Another named, checkable example reinforces why proportion matters. In January 2010, in the United Kingdom, Paul Chambers posted a joke on Twitter about blowing up Robin Hood Airport in

Doncaster after his flight was cancelled. The tweet led to arrest and prosecution, and the conviction was eventually overturned in 2012. The case is remembered because it collided humour with institutional response, and because it demonstrated how a casual post can be interpreted outside its intended register. Even when the legal outcome changes, the social record remains. The internet keeps receipts; institutions sometimes do too.

Show: a post intended as humour is interpreted as threat, harassment, or evidence of character. Name: interpretive drift. Explain: as audiences change and stakes rise, the same text is read differently; platforms preserve text without tone, and readers supply their own. Implication: tidying is partly about recognising that your future audiences will not share your past context.

A practical way to think about pruning is to distinguish between three classes of material: content that is harmless but noisy, content that is personally revealing, and content that is relationally risky. Harmless noise—old memes, casual reactions—can be left alone unless it clutters your visibility. Personally revealing content includes addresses, routines, children's schools, travel patterns, workplace disputes, and anything that could help someone locate you or predict your habits. Relationally risky content includes posts that involve other people who did not consent to being part of your public narrative: friends' crises, family arguments, children's moments, identifiable photos of others in sensitive settings. The moral centre of privacy, especially on social platforms, is often respect for other people's boundaries.

Show: an old "about" field reveals a full birth date, hometown, workplace, and relationship status. Name: profile overspecification. Explain: platforms encourage rich profiles because rich profiles drive connection and targeting; overspecification turns a profile into an identity dossier. Implication: reducing profile fields can lower risk without changing your social participation at all.

Friend lists deserve special attention because they are often treated as neutral. They are not. A visible friend list reveals who you trust, who you associate with, and how someone might reach you through social engineering. It can also expose other people who did not choose visibility. For some users—teachers, public-facing professionals, people with complex family situations—relationship visibility can be more sensitive than posts.

Tagging controls are a similar lever. Many platforms offer some version of tag review: whether tagged content appears on your profile automatically, whether you are notified for approval, whether others can tag you at all, whether facial recognition suggestions are enabled. These settings are often buried because they reduce friction for the platform, and friction is the enemy of growth. But these are precisely the controls that keep your profile from becoming a public ledger of other people's cameras.

Then there is the question of likes and reactions. People treat likes as ephemeral gestures, but likes can be visible, searchable, and politically or socially legible. They can reveal affiliations and interests that you no longer hold. They can also be used to profile you by advertisers or data brokers when platforms allow such inference. A decade of likes is a behavioural biography written in taps.

Show: you scroll through your past likes and find pages and posts that no longer represent you. Name: preference sediment. Explain: preferences accumulate like layers; they remain attached to your account even after your beliefs, tastes, and communities change. Implication: pruning likes is not performative; it is reducing stale signals that may misrepresent you or be used to infer things you would not volunteer now.

The attic motif returns here because it captures the emotional reality of this work. Tidying a profile can feel like meeting old versions of yourself: earnest, awkward, angry, performative, lonely, brave. There is a temptation either to punish that earlier self or to defend it reflexively. Neither is necessary. The task is simpler and kinder: decide which boxes should remain visible to strangers and which should be stored away.

Warmth matters because privacy is often framed as paranoia. It is not paranoid to prefer that strangers cannot see your child's school. It is not paranoid to prefer that a former colleague cannot browse your family photos. It is not paranoid to prefer that your profile does not function as a free dossier. These are ordinary boundaries, translated into digital terms.

The final movement of tidying is about search visibility, both inside and outside platforms. A profile can be "private" in the sense that posts are restricted, and still be discoverable in the sense that your name, photo, workplace, and friends are visible to anyone. Search settings determine whether someone can find you with an email address, a phone number, or a name plus a location. External indexing determines whether your profile appears in Google results. These are not cosmetic settings. They determine whether your profile is a locked door on a busy street or a door in a quiet corridor.

The forward test that closes this section is deliberately personal and slightly austere: if a stranger—an employer, a client, a hostile ex, a scammer, or simply a bored acquaintance—looked at your profile for five minutes, would they see a living room you chose to show, or an attic you forgot to lock?

Sharing With Boundaries

In September 2015, in Paris, the French National Commission on Informatics and Liberty (CNIL) launched a public campaign reminding parents that sharing photos of children online can implicate the child's rights, and that, in principle, the child may later have grounds to object. The campaign was not a moral panic. It was a legal-cultural signal: societies were beginning to notice that "family sharing" had become a form of identity publication, and that the subject of that publication often had no say. A baby cannot consent. A platform does not wait.

Posting is irreversible in practice.

The interface suggests otherwise. You can delete. You can archive. You can change privacy settings. You can untag. Yet the social reality of sharing is that copies escape: screenshots, forwards, caches, private archives, downloaded albums, reposts in other spaces. Even without copying, the platform itself keeps internal records for varying periods and purposes. So the question is not whether you can delete later. The question is whether you are willing to publish now.

Social networks reward the exact opposite instinct. They reward immediacy. They reward confession. They reward outrage. They reward the photograph that feels too personal to share and therefore attracts attention. They reward the "raw" update that signals authenticity. A boundary is, by definition, a refusal to pay for attention with exposure. That refusal can feel awkward because platforms are designed to make boundary-setting feel antisocial. In reality, boundaries are a form of care: care for your future self, care for the people whose lives are entangled with yours, care for children who will one day inherit a digital footprint you helped create.

Show: a parent posts a "first day of school" photo with the child's name and school crest visible, receives warm comments, and moves on. Name: inadvertent doxxing. Explain: personal details embedded in images—uniforms, signage, routine locations—can make a child identifiable and locatable; what feels like harmless pride becomes a breadcrumb trail. Implication: small sharing choices can create disproportionate risk because they combine identity with location and routine.

Boundaries begin with recognising that sharing is not one thing. There is sharing about the self, sharing about others, and sharing that uses others as props. The last is common and rarely intended. A person posts a story about a difficult family member. A friend is named in a rant about work. A child's tantrum becomes a comic clip. These are often framed as "my story", and therefore treated as the poster's right. Yet the story is not only the poster's. It includes other people's privacy, dignity, and future.

The right word here is consent, but consent is not a checkbox. In families it is a practice: asking, noticing, respecting "no", and recognising that "yes" at one age may not remain "yes" later. A toddler cannot consent. A teenager can, and often does, but may feel pressure to agree because adults control the narrative. A partner can consent, but consent can be compromised by emotional dynamics. A friend may consent in the moment and regret later. The ethical challenge is to treat consent as a living relationship rather than as a one-off permission slip.

Show: a teenager asks a parent to remove an old childhood photo that feels humiliating. Name: retroactive boundary. Explain: identity changes with age; what was cute at five can feel exposing at fifteen; children grow into their own sense of dignity and privacy. Implication: sharing that involves children must anticipate future autonomy, not merely present delight.

A second checkable example shows how quickly "private sharing" can become public content. In March 2019, Facebook acknowledged that hundreds of millions of user passwords had been stored in plaintext in internal systems, a fact reported widely and investigated by regulators. The incident was not a story about users oversharing. It was a reminder that even when users share within a platform under expected controls, the platform's internal handling can introduce risk. A boundary is not only about who you choose as an audience; it is about the fact that the platform itself is an intermediary with its own fallibilities.

Still, a credible limitation belongs here: humans need to share. Social connection is built on disclosure. Parents share joy because it keeps families connected across distance. People share hardship because it attracts support. Communities share stories because it creates belonging. A boundary that forbids sharing altogether is brittle; it will break, and the break will be messy. The reconciliation is to make boundaries workable: not a vow of silence, but a personal policy that keeps you connected while reducing avoidable exposure.

The phrase "personal policy" matters because it shifts the work from a moral performance to a design problem. You are not trying to be a saint. You are trying to set defaults for yourself that hold up under stress, excitement, grief, and boredom—the states in which most oversharing happens. In the earlier chapters, settings mattered because humans live in defaults. The same is true of behaviour.

Show: someone shares most recklessly when emotionally elevated—celebrating, furious, lonely. Name: mood-driven disclosure. Explain: heightened emotion narrows judgement and increases impulsivity;

platforms amplify this because engagement spikes when emotion spikes. Implication: boundaries must be designed for your worst moments, not your best intentions.

Children are the sharpest case because they embody the asymmetry of power. Adults control cameras, accounts, and audiences. Children live with the consequences. This is not abstract. A child's name, face, school, and routines are identifiers. Combined, they can be used to locate, impersonate, or harass. More commonly, they create reputational artefacts a child cannot edit away: embarrassing stories, vulnerable moments, early social labels. The ethical problem is not only safety. It is dignity.

Dignity survives screenshots.

That five-word sentence belongs here because it captures the point: even when safety risks are low, dignity risks remain. A child might never be targeted by a stranger, and still be harmed by the knowledge that their most private moments were turned into content.

The boundary question therefore becomes: what kind of archive are you building on your child's behalf? The best archive for a child is not the public feed. It is the private family album with controlled access and time-bounded sharing, the kind of archive we discussed in cloud photos. The public feed is not an album. It is a stage. Stages reward drama, not privacy.

Consent inside families is also messy because family itself is an audience. Grandparents want photos. Relatives feel entitled to updates. Family group chats create pressure to produce content as proof of connection. Some families treat sharing as love. Refusing to share can be misread as withholding. This is where boundaries must be communicated as values rather than as accusations. The aim is not to shame relatives. It is to align the family on a shared sense of what is appropriate to publish about a child who cannot choose.

Show: a grandparent reposts a child's photo publicly because "everyone should see", believing it harmless. Name: boundary drift. Explain: different generations have different intuitions about audience and permanence; what feels like neighbourhood sharing becomes global distribution online. Implication: boundaries must include shared expectations, not just individual restraint.

Boundaries also apply to the self. A common mistake is to assume privacy means never sharing personal moments. The more subtle mistake is to share personal moments that contain too much structured information: address visible in the background, travel dates, workplace identifiers, routine locations, and, most of all, the small clues that scammers use to mimic intimacy. Many scams succeed because the attacker can reference details scraped from public posts: a pet's name, a parent's nickname, a recent trip, a child's school event. Sharing with boundaries is therefore partly about refusing to publish the raw materials of impersonation.

Show: a public post reveals a mother's maiden name in a nostalgic story, or a pet's name in a birthday caption. Name: trivia leakage. Explain: "innocent" details are often used as security questions or as authenticity signals; they help attackers craft credible messages. Implication: privacy boundaries can reduce fraud risk without reducing genuine connection.

Tagging is another quiet vector. Tagging turns people into searchable links. It binds identity to content in a machine-readable way, making it easier for others to browse networks and infer relationships. When you tag a friend, you do not merely credit them. You publish association. When you tag a location, you do not merely set a scene. You publish routine. The platform likes this because it increases connectivity. Privacy dislikes it because it increases legibility.

Show: a person tags a new partner repeatedly in early posts, then later wants privacy during a difficult period. Name: relational overexposure. Explain: early enthusiasm produces dense public signals; later changes are harder because the archive already exists; platform memories can resurface old posts. Implication: boundaries are most valuable at the beginning of relationships, when exposure is easy and reversal is hard.

A second limitation is worth stating plainly: boundaries cannot control other people's behaviour completely. Friends may post about you. Family may share photos you would not share. Children may later post their own content. The reconciliation is to treat boundaries as influence rather than as command. You can ask people to avoid posting certain things. You can model restraint. You can refuse to engage with posts that violate your boundary. You can control what you publish. You cannot control the entire network.

This is why the most robust boundaries are those that do not require perfect compliance from others. For example, choosing not to post identifying information about children does not depend on anyone else. Choosing not to share travel dates in real time does not depend on anyone else. Choosing to keep sensitive family moments off public feeds does not depend on anyone else. These boundaries reduce exposure regardless of what relatives do.

The motif that ties this together is the stage versus the album. The stage is performance; the album is memory. The stage demands immediacy; the album can wait. The stage rewards exposure; the album rewards intimacy. Many people accidentally use the stage for what belongs in the album because the stage is where the upload button lives.

So the intellectual work of this section is to treat posting as publication, even when the audience is "friends". Publication carries responsibilities: to accuracy, to proportion, to consent. It also carries a question that is both ethical and practical: if this post were still visible in five years, would it represent you fairly, and would it represent the people in it kindly?

The forward test at the end is simple enough to hold in mind when thumbs are moving faster than judgement: when you are about to share, are you building an album your family will be grateful for—or feeding a stage that will ask for more and more of your life until boundaries become impossible to rebuild?

Chapter 8
Home Network And Devices

In October 2016, much of the internet briefly buckled under a wave of traffic driven by malware called Mirai, which had quietly recruited insecure internet-connected devices—cameras, routers, and other domestic hardware—into a botnet. The attack is remembered for the sites it disrupted, but the more intimate detail sits closer to the kettle and the hallway coat rack: ordinary homes had become part of critical infrastructure without being asked. A baby monitor, a bargain router, a "smart" camera installed for convenience had been conscripted into an event that made the news, not because the owners were reckless, but because the devices were designed to be easy to install and hard to maintain.

The home is now a network.

That sentence changes how one should think about privacy. For decades, the boundary between "inside" and "outside" was physical: a front door, a key, a curtain. The domestic sphere was private by default because it was hard to observe without being present. Now, a surprising amount of home life flows through radios and cables and cloud accounts: streaming, messages, homework, work calls, thermostats, voice assistants, doorbells, televisions. The privacy of the home increasingly depends on the invisible plumbing that connects it to everything else. The house is still a refuge, but its walls have become porous in a new way—porous to data.

This chapter is about the parts of digital privacy that most people never think about because they never look like "privacy". They look like broadband. They look like a printer that sometimes refuses to print. They look like a television that asks for an update at the wrong moment. They look like a friendly cylinder that plays music when you say its name. They look like a child's tablet on the sofa. Yet these objects are not neutral. They are computers with microphones, cameras, storage, and network access, and they behave according to defaults chosen by manufacturers whose incentives do not neatly align with domestic calm.

The router sits at the centre of this story, not because it is glamorous but because it is the gateway. It is the border post through which most household traffic passes. People treat routers like appliances—set it up once, forget it. Manufacturers encourage this by shipping devices with predictable default settings, cheerful setup apps, and minimal incentives to update. But a router is closer to the front door lock than to a toaster. If it is poorly configured, the house becomes easier to map from the outside. If it is well configured, much of the rest of household privacy becomes easier.

There is a psychological trap here. People assume threats arrive through the screens they can see: a dodgy website, a suspicious message, a sketchy attachment. Those matter. But home networks create a different kind of exposure: background devices that chatter constantly, often to remote servers, often with unclear data practices, often with weak security because the market rewards speed and cheapness more than restraint. A phone might be hardened carefully, while a smart TV quietly gathers viewing habits and sends them back as "analytics". A laptop may have strong passwords and encryption, while a printer stores a contact list and offers a web interface with a default password that no one changed.

Show: a person buys a smart doorbell for safety, installs it in ten minutes, and forgets it until a firmware update notification appears months later. Name: install-and-forget. Explain: consumer devices are designed for quick installation; ongoing maintenance is left to the user, who has neither time nor expertise incentives. Implication: the home fills with semi-maintained computers, each a small point of potential leakage.

This chapter does not ask anyone to become a network engineer. It focuses on the small set of actions that change the risk profile disproportionately. Changing default router passwords and updating firmware is not glamorous, but it closes a large class of avoidable exposure. Naming Wi-Fi sensibly sounds trivial, yet it can reduce inadvertent information disclosure and discourage sloppy sharing. Enabling guest networks can prevent a visitor's compromised device from having the same access as a work laptop. These are the domestic equivalents of locking doors and not leaving spare keys under the plant pot.

The next layer involves children, not as threats but as citizens of the home network. Children's devices are often the least controlled not because parents are negligent but because childhood is messy and technology is baked into education and social life. Many adults oscillate between two unhelpful extremes: surveillance dressed up as safety, or permissiveness dressed up as trust. This chapter takes a calmer line. Separating children's devices from adult work machines reduces risk without peering into a child's private messages. Parental controls can be used to reduce exposure to the worst of the internet without pretending that any filter produces innocence. The aim is not to monitor children as suspects. It is to build an environment where mistakes are less costly.

A subtle motif threads through the chapter: doors within doors. A home has internal doors—bedrooms, cupboards, filing cabinets—because not everything belongs everywhere. A home network needs internal doors too. A guest network is an internal door. Separate device groups are internal doors. Even choosing which devices can talk to one another is a kind of internal architecture. Most households currently live in a single open-plan network where everything can see everything. That is convenient. It is also unnecessary.

Then come smart home devices: speakers, cameras, thermostats, bulbs, plugs, and a growing menagerie of "assistants" and sensors. These devices bring microphones and cameras into intimate spaces under the banner of convenience. Some behave respectfully. Some do not. Many are opaque. They can record, transmit, and store data in ways that are not obvious from their physical form. A smart speaker does not look like a microphone. A television does not look like a listening device. A doorbell does not look like a cloud service with retention policies. Yet all of these can be true at once.

The conversation around smart devices often becomes ideological: either giddy futurism or paranoid refusal. Neither posture helps normal households. The practical question is: what data does the device generate, where does that data go, who controls it, and what happens when the device is sold, recycled, or simply abandoned? A gadget that is harmless while it is in your home can become a privacy leak when it changes hands. A device that feels private because it is "in your house" can be broadcasting to servers in another country. The domestic setting does not confer privacy. The design does.

Printers, televisions, and other "oddities" are where the chapter becomes almost comedic, because the absurdity is real. A printer is a computer. It can store a history. It can store contacts. It can have cloud features and remote access. A television can have a microphone, camera capabilities, and tracking systems that infer viewing habits and sometimes more. A set-top box can be a telemetry engine. A games console can be a social platform with voice chat and logging. Even a fridge, if it has a screen and Wi-Fi, becomes part of the network's exposure surface. These are forgotten computers, and forgotten computers are the easiest to neglect.

Still, there is an honest counterpoint that must be acknowledged. Many network risks remain hypothetical for many households. A properly configured device may never be targeted. A guest network may feel like unnecessary fuss in a quiet household. A smart speaker may never cause an obvious harm. And yet, the absence of obvious harm is not evidence of absence. Network and device risks are often invisible by nature. Data collection can be quiet, automated, and long-term. The problem is rarely one dramatic breach. It is the steady accumulation of exposure through defaults.

This chapter therefore aims for a specific kind of competence: the kind that feels like home maintenance rather than like a crusade. The intellectual payoff is that privacy stops being only about phones and passwords and becomes something broader: the design of your domestic environment. The emotional payoff is relief. When the home network is tidy, many other worries shrink. The phone feels less besieged. The laptop feels less exposed. Children's devices feel less like portals to chaos. Even the smart gadgets feel less like strangers.

The momentum at the end of this introduction points towards a concrete question that is also a moral one. A home is a place where people are supposed to relax, to speak freely, to be unobserved. The modern home is full of devices that profit from observation, even when observation is "only for product improvement". The task is not to reject modern life. It is to decide which doors inside the home should stay open and which should be closed—because a private home is not one without technology, but one where technology stays in its place.

Router And Wi Fi Basics

In October 2016, a wave of disruption rippled across the United States when Dyn, a company providing DNS services, was hit by a distributed denial-of-service attack fuelled by the Mirai botnet. The detail that keeps it tethered to ordinary life is what powered it: insecure consumer devices sitting in homes—routers among them—doing what they had been designed to do, which was to be easy to set up and easy to forget. Somewhere, in a kitchen or a spare room, a small plastic box with blinking LEDs and a faintly warm casing kept forwarding packets while its owner made tea, unaware that the box's defaults had turned it into an uninvited participant in a public event. The internet wobbled. The router stayed quiet. Small boxes. Big consequences.

A home router is not glamorous, and that is exactly why it matters. It sits where the domestic meets the global, like a front door that opens onto a city you cannot see. Every message, stream, update, and school assignment passes through it, and most households never look at it again after the first evening of setup. That is a rational human choice—life is busy—but it creates a predictable pattern: the most important gateway in the home is often governed by the oldest decisions, the least reviewed settings, and the weakest passwords.

Show: a household keeps a router installed by an ISP, still using the credentials printed on the sticker, still running firmware from the year it was shipped. Name: default inheritance. Explain: defaults are designed for rapid deployment at scale; they minimise support calls, not risk; they persist because changing them feels optional until it is urgent. Implication: a large portion of home-network exposure is not the result of sophisticated attack, but of time acting on unaltered defaults.

The "front door" analogy is useful only if it remains concrete. A front door has three features: an address, a lock, and a habit of being left open by accident. A router has the same. The address is how it can be reached—internally by devices in the home, and sometimes externally if remote administration is enabled. The lock is its administrative access and its Wi-Fi encryption. The habit is the steady creep of convenience features: quick setup wizards, sharing buttons, remote management, "smart" security add-ons, and the small compromises we make because they remove friction. Security happens when those three features are made deliberate.

The first distinction worth holding is between the Wi-Fi network and the router's administrative interface. Many people think "Wi-Fi password" and imagine that they have "secured the router". They have not necessarily done so. The Wi-Fi password controls who can join the wireless network. The administrative password controls who can change the router's settings—who can rename networks, expose ports, change DNS, redirect traffic, or install new firmware. Treating the Wi-Fi password as the only lock is like putting a good padlock on the garden gate while leaving the front door key under the doormat.

Show: a visitor cannot join the Wi-Fi because the password is strong, yet the router's admin interface still uses a factory default username and password. Name: split control. Explain: Wi-Fi access and administrative control are separate surfaces; manufacturers ship defaults for both; users often change only one. Implication: a household can feel secure while leaving the more powerful lock untouched.

This is why default passwords are so corrosive. They are not merely "weak"; they are predictable. Predictability is what makes automation possible. An attacker does not need to guess one household's password if a million households share the same model and many of them never changed the credentials printed in the manual. Even when the admin password is unique per device, sticker credentials are often stored in plain view on the router itself, which is convenient for the owner and equally convenient for anyone with physical access. The risk is not only malicious strangers. It is the messy reality of domestic space: guests, tradespeople, flatmates, short-term rentals, and the simple fact that routers are often placed in hallways or living rooms because that is where the socket is.

A second, named, checkable example sharpens the point that Wi-Fi security is not only about who joins your network but about the protocol itself. In October 2017, the security researcher Mathy Vanhoef (at KU Leuven in Belgium) published details of the KRACK attack, a weakness in the WPA2 protocol's four-way handshake. The headlines sometimes sounded like "WPA2 is broken", which was too blunt, but the event was instructive: the safety of Wi-Fi depends on both the password you choose and the correctness of the underlying implementation. The fix, in many cases, was patches on client devices as well as updates to routers. The implication for normal households was not to panic. It was to internalise that "set and forget" is a poor match for infrastructure that needs patching.

Show: a household continues using a router that never receives firmware updates, even as vulnerabilities are published and patched elsewhere. Name: patch gap. Explain: routers are long-lived and often poorly maintained; manufacturers may stop issuing updates; users may never check; ISPs may delay firmware releases. Implication: the router can become the oldest, least defended computer in the home.

Firmware updates deserve their own realism. A router firmware update can feel like something only experts do, partly because the experience is often dreadful: confusing interfaces, unclear version numbers, risk of temporary outage, fear of breaking connectivity. Yet router firmware is simply the operating system for a critical gateway. If the gateway is never updated, the household remains exposed to known problems for years. The point is not that every home router is constantly under attack. The point is that the cost of updating is concentrated—a short burst of effort—while the benefit persists.

Still, a limitation should be stated plainly: updating the router does not fix everything. Many household privacy harms come from devices and services that behave intrusively even on a perfectly secured network. A smart TV can track viewing habits through the apps you log into. A phone can share location through a permissions setting. A laptop can be compromised by a malicious download. Router hygiene is necessary, not sufficient. The reconciliation is that the router is the place where broad, low-effort improvements are possible. It reduces a class of avoidable, structural risk, even if it cannot eliminate all risk.

The second major surface is open or weak Wi-Fi encryption. Here the temptation is to imagine shadowy figures in cars "hacking Wi-Fi". That can happen, but the more common issue is simpler: if your Wi-Fi is open or uses outdated encryption, anyone within range can join or observe traffic. Modern web traffic is often protected by HTTPS, which encrypts content between your device and the website. That is a genuine improvement over the early web. Yet even with HTTPS, an open network can leak metadata such as which domains are being contacted, and it can enable local attacks against devices, especially those that expose services on the local network. Security is rarely one dramatic collapse; it is a series of small, avoidable exposures.

Show: a neighbour's device connects to an open network by accident, because phones and laptops remember known networks and auto-join when signal is strong. Name: accidental membership. Explain: devices prioritise connectivity; open networks remove the "are you sure?" barrier; the boundary between households becomes porous. Implication: open Wi-Fi is not merely generous; it is an invitation to confusion and risk.

Then there is the question of naming the network—the SSID. People often treat network names as jokes: "FBI Surveillance Van", "Pretty Fly for a Wi-Fi", or the default name that reveals the router model and sometimes the ISP. Humour is harmless until it becomes information. A network name is a broadcast. It can reveal the household's surname, address, or device type. It can also reveal whether you are using a widely known router model with known vulnerabilities. The goal is not to create paranoia about someone driving around collecting Wi-Fi names, though that does happen as part of mapping. The goal is to avoid unnecessary disclosure. A front door does not need to display your full CV.

Show: a network name includes a surname and house number, and is visible to anyone standing outside. Name: ambient identification. Explain: Wi-Fi network names are broadcast; devices scan for them constantly; passers-by can see them without connecting. Implication: a seemingly trivial naming choice can link identity to location and make the household easier to target or to gossip about.

The administrative interface contains another common footgun: remote administration. Many routers allow configuration from outside the home network so the owner can manage it while away. The feature is sometimes useful. It is also a classic source of trouble because it exposes the router's management surface to the public internet. If remote access is enabled unnecessarily, the router's "front door" is effectively propped open onto the street. A domestic network does not need that by default.

And then there is WPS—Wi-Fi Protected Setup—which was designed to make joining a network easier, often via a push-button or PIN. Ease is the selling point. The problem is that ease features often create new attack paths. WPS, especially in older implementations, has been criticised by security practitioners because the PIN method can be vulnerable to brute-force attacks. Some routers allow WPS to be disabled. Some hide it. Some keep it on. The broader principle matters more than the acronym: any feature that exists to bypass a password should be treated with suspicion unless you actively need it.

Show: a router offers a one-button pairing feature that allows devices to join without typing the Wi-Fi password. Name: convenience bypass. Explain: bypass mechanisms expand the ways access can be gained; they are attractive because they remove friction; they can also remove security assumptions. Implication: a household may strengthen the Wi-Fi password while leaving a shortcut that undermines it.

Wi-Fi encryption standards are another area where clarity helps. WPA2 has been the long-standing baseline, with WPA3 introduced later to improve protection, particularly against certain forms of password-guessing and to strengthen security on public networks. Not all devices support WPA3. Many households run mixed environments: an older printer, a new phone, a smart plug bought on sale. Mixed environments create awkward compromises, because the network's security settings must often accommodate the least capable device. That reality does not require perfectionism; it requires awareness. If a network must be configured for compatibility, that should be a conscious trade-off rather than an accident.

Show: a household keeps weaker settings because one old device will not connect otherwise. Name: compatibility drag. Explain: networks are shared infrastructure; older devices can dictate security levels; replacing or isolating those devices can change what is possible. Implication: privacy and security often depend on the oldest object in the room, not the newest.

Notice how each of these issues returns to the motif of doors. The router is the front door. The Wi-Fi password is the latch. The admin password is the deadbolt. Remote administration is leaving the door accessible from the street. WPS is leaving a spare key under the doormat. Firmware updates are the act of repairing a lock when the manufacturer announces a defect. Once you see the router this way, the work stops feeling like "tech stuff" and starts feeling like basic household stewardship.

The phrase "under an hour" matters, but not as marketing. It matters because the human brain budgets attention, and attention is scarce. Router hygiene works best when it is treated as a one-time domestic task with occasional light check-ins, rather than as an ongoing hobby. It is closer to changing the batteries in a smoke alarm than to rebuilding an engine. The task is finite. The benefits endure.

A final note on risk without melodrama: the strongest reason to secure your router is not that an adversary is personally interested in you. It is that routers are general targets. They are useful to attackers precisely because they are common and neglected. They can be used to reroute traffic, to spy on DNS queries, to insert adverts, to recruit devices into botnets, or to provide a foothold into the home network. That is not science fiction. It is a pattern observed repeatedly in the wild, including in events like Mirai in 2016 and in vulnerability disclosures like KRACK in 2017. The household is not the headline. It is the infrastructure.

The forward test that follows you out of this section is deliberately simple, because simplicity is what survives real life: if your home network is a front door to everything you do—work, school, banking, private conversation—does it still have a factory key under the doormat, or have you made it your own?

Guest Networks And Kids

On 25 May 2018, the General Data Protection Regulation (GDPR) became enforceable across the European Union, and suddenly "data protection" was no longer a specialist term reserved for lawyers and compliance departments. It entered kitchens and school WhatsApp groups in a gentler form: parents began asking what apps collected about their children, what schools uploaded to third parties, what "free" services meant in practice. The law did not solve domestic privacy. It did something subtler and more useful. It made the idea of children having privacy *legible* in ordinary conversation. A child's digital life was no longer only a parenting matter. It was a rights matter.
Rights begin at home.

Home networks, however, are not built for rights. They are built for convenience. Most households run a single, flat Wi-Fi network where every device—work laptop, child's tablet, guest's phone, smart TV, printer—shares the same digital space. This is the open-plan living room of networking. It feels sociable. It is also unnecessary. Separation inside a home network is the equivalent of internal doors: not because everyone is untrustworthy, but because different activities have different stakes.

Show: a friend visits, asks for the Wi-Fi password, joins the same network as the work laptop that holds confidential files and remote access tokens. Name: network cohabitation. Explain: when devices share one network, they can often "see" one another more than people realise; even if modern operating systems are safer than they once were, shared networks expand the blast radius of mistakes. Implication: a simple act of hospitality can quietly increase exposure for the most sensitive device in the home.

A guest network is the most straightforward form of separation. It is a second Wi-Fi network provided by the same router, usually with a different name and password, designed for visitors and low-trust devices. The key idea is not secrecy; it is containment. If a guest's phone is compromised, or simply noisy, it should not sit shoulder-to-shoulder with devices that matter more. If a visitor's device begins scanning the local network—as many devices and apps do routinely—it should not have a clear view of the family printer's address book or the file-sharing service on a laptop. Containment is kindness to the future.

Containment prevents collateral damage.

That five-word sentence is the whole thesis of this section. Many domestic incidents are not "attacks" in the cinematic sense. They are accidents with consequences: a child installing an untrustworthy game, a guest's laptop carrying malware from a workplace incident, a smart gadget phoning home in ways you did not anticipate. Separation turns a potential household-wide problem into a local one.

The quiet motif from the chapter introduction returns here: doors within doors. A home has internal doors because privacy is layered. You do not put the filing cabinet in the front garden. You do not hand every visitor a key to every room. Digital life benefits from the same architecture. A guest network is a door. A child-specific network can be another. Some routers and home systems allow more granular segmentation—separate networks for smart home devices, for example—but even a basic guest network is an internal door that most people can create without acquiring new equipment.

Show: a router offers a "Guest Wi-Fi" toggle in its settings, and enabling it creates a separate network with "isolation" so guest devices cannot directly reach devices on the main network. Name: device isolation. Explain: guest networks often include client isolation, limiting device-to-device communication; the main network remains for trusted devices. Implication: isolation reduces the risk of lateral movement inside the home, even when the guest network password is shared widely.

The phrase "shared widely" is not a hypothetical. Wi-Fi passwords travel. They sit in phones. They are typed into tablets. They get saved to contact cards. They get written on chalkboards in holiday cottages and copied into notes apps. They get shared with babysitters and visiting relatives and builders. If your home uses one Wi-Fi password for everything, the password is not merely a secret you possess. It is a social object. Guest networks allow that social object to be less powerful.

Now place children in this picture. Children are not adversaries. They are learners with different incentives. They explore. They click. They trade links. They install whatever their friends install. They may not read warning screens because warning screens are designed to be ignored. Their devices therefore should not share the same trust tier as a work laptop used for confidential documents or a machine that controls bank accounts.

Show: a child taps "Allow" to a permission request, not out of malice but out of impatience to reach the game. Name: friction skipping. Explain: children (and adults) optimise for fun and belonging; apps exploit this with prompts; permissions can be granted without understanding. Implication: treating children's devices as lower-trust by default is not an insult; it is accurate design.

This leads to the second half of the section: parental controls and limits. The tone matters. Controls are not a substitute for parenting, and they are not a licence to surveil. The purpose of domestic controls, used well, is to reduce exposure and to support rhythms—sleep, homework, family time—without turning the child into a monitored employee. Surveillance corrodes trust; boundaries can build it. The difference is not in the software. It is in the intent and the transparency.

Show: a parent secretly monitors a child's messages and location, then discovers something worrying but has poisoned the relationship needed to talk about it. Name: trust erosion. Explain: covert monitoring trades short-term information for long-term relational damage; children learn to hide rather than to ask for help. Implication: privacy-aware parenting is not permissive; it is strategic about which problems are solved by technology and which require conversation.

A credible limitation must be stated early: no filter is perfect. Content classification fails. Kids find workarounds. Platforms change. New apps appear faster than parents can learn their names. Anyone promising a "set and forget" safe internet for children is selling fantasy. The reconciliation is to treat controls as guardrails rather than as walls. Guardrails reduce the consequences of a swerve. They do not prevent all swerving. They make it more likely that a mistake becomes a teachable moment rather than a crisis.

The simplest and most durable controls are often time-based rather than content-based. Time-based limits align with physiology and family routine. Children need sleep. They need offline time. They need boring time. They need time where their attention is not tugged by an endless feed engineered to keep them scrolling. Time controls do not pretend to judge what is "good" content. They manage exposure by managing hours.

Show: a child's device remains accessible late into the night, and attention spills into sleep deprivation and irritability the next day. Name: attention bleed. Explain: devices extend social time indefinitely; sleep is vulnerable; fatigue reduces judgement and increases vulnerability to manipulation and conflict. Implication: limits that protect sleep are privacy-adjacent because they reduce the hours in which children are most persuadable and least resilient.

Age-appropriate boundaries differ, and any one-size policy becomes brittle. A seven-year-old's risk profile is different from a fifteen-year-old's. Younger children benefit from more structure because their online worlds are mediated by games and videos and they lack the experience to detect manipulation. Teenagers benefit from more autonomy because they are building identity and relationships, and authoritarian control often triggers secrecy. The constant across ages is that boundaries work best when they are legible and consistent, and when children understand the "why" without being frightened into compliance.

Show: a teenager is given an unexplained restriction and responds by creating a new account or using a friend's device. Name: displacement. Explain: restrictive controls can shift behaviour rather than change it; they may push activity into less safe channels where adults have even less visibility and influence. Implication: the goal is to reduce risk while keeping channels for help open, not to win a cat-and-mouse game.

Here is where network segmentation and parental controls can cooperate without becoming intrusive. A child-specific network can make it easier to apply coarse protections without micromanaging: basic content filters at the network level, safe-search enforcement where supported, and simple schedules for when the internet is available for certain devices. These controls do not read private messages. They do not inspect every click in detail. They shape the environment.

Environment shapes behaviour.

Five words again, and again they matter. Much of privacy and safety work is environmental design: making the easiest path the safer path.

Another named, checkable example illustrates why environment matters more than intention. In September 2021, Facebook's internal research—reported by *The Wall Street Journal* in its "Facebook Files" series—became public discussion material, including findings about how Instagram could affect some teenagers' wellbeing. Whatever debates followed, the relevant point for this chapter is that platforms are engineered to maximise engagement, and they measure the results. This is not a moral accusation. It is a business model. A child's device therefore sits inside an attention economy whose incentives do not prioritise family rhythms. Domestic boundaries are a way of reasserting a different set of incentives: sleep over clicks, homework over autoplay, privacy over performance.

Guests, meanwhile, present a different sort of unpredictability. You can love your friends and still not want their devices on your network. Not because they are irresponsible, but because you do not know the state of their devices. Their phone might be full of old apps with wide permissions. Their laptop might have been compromised at work. Their child might be using their tablet. Their browser extensions might be questionable. Guest networks treat this uncertainty as normal, not as insulting.

Show: a tradesperson asks for Wi-Fi to download documents, and you provide guest access that works without exposing the main network. Name: polite containment. Explain: guest networks allow hospitality while keeping internal devices compartmentalised; this is etiquette translated into network design. Implication: privacy can be woven into social life without awkwardness.

One of the more subtle exposures in households with children is device sharing. A shared iPad on the coffee table becomes a repository of multiple accounts, multiple messages, multiple browsing histories, and multiple saved passwords. Sharing devices is not wrong; it is common. But it makes privacy boundaries ambiguous. A child might access an adult account by accident. An adult might see a child's messages by accident. A sibling might snoop. In a flat network, the ambiguity spreads further. Separate accounts on devices help, but network separation can reduce cross-device visibility and prevent a child's device from talking to shared storage or printers where it does not need to.

Show: a shared device remains logged into an adult email account, and a child opens it while searching for a game code. Name: accidental disclosure. Explain: shared devices collapse boundaries; persistent logins make private information easy to stumble upon; the harm is not only data leakage but emotional confusion. Implication: reducing sharing friction through clear boundaries can protect both privacy and relationships.

The closing tension of this section sits in a parenting paradox: children need privacy to grow, and they need protection to be safe. Those needs can conflict. A household that chooses only privacy may neglect hazards; a household that chooses only protection may create secrecy and resentment. The aim here is not to solve that paradox with a gadget. It is to manage it with architecture and honesty: build internal doors in the network, use controls as guardrails, and reserve surveillance for genuinely exceptional circumstances rather than making it the default shape of family life.

The forward test is therefore a decision you will face the next time someone asks, "What's your Wi-Fi password?" or the next time a child's device becomes the site of a conflict: will your home network treat everyone as if they belong in the same room with the same keys, or will it quietly reflect the truth that different devices—and different ages—deserve different doors?

Smart Home Device Risks

In May 2019, in Boston, researchers associated with Northeastern University and Imperial College London published a study of smart speakers that described how the devices could be triggered into recording by words that merely *sounded* like wake words, producing what they called "accidental activations". The claim was not that the speakers were plotting. It was that a microphone designed to listen for a cue will sometimes listen when it should not. In a living room, that difference can be the muffled sound of a kettle boiling, the rasp of a laugh, the low hum of a television; small noises that feel private because they are ordinary. In a dataset, ordinary is still data. Mistakes scale in silence.

Smart home devices are seductive because they turn the home into a responsive environment. Lights obey a voice. The doorbell shows a face. The thermostat anticipates comfort. The camera offers reassurance. Convenience becomes intimacy: the house begins to behave as if it knows you. The risk is that "knowing you" is not only local knowledge. It often involves remote servers, persistent accounts, and telemetry that travels far beyond the walls that make a home feel like a home.

The earlier sections established the home network as a gateway and guest networks as internal doors. Smart devices are the reason those doors matter. They are not just computers. They are computers with senses. A smart speaker is a microphone with a personality layer. A camera is a lens attached to an internet account. A doorbell is a sensor that records your social boundary—who arrives, when, and how often. Even "simple" devices like smart bulbs and plugs can reveal patterns: when people are home, when they sleep, whether they travel. These devices do not need to capture content to create exposure. Timing is enough.

Show: a smart plug reports on/off events to a cloud service, and those events reveal when the household wakes, eats, and leaves. Name: behavioural telemetry. Explain: sensor data is often logged for "reliability" or "analytics"; patterns emerge from timestamps without any audio or video. Implication: privacy is not only about what is said or seen; it is about what can be inferred.

The word "infer" deserves attention because it is how modern surveillance becomes socially acceptable. People hear "microphone" and imagine eavesdropping; they hear "bulb" and imagine harmlessness. Yet inference collapses that distinction. A bulb can disclose a routine. A thermostat can disclose occupancy. A vacuum robot can disclose floor plans. A speaker can disclose voice characteristics and household dynamics, even if content is protected. Inference is the quiet power that makes innocuous devices sensitive.

This is not an argument against smart devices as a category. It is an argument against treating them as toys. A smart device brings three kinds of risk: data risk (what it collects and stores), access risk (who can control it), and dependency risk (what happens when it fails, when the company changes policy, or when the device is abandoned). A fourth risk sits underneath all three: placement. Where you put a device determines what it can sense, and therefore what it can turn into data.

Placement is policy.

Five words, and they are almost always ignored in household setups. People place devices where they work best: the speaker near the kitchen, the camera facing the hallway, the smart display in the bedroom. Those placements often maximise convenience and minimise thought. Yet a bedroom is not a hallway. A child's play area is not a porch. A device that belongs near the front door may not belong near a dining table where family conversations happen, or near a desk where confidential work calls happen. Placement is the first control because it is the only control that cannot be bypassed by a software update.

Show: a smart speaker sits on a bedside table because it plays music, and it becomes a night-time listener by default. Name: intimacy amplification. Explain: sensors in intimate spaces capture the most revealing slices of life; even if nothing "sensitive" is said, the context is sensitive. Implication: convenience can pull sensors into the very places privacy matters most.

The second control is muting and physical indicators. Many smart speakers and some cameras include hardware mute buttons or physical shutters, sometimes accompanied by lights that signal active listening or recording. These features are valuable because they are not purely software. Software can be changed remotely. A physical switch is closer to an internal door—an architectural boundary rather than a policy setting. Still, physical indicators can be misunderstood. A light that indicates "listening" may indicate only that the device is actively processing, not whether it is capturing and buffering audio locally. A shutter may cover a camera lens but not silence a microphone. Understanding what the hardware switch actually does is therefore part of control.

Show: a user presses mute on a smart speaker and assumes it is inert, yet the device still connects to the internet for updates and telemetry. Name: partial muting. Explain: muting often disables audio capture, not network activity; the device remains a networked computer. Implication: mute is a meaningful boundary for content, but not a complete privacy solution.

A named, checkable example illustrates the stakes around access risk. In December 2019, Ring acknowledged a series of incidents in which users reported unauthorised access to their cameras, with media coverage describing cases where strangers spoke through devices. The pattern was not always a "hack" of Ring's infrastructure; it frequently involved credential reuse, weak passwords, or compromised accounts. The important point is that a camera is not merely a camera. It is an account. If the account is compromised, the device becomes an instrument of intrusion inside the home. The lesson is architectural: attaching sensors to accounts raises the stakes of account security.

Show: a camera is installed to reduce anxiety about security, and an account compromise increases anxiety by turning the camera into a channel for intrusion. Name: inversion of purpose. Explain: security devices can become threats when access controls fail; the device's core function becomes a vector. Implication: smart home devices should be evaluated not only by what they promise but by what they could become under failure.

Another checkable example speaks to data risk. In July 2022, Amazon agreed to pay penalties related to two issues involving Ring and Alexa, including allegations about employees' access to customer video recordings and the handling of children's voice recordings, as reported by the U.S. Federal Trade Commission. Whatever the legal details, the broader point is stable: cloud services create internal audiences. The "you" who uses the device is not the only party who can, under certain conditions, access stored data. There may be contractors, support teams, machine learning pipelines, or law enforcement requests depending on jurisdiction and policy. A private home becomes entangled with institutional processes.

Show: a household assumes its doorbell footage is "ours", then realises footage is stored in a third-party cloud governed by terms, retention rules, and internal access policies. Name: outsourced custody. Explain: when data is stored remotely, you are delegating custody; custody implies access by others under defined conditions. Implication: domestic privacy depends on corporate governance as much as on household intent.

Still, an honest limitation matters here too. Not all smart devices are equally invasive, and not all use-cases are frivolous. Some people rely on smart speakers for accessibility. Some rely on cameras for caring responsibilities, or for monitoring a property in ways that reduce real risk. Some devices can be configured to minimise data retention. Some vendors offer stronger privacy practices. The reconciliation is to avoid absolutism. The goal is not to create a home that refuses convenience. The goal is to align convenience with boundaries.

Alignment requires understanding what data types are in play. Smart speakers capture audio around wake-word events and may log voice interactions to improve recognition and services. Cameras capture video and audio, sometimes continuously, sometimes on motion. Doorbells capture visitors, deliveries, neighbours, and passers-by. Smart TVs may capture viewing behaviour and sometimes voice input. Sensors can include motion, temperature, humidity, light levels, and more. Each data type has its own sensitivity profile. Audio and video feel most intimate, but pattern data can be revealing in aggregate.

Show: a motion sensor logs movement patterns throughout the day, revealing when the home is empty even without video. Name: occupancy signature. Explain: repeated sensor events create signatures that can indicate routines and absences; these signatures can be valuable for targeting or inference. Implication: "low-content" sensors still create high-value behavioural data.

Control, then, becomes a series of decisions about minimisation. Minimisation is not a slogan. It is a practice: minimise the number of sensors, minimise the sensitivity of placement, minimise retention, minimise the audience, minimise the connectivity. Saying "no" to some gadgets is part of this, not as moral posturing but as design discipline. Every device you do not install is a device you do not maintain, patch, account-manage, or explain to a family member.

The "doors within doors" motif becomes practical again when we consider network segregation. A separate network for smart devices—distinct from laptops and phones—reduces how far an issue can spread. If a smart plug has weak security, it should not be a stepping-stone to a work machine. Segregation also makes it easier to manage behaviour at the network level: you can see what kinds of devices are connected, and you can choose to restrict or disable internet access for certain categories when not needed. The point is not to micromanage. It is to contain.

Show: a household places smart devices on a separate Wi-Fi network so the devices cannot directly reach the laptop used for work. Name: compartmentalisation. Explain: separating device classes limits lateral movement and reduces the consequences of compromise in any one class. Implication: network design can compensate for the fact that many smart devices are poorly designed or poorly maintained.

Dependency risk is the least discussed and often the most irritating. Smart devices depend on remote services. Companies change terms. Products are discontinued. Servers are shut down. A light switch that requires an app and a cloud login is not simply a light switch; it is a contract with a vendor's continued existence. This matters for privacy because dependency increases coercion: if the device stops working without data sharing, the household may accept data sharing as a fee for functionality.

Show: a device prompts a mandatory account upgrade or new privacy terms, and the user cannot use the device without acceptance. Name: consent under duress. Explain: dependency turns "choice" into compliance; refusing becomes costly because the device is already installed in the home. Implication: privacy choices are easier before purchase than after installation.

This is where the phrase "tame the ones you already own" earns its weight. Many households already have smart devices. The work is not to scold. It is to bring the devices back into the architecture of the home: place them thoughtfully, use hardware controls where available, limit data retention where settings allow, keep accounts secured, reduce unnecessary integrations, and separate networks where feasible. Even small adjustments can shift the exposure profile because smart devices operate continuously.

A final human complication must be acknowledged: household members differ. One person loves voice control; another finds it intrusive. One person wants cameras; another feels watched. Children may find smart devices fun and therefore disclose more around them. Guests may not realise they are being recorded. Privacy inside a home is also interpersonal. A device placed in a common area becomes a household policy imposed by one person's purchase. That is not inherently wrong, but it requires conversation. Otherwise technology becomes a proxy for power.

The forward test that closes this section is deliberately uncomfortable, because it mirrors the real decision smart devices ask you to make. A smart home is not only a set of gadgets. It is a set of permissions granted to companies, to accounts, and to sensors placed inside private life. When you next consider adding a microphone, camera, or "helpful" sensor to an intimate space, will you treat the device as a tool that must earn its place—or as a guest you invite in and then forget to watch?

Printers, TVs, And Oddities

In February 2015, in Seoul, Samsung issued a public statement after reports drew attention to the company's smart TV privacy policy, including a warning that spoken words captured through voice-recognition features could be transmitted to third parties. The story travelled not because it revealed a single villain, but because it punctured a comforting assumption: a television feels like furniture, and furniture does not listen. Yet the modern television is a networked computer with microphones, app stores, identifiers, and update mechanisms. The soft glow in the corner of a sitting room had quietly acquired the same appetite for data as a phone. The lounge has an operating system.

Once you recognise that sentence as literal, a great deal of domestic privacy becomes easier to manage. The "forgotten computers" are rarely the devices people obsess over. People worry about laptops, because laptops look like computers. They worry about phones, because phones contain their lives. They rarely worry about printers, because printers look like bureaucratic appliances from a more innocent age. They rarely worry about televisions, because televisions feel passive. They rarely worry about set-top boxes, game consoles, smart speakers tucked behind books, or the router's "helpful" ISP app. These objects are overlooked precisely because they perform familiar roles. A printer prints. A TV plays programmes. A console plays games. The privacy shift happens when familiar roles become wrapped in persistent accounts and constant connectivity.

Show: a household prints a bank statement, scans it, and sends it by email, believing the printer is merely a conduit. Name: appliance illusion. Explain: many modern printers store job histories, document previews, scanned files, and address books; some offer cloud printing and remote access; they are small servers on the home network. Implication: a device treated as a transient tool may quietly become a repository of sensitive data.

The core challenge with oddities is not technical complexity. It is categorisation. A household needs a method for identifying which devices are merely "dumb endpoints" and which are computers with storage, sensors, and accounts. The ones that matter for privacy usually have at least one of these traits: they sign into something, they store something, they speak to the internet when they are "idle", or they have features that suggest memory—recommendations, history, personalised settings, voice profiles, user accounts, contact lists. Any of these is a signal that the device is not only doing a task. It is building a relationship.

That relationship has two sides: what the device knows about you, and what someone else could learn through the device. The first is about data collection and profiling. The second is about access—either unauthorised access by outsiders or accidental access by the next owner when the device changes hands. Both matter. The second is often neglected because people think about privacy as surveillance by corporations, not as a practical problem of second-hand electronics.

Show: a family sells a smart TV and resets only the streaming apps, leaving the TV still logged into a manufacturer account with household Wi-Fi history and personal settings. Name: residual identity. Explain: consumer devices often maintain a "root" account separate from app logins; factory reset is the boundary, not uninstalling an app. Implication: resale and recycling can leak personal data even when the seller believes they have "signed out".

A named, checkable example illustrates how data can persist in unexpected places. In January 2010, CBS News reported on a study by the US National Association for Information Destruction (NAID) in which used photocopiers were found to contain hard drives storing copies of documents previously scanned, including sensitive records. The photocopier is simply the office analogue of the modern home printer and multifunction device: a machine that seems mechanical but contains storage. The point is not to frighten people away from using devices. It is to correct the mental model. If a device can scan, it can store. If it can store, it can leak.

The mental model, once corrected, becomes powerful. A smart TV is not a screen with apps. It is an advertising and analytics platform disguised as a screen, sometimes subsidised by data. This does not mean every TV is malicious. It means that "free" features—voice search, personalised recommendations, automatic content recognition—often exist because they generate valuable signals. Automatic content recognition (ACR), for example, is a class of technology used to identify what is being watched, often by analysing on-screen content or audio fingerprints. Where ACR is present, it can support targeted advertising and measurement, and it can operate independently of which streaming apps you use. Watching becomes measurable in ways that feel alien to the cultural role of television.

Show: a TV offers "improved recommendations" and "enhanced viewing experience" toggles during setup, and accepting them enables extensive analytics. Name: consent theatre. Explain: setup screens bundle disparate data practices behind soothing language; users click through to reach the programme; "choice" becomes ritual rather than informed decision. Implication: the most consequential privacy decisions for these devices often happen in the first five minutes of ownership.

Printers have their own version of this. They often present cloud features as convenience: scan-to-email, mobile printing, remote management, "smart" ink ordering. Each convenience creates an account and a data flow. Scan-to-email can create a list of recipients or recent destinations. Mobile printing can expose printer discovery to the local network. Remote management can expose administrative interfaces in ways that resemble the router problems described earlier. And printers have another oddity: they tend to be shared. Shared devices invite broad access by default. A printer's address book can become, in practice, a family directory.

Show: a printer is used for school forms, work documents, medical letters, and travel itineraries. Name: cross-domain aggregation. Explain: shared household devices collect fragments from multiple domains of life; aggregation increases sensitivity because it links contexts. Implication: a mundane device can become a concentrated record of household activities.

One might object, fairly, that these risks are often theoretical. Many households will never experience a printer breach, and many smart TV data practices feel abstract compared to the immediate joys of watching a film. This limitation matters because privacy writing can become unmoored from lived experience. The reconciliation is to focus on two realities that do not depend on being personally targeted. First, data collection is routine even without harm: many devices are designed to report telemetry as a default. Second, device turnover is routine: households upgrade, move, give away devices, return them under warranty, or recycle them. Turnover is where quiet leaks become concrete, because the next owner is not hypothetical. It is a person who now possesses a device that may still remember you.

Turnover is the danger zone.

Five words again, and they are not dramatic. They are domestic. Turnover happens during house moves, renovations, relationship changes, clear-outs, and the slow churn of technology. It is precisely when people are busy and distracted that they forget to reset devices properly.

The question then becomes: what does "properly" mean without descending into instruction manuals? At the conceptual level, proper handling of oddities involves three actions: identify what the device stores, decide what the device should be allowed to transmit, and clear identity before disposal. Identification is partly about recognising accounts and memory. Transmission is partly about disabling features that are not genuinely needed, especially those that create ongoing reporting. Clearing identity is partly about understanding what a factory reset does and does not do.

To make this vivid, consider the ordinary act of watching. A television can collect a log of what apps are opened, which channels are selected, how long the TV is on, and sometimes what content is displayed if ACR is enabled. This log can be linked to an advertising identifier and perhaps to an account if one is created. Even if you never type your name, the TV can still create a household profile from patterns and IP address associations. Now consider the ordinary act of printing. A printer can store recent jobs, store scans temporarily or persistently, and store contact lists for scan-to-email. If the printer is networked, it can also be visible to devices on the network, and sometimes accessible through a web interface.

The key insight is that both devices can become "privacy multipliers" because they operate in shared spaces. A phone is usually personal. A TV is communal. A printer is communal. A communal device creates social privacy issues: it can expose one person's activity to another person in the home, and it can create shared logs that outlast context. Privacy in a household is always, in part, privacy from the household itself. That does not mean families should be suspicious. It means shared devices deserve more careful boundaries than personal ones.

Show: a teenager's YouTube recommendations appear on the family TV, revealing interests to siblings and parents. Name: ambient disclosure. Explain: shared screens surface personal preferences; platform accounts and device profiles leak identity across family members. Implication: device privacy is not only about outsiders; it is also about managing internal visibility.

Oddities extend beyond printers and TVs. Set-top boxes often have persistent identifiers and usage logs. Game consoles can store messages, friend lists, payment information, and voice chat history. Smart speakers and displays can capture voice interactions that inadvertently reveal household relationships. Even the router's ISP-provided management app can collect diagnostics and behavioural data. Each device has its own menus and terms, and the point is not to memorise them. The point is to treat each device as either a tool or a relationship. Tools do a task and forget. Relationships remember, report, and sometimes monetise.

A practical, human way to handle this is to adopt a household habit of "setup with suspicion" and "goodbye with care". Setup with suspicion means that when a device offers optional cloud features, voice features, personalised recommendations, or data sharing for "improvement", you treat those as trade-offs rather than as defaults to accept. Goodbye with care means that before a device leaves your control—sold, given away, recycled—you treat it like a phone: sign out of accounts, remove it from associated account dashboards if possible, and perform a factory reset rather than a superficial cleanup.

The earlier motif of doors within doors applies here too. A smart TV in the lounge is a door to the internet, but it is also a door from the internet into your home environment through microphones, cameras (in some models), and account links. A printer is a door from documents into the network. These are not the doors most people think about, which is why they are so often left unlocked.

The forward test at the end of this section is the kind that reveals whether a household has truly internalised the modern shape of privacy. When you look around your home—at the television, the printer, the set-top box, the console, the smart display—do you see appliances that merely *do*, or computers that also *remember*?

Chapter 9
Kids, Teens, And Families

On 2 September 2021, in the United Kingdom, the Information Commissioner's Office began enforcing the Age Appropriate Design Code, often shortened to the Children's Code. It sounded, to many parents, like a distant regulatory rumble. Yet its real significance arrived in ordinary places: a primary school newsletter, a new "please tick here" consent form, a settings page that suddenly offered a choice rather than a shrug. In a corridor that smelled faintly of disinfectant and poster paint, an adult's old assumption—that children's online lives were mostly a matter of family rules—met a new public claim: children are owed privacy by design, not merely by parental vigilance. The law did not raise a child. It did something more subtle. It changed what we could reasonably demand from the machines around them.

Families are where privacy becomes real, because families are where privacy becomes interpersonal. A solitary adult can treat privacy as an individual project: a password manager, a new browser, a few permissions toggled, a router tidied. Children complicate that neatness, not because they are problems to be managed, but because privacy is partly a social contract, and children are learning the contract while adults are still improvising it. The questions shift. It is no longer only "What does this company collect?" or "How secure is this device?" It becomes "What is fair to know about another person in your home?" and "What do we owe each other when technology makes knowing effortless?"

The awkward truth is that most people first learn privacy at home, long before they learn it online. They learn it through doors, drawers, diaries, tone of voice. They learn it through what adults do when someone walks into a room, through whether conversations are repeated outside their context, through whether a child's story is treated as entertainment. Digital life amplifies these early lessons because it makes sharing frictionless and forgetting difficult. A photo posted in seconds can remain searchable for years. A message sent in anger can be screenshotted, forwarded, archived. A child's embarrassment, once local and fleeting, can be made durable.

This is why "kids and privacy" is not a niche topic for anxious parents. It is the heart of what privacy means in a normal life: the ability to grow, to experiment, to make mistakes, to change one's mind, and to have those changes respected. Childhood is essentially a long rehearsal for adulthood. When technology turns rehearsals into permanent records, it changes the terms under which growing up happens.

There is a paradox at the centre of family privacy that no one can fully escape: adults are responsible for children, and yet children are separate people. Responsibility pulls towards oversight. Personhood pulls towards autonomy. The task is not to choose one and defeat the other. The task is to negotiate a moving boundary that shifts with age, temperament, and circumstance. The worst approach is to pretend the boundary does not exist until the first crisis, because then the only tools left are panic and punishment.

A parent may say, sincerely, that they want their child to be safe online, and then share a child's photo in a public forum without asking because it feels affectionate, because grandparents enjoy it, because everyone else is doing it. That tiny act carries a message louder than any lecture. It says: privacy is something you request from strangers, not something you practise with loved ones. Children are exquisitely sensitive to hypocrisy, not out of cynicism, but because they are learning what rules really mean. If adults treat a child's identity as communal property, later demands for restraint can feel arbitrary. If adults treat consent as normal—"May I post this?" "Do you want your name attached?"—then boundaries begin to feel like part of family culture rather than a sudden clampdown.

The chapter begins, then, with modelling, because modelling is the only technique that scales. Settings change. Platforms change. The deep habit of asking, pausing, and considering the downstream audience is portable. It travels across apps and years. It also turns privacy from a fearful reaction into a positive ethic: respect. There is no need for melodrama here. A child does not need to be told that the internet is a pit of monsters. They need to be shown that the self they are becoming is worth protecting.

From modelling, the conversation moves into rules—specifically, rules that evolve. A seven-year-old and a fifteen-year-old are not variants of the same user. They occupy different worlds. The younger child's internet is often mediated through games and videos and the accidental oddities of autoplay. The teenager's internet is social. It is reputation. It is belonging. It is romantic confusion and friendship turbulence and the peculiar cruelty of group dynamics. When adults impose the same structure on both, the rules fail twice: they restrict the younger child in ways that do not address the real risks, and they provoke the older child into secrecy because the rules do not respect the reality of adolescence.

The temptation, for busy families, is to treat "screen time" as a single dial. Yet time is only one variable. Context matters. A child messaging friends after school is not the same as a child watching videos alone at midnight. A teenager researching coursework is not the same as a teenager doomscrolling when anxious. A device in a shared space is not the same as a device behind a closed bedroom door. What works is not a perfect plan but a pattern of revisiting: rules as a living document, revised as children show they can handle more, tightened when circumstances demand it, always explained without turning technology into mythology. Horror stories are lazy. Competence is kinder.

Still, any honest family knows that rules are not only rational. They are emotional. Devices are not just tools; they are comfort, boredom relief, social oxygen, status symbols. Adults sometimes reach for controls when what they really need is a way to talk about attention, sleep, conflict, and belonging. The aim of this chapter is to make those conversations easier by removing unnecessary complexity. The household does not need to win an arms race against apps. It needs to create an environment in which the easiest choices are not the worst ones, and in which children can ask for help without fear of disproportionate punishment.

That leads naturally to schools, clubs, and teams—the great forgotten collectors of children's data. A child's privacy is not negotiated only within the family. It is negotiated with institutions that are often well-meaning, overstretched, and increasingly reliant on third-party platforms. A school may use a learning app, a photo-sharing service, a behaviour tracking system, a newsletter platform, a cafeteria payment system. Each has its own policies and its own defaults. Parents are often asked to consent in bulk, as if consent were a single signature rather than a set of choices. The institutional burden is real: staff do not have time for bespoke negotiations. Yet the stakes are also real: children's data is uniquely sensitive because it precedes them. It shapes opportunities, reputations, and sometimes risks in ways that adults can only partly foresee.

Advocacy in this context is a delicate art. The caricature of "that parent" exists for a reason: schools face unreasonable demands. But silence has its own cost. A parent who never asks what a platform collects has delegated not only convenience but duty. The chapter's stance is pragmatic: ask a small number of good questions, choose battles, and understand that opting out is sometimes possible, sometimes not, and often requires social tact. Privacy is a form of stewardship. Stewardship does not require antagonism.

Then there are teenagers, where privacy talk can become clumsy very quickly. Many adults approach teen online behaviour with a mix of nostalgia and panic—nostalgia for a childhood that could be contained by geography, panic because containment no longer works. Blanket bans tend to fail for the same reason prohibition often fails: it treats a complex desire as a single misbehaviour and drives it into the shadows. Teenagers are not simply risk. They are agency in training. They need tools that respect their intelligence: how to adjust settings without turning it into a ritual of paranoia, how to block and report without feeling petty, how to understand that a screenshot is a kind of permanence, how to recognise pressure when it arrives dressed as affection or popularity.

The chapter's tone towards teenagers is deliberately respectful because respect is practical. Teenagers who feel patronised stop listening. Teenagers who feel treated as partners become more capable of making good decisions when adults are not present. That partnership is not permissive. It is strategic. It recognises that teens will do things adults do not like, and it focuses on reducing harm rather than demanding purity. It also recognises something adults often forget: a teenager's worst fear is often not danger in the abstract, but social humiliation. A privacy mistake can be terrifying because it can become social currency. To help teens manage data is therefore to help them manage status, conflict, and the persistence of digital artefacts.

A quiet image runs through this chapter: the family home as a place with internal doors. Earlier chapters used doors as a way to think about networks and devices. Here, the doors become human. A bedroom door. A closed notebook. A phone turned face-down during dinner. A request before posting. An apology when a boundary is crossed. These are small acts, but families are made of small acts. Technology doesn't abolish the need for internal doors. It raises their value.

And yet, certainty is impossible. No parent can guarantee that a child will never see something disturbing, never be misled, never feel pressured, never make a mistake. The point is not perfect safety. It is resilient competence: a child who knows how to recover, who knows how to ask for help, who can distinguish between private and public, between temporary and permanent, between attention and care. The highest achievement of family privacy is not control. It is trust that survives error.

The momentum at the end of this introduction turns on a question that families cannot avoid for much longer, because the devices will not wait: when a child grows up under constant capture—photos posted, locations shared, messages monitored, school platforms logging every click—what kind of adult does that produce? The answer is not predetermined. It depends on whether the adults around them treat privacy as a rule to enforce or as a culture to model.

Modelling Healthy Privacy

In March 2018, in Vienna, a mother filed a case against her parents for posting hundreds of photographs of her online as a child without her consent, arguing that the images had followed her into adulthood like an unwanted shadow. The details were reported in European media with the familiar mix of outrage and amusement, as if the problem were merely generational etiquette. Yet the case landed because it made a private discomfort public: a life can be documented into permanence by people who love you. The glow of a phone screen in a family kitchen—thumb scrolling, a soft notification sound, the brief pause before "Share"—became, in retrospect, a kind of authorship. Someone was writing a child into the internet.

Love can still overstep.

That is the first fact of modelling healthy privacy. Children do not learn privacy from lectures. They learn it from what adults treat as normal. They learn it from the reflexive behaviours that happen when no one is making a speech: whether adults knock before entering a bedroom, whether an adult reads a message over a child's shoulder, whether family stories are told as jokes to strangers, whether a parent takes a photo of a child crying and treats it as content. Adults often imagine that children are too young to notice these things. Children notice. They may not have the language to name what they are seeing, but they absorb the rules.

Show: a parent posts a child's first day of school photo with the school name visible in the background. Name: ambient disclosure. Explain: small contextual details in images and captions can reveal location, routine, and identity; adults often share them to celebrate, not to disclose. Implication: what begins as pride becomes a trail that others can follow.

The core argument here is not that families should stop sharing. It is that sharing is a skill, and children deserve to be raised by adults who practise it. Privacy is sometimes described as secrecy, but within families it is better understood as boundary-making: deciding what belongs where, and who gets to decide. The shift is subtle. If privacy is secrecy, then the adult's job is to hunt for hidden things. If privacy is boundary-making, the adult's job is to build a household culture in which boundaries are negotiated and respected.

The second fact is more uncomfortable: modelling privacy is also modelling power. Adults control the cameras, the accounts, the phones, the rules. Children have little recourse. A child cannot easily opt out of a parent's social media habits. They cannot rewrite an embarrassing caption. They cannot untag themselves if they do not have an account. They cannot prevent relatives from forwarding pictures in group chats. This asymmetry means that adult choices carry ethical weight even when they feel casual.

Show: a relative shares a bath-time photo in a family group chat because it is "only family". Name: private-public slippage. Explain: digital messages are easily forwarded, screenshotted, backed up, and stored; "only family" is not a technical category. Implication: adults may create exposures they cannot later retract, and children bear the consequences.

A named, checkable example grounds the cultural change. In September 2019, the French data protection authority CNIL published guidance reminding parents that sharing children's images online can create risks and that children have rights over their data. The specific jurisdiction matters less than the shift it represents: children's privacy is not merely a parental preference; it is increasingly recognised as a right with a lifespan. A child grows up. Their boundaries should grow too. When adults share, they are not only communicating with today's audience. They are making a decision on behalf of a future person.

Future selves matter.

Five words, and they are the hinge of this chapter. Most family sharing decisions are made as if the child will always be five years old, always delighted, always indifferent. The child will not remain five. The photo will remain. That mismatch—temporary child, durable record—is what makes modelling privacy urgent now in a way that previous generations did not face.

Modelling begins with the simplest visible habit: asking. Asking is not performative politeness; it is training. When an adult asks a child, "May I post this?" or "Do you want your face in this?" the adult is doing three things at once. They are acknowledging the child as a person with preferences. They are demonstrating that consent can exist in a family, not only in formal settings. And they are teaching the child to consider audience. Even when a young child cannot fully grasp the implications, the act of asking lays the rails along which later understanding can travel.

Show: a parent holds a phone up at the dinner table and pauses, asking permission before taking a photo. Name: consent rehearsal. Explain: children learn consent through repetition in low-stakes moments; the muscle is built before it is tested. Implication: when higher-stakes situations arrive—peer pressure, rumours, intimate images—the child has a lived example of consent being normal.

The question is often raised: what if a child always says no? That question reveals the adult fear that consent will be inconvenient. Consent is inconvenient. That is its point. It forces a pause where impulse would otherwise rule. In practice, children rarely say no to everything; they say no when something feels embarrassing, or when they are tired, or when they sense they are being turned into a performance. If a child says no often, the adult has learned something important: the child experiences the adult's camera as intrusive. That is not a moral failure. It is information.

Modelling is not only about photos. It is about conversations. Adults narrate children's lives to other adults: to friends, colleagues, relatives, sometimes strangers. They share stories about tantrums, school struggles, crushes, awkward questions. Some sharing is normal; families are social. The privacy question is whether the child's life is treated as a public resource. A child who grows up hearing their private moments retold as jokes learns that privacy is fragile and that adults cannot be trusted with vulnerability.

Show: a parent repeats a teenager's private confession at a family gathering for humour. Name: relational leakage. Explain: information shared in one context is re-used in another; the child experiences betrayal; trust becomes costly. Implication: privacy modelling is also trust modelling, and trust is hard to rebuild once broken.

Trust, however, can sound abstract until it is paired with behaviour. A trusting household is one in which people do not routinely read one another's messages, do not broadcast one another's difficulties, and do not treat surveillance as love. This is not sentimental. It is functional. Children who believe that adults will respond calmly to mistakes are more likely to disclose problems early. Children who expect punishment or humiliation learn to hide. Hiding is often more dangerous than the behaviour adults are trying to prevent.

A credible limitation must be admitted: sometimes adults do need to intervene. Young children are not equipped to manage every risk, and certain situations demand decisive action. The reconciliation is that intervention should be exceptional and explainable, not ambient and secret. Secret monitoring teaches children to become better at secrecy. Visible boundaries teach children how boundaries work.

Show: a parent quietly checks a child's device nightly without disclosure, then is surprised when the child develops elaborate hiding habits. Name: surveillance spiral. Explain: covert monitoring increases concealment; concealment increases monitoring; the relationship becomes adversarial. Implication: modelling privacy is partly about resisting the slide into a household where everyone becomes a detective.

The home itself offers a set of physical analogies—doors, drawers, curtains—that can be translated into digital habits. A household that knocks before entering a bedroom is already modelling that privacy is not synonymous with wrongdoing. A household that keeps certain conversations private is already modelling that boundaries are normal. Translating those habits into digital space means treating devices as rooms: a phone is a bedroom, not a noticeboard; a private message is a closed letter, not a family announcement; a location log is a diary of movement, not a family scoreboard.

Show: an adult picks up a child's phone to "just check something" without asking. Name: boundary bypass. Explain: casual boundary violations teach that boundaries are optional when power is available; children learn to do the same to siblings and peers. Implication: everyday moments either reinforce or erode the idea that privacy is real.

There is another reason modelling matters: children watch how adults negotiate with institutions. When a school asks for blanket consent to share photographs, does the parent shrug and sign, or do they read and ask a question? When an app asks for contact access, does the adult tap "Allow" without thinking, or do they pause? When a family member forwards a child's photo outside the family group chat, does anyone object? These are not grand battles. They are micro-choices. Children learn from micro-choices because micro-choices are what life is made of.

Here the earlier motif of internal doors returns in human form. A family home with internal doors signals that different spaces have different levels of privacy. Digital life needs the same architecture. Some information belongs in the family. Some belongs with close friends. Some belongs with a teacher. Some belongs nowhere outside the child. Adults model this architecture by how they share. Not sharing is not the only option. Sharing well is.

A second named, checkable example helps anchor the idea that modelling is cultural, not merely personal. In 1997, the sociologist Annette Lareau published *Unequal Childhoods*, a study of how different families cultivate different forms of competence through everyday practices. While not a book about digital privacy, its relevance is structural: children learn skills and expectations through daily routines, not through abstract instruction. Privacy competence—knowing what to share, when, and with whom—fits that pattern. Families that practise consent, boundary respect, and careful sharing are not merely being "careful". They are teaching a form of social intelligence that will matter in friendships, romance, workplaces, and civic life.

Modelling also requires adults to face their own incentives. Social platforms reward sharing. Family group chats reward constant updates. Adults sometimes share because they are lonely, or proud, or seeking affirmation, or trying to reassure distant relatives. Those motives are human. The privacy question is whether adult emotional needs are being met by spending a child's privacy as currency. That is a harsh way to phrase it, and it is accurate enough to be useful. It forces a pause. It turns "It's just a cute photo" into "What am I buying with this, and who pays?"

Show: a parent receives a rush of likes and supportive comments after posting a child's vulnerable moment, and begins to share more of the child's life in search of that feeling. Name: attention substitution. Explain: platforms turn family life into content; feedback loops can encourage oversharing; the child becomes part of the adult's online identity. Implication: modelling privacy sometimes means adults managing their own attention habits so children are not recruited into them.

None of this requires perfection. Families are messy. Adults make mistakes. The point is that modelling creates a default trajectory. When a child sees an adult correct themselves—removing a post, apologising for sharing too much, asking before reposting—children learn that privacy is not a rigid doctrine but a living practice. That may be the most valuable model of all: that boundaries can be adjusted without shame, that respect is not brittle.

The closing tension, then, is a forward test that will surface repeatedly as children grow and the platforms evolve. When an adult's impulse is to share—whether a photo, a story, a location, an anecdote—does the adult pause long enough to ask whose identity is being broadcast, and whether the person being broadcast would choose it?

Setting Age Appropriate Rules

In January 2020, in Washington, D.C., the American Academy of Pediatrics updated its long-running advice on children and media, shifting emphasis away from blunt "screen time" caps towards what it called a *Family Media Plan*—a framework that treats media use as part of the texture of family life rather than as a toxin to be measured by the minute. The update was widely reported, and it landed with parents not because it offered a magic number, but because it admitted something parents already knew in their bones: the same rule cannot govern a toddler, a primary school child, and a teenager. The glow from a tablet in a darkened lounge is the same glow; the mind behind it is not.

Age changes the equation.

That five-word sentence is not sentimental. It is operational. If family rules do not change with age, children learn the wrong lesson: that rules are not about growth, but about control. They then treat rules as obstacles rather than as scaffolding. Scaffolding can be removed as competence increases; obstacles must be circumvented. When adults want children to internalise good judgement, rules must feel like a path to adulthood, not a gate barring it.

The first move in setting age-appropriate rules is to decide what the rule is *for*. Rules that exist only because "this app scares me" or "everyone else is doing it" are brittle. They collapse under negotiation, peer pressure, or adult fatigue. Rules that exist to protect sleep, reduce exposure to persuasive design, prevent costly mistakes, or preserve family rhythms are sturdier because they can be explained without melodrama. Explanation matters. Children do not need a horror story to take something seriously. They need a reason that respects their intelligence.

Show: a parent announces a new phone rule after reading a headline about online dangers, and the child hears panic rather than principle. Name: fear-driven governance. Explain: rules made in fear tend to be sweeping, inconsistent, and poorly articulated; children respond with resistance or secrecy. Implication: the emotional origin of a rule shapes whether it becomes a shared norm or an adversarial struggle.

A better approach begins with observable constraints that most children can recognise: tiredness, distraction, conflict, missed homework, arguments over devices at dinner, the way late-night scrolling spills into morning irritability. These are not moral failures. They are feedback. Rules can be framed as responses to feedback rather than as arbitrary restrictions. The aim is not to remove pleasure. The aim is to manage costs.

This reframing becomes crucial when parents meet the limits of control. By the time a child reaches adolescence, controlling everything is not only unrealistic; it is counterproductive. A teenager can borrow devices, create new accounts, use web versions of apps, or live online through friends. A family that treats control as the goal ends up in an arms race, and arms races create two outcomes: either the adult wins through surveillance and coercion, at which point trust is damaged, or the teen wins through concealment, at which point risk increases. Neither is the stated aim.

Show: a teenager is banned from a platform and immediately uses a friend's account, losing whatever safety settings the family had agreed. Name: displacement. Explain: prohibition can shift behaviour into less visible, less governable spaces; risk does not vanish, it moves. Implication: effective rules often focus on behaviours and contexts rather than on single platforms.

Behaviour and context are where "age appropriate" becomes practical. A seven-year-old generally needs more structure around discovery and impulse. A fifteen-year-old generally needs more support around social complexity and reputation. Younger children's online risks often look like accidental exposure, scams disguised as games, or persuasive design nudging them into purchases and endless loops. Teenagers' risks often look like social manipulation, coercion, screenshot permanence, and the collision between private desire and public performance. A rule that makes sense for one can be absurd for the other.

Consider bedtime. The rule "no devices in the bedroom" looks like a blunt instrument until it is understood as protecting sleep, protecting attention, and protecting vulnerability. Younger children may accept it readily because they have not yet built a social life that extends into the night. Teenagers may resist because night-time is often when private friendships and confessions happen. The age-appropriate version is not "allow everything"; it is to recognise that the rule is trying to protect a biological need without denying a social need. That tension is real. A family can face it honestly rather than pretending it does not exist.

Show: a teenager scrolls and messages late into the night, then struggles at school. Name: attention bleed. Explain: devices extend social time indefinitely; fatigue reduces judgement and increases susceptibility to pressure and conflict. Implication: rules that protect sleep are not moralistic; they are protective of capacity.

"Capacity" is a useful word here because it is measurable without becoming clinical. Capacity is the ability to concentrate, to regulate emotion, to resist persuasion, to recover from conflict. Families can often see when capacity is depleted. Age-appropriate rules can therefore be described as capacity management, not punishment. When a child is well-rested and coping, they can handle more freedom. When they are depleted, boundaries tighten. This makes rules dynamic rather than rigid. It also avoids the trap of turning the device into the villain.

The second move is involvement. Involving children in rule-making is not a gimmick. It is training in self-governance. A child who can articulate why a rule exists, and propose adjustments, is learning to manage their own technology use. A child who is merely policed is learning to evade. Even young children can participate in simple forms: choosing where devices are charged, agreeing on screen-free meals, deciding which apps feel "too much". Teenagers can participate in more complex negotiation: what counts as appropriate sharing, what to do when pressured, how to handle conflicts, how to manage privacy settings, what should happen if something goes wrong.

Show: a family agrees that phones charge overnight in the kitchen, and the rule is framed as a household norm rather than a child-specific punishment. Name: shared constraint. Explain: rules that apply to everyone feel less like control and more like culture; they reduce resentment and model adult discipline. Implication: consistency makes enforcement less exhausting and more legitimate.

Legitimacy is not a soft concept. It is a predictor of compliance. Children comply more when they believe a rule is fair. Fairness does not mean "I like it". It means "I can see the reason, and I can see that it applies consistently." Adults often underestimate how much children value fairness. They also underestimate how much children are willing to accept restrictions when they feel respected.

A credible counter-example must be acknowledged: some children cannot safely be given the same autonomy, even at the same age. Temperament varies. Some children are impulsive. Some are anxious. Some are especially vulnerable to social pressure. Some have specific needs. Families also vary in circumstance: public-facing parents, blended families, high-conflict households, children moving between homes. In those situations, rules may need to be tighter or differently structured. The reconciliation is to avoid turning age into destiny. Age is a baseline. The rule must fit the child, not merely the birth certificate.

Show: two thirteen-year-olds use the same platform; one treats it as casual entertainment, the other spirals into conflict and obsessive checking. Name: differential susceptibility. Explain: the same environment can affect children differently depending on temperament, peer context, and stressors. Implication: age-appropriate rules are necessary but not sufficient; they must be adjusted to the child's lived reality.

This is where the "no horror stories" instruction becomes important. Children do not need to be terrified to be careful. Fear can backfire. It can create either denial ("that won't happen to me") or obsession ("the world is unsafe"). The better method is to describe risks as ordinary possibilities and to pair them with competence: what can be done when something feels wrong, how to exit a situation, how to ask for help. Competence reduces anxiety. It also builds trust.

Trust grows through predictability. Children need to know what will happen if they disclose a mistake. If the consequence is humiliation or severe punishment, they will not disclose. If the consequence is calm problem-solving and proportionate boundaries, they will. This is why rules must include not only restrictions but procedures. Procedure is the quiet backbone of safety: "If you see something upsetting, tell us." "If someone pressures you, you can say you blame your parents." "If you're worried about a message, show us and we'll decide together." These are not lists to memorise. They are scripts that make disclosure easier under stress.

Show: a child receives a suspicious message asking for a photo or a code, hesitates, and remembers that the household response to mistakes is calm rather than punitive. Name: safe disclosure channel. Explain: children disclose when they expect support; support is a learned expectation built by past reactions. Implication: the quality of adult response is itself a protective factor.

Now consider apps specifically. Many parents focus on which apps are "allowed" as if app names were stable categories. App names change, features mutate, companies merge. A more durable approach is to focus on functions: messaging, posting, live streaming, disappearing content, location sharing, payments, and contact discovery. Each function has a different risk profile at different ages. A young child may safely play a game that has no chat; the same game becomes riskier when chat is added. A teenager may handle messaging well but struggle with public posting. Focusing on functions keeps rules relevant even as platforms evolve.

The chapter's quiet motif of internal doors fits here. Rules can be framed as doors that open as children demonstrate competence. A younger child may have a door that opens only into a few rooms: limited apps, shared spaces, devices used at certain times. As competence grows, more doors open: private messaging, more autonomy, more discretion. Doors are not prisons. They are architecture. They teach that freedom is built, not granted.

Show: a parent treats access to a new app as a privilege earned by demonstrating good judgement in smaller contexts. Name: graduated autonomy. Explain: competence grows through staged exposure; small responsibilities prepare for larger ones. Implication: rules become a developmental pathway rather than a perpetual restriction.

There is also a family-wide reality that must be faced: parents are often exhausted. Rules that require constant policing fail because no one can police constantly. Age-appropriate rules should therefore be designed for low-friction enforcement. The best rules reduce the number of daily battles rather than multiplying them. A rule that relies on arguing every night is not a rule; it is a recurring negotiation. Negotiation is fine, but it should happen at predictable intervals, not in the heat of conflict.

The final move is revision. Children grow. Their peer group shifts. School demands change. A new device arrives. A parent changes job. A move happens. Rules should be revisited like any household system: periodically, calmly, with attention to what is working and what is not. Revision is not weakness. It is governance. When a child sees a parent revise a rule based on evidence—"We tried this for a month; here's what we noticed"—the child learns that rules respond to reality. That lesson will matter long after childhood, when the child must govern their own habits without external enforcement.

The unresolved tension that closes this section is the one families live with daily, often without naming it: are rules being designed to produce obedient children, or competent adults? The two can overlap. They can also diverge sharply. The next time a new boundary is proposed—about bedtime, apps, or devices—the diagnostic question is simple and demanding: does this rule teach the child how to choose well when no one is watching?

Schools, Photos, And Consent

In August 2019, in Skellefteå in northern Sweden, the municipality's attempt to automate school attendance with facial recognition ended not with a triumph of efficiency but with a reprimand: the Swedish Data Protection Authority ruled that the trial had breached data protection law and issued a fine. The headline detail was the technology—cameras, faces, a system trained to identify children as they entered a classroom—but the deeper story was older than computing: a school had treated consent as a convenience. In a corridor where trainers squeaked on polished linoleum, the ordinary ritual of registration had been turned into a biometric checkpoint, and the adults involved had misjudged what children's data signifies. Consent is not a checkbox.

The incident matters because it punctures a common parental illusion: that a child's privacy is negotiated mostly at home, through household rules and device settings. Schools, clubs, teams, music tutors, holiday camps, exam boards, and youth organisations collect and generate data as a by-product of care, education, and administration. Most of this collection is not sinister. It is paperwork modernised. Yet the volume and portability of the resulting data creates a different landscape from the one many adults grew up with. A school photograph used to live in a corridor frame or a printed newsletter. Now it is a digital asset that can be uploaded, tagged, reposted, and indexed. A homework assignment used to be a crumpled sheet at the bottom of a bag. Now it is a cloud document tied to a platform account, with logs and metadata that can outlast the school year.

Show: a parent receives a start-of-term "permissions pack" with several consent forms, and signs quickly because the child is already late for a club. Name: consent fatigue. Explain: schools bundle multiple decisions into a single administrative moment; parents comply to keep life moving; the details become background noise. Implication: the most consequential choices about a child's data are often made at the point of maximal distraction.

When people talk about "children's data", they often imagine the obvious categories: name, address, date of birth. Schools hold those, certainly. They also hold the intimate and the banal: behaviour notes, learning support plans, pastoral records, attendance patterns, medical details relevant to care, disciplinary incidents, exam accommodations, safeguarding concerns. Even when a school is careful, third-party tools can expand the circle of access. A spelling app may collect performance data. A classroom management tool may collect usage logs. A communication platform may store message histories and parent contact details. A photo-sharing service may store images and identifiers for years. The shape of the issue is less about one dramatic breach and more about accumulation: small, justified collections that add up to a portrait.

Show: a child uses a reading platform at school, a sports club app for fixtures, and a music tutor's booking system, each requiring an account. Name: institutional sprawl. Explain: children are enrolled into multiple systems across organisations; each system creates an identity; identities persist unless deliberately retired. Implication: a child's data footprint is not a single file in a school office, but a constellation spread across vendors.

Parents often feel a tug of competing goods here. They want their child included in school life. They like seeing photos of assemblies, sports day, the school play. They want teachers to have tools that make learning smoother. They also want to avoid being perceived as difficult. The caricature of "that parent" sits in the background of every email drafted to a school administrator. This social friction is not trivial; it shapes behaviour. Many families accept defaults simply to avoid embarrassment or conflict.

Still, it is possible to advocate without turning the relationship adversarial, and the key is to speak in the language schools already use: duty of care, proportionality, fairness, and workload. Advocacy fails when it arrives as accusation. It works when it arrives as clarity. A parent does not need to recite regulations to make a sensible request. They can ask what any competent organisation should be able to answer: what is collected, where it is stored, who can access it, how long it is kept, and what alternatives exist if a parent declines. Those questions do not imply distrust. They imply seriousness.

Show: a school announces a new third-party learning platform and parents are asked to "activate accounts" by Friday. Name: deadline pressure. Explain: schools often adopt tools under time constraints; parents are nudged into rapid onboarding; dissent feels like disruption. Implication: parents who want choices must act early, because once an entire class is onboarded, alternatives shrink.

Photos are where the emotional stakes are highest because photos feel like love. They also carry the most misunderstood risk because people assume privacy is about secrets, and a child's school photo is not a secret. Yet privacy is also about context and control. A photo of a child in uniform, with a school name visible, posted publicly, is not merely "a nice picture". It is a location marker, a routine marker, sometimes a peer network marker. It can be indexed by search engines. It can be copied without permission. It can surface years later in contexts the child would not choose. Even when the risk of malice is low, the loss of agency is real.

Show: a school posts a public gallery of a sports match, and a parent notices that name tags on kit bags are visible in several images. Name: incidental identifiers. Explain: images capture details the photographer did not intend to share; once posted, those details become part of the public record. Implication: "harmless" images can reveal more than anyone planned, especially when combined with other public information.

There is also the matter of consent itself. Schools often ask for consent for photos at enrolment, and then treat that consent as evergreen. The child, meanwhile, grows. What a parent agrees when a child is five may not match what a child wants at eleven. A child may become more private, more self-conscious, more aware of peer judgement. Consent that does not evolve becomes, quietly, a breach of respect. A school's administrative convenience can clash with a child's developing autonomy.

Show: a teenager asks not to be photographed at a school event, but the default procedure is to photograph everyone and "sort it later". Name: default capture. Explain: institutional routines are built for speed; individual preferences are treated as exceptions; exceptions are easy to forget. Implication: children who want privacy can be made to feel unreasonable for wanting ordinary control.

The Skellefteå facial recognition case makes this clash stark because biometrics remove ambiguity. A school can plausibly argue that posting a photo is part of community building. It cannot plausibly argue that scanning children's faces to automate attendance is simply "normal school life". The principle, however, travels: schools should collect only what they need, not what is possible. Technology expands what is possible faster than institutions can expand their ethical judgement.

A second named example shows how parent and public pressure can change institutional data practices. In April 2014, inBloom, a non-profit backed by major philanthropic funding, shut down after backlash from parents and privacy advocates who objected to the creation of a large-scale student data platform used by districts in the United States. Whatever one thinks of the project's intentions, its collapse illustrates a crucial point: schools and education systems do not operate in a vacuum. Consent is partly political. Families can influence what is treated as acceptable. They do not need to be extremists to do so. They need to be persistent and clear.

Show: parents object not to the existence of digital records, but to centralisation and vendor access. Name: boundary contest. Explain: disputes often centre on who controls the boundary between educational need and commercial interest; when that boundary feels porous, trust collapses. Implication: maintaining trust requires institutions to explain boundaries plainly, not hide them behind technical language.

Third-party learning platforms deserve special attention because they sit at the intersection of education, commerce, and childhood. Many platforms are genuinely useful. Teachers are not villains for adopting tools that make classroom life workable. The risk is not that "schools are spying". The risk is that vendors, analytics, and long retention periods can transform educational support into long-lived profiles. A child's struggles can become a dataset. A child's progress can become a metric that travels beyond the classroom.

This is where a credible limitation belongs, because it is easy to drift into suspicion and forget realities on the ground. Schools have limited budgets and limited staff time. Many digital systems exist precisely because paper systems fail: they lose homework, misplace forms, exclude parents who cannot attend meetings, and make it hard to support children consistently. A blanket refusal of all digital tools can harm a child by isolating them from normal school processes. It can also harm staff by creating extra work. The reconciliation is not to reject tools wholesale, but to insist on proportionality and choice where feasible, and to understand that "choice" sometimes means "a slower alternative" rather than "an identical service without data collection".

Show: a parent refuses a communication app and the teacher must remember to send duplicate messages manually. Name: workload spillover. Explain: opt-outs can create administrative burden; schools may resist not out of malice but out of capacity limits. Implication: successful advocacy often offers a workable alternative and acknowledges staff constraints, turning conflict into collaboration.

A useful way to think about this is to treat the school as a steward and the vendor as a contractor. Stewardship implies duty: a school should be able to explain why a tool is used and what protections exist. Contracting implies boundaries: a vendor should not be permitted to use children's data for unrelated purposes. Parents do not need to master contractual law to care about this. They need to notice when explanations are absent or evasive.

Notice the language schools use when introducing tools. "Improves engagement." "Supports personalised learning." "Streamlines communication." These may be true. They also often function as gloss. A parent can request specifics without being combative: what data the platform collects, whether it requires personal accounts, whether there are advertising identifiers, whether data is deleted after a set period, and whether the school has assessed the tool's privacy impact. Asked politely, such questions are not outrageous. They signal that the parent is paying attention.

Paying attention is modelling.

The earlier theme of the home having internal doors applies here in institutional form. Schools have their own doors: the classroom, the staff room, the safeguarding file, the public website, the parent portal. Good data practice keeps those doors distinct. A child's learning data belongs behind one door. A public marketing photo belongs behind another. Problems arise when doors are left ajar for convenience: when public galleries are created with minimal access control, when children's names are paired with images publicly, when third-party tools are adopted without clear boundaries, when retention is indefinite because no one owns the task of deletion.

Show: a club posts a team list with children's full names and match locations on a publicly accessible page. Name: unnecessary exposure. Explain: information intended for community coordination becomes public by default; convenience overrides discretion. Implication: children can be made findable in ways no adult would tolerate for themselves.

There is also an often-overlooked psychological dimension: children learn their own worth partly through how institutions treat their data. When an institution is casual with privacy, children internalise that casualness. They learn that being documented and shared is normal, that refusal is awkward, that privacy is something only the anxious request. Conversely, when institutions make room for choice and treat it as normal, children learn that boundaries are legitimate.

Show: a school offers a discreet way for children who do not wish to be photographed to indicate so, and staff respect it without comment. Name: dignified opt-out. Explain: privacy choices can be implemented without singling children out; respect can be built into routine. Implication: children learn that autonomy can coexist with community participation.

The practical difficulty, and the one that trips many parents into silence, is social: how to ask without becoming the parent everyone dreads. The answer lies in tone and timing. Ask early, before systems are entrenched. Ask privately, not in public forums designed for group bonding. Ask for understanding rather than demanding perfection. A parent who begins with "I know you're busy, and I appreciate what you're doing" is not being obsequious; they are aligning with reality. A parent who asks for the simplest workable accommodation is often more effective than one who seeks to litigate every detail. The goal is not to win an argument. It is to shape a child's data environment.

This subchapter cannot promise that every school will be responsive, or that every vendor will behave impeccably. Some institutions will be exemplary. Some will be overwhelmed. Some will be defensive. Parents cannot control these outcomes. They can control whether they sleepwalk through consent forms and public galleries, or whether they treat them as meaningful decisions. They can also decide how to bring their child into the conversation, especially as the child grows older: asking what the child is comfortable with, explaining why the family cares, and practising the language of boundary-setting in low-stakes contexts.

The forward test that remains is both simple and uncomfortable, because it asks parents to trade convenience for deliberation. When a school, club, or team offers a new platform or posts a new gallery, does the family accept the default because it is easier, or do they pause long enough to ask which door the child's data is being pushed through—and whether that door should really be open?

Helping Teens Manage Data

In 2003, in Québec, a teenager named Ghyslain Raza recorded a short, awkward video for private amusement. It leaked, then spread, then became a global joke with a nickname that stuck. The details differ depending on who tells the story, but the outline is stubbornly checkable: a schoolboy clip, copied beyond its intended audience, became a durable artefact that followed him long after the moment should have faded. The technology of the time was almost quaint—early sharing sites, file transfers, the clumsy viral mechanics of a younger web—yet the social mechanism has barely changed. A private moment escapes. The audience grows. The meaning hardens. The internet keeps receipts.

That five-word sentence is not a slogan. It is a description of an environment. Teenagers live in an archive disguised as a conversation, and the task is not to frighten them into silence but to help them steer within that archive without pretending it can be abolished. Adult instincts often reach for the blunt tool—ban the platform, confiscate the phone, shut it all down—because blunt tools are satisfying. They produce a visible action. Yet they rarely produce durable skill. Teens do not need adults to win a temporary standoff. They need adults to help them build judgement under real conditions: social pressure, boredom, desire for belonging, occasional loneliness, and the relentless persuasion of apps designed to maximise attention.

Show: a teenager deletes a post in embarrassment and assumes it is gone. Name: persistence gap. Explain: deletion removes a visible copy but not necessarily screenshots, backups, re-uploads, or platform retention; the teen's mental model of "gone" may not match the system's. Implication: managing data begins with updating the mental model, not with moralising about posting.

If the earlier chapters treated privacy as doors and locks, teenage privacy is more like an audience with shifting boundaries. Adults often talk as if the primary threat is an unknown stranger. For many teenagers, the more immediate risk is a known peer with a phone and a grievance, or a group chat that turns cruel, or a moment of oversharing captured at precisely the wrong time. "Risk" here is not abstract. It is reputational, social, and sometimes painfully local. That is why teenagers respond poorly to lectures about faceless danger: the lecture does not match the lived terrain.

Show: a message meant for one friend is shared into a larger chat during a disagreement. Name: context collapse. Explain: digital communication makes it easy to move content between contexts; the sender cannot control redistribution once trust breaks. Implication: reputational safety depends less on perfect privacy settings and more on understanding how quickly context can collapse.

This does not mean privacy settings are pointless. It means settings are only one layer, and the most useful way to talk about them is not as technical toggles but as audience design. A teenager chooses an audience every time they post, even when they pretend they are "just sharing". The choice may be deliberate—close friends, a small account, a private story—or it may be accidental—public defaults, searchable profiles, open follower requests accepted without thought. Adults can help teens by translating settings into outcomes: who can see, who can search, who can contact, who can tag, and what happens when someone tries to share content onward. The most important shift is from "I trust my friends" to "I'm choosing an audience, and audiences change".

Show: a teenager keeps a profile public because "it's easier", then receives unwanted messages. Name: friction avoidance. Explain: teens often accept defaults to reduce hassle; platforms benefit from this because publicness increases engagement and data. Implication: small amounts of friction—waiting, approving, limiting—often buy disproportionate privacy.

Blocking and reporting sound mundane, even petty, until they are understood as boundary enforcement. Adults sometimes treat blocking as rude, as if social life were a dinner party where one must remain polite while being insulted. Teenagers, however, experience online contact as persistent and invasive in a way most adults did not at their age. A boundary that can be enforced quickly is not a social failure; it is a safety tool. The same is true of reporting: not because every report leads to swift justice—it often does not—but because reporting creates a record and, in many systems, shifts what the platform shows next. Reporting is not tattling. It is signalling: "This is not normal."

Show: a teen mutes and blocks an account after repeated harassment, then feels guilty for "overreacting". Name: boundary shame. Explain: social norms can frame self-protection as drama; platforms amplify this by making conflict public. Implication: one of the most protective lessons is that disengagement is a valid response, and guilt is not evidence of wrongdoing.

The motif of receipts becomes practical here. Teens already live with screenshots as a social fact. The useful move is to make screenshot awareness neither paranoid nor naïve: treat it as the default possibility, especially in conflicts, flirtations, and emotionally charged conversations. The point is not to ban intimacy or vulnerability. It is to place vulnerability in contexts where betrayal is less likely and consequences are manageable. Adults can respect teens by admitting that teens will talk about sensitive things; the question is whether teens have a working model of what can be captured and re-used.

Show: a teenager shares a private joke or confession in a disappearing-message feature and assumes it cannot be saved. Name: ephemerality illusion. Explain: "disappearing" refers to the sender's interface, not to the recipient's ability to capture; screenshots, second devices, and screen recordings exist. Implication: the safest assumption is that anything viewable can become a receipt.

This is where conversations about intimate images often appear, and they must be handled with care. The reality is that teenagers may face requests for images, may be pressured to share, may be threatened if they refuse, or may be targeted by scams that mix flattery with coercion. Speaking about this without turning it into a horror story requires a simple insistence: consent is the centre. The most dangerous moments often involve pressure—"prove you care", "everyone does it", "if you don't, I'll leave", "I'll show people what you already sent". Pressure is not romance. It is manipulation.

Show: a teen receives a request framed as affection, then a second message framed as urgency. Name: coercive escalation. Explain: manipulators often move quickly from warmth to threat because speed prevents reflection; the goal is compliance, not mutuality. Implication: teens who can name escalation can pause, and pausing is protective.

A respectful approach treats teens as capable of understanding trade-offs. Some teens will choose not to share intimate images at all. Some will choose to share within relationships, believing trust will hold. Adults cannot make that choice for them, and attempts to do so often backfire. What adults can do is clarify asymmetries: once an image exists outside the sender's control, it can be copied; once copied, it can travel; once it travels, it can be hard to retrieve. This is not a moral judgement. It is a technical and social property of digital media. It also intersects with law in many places, particularly when minors are involved; laws vary by jurisdiction, and families should avoid improvising legal interpretations under stress. The practical point remains: reduce situations where someone else holds leverage over a teen's privacy.

Show: a scammer impersonates a peer and requests an image, then threatens exposure. Name: social engineering. Explain: scams rely on impersonation, urgency, and shame; the target is not the device but the person's emotions. Implication: the antidote is not cleverness but having a plan for disclosure that does not trigger punishment or humiliation.

Here a limitation deserves honesty. Not every risk can be mitigated through personal skill. Some harms come from structural features: platforms that default to publicness, schools that require specific tools, group dynamics that punish refusal, or abusive individuals determined to cause damage. Even perfect privacy behaviour cannot guarantee perfect outcomes. The reconciliation is that skill still matters because it changes probabilities and recovery time. A teen who knows how to lock down an account, document harassment, and ask for help early is not invincible; they are more resilient.

A second named, checkable example helps to ground persistence in something beyond schoolyard drama. In May 2014, in Luxembourg, the Court of Justice of the European Union decided *Google Spain SL, Google Inc. v Agencia Española de Protección de Datos (AEPD) and Mario Costeja González*, a case that became famous for shaping what is often called the "right to be forgotten" in European data protection discourse. Whatever one's view of the decision, it crystallised a tension that matters for teenagers: the web's memory is not naturally humane. Societies sometimes have to *deliberately* create forgetting mechanisms because systems prefer accumulation. For teens, the practical echo is clear: reputations form early, often around moments that should be transient. A teen does not need to memorise European case law to benefit from the underlying idea—persistence is a default, and forgetting requires work.

Show: a teenager searches their own name and finds old content they assumed had vanished. Name: self-indexing. Explain: search functions as an external mirror; it reveals how platforms and other people present you to the world. Implication: reputation management is not vanity; it is understanding what the world can learn with minimal effort.

Reputation is not only about outsiders. It is also about the future self. Teenagers are in the business of becoming someone else. They try identities, aesthetics, opinions, friendships. This is normal developmental work. The danger is that online systems reward permanence: you are encouraged to build a "brand", to be consistent, to gather followers, to archive your self as if you were a product. Helping teens manage data includes giving them permission to change—while giving them tools to prevent old selves from being weaponised.

Show: a teen leaves an old account untouched because it feels embarrassing to revisit it. Name: abandonment risk. Explain: dormant accounts can still reveal information and can sometimes be compromised; embarrassment discourages maintenance. Implication: tending to old accounts is a form of self-respect, not a tedious chore.

There is a practical skill hidden inside this: separating identity contexts. Teens already do it informally—one account for close friends, one for broader circles, one for public interests. Adults sometimes misread this as deception. It can be. It can also be healthy privacy architecture: internal doors again, but for identity. The ethical line is not whether a teen has more than one context; it is whether those contexts are used to harm others or to evade accountability. A teen who uses a private account to share art with friends is not the same as a teen who uses anonymity to bully. Context separation is a tool. Tools inherit the intent of the user.

Show: a teen keeps a "close friends" circle for personal updates and a separate public profile for hobbies. Name: compartmentalisation. Explain: different audiences warrant different disclosures; mixing them increases risk of misunderstanding and redistribution. Implication: teaching teens to manage audiences is more realistic than demanding one unified, constantly public self.

Blocking, reporting, and settings deal with known threats. Another strand of teenage data risk is the unknown: automated profiling, recommendation systems, and, increasingly, synthetic media. As of the mid-2020s, generative tools have made it easier to fabricate convincing images, voices, and screenshots. This does not mean every teen is at constant risk of sophisticated forgery; it does mean that "seeing is believing" has weakened, and the social use of falsified material is more plausible than it was a decade ago. The practical implication is not panic. It is caution about evidence: pause before reacting, verify with a direct channel, and remember that outrage is a lever others can pull.

Show: a teen receives a screenshot of a message allegedly sent by a friend and is urged to "look what they said about you". Name: manufactured conflict. Explain: altered screenshots and miscontextualised content can inflame groups; anger spreads faster than verification. Implication: reputation management includes emotional management—slowing down before responding.

Throughout all of this, the decisive factor is the relationship between teens and the adults who can help them. Teenagers are more likely to seek support when they believe the adult response will be calm, proportional, and focused on solving the problem rather than assigning shame. Shame is the enemy of disclosure. It drives mistakes underground. A teen who fears that asking for help will result in total phone confiscation is a teen who will delay asking until the problem is larger.

Show: a teen hesitates to report harassment because they fear losing their device, which is also their social lifeline. Name: help-seeking barrier. Explain: punitive responses make help costly; teens weigh that cost against the harm they're facing and often choose silence. Implication: adults who want early disclosure must make early disclosure safe.

The most respectful stance treats teens as partners: capable of understanding the environment, capable of choosing, capable of making mistakes, and capable of learning. Partnership does not mean adults abdicate responsibility. It means adults shift from policing to coaching. Coaching looks like asking what happened, what the teen wants, what the likely consequences are, and what the smallest next move is that reduces harm. It looks like treating privacy settings as routine maintenance rather than as a moral referendum. It looks like practising boundary phrases that make refusal easier under pressure, and practising them when no one is in note-perfect crisis mode.

The forward test is as sharp as it is ordinary. When a teenager's phone lights up with something that feels urgent—flattering, threatening, humiliating, intoxicating—do they have enough internal space to pause before they respond, and do they have at least one adult relationship where asking for help does not come with a price that feels unbearable?

Chapter 10
Travel And Location Privacy

In October 2013, in Paris, a young data analyst named David Thompson set out to prove a point that sounded abstract until he made it embarrassingly concrete. He took a set of anonymised location traces—mere latitude and longitude points, stripped of names—and showed how easily a person could be singled out by routine: the place they slept, the place they worked, the café they visited on Tuesdays. The work was published in *Nature* that month, and it carried a quietly unsettling implication for anyone who has ever treated their movements as "just background": location is identity, even when the labels are removed. A suitcase zip rasping shut in a hotel room, the stale smell of airport coffee, the vibration of a phone as it latches onto a foreign network—these are sensory details of travel, but they are also the sound and texture of a dataset forming.

Travel makes you legible.

That is the paradox at the heart of modern mobility. Travelling is supposed to loosen the grip of routine. It is a voluntary untethering: different streets, different time zones, different weather, a small rupture in the calendar. Yet the same devices that make travel effortless—maps that whisper turn-by-turn instructions, boarding passes that live inside an app, translation tools that remove friction, ride-hailing services that summon a car with two taps—also tighten the net of traceability. The traveller gains convenience and loses opacity. A person can be physically far from home while being digitally more exposed than usual.

The shift happens because travel changes the conditions under which privacy decisions are made. At home, devices sit inside familiar boundaries: trusted Wi-Fi, predictable routines, a drawer where passports and spare keys live, a front door and a bed. Away from home, those boundaries fray. The phone is used in crowds.

Laptops open on café tables. Screens are read over shoulders. Connections are improvised. The risk is not only technical. It is situational. A crowded airport lounge is not merely a room; it is a theatre of accidental disclosure, where people speak loud enough for microphones, type on keyboards in full view, and leave devices unattended for a moment that turns out to be long enough.

Show: a traveller checks into a hotel, hands over a passport, connects to "Free Wi-Fi", and taps through a splash page without reading. Name: travel autopilot. Explain: travel is cognitively demanding—tickets, timing, fatigue, unfamiliar signage—so people default to speed over deliberation; systems are designed to capitalise on this. Implication: the moment you most need careful boundaries is precisely when you are least inclined to maintain them.

This chapter sits at the crossroads of two themes already running through the book: the idea that privacy is not secrecy but control, and the recognition that control must be adapted to context. Travel is the purest test of that adaptability. The same settings that feel sensible at home can be wrong on the road, not because your morals change, but because the audience changes. At home, the audience for your digital life is mostly your chosen circle—family, colleagues, the platforms you use. During travel, the audience expands to include strangers in shared spaces, network operators in unfamiliar jurisdictions, and, sometimes, officials whose job includes scrutiny. The question is not whether travel is "safe" or "unsafe". The question is how to carry only what you intend to carry, and how to remain calm when conditions are not yours to control.

Consider the modern travel itinerary. Even a short trip can produce a thick braid of data: airline booking records, hotel check-ins, payment card transactions, location histories, roaming logs, ride receipts, digital keys, photos tagged with place and time. Some of this data is necessary. Some is optional. Much is created without anyone consciously choosing it. A person can spend an evening wandering an unfamiliar city feeling anonymous in the crowd, and still generate a precise timeline of movement in the background, captured by apps, devices, and services that treat location as a default signal.

Show: a traveller opens a map to find a museum, then keeps the app running while walking, then uses the same phone to pay for lunch, then posts a photo of the meal. Name: chain correlation. Explain: separate services can be linked via time, location, device identifiers, and account logins; travel compresses these signals into a dense, easily correlated set. Implication: travel does not merely create more data; it creates data that is easier to connect.

The stakes are not uniform. For some, the chief worry is petty theft: a phone left in a taxi or lifted in a crowd. For others, the stakes include professional confidentiality, activism, sensitive research, or the simple fact that being publicly "found" in the wrong place can create social risk. For still others, the risk is less dramatic but still costly: account takeover after using a dubious network, or a family photo archive exposed by an over-broad sharing link sent from an airport gate. The same trip can be a lighthearted holiday and, simultaneously, a shift in one's risk profile. The sensible response is not paranoia. It is proportional preparation.

And yet, travel preparation often focuses on the tangible: chargers, adapters, passports, insurance documents. Digital preparation is treated as an optional add-on—something for the unusually cautious, the kind of person who travels with a money belt. The irony is that many travellers already carry their most valuable asset in their pocket: not the phone as an object, but the access it grants. A modern phone is a master key. It opens email, banking, photos, work accounts, messaging histories, boarding passes. Losing the device is annoying; losing control of what the device unlocks is the real cost.

Show: a traveller realises their phone is missing and panics less about the hardware than about the accounts attached to it. Name: access gravity. Explain: accounts cluster around the primary device; authentication, saved passwords, and trusted sessions turn the phone into a hub. Implication: the goal is not to guard a gadget like a jewel; it is to reduce how much the gadget can expose if it vanishes.

That reduction begins before departure, in a set of choices that feel almost boring: updating, backing up, and deciding what does and does not need to be on the device. These are not "security theatre". They are the preconditions for calm. A traveller who knows their data is backed up is freer to use stronger locks, to log out of certain accounts, and to make more conservative choices about what to carry. A traveller who has postponed updates and left everything logged in is travelling with the digital equivalent of an unlocked suitcase.

Travel also forces a confrontation with networks. The air itself feels different when your phone switches carriers: the little letters in the status bar, the new roaming icon, the sudden flood of notifications as a connection returns. Public Wi-Fi is tempting not because people are foolish, but because travel is expensive and connectivity is a habit. A hotel network, an airport lounge, a café chain—these offer familiarity and relief. They also create shared spaces where the boundary between "my connection" and "our connection" is thinner than most people intuitively grasp.

A credible limitation belongs here, because network risk is often dramatised. Many everyday internet services are now protected by HTTPS, which encrypts the content between the device and the website or app, making casual eavesdropping harder than it once was. This is real progress. It does not mean public Wi-Fi is harmless. It means the risks have shifted: the most common hazards are now often about malicious hotspots, captive portals, device exposure, and the leakage of metadata and behaviour patterns rather than someone casually "reading your emails" like a spy in a film. The reconciliation is simple: public networks are not automatically catastrophic, but they are rarely the place to do your most sensitive work.

Show: a traveller uses airport Wi-Fi to browse general information without incident, then later uses it for a sensitive login and receives a suspicious prompt. Name: risk mixing. Explain: people treat a network as either "safe" or "unsafe" and then behave consistently, but risk varies by activity; authentication events are higher stakes than casual browsing. Implication: the most useful habit is not blanket avoidance but activity triage.

Then there are borders. Border crossings are liminal spaces: queues, fluorescent lighting, the fatigue of travel, the subtle pressure to be compliant and quick. In some jurisdictions, devices may be inspected; in others, the legal landscape is different; in all cases, the traveller is in a place where the ordinary assumption of privacy is reduced. People often do not think about this until they are standing at a desk being asked to unlock a phone, at which point the decisions become stressed and reactive. The more interesting question is not what to do in that moment—this is not legal guidance, and laws vary—but how to avoid having to improvise under pressure. Planning is privacy's quiet superpower.

Show: a traveller reaches a border checkpoint with a phone full of work documents, personal messages, and family photos, and realises there is no clear separation between "what I need for the trip" and "everything I am". Name: carry burden. Explain: devices accumulate; travel exposes the accumulation to contexts where scrutiny is possible; the burden is psychological as much as technical. Implication: deliberate reduction of on-device data is not about secrecy; it is about choice and peace of mind.

Location itself is the final strand. Travel is, by definition, movement through space, and space is now logged by default. Maps, ride-hailing, weather apps, photo libraries, fitness trackers, airline apps, car infotainment systems—all of these can record location histories. Some do so overtly with timelines; others do so quietly via permissions and analytics. The result is that a trip can be reconstructed after the fact with unsettling precision, sometimes by the traveller themselves when a "memories" feature resurfaces a photo tagged with a place they had forgotten. Location logs can be useful—safety check-ins, finding a lost phone, retracing a route. They can also be revealing in ways the traveller did not intend.

The modern car adds a twist. Many cars now behave like rolling computers: connecting to phones, syncing contacts, remembering destinations, storing call logs, keeping paired devices. A hire car or a friend's vehicle can become an unintentional archive of a trip. The traveller who carefully manages phone settings may still leave traces in the car's system without noticing. This is not a reason to refuse modern convenience. It is a reason to treat travel as a temporary state with its own defaults, rather than as life-as-usual in a new postcode.

Show: a traveller pairs their phone with a rental car for navigation, then returns the car without considering what the car retained. Name: peripheral memory. Explain: devices around us—cars, TVs, tablets—store fragments of our data when connected; travel increases the number of unfamiliar devices we connect to. Implication: privacy is not only in the phone; it is in the web of machines we casually touch.

If this sounds heavy, it need not be. The tone of this book has never been to demand an impossible purity. The promise is smaller and more humane: reduce the amount you expose when you are least able to monitor it. Travel is the moment when small, deliberate choices pay unusually large dividends, precisely because the environment is noisy and unpredictable. A traveller cannot control whether a bag is jostled in a crowd, whether a café Wi-Fi is misconfigured, or whether a queue is long and tiring. A traveller can control how much sensitive material is sitting unlocked behind a screen, how easily their accounts can be re-entered if something goes wrong, and how much of their movement is logged by default.

The closing question that carries this chapter forward is not "How can a person travel without leaving traces?"—that is rarely realistic. It is sharper, and more liberating: when a trip is over, what do you want the record of it to look like, and who do you want to be able to read it?

Preparing Devices For Travel

In October 2017, in Washington, D.C., U.S. Customs and Border Protection published a set of figures that made an old truth newly specific: border officials were searching tens of thousands of electronic devices each year. The number for fiscal year 2017 was 30,200, CBP said in its own reporting that autumn; the point was not the exact tally so much as the fact that device search had become a normal administrative act rather than a rare drama. Imagine the scene at almost any international arrivals hall—the hard shine of floor tiles, the stale warmth of recycled air, the low electrical buzz of lighting—and add one modern intimacy: the small rectangle in a traveller's hand that contains their work, their family, their private jokes, their anxieties, their banking keys, their photos. A passport has always been a travel document. A phone has become one too, except it carries far more than anyone ever intended to present at a desk. Pack light, digitally, for once.

Travel changes a person's risk profile for the same reason it changes their posture. At home, devices live inside a domestic rhythm: familiar networks, predictable places to charge, the quiet assumption that if something goes wrong it can be handled tomorrow. Travel breaks that rhythm. Devices are used in queues, in crowds, in taxis, on café tables, in unfamiliar jurisdictions and languages, often under fatigue. The threat is not a single villain with a single plan. It is the accumulation of small exposures: a shoulder glance at a passcode, a lost bag, an opportunistic theft, an insecure network, an unexpected request to unlock a device, the simple fact of being physically separated from one's usual support systems. What feels like "just using the phone" at home becomes, while travelling, a sequence of risk-bearing acts performed in public.

Show: a traveller checks in at an airport kiosk, then opens email to find a boarding pass, then toggles to a banking app to confirm a transaction, then messages a colleague about a meeting, all while standing in a line that inches forward under fluorescent light. Name:

exposure stacking. Explain: travel concentrates sensitive actions into shared spaces, and shared spaces expand the audience—people, cameras, network operators, sometimes officials—whether or not anyone is actively hostile. Implication: the same device settings and habits that feel adequate at home can be insufficient when the audience quietly multiplies.

The first move in preparing devices for travel is conceptual, not technical. It is the decision to treat the trip as a temporary state with its own defaults. A person does this instinctively with luggage: they do not take every possession they own, because carrying everything is exhausting and unnecessary. Digital life, however, is often carried by default, because devices are designed to make carrying effortless. Accounts stay signed in. Photos sync automatically. Password managers and email clients hold the keys ready. The result is a device that functions like an overpacked suitcase: convenient until it is dropped, lost, or opened by someone else.

Show: a traveller loses a phone in a taxi and feels a specific kind of panic—less about the cost of replacement hardware and more about the unlocked access sitting inside. Name: access concentration. Explain: modern devices are hubs, not mere tools; they hold authentication tokens, saved sessions, and recovery pathways that can lead into other accounts. Implication: "losing a phone" is increasingly "losing a bundle of doors", which is why preparation is less about guarding objects and more about limiting what those objects can reveal.

This is where updating and backing up—two chores everyone knows and many postpone—become travel hygiene. Updates matter in a banal way: they close known vulnerabilities and fix security flaws that have already been observed in the wild. Backups matter in a psychological way: they reduce the fear of loss, and fear is the reason people keep devices configured for maximum convenience. A person who is confident their data exists elsewhere can tolerate stronger local protections and more selective syncing. A person who is not confident tends to keep everything available, everywhere, all at once, because the device feels like the only copy.

Show: a phone displays a long-postponed update notice the night before departure, and the traveller dismisses it because "now isn't the time". Name: departure procrastination. Explain: the moments before travel are busy; people prioritise the visible tasks—packing, tickets, routes—over invisible risk reduction. Implication: travel preparation works best when it is framed as removing future stress, not as performing a virtuous ritual.

Reducing what a device carries does not require theatrics. It begins with an inventory: what genuinely needs to travel, and what is merely along for the ride because it has always been there. Many travellers carry entire photo libraries when they only need a handful of documents. Many carry full work chat histories when they only need today's contacts. Many keep every account logged in because logging out feels like friction with no immediate payoff. Travel makes the payoff immediate, even if the traveller would prefer not to think about it: theft is more common in crowded tourist corridors; devices are handled more frequently; the chance of a momentary lapse increases. The traveller is not becoming paranoid by acknowledging probability. They are thinking like an adult.

Show: a traveller leaves for a week and realises, only after arriving, that a device contains years of archived messages and saved documents that have nothing to do with the trip. Name: default carry. Explain: devices default to keeping data close because closeness increases engagement and convenience; users rarely revisit that default. Implication: travel is an opportunity to practise deliberate carrying—an exercise in choosing what is worth having in the pocket.

Sometimes the cleanest way to reduce carry is separation: keeping high-sensitivity accounts or datasets off the travel device entirely. People vary in what counts as "high-sensitivity". For one person it is work research. For another it is family photos. For another it is health-related records. The point is not to declare a universal hierarchy but to notice that travel introduces new audiences and therefore changes what "appropriate exposure" looks like. Some travellers use a separate email identity for travel logistics. Some use temporary accounts for hotel booking sites that do not need to know a lifetime's history. Some keep a dedicated travel device with only the essentials, the way one might keep a spare key.

Show: a researcher travels to a conference with a laptop containing a full archive of interviews and participant notes, then realises the archive is both precious and irrelevant to the trip itself. Name: relevance trimming. Explain: carrying data "just in case" is often a failure to distinguish between what might be useful and what would be catastrophic to lose. Implication: travel preparation is an exercise in relevance: the smaller the carried dataset, the smaller the potential harm.

A second named example makes the stakes vivid without sensationalising them. In August 2013, at Heathrow Airport in London, David Miranda—partner of journalist Glenn Greenwald—was detained under Schedule 7 of the UK Terrorism Act 2000 while transiting through the airport, and electronic devices were seized. The incident became internationally reported and legally contested, and it sits in the travel imagination because it shows how quickly routine movement can collide with scrutiny, especially when a traveller's work or associations attract attention. Most readers will never be in that situation. That is precisely the point. A traveller does not need to predict a particular encounter to recognise the general principle: once a device holds everything, any unexpected scrutiny becomes more consequential.

Show: a person assumes travel risk is mostly about pickpockets, then hears of a transit detention involving device seizure and realises the risk landscape includes institutional power as well as opportunism. Name: threat expansion. Explain: travel shifts the balance of power; a traveller can encounter both petty theft and official scrutiny, and devices are relevant in both scenarios. Implication: preparation that reduces on-device exposure is valuable even when the traveller is law-abiding and uninteresting, because it reduces the stakes of surprises.

None of this implies that everyone should travel with a "clean" phone or a wiped laptop. That would be unrealistic for many jobs, families, and research contexts. It would also be, in some cases, counterproductive—devices that appear unusually blank can attract curiosity, and some travellers need access to accounts to function. The limitation is real: travel preparation is constrained by necessity. The reconciliation is equally real: constraint does not remove choice; it shifts choice towards compromise. A person who must carry work data can still reduce personal archives. A person who must carry personal archives can still reduce the number of logged-in services. A person who cannot carry a separate device can still separate identities within the device by using different accounts, different browsers, or different app profiles where available.

Show: a consultant travelling for work cannot avoid carrying confidential documents, because the trip exists for the documents. Name: necessity constraint. Explain: the value of travel lies in what must be done on the road; preparation cannot wish that away. Implication: privacy does not demand purity; it demands proportionality—reduce what you can, accept what you must, and understand the trade.

There is also a quiet human factor: stress. Many people keep everything signed in because they fear being locked out while abroad. This fear is not irrational. Account recovery can be harder when the usual phone number is roaming, when a security prompt triggers in a different country, or when multi-factor authentication depends on an app that has been lost with the phone. Travel preparation therefore includes thinking about continuity—not in the sense of creating an invulnerable system, but in the sense of reducing single points of failure. If the phone is the only device that can receive a code, the phone becomes a chokepoint. If a password manager exists only on one device and the device is lost, the trip becomes miserable. The aim is to build a little redundancy without building a shrine to preparedness.

Show: a traveller reaches a hotel and cannot sign into a key account because the second factor is tied to a device that has just been misplaced. Name: authentication choke. Explain: security mechanisms often assume stable access to devices and networks; travel destabilises both. Implication: travel readiness includes designing access pathways that can survive loss, because resilience is part of privacy.

The metaphor of packing light helps here because it makes trade-offs honest. Packing light is not about deprivation. It is about choosing what matters. A traveller who reduces on-device data is not trying to be invisible. They are trying to keep the trip's inevitable risks from turning into a life-wide breach. They are choosing, in advance, what they are willing to lose. That choice can be made calmly at home. It is far harder to make in a crowded terminal after discovering a missing bag.

Show: a person prepares a travel device so that, if it disappears, the loss is bounded to travel logistics rather than personal history. Name: bounded loss design. Explain: by limiting what is stored locally and what remains logged in, the harm radius of a single incident shrinks. Implication: the traveller gains a kind of freedom—the freedom to respond to problems without existential dread.

This boundedness extends beyond data to identity signals. Travel involves frequent identity checks: airline apps, hotel reservations, ride accounts, loyalty programmes. Each check often invites additional disclosure—middle names, dates of birth, passport numbers, personal preferences—sometimes for legitimate reasons, sometimes out of habit. While this book avoids legal and financial advice, it can still point to an educational principle: disclosure should be proportionate to purpose. Travellers who treat forms and sign-ups as negotiable rather than compulsory often end up disclosing less without losing the service. The device, meanwhile, should not become a permanent repository of every identity artefact used during the trip.

Show: a traveller uses a booking app that retains passport details after check-in, then forgets it does so. Name: identity residue. Explain: travel services store identifiers for convenience and repeat business; users rarely return to remove them. Implication: travel preparation includes thinking beyond the trip—what identifiers will remain cached, and where?

The motif returns because it is more than a neat analogy. Packing light is a moral stance towards technology: it refuses the idea that convenience must always mean accumulation. It also protects against the most common travel mishaps. Theft is not exotic. Misplacement is not rare. Lapses happen. A device prepared with a smaller footprint turns those lapses into manageable problems rather than catastrophes.

There is one more subtle benefit to preparation: it changes how a person uses devices during travel. When a phone holds everything, it invites constant use. When it holds only what matters for the trip, its role becomes clearer: navigation, communication, logistics, perhaps a small set of work tasks. Clarity reduces compulsive checking, and reduced checking reduces exposure. The traveller becomes slightly less "chattery", not by force, but by design.

Show: a traveller with a pared-back device finds themselves less tempted to scroll through private archives in public spaces. Name: behavioural drift control. Explain: the contents of a device shape behaviour; fewer temptations mean fewer moments of inadvertent exposure. Implication: privacy is not only settings; it is behaviour shaped by design.

The forward test is simple and, for many, uncomfortable precisely because it asks for an explicit decision. Before a trip begins, what is the smallest set of data and access that still allows the journey to function—and what, if lost, would become an avoidable disaster?

Using Public Wi Fi Wisely

In October 2017, in Leuven, Belgium, the security researcher Mathy Vanhoef disclosed a practical attack against WPA2—the Wi-Fi security standard that most people assumed was "the safe one". The disclosure, quickly nicknamed KRACK, mattered less for its acronyms than for its timing: it arrived after years in which cafés and airports had persuaded travellers that the danger lay mainly in obvious, passwordless networks. The scene is easy to picture because it repeats daily in softer form: a hotel lobby with a faint chlorine tang drifting from a nearby pool, the constant hush of air conditioning, a phone tilting towards a "Free Wi-Fi" network as if the name itself were a promise. What Vanhoef's work made plain is that public connectivity is never a single risk with a single fix; it is a moving target made of standards, implementations, and human habits, all layered together in a place where strangers share the same invisible medium. Assume the air is shared.

That phrase sounds like paranoia until one thinks about what Wi-Fi is: not a private wire, but a shared radio space. The convenience is precisely that nothing needs to be plugged in. The cost is that the boundary between "my connection" and "our environment" is thinner than intuition suggests. People rarely feel this because the interface hides it. A padlock icon appears in a browser, a network name appears on a list, and the mind supplies a story: connection achieved, problem solved. Travel invites this story because travel is full of friction—queues, delays, unfamiliar signs—so any friction removed feels like a gift. The trick is to accept the gift without handing over the keys.

Show: a traveller in an airport lounge joins a network labelled with the airline's name, taps through a captive portal, then opens their inbox to pull up a meeting link. Name: borrowed trust. Explain:

public Wi-Fi often asks for trust based on branding rather than proof, and branding is easy to mimic; the interface makes networks look like places, when they are really signals. Implication: the wisest stance is not fear, but scepticism—treat a network like a room full of people, not like the privacy of one's kitchen.

What can someone on the same network actually see? The honest answer is: less than sensational headlines imply, but more than most people assume. Modern web traffic is often protected by HTTPS, which encrypts the content between a device and a website; that is why a stranger in the next seat cannot typically read the text of an email or the contents of a banking page simply by "listening" to the network. This is a real improvement, and it deserves the credit. Yet encryption of content does not erase the existence of communication. It does not erase patterns. It does not erase the fact that your device is making connections, to particular services, at particular times, from a particular place, while broadcasting technical identifiers that help networks function. Even when a message is sealed, the envelope still travels.

Show: a laptop connects to a hotel network and immediately begins talking—checking for updates, syncing messages, refreshing cloud files—before the traveller has opened a single app. Name: background chatter. Explain: devices maintain a steady pulse of network activity for convenience and reliability; public networks expose that pulse to more observers and more intermediaries. Implication: the question is not only "what could be read?" but "what could be inferred?"—and inference is often enough to create discomfort or risk.

In practical terms, there are three broad categories of risk on public Wi-Fi, and they overlap. The first is passive observation: seeing unencrypted traffic, capturing metadata, watching which domains are queried via DNS, noticing device names that users never meant to share. The second is active interference: a malicious hotspot that imitates a legitimate one, a network operator or attacker who manipulates traffic, a captive portal that nudges a user towards a fake login screen, a local attacker who exploits weak device settings to probe for open services. The third is the human layer: people mistyping network names, clicking security warnings away, reusing passwords, leaving devices unlocked while a connection is "sorting itself out". Public Wi-Fi is rarely dangerous because of one cinematic manoeuvre. It is dangerous because it offers many small handles.

A historical moment makes the point without melodrama. In October 2010, in San Diego, the developer Eric Butler released Firesheep, a browser extension that demonstrated session hijacking on open Wi-Fi. The demonstration mattered because it was not obscure; it was easy. Firesheep did not crack passwords by brute force. It took advantage of a then-common pattern in which websites protected the login page but not the session cookie that kept a user logged in. In plain terms, a person could watch another person's session and step into it. The ensuing public discussion helped push the web towards wider adoption of full-session HTTPS. That is the limitation, and it is a hopeful one: public demonstrations can drive better defaults. The reconciliation is equally important: improved defaults reduce certain attacks, but they do not turn a shared network into a private one, and they do not protect against every kind of manipulation or mistake.

Show: a traveller hears that "everything is encrypted now" and relaxes into doing high-stakes tasks on any network that offers a signal. Name: encryption complacency. Explain: HTTPS blocks many forms of casual snooping, but it does not validate that a network is honest, and it does not prevent every form of deception—especially when users override warnings or when attackers exploit the edges. Implication: progress is real, but it is not permission to abandon judgement.

Judgement becomes easier when abstract "risk" is tied to visible behaviours. Consider what changes when a device joins public Wi-Fi. The device typically accepts an IP address, a default gateway, and a DNS resolver offered by the network. That DNS resolver—essentially a directory service translating names into addresses—often reveals which services a device is trying to reach. Even if the content is encrypted, the fact of the query can be informative: email provider, social network, corporate login, medical portal, travel itinerary. Some of these signals are blunt; some are subtle. A network operator can log them. A malicious actor on the network can sometimes nudge or poison them, depending on the environment and the device's safeguards. This is not guaranteed catastrophe; it is an exposure surface.

Show: a café's Wi-Fi uses an advertising-supported provider that logs browsing-related metadata in exchange for "free" connectivity. Name: subsidised access. Explain: a service must pay for bandwidth, hardware, and maintenance; "free" often means monetised via data collection, marketing, or behavioural profiling. Implication: the cost of public Wi-Fi is frequently paid in information rather than cash, and the traveller should decide which currency is acceptable.

The second layer is the hotspot itself. "Evil twin" attacks—where an attacker creates a hotspot with a plausible name—are a classic because they exploit the easiest weakness: people's expectations. Hotels and airports often have multiple networks. Names vary by terminal or floor. The legitimate network may be "Airport WiFi", "Airport_Free", "Airport Guest", "Airport-Public". A malicious hotspot need only be nearby and more convincing. When a device auto-joins known network names, the risk increases. When a user is tired and in a hurry, the risk increases again. The most powerful security measure is not a complex tool; it is the habit of treating network names as claims that require verification.

Show: a traveller sees two similar network names and chooses the stronger signal without noticing the subtle spelling difference. Name: signal bias. Explain: humans are trained to interpret stronger signal as better service; attackers can exploit this by offering a stronger, closer hotspot. Implication: in shared spaces, the most persuasive cue is not always the safest cue.

A third layer is what a local attacker can do even without reading encrypted content. On many public networks, devices can "see" each other at least partially—sometimes they can discover other devices, sometimes they cannot, depending on how the network is configured. Even when a network uses client isolation, mistakes happen, and not all venues configure networks thoughtfully. A device that exposes file sharing, remote administration tools, or poorly secured services can become visible. The technical details vary by platform and settings, but the underlying point is constant: public networks widen the circle of potential proximity attacks, and proximity is powerful. A stranger does not need to break encryption if they can find a misconfigured service on the device itself.

Still, it is worth being honest about probabilities. The average traveller in a café is far more likely to be targeted by generic scams—phishing prompts, fake login pages, opportunistic theft—than by a sophisticated network-level attack. That is not comforting; it is clarifying. It means that "using public Wi-Fi wisely" is chiefly about preventing ordinary failures under ordinary pressure. Wisdom is a posture of triage: deciding which tasks are acceptable on borrowed infrastructure and which are not.

Show: a traveller uses hotel Wi-Fi for a low-stakes activity, then later attempts a sensitive login and receives an unusual prompt that they dismiss because they are already late. Name: task mixing. Explain: when all tasks share the same network context, the mind treats them as equivalent; fatigue compresses nuance. Implication: a simple personal rule—about which tasks can wait—reduces the moments when fatigue and high stakes collide.

That personal rule does not need to be elaborate. Think in terms of "reversible" and "irreversible" actions. Reading a news article is reversible; if something odd happens, closing the tab ends the exposure. Logging into an email account, approving a payment, changing account recovery settings—these actions are not easily reversible, because they create new states and new permissions. Public Wi-Fi is not automatically hostile, but it is inherently less controllable. A wise traveller treats uncontrollable infrastructure as a poor place for irreversible actions. The rule is not moral. It is practical.

Show: an airport Wi-Fi works perfectly for browsing maps and checking gate information, but feels less suitable for resetting a password or approving a sensitive transfer. Name: reversibility test. Explain: the more permanent the consequence, the more a traveller benefits from using a more trusted channel, such as a known mobile connection. Implication: privacy becomes a series of small design choices rather than a vague aspiration.

Mobile data occupies a peculiar place in the imagination. People sometimes treat it as "more secure" in a mystical way. It is not magic; it is simply different. A mobile connection generally removes the shared local Wi-Fi environment and its easiest proximity attacks. It also reduces the chance of joining a malicious hotspot by accident. That is a real advantage. It does not eliminate every risk: mobile carriers can still observe metadata, roaming introduces its own complexities, and a compromised device remains compromised regardless of network. The point is not to crown mobile data as virtuous, but to recognise it as a different trade-off that, in many travel situations, aligns better with sensitive tasks.

Show: a traveller uses mobile data for an important login because the channel is not shared with the strangers around them. Name: channel separation. Explain: separating high-stakes actions from high-exposure environments reduces the number of variables that can go wrong at once. Implication: a traveller gains calm not by seeking perfect safety, but by reducing simultaneous uncertainty.

Tools like VPNs often appear here, wrapped in marketing. It is worth stripping the idea down to its mechanics. A VPN encrypts traffic between the device and a VPN provider, which can reduce what local network operators and nearby attackers can observe or manipulate. That is the benefit. The cost is that the VPN provider becomes a new point of trust: it can see certain metadata, and the user is substituting one intermediary for another. This is not an argument for or against VPNs as a category. It is an argument for understanding what is being swapped. Public Wi-Fi already asks for borrowed trust. A VPN rearranges who is being trusted, not whether trust is involved.

Show: a traveller installs a VPN app in a panic after reading a headline, without considering who runs it or what it logs. Name: trust displacement. Explain: encrypting a channel to a third party is only as comforting as the third party is reliable; the security story changes shape, but it does not vanish. Implication: wise use of protective tools begins with naming the new trust relationship rather than pretending it is neutrality.

The fishbowl motif fits because public Wi-Fi is not only a technical environment; it is a social one. People behave differently when they feel observed, and they misbehave when they forget they might be. A hotel lobby is a fishbowl: glass doors, cameras, passers-by, the quiet sense of being in public even when one is alone. Wi-Fi extends that fishbowl into the invisible layer of communication. The traveller does not need to imagine a hostile audience at every table. They only need to remember that the room is not theirs.

This is where "secure connections" become less about a checklist and more about an attitude. A secure connection is not only a padlock icon. It is also the refusal to override certificate warnings casually. It is the habit of noticing when a network requires unexpected reauthentication. It is the discipline of keeping high-stakes work inside environments one can better evaluate. The traveller who cultivates these habits becomes less vulnerable to the most common public Wi-Fi tricks, which depend on hurried compliance rather than advanced exploitation.

A second named, checkable example underlines how venue networks can become attack surfaces without being obviously "bad". In 2014, Kaspersky Lab published reporting on what it called "DarkHotel", a campaign that targeted business travellers via hotel networks, using techniques such as delivering trojanised software updates through captive portals. The details of the campaign belong to security history, but the enduring lesson is simpler: hotels are not security companies, yet they run infrastructure that travellers treat as a neutral utility. The attack exploited that mismatch. Hotels wanted guests online. Travellers wanted frictionless connectivity. Attackers wanted a believable distribution channel. The fishbowl acquired a hidden drain.

Show: a traveller accepts a prompt to install an "update" because it appears in the context of a reputable hotel, and reputability is mistaken for technical integrity. Name: contextual authority. Explain: humans outsource trust to surroundings; the nicer the venue, the less likely they are to suspect deception. Implication: wise use of public Wi-Fi includes resisting prompts that piggyback on the venue's authority.

None of this requires a bunker mentality. It requires clarity about what public Wi-Fi is for. It is for convenience when the stakes are low, and for bridging gaps when one has no better option. It is not the ideal channel for the most sensitive, irreversible actions—those can often wait for a more trusted network, or be routed through a channel whose trust story is understood. The goal is not to "win" against public Wi-Fi. The goal is to stop donating the most consequential moments of one's digital life to the least controllable environments.

The forward test, then, is not a demand for perfection. It is a diagnostic question that can be asked before fingers move: is this action reversible, and is this a fishbowl?

Border Crossings And Devices

In August 2013, at Heathrow Airport in London, David Miranda was stopped while in transit and detained for nine hours under Schedule 7 of the UK Terrorism Act 2000; his electronic devices were seized. The details became public, argued over, litigated, and turned into a kind of modern parable—not because most travellers will ever meet that particular kind of attention, but because it clarified what a border is. It is not merely a line on a map. It is a threshold where ordinary assumptions loosen. The carpet underfoot feels slightly tacky from thousands of rolling suitcases; the air smells faintly of coffee and jet fuel; fluorescent light flattens faces into passport-photo seriousness. A traveller arrives carrying the story they tell about themselves. They also arrive carrying a device that contains stories they never intended to tell at all. Borders are different.

That difference is not mystical. It is administrative. States reserve special powers at borders that they do not exercise in the same way elsewhere, and those powers can include questioning and, in some jurisdictions and circumstances, inspection of belongings, including electronic devices. For privacy-minded travellers, the key shift is psychological: a border crossing is one of the few places where a person may be asked, unexpectedly, to justify access to their own digital life. The question may never come. It may come softly, as routine procedure. It may come sharply, as suspicion. Either way, it is easiest to handle when it has been thought about *before* the queue begins to move.

Show: a tired traveller, shuffling forward between retractable belt barriers, suddenly remembers that their phone is still logged into work email and that it contains years of messages unrelated to the trip. Name: queue-pressure vulnerability. Explain: time pressure narrows judgement; fatigue makes people agree to things they would negotiate calmly at home. Implication: planning is privacy's antidote to the queue, because it replaces improvisation with prior decisions.

There is a common misunderstanding worth clearing without theatrics. "Device search" is often imagined as a single act: someone scrolls through photos, reads messages, nods grimly, and hands the phone back. In reality, "attention to devices" is a spectrum. Sometimes it is no more than noticing a device during a bag check. Sometimes it is asking a traveller to unlock a phone for a quick look. Sometimes it is retaining a device for longer examination. The same object—a phone, a laptop—can be treated as a personal diary, a corporate asset, an evidential artefact, or an inconvenient complication, depending on the context and the officer's mandate. That ambiguity is part of the stress. It is also the reason that privacy preparation for borders focuses less on clever tricks and more on reducing stakes.

Show: a traveller hears rumours of "phone searches" and imagines only one scenario, then becomes startled when reality presents a different one. Name: scenario lock. Explain: fear narrows imagination; narrow imagination produces poor preparation. Implication: wise travellers prepare for a range of outcomes by shrinking what the device can reveal, rather than betting on one story.

The most practical concept here is the one introduced earlier in this book: bounded loss. At a border, the relevant question is not only "What is on the device?" but "What could be exposed if the device is unlocked, copied, retained, or simply observed?" Exposure can be direct—photos, chats, documents. It can be indirect—account sessions that enable access to cloud stores, password managers, work systems. It can be contextual—notifications popping up on a lock screen, contact names visible in recent calls, calendar entries announcing where someone will be tomorrow. The border amplifies these small disclosures because the setting carries authority. A notification that would be mildly embarrassing at home can feel catastrophic when it appears under questioning lights.

Show: a phone receives a message preview at the wrong moment, revealing a contact name or a private topic without anyone opening the app. Name: incidental disclosure. Explain: devices leak information at the edges—lock screens, widgets, recent items—because they are built to be helpful. Implication: at borders, "helpful" can become "revealing", and the traveller benefits from recognising the leak points.

A second named example shows how law and technology can diverge across jurisdictions even within broadly similar democracies. In 2013, in the United States, the Ninth Circuit Court of Appeals decided *United States v. Cotterman* (en banc), a case involving a forensic search of a laptop seized at the Arizona border. The court distinguished between a quick manual look and a more intensive forensic examination, and held that the latter required reasonable suspicion. That decision sits inside a complex landscape of U.S. border-search doctrine, but the educational takeaway is straightforward: borders create categories of search that do not map neatly onto everyday expectations. A traveller may assume that a device is either private or not private. Legal systems often treat it as both, depending on the depth and method of inspection. The border is a threshold not only between countries, but between ordinary intuitions and specialised rules.

Show: a traveller assumes a phone is treated like a wallet, then learns that authorities may distinguish between a glance and a forensic extraction. Name: depth distinction. Explain: the "how" of a search matters—manual browsing differs from technical analysis—even when the object is the same. Implication: privacy preparation should not depend on a single simplistic belief about what "search" means.

Yet it would be dishonest to imply that border device scrutiny is universal. It is not. Many people cross borders repeatedly without any device-related questions at all. Many are waved through with a glance. Many experience nothing more than the usual inspection of documents and luggage. This is the credible counter-example, and it matters because it prevents the chapter from sliding into superstition. The reconciliation is equally important: infrequent does not mean irrelevant. People buy travel insurance not because they expect a crash, but because the cost of a crash is high and the policy is purchased when calm. Privacy preparation works the same way. It is not an admission of guilt or fear. It is an act of adult risk management.

Show: a traveller has flown internationally for years without a problem and therefore treats preparation as unnecessary fuss. Name: smooth-history bias. Explain: past ease can make low-frequency risks feel imaginary. Implication: the traveller's aim is not to predict scrutiny, but to ensure that scrutiny—if it happens—does not become a life-wide event.

There is also a temptation, especially among smart and busy people, to turn border privacy into a puzzle: to search for the perfect technique that defeats inspection while preserving full convenience. That temptation usually ends in disappointment, because borders are not a purely technical environment. They are a human environment shaped by law, discretion, and power. Any approach that relies on "outsmarting" the process can backfire simply by creating friction or raising questions. The calmer approach is to make peace with the fact that, at a border, persuasion and clarity often matter as much as cryptography, and that the simplest way to protect privacy is to carry less of it on the device.

Show: a traveller rehearses a complicated set of manoeuvres and then realises, in the queue, that complexity increases stress and mistakes. Name: complexity trap. Explain: complex systems fail under pressure; travel is pressure. Implication: travellers benefit from simple, explainable arrangements that reduce exposure without depending on theatrics.

The word "carry" does heavy work here because it connects to travel's physical reality. People accept that a suitcase should not contain everything they own. Digital life, however, tends to accumulate until a phone becomes a pocket-sized archive of years. At borders, this accumulation turns an ordinary object into an extraordinary liability. Reducing on-device data is therefore less about secrecy and more about proportionality. What is proportionate to bring? Travel documents, current communications, maps, tickets, the minimal set of work materials needed for the trip. What is not proportionate? Entire photo libraries, long chat histories, dormant accounts that remain signed in out of inertia, caches of confidential material unrelated to the journey. The point is not that any of these are shameful. The point is that their presence at the threshold is often unnecessary.

Show: a traveller carries a laptop because it is needed for a presentation, and the same laptop also carries years of unrelated personal archives because no one has ever pruned it. Name: accidental archive. Explain: devices retain data because retention is the default; deletion takes intention. Implication: borders punish default accumulation by turning irrelevant data into potential exposure.

Cloud services complicate this picture in an unintuitive way. Many people assume that if something is "in the cloud" it is not "on the device". Sometimes that is true. Sometimes it is half true. Devices cache files for offline access, store thumbnails, keep "recent" copies, and maintain authenticated sessions that can pull content instantly. A traveller may delete a file locally while leaving it accessible through an app. Or they may remove the app while leaving access tokens elsewhere. The cloud is not a location; it is a relationship—a set of permissions and sync behaviours that determine what content is immediately reachable. At a border, "reachable" can matter almost as much as "stored".

Show: a traveller confidently says "it's not on my phone" and then realises the phone can download it in seconds because the account is still logged in. Name: reachability illusion. Explain: cloud services blur storage and access; the device becomes a remote control for a much larger repository. Implication: border privacy depends on understanding access pathways, not merely file locations.

This is where education must be careful. Laws differ across the UK, the United States, and EU member states; practices differ between ports of entry; and travellers' circumstances differ wildly. The safe stance is not to prescribe legal moves, but to describe a planning principle: avoid making significant privacy decisions while standing at the threshold. If a traveller anticipates that a device might attract attention—because of the nature of their work, their public profile, their research, their activism, or simply the jurisdictions involved—they benefit from thinking ahead about what they would be comfortable revealing, what would be professionally sensitive, and what would be personally harmful if seen. This is not an invitation to conceal wrongdoing. It is an invitation to avoid accidental overexposure.

Show: a journalist travels with contact lists and notes that, if exposed, could affect other people's safety and privacy. Name: third-party burden. Explain: travellers often carry data about others—clients, participants, family—who did not consent to their information being exposed in a border context. Implication: preparation is not only self-protection; it is ethical stewardship of other people's data.

The third-party burden is where border device issues become morally sharper. A phone does not only contain one person's privacy. It contains messages from friends, photos of children, confidential work chats, research participants' stories, colleagues' addresses, doctors' appointment reminders, and the quiet intimacies of ordinary relationships. A traveller may be perfectly willing to disclose their own details but unwilling to expose someone else's. At a border, that unwillingness can collide with authority in uncomfortable ways. Planning ahead does not eliminate that collision, but it can narrow the amount of third-party data that is needlessly present.

Show: a traveller scrolls through their own photo roll and sees images that include other people who never agreed to be part of any official scrutiny. Name: collateral exposure. Explain: digital archives are social; they contain other lives. Implication: carrying less is a form of respect for others, not merely a tactic.

There is also a professional dimension that time-conscious readers will recognise instantly: corporate policies. Many organisations treat travel as a special security context and issue guidance about devices, accounts, and sensitive data. This is not corporate paranoia; it is an acknowledgement that borders are thresholds where legal regimes and technical environments shift. When a traveller uses a personal device for work—common in modern life—they merge personal and organisational risk. When they travel with work devices, they may carry data governed by confidentiality obligations. The border does not care about the traveller's internal story of "personal" versus "work". The device contains both, and the traveller feels the pressure.

Show: a professional opens a work laptop in a terminal and sees confidential documents alongside personal browser tabs. Name: boundary bleed. Explain: convenience collapses domains; travel exposes the collapse. Implication: separating domains—whether by device, account, or habit—reduces the chance that one context contaminates another at the threshold.

The motif returns because it keeps the focus honest. The threshold is not only a place. It is a moment where decisions become harder and consequences more immediate. The traveller who prepares at home retains agency; the traveller who improvises at the desk may feel cornered. That is why the most valuable outcome of preparation is psychological calm. Calm does not guarantee a favourable interaction. It does reduce errors: blurting, overexplaining, consenting to things without reflection, making panicked deletions that create confusion, or promising actions one cannot later sustain.

Show: a traveller faces unexpected questions and feels the urge to start deleting, changing settings, or inventing explanations on the spot. Name: reactive scrambling. Explain: under authority, people try to regain control through quick action; quick action often creates mess. Implication: the best time to decide what belongs on a travel device is when no one is watching.

A useful mental model is to treat border scrutiny as a possibility rather than a prophecy and to ask a diagnostic question that respects reality: if this device were retained for a day, or inspected more closely than expected, what is the worst plausible outcome—and is that outcome acceptable? "Acceptable" is personal. For some, the worst outcome is embarrassment. For others, it is professional breach. For others, it is risk to family or contacts. The question matters because it pushes privacy out of the realm of vague dread and into the realm of concrete planning. The traveller is not asked to become invisible. They are asked to become deliberate.

Show: a traveller realises that the most sensitive material on the device is not the obvious "secret", but the mundane archive of conversations that reveal patterns, associations, and obligations. Name: pattern exposure. Explain: devices disclose not only content but networks—who someone knows, how often they communicate, what they work on. Implication: reducing exposure is as much about protecting patterns as hiding particular facts.

The final tension is that borders, by design, are places where individuals have less control than they prefer. Privacy preparation cannot change that. It can only change what control remains. That is why this subchapter refuses the fantasy of perfect technique and instead emphasises the quieter competence of planning: decide what you carry, understand what your cloud sessions make reachable, respect the third-party burden, and avoid improvising at the threshold. The traveller will still face trade-offs—convenience versus exposure, simplicity versus completeness, peace of mind versus friction. The value of preparation is that those trade-offs can be chosen in advance rather than endured in a queue.

The forward test is as plain as a stamped passport: when the threshold arrives, does the device in your pocket contain only what you meant to carry?

Location Trails And Cars

In January 2018, Strava published its Global Heatmap, and within days people were tracing bright, looping lines across dark deserts—jogging routes and patrol circuits glowing against places that, by design, were meant to be dull on maps. In Helmand Province, Afghanistan, the pattern looked like a necklace laid on sand: repeated laps around a perimeter, a straight line to a gate, a scatter of smaller paths where someone had wandered off-route. The sound in that world is often rotor-thump and wind; the texture is grit that gets everywhere. Nothing about those runners was secret in the cinematic sense. They were not hiding in caves. They were exercising with a fitness app. The surprise was how easily private habit became public geography, and how quickly a harmless convenience could turn into a trackable signature. Location is a quiet biography.

That incident is easy to misread as a story about soldiers, deserts, and extraordinary danger. Its real subject is ordinary life. It is the way small location traces—*breadcrumbs*, left without malice—accumulate into something legible to strangers. A fitness route becomes a work schedule. A school run becomes a home address. A series of late-night stops becomes a pattern that someone else can interpret, wrongly or rightly, but never neutrally. Once the story can be told, it can be sold, subpoenaed, guessed at, or weaponised in petty ways. The modern device is not only a tool that knows where you are. It is a narrator that remembers where you have been.

Show: a phone pings location as a map app searches for "coffee near me". Name: ambient location collection. Explain: location is not one sensor reading but a stream, stitched together from GPS, Wi-Fi networks, mobile towers, and sometimes Bluetooth beacons; the device keeps refining a guess because accuracy improves experience. Implication: a single glance at a map is rarely a single act; it can be a burst of signals that leave residues across systems the user never sees.

The residue is the part most people never meet directly, because the interface is built to feel like a moment. "Where am I?" "How do I get there?" "Which train platform?" The experience is a clean question and a clean answer. Underneath, location is treated as an asset: a useful input for navigation, yes, but also a powerful ingredient in advertising, analytics, fraud detection, and product design. Even when content is encrypted, location remains valuable because it ties the digital to the physical. A device that knows where you were at 07:42 does not merely know a coordinate; it knows a context—home, commute, workplace, hospital, courtroom, rival shop. Context is the currency.

Show: a ride-hailing app records pick-up and drop-off points as part of providing a service. Name: service necessity. Explain: some location collection is essential; without it, the service collapses. Implication: the privacy question is not "can we eliminate location?" but "can we limit it to what is proportionate and necessary, and can we control what happens afterwards?"

This is where the idea of "default broadcasting" becomes concrete. Phones often offer location as an always-available tap. Apps ask for it once, and the user grants it once, because friction is annoying and the request seems reasonable in the moment. The permission then persists. Months later, the app still has access while the original reason has evaporated. A restaurant app wants location for finding nearby branches. A weather app wants it for local forecasts. A torch app—absurdly—may want it because it wants the same advertising profile as everything else. The result is not a single leak but a culture of casual access: location granted as background noise.

Show: an app that rarely needs location continues to request it in the background, because background access makes analytics richer.

Name: permission drift. Explain: permissions are negotiated once but exercised repeatedly; the user's mental model is "I agreed to this for that one task", while the system's model is "access granted until revoked". Implication: location privacy is won not through paranoia but through periodic re-negotiation of old agreements.

A second named example shows how location can feel intimate even when no one reads a single message. In June 2018, the United States Supreme Court decided *Carpenter v. United States* in Washington, D.C., holding that police generally need a warrant to access historical cell-site location information over extended periods. The case was not about a GPS dot on a screen; it was about the narrative power of movement—where a person sleeps, works, worships, socialises, and repeats themselves. The Court's language acknowledged something people already feel in their bones: long-term location history is not a trivial record. It is a reconstruction of life.

Show: a person's location history over weeks can indicate routines and relationships without any confession. Name: inference. Explain: humans are creatures of habit; repeated movement creates patterns that are easy to classify. Implication: location data is often more revealing than people expect because it answers questions they did not think they were asking.

Modern cars bring this problem closer to home because they turn the road itself into a data surface. Many vehicles now contain infotainment systems that mirror phones, embedded SIMs that provide connected services, and telematics units that send data back to manufacturers or service providers. Some of this exists for legitimate reasons—emergency assistance after a crash, remote diagnostics, stolen-vehicle recovery, live traffic. Some exists because companies, like all companies, want to measure how products are used. The car becomes a moving computer, and computers produce logs. The driver thinks they are driving. The system thinks it is recording.

Show: a car's navigation system stores recent destinations so the driver can return quickly. Name: local location memory. Explain: many head units cache addresses, call logs, and paired devices; the data persists because persistence is convenient. Implication: location privacy is no longer only about the phone in a pocket; it is about the dashboard in the driveway.

The dashboard has a peculiar authority. People treat it like an appliance: a radio, a map, a helpful voice that says "turn left" at the right moment. Yet it often behaves like a social device, linked to accounts, paired to phones, and capable of synchronising contacts and messages. When a person rents a car, borrows one, shares one with family, or sells one, the dashboard can quietly retain the previous owner's life. The risk is rarely a master hacker. It is the next driver tapping "recent destinations" and seeing something unexpectedly personal.

Show: a second-hand car changes hands and the new owner finds a list of addresses still present in the system. Name: residual intimacy. Explain: location storage turns ordinary convenience into an unintended record of someone else's patterns. Implication: a person's physical movements can become someone else's inheritance, without anyone choosing that outcome.

A credible limitation needs saying plainly: location sharing is not inherently bad. It can be genuinely protective. People use "share my location" to meet friends in unfamiliar places, to coordinate family pick-ups, to let someone know they arrived safely, to call for help, to recover lost devices. During travel, location is often the difference between getting home and getting stuck. In cars, emergency call systems exist for a reason. The reconciliation is not to reject location. The reconciliation is to shift from always-on, default access to deliberate, contextual sharing—*breadcrumbs* dropped on purpose, for a defined journey, rather than scattered unconsciously for years.

Show: a person shares live location during a late-night walk home, then switches it off once they arrive. Name: bounded sharing.

Explain: time-limited sharing matches the real purpose—safety during a specific window—without creating a permanent archive. Implication: privacy and safety are not enemies when sharing is treated as a tool rather than a constant setting.

The most useful distinction is between location used "in the moment" and location stored "for later". Navigation needs the moment. Traffic prediction often needs aggregated patterns, not individual histories. Advertising and profiling thrive on later. So do investigations, disputes, and the messy business of memory. A system designed to retain will retain more than the user imagines: not only where you went, but when, how often, and with what device. When location is stored for later, it acquires a second life: it can be accessed by more parties, under more conditions, for more reasons, than the original moment suggested.

Show: a person visits a clinic once; the visit is forgettable in daily life but permanent in a location timeline. Name: permanence mismatch. Explain: human attention forgets quickly; databases do not. Implication: a single, sensitive stop can outlive its relevance, available for re-interpretation in a context the person never anticipated.

This is also where marketing becomes less abstract. Location is commercially valuable because it improves targeting and measurement: did someone see an advert and then visit a shop? Did a commuter pass a billboard and later purchase? Companies do not need to know the intimate meaning of a place to profit from its category. "High-end retail" and "gym" and "airport" and "primary school" are enough. The person becomes a moving segment. A moving segment is easy to monetise.

Show: a phone spends most weekdays in one small cluster, then repeatedly visits another cluster in the evening. Name: home-and-work discovery. Explain: even crude analysis can identify home and workplace from repeated overnight and daytime locations. Implication: once those anchors are inferred, many other movements become interpretable, because distance, time, and frequency form a readable script.

Cars add a further twist: location is often shared not only with the manufacturer but with service partners. Insurance products may offer telematics-based pricing. Fleet vehicles may be monitored for operational reasons. Roadside assistance may use live location. Each relationship may be justified. Each relationship also broadens the circle of knowledge about movement. Privacy here becomes an exercise in noticing who is in the car with you, invisibly, and whether their presence is invited.

Show: a driver signs up for a connected feature to get remote unlocking, and in doing so authorises ongoing data exchange with a vendor. Name: feature-for-data trade. Explain: connected features are rarely free in an informational sense; they are often funded or improved through telemetry. Implication: the practical question is whether the feature is worth the expanded audience for one's movements.

It is tempting to search for a single switch that solves all this. Reality is messier because location trails are distributed. Some live with the operating system. Some live inside specific apps. Some live with cloud services that keep timelines and memories. Some live in the car. Some live with third parties that aggregate signals from many sources. The privacy skill, therefore, is not memorising one setting; it is learning to *review* and *limit* in layers. Review is a habit of looking back at what has been collected. Limit is the habit of narrowing future collection to what is proportionate. The reader who learns those two verbs gains control across changing technologies, because the details will change. The pattern will not.

Show: a person checks a location history feature and feels startled by how mundane entries add up—petrol stations, supermarkets, school gates. Name: accumulation shock. Explain: isolated points feel harmless; the assembled trail feels intimate. Implication: reviewing history is not about guilt; it is about recalibrating intuition to match reality.

The car layer is particularly stubborn because it is not updated like a phone. Vehicles remain on the road for a decade or more, and their software may outlive the assumptions under which it was designed. A phone user can switch apps. A driver cannot swap an infotainment system as casually. That means car privacy often hinges on two unglamorous disciplines: understanding what the vehicle stores locally, and understanding what it transmits. Local storage affects resale, lending, rentals, and shared family vehicles. Transmission affects the ongoing relationship with manufacturers and service providers. Both are solvable only through attention, not through wishful thinking.

Show: a family shares one car and multiple phones connect over time, leaving a tangle of paired devices and synced contacts. Name: shared-vehicle spillover. Explain: shared environments blur personal boundaries; the system retains what it is given. Implication: location and identity leak not because anyone intended it, but because shared infrastructure behaves like a memory without a sense of propriety.

A second limitation is worth admitting: even careful people cannot fully control every downstream copy of location data once it has been shared. A ride receipt may include a pick-up address in an email. A calendar entry may store a meeting location. A photo may retain location metadata. A car's service records may note mileage and dates. Convenience generates paper trails, and paper trails create digital trails. The reconciliation is not defeat. It is prioritisation: focus on the largest, most persistent trails—the ones that run automatically, daily, and invisibly—because reducing those has outsized effect.

Show: a person turns off one app's location access but continues to broadcast location through another service they forgot was running. Name: partial control. Explain: systems overlap; control is rarely total. Implication: privacy is improved through reducing volume and persistence, not through chasing total silence.

The motif returns one last time because it keeps the emotional truth in view. *Breadcrumbs* can be a safety device: a deliberate trace left so someone can find you. Breadcrumbs can also be the opposite: an unthinking trail that makes it easier for others to follow. The difference is intent, scope, and retention. A safety check-in is a breadcrumb placed carefully and retrieved quickly. A permanent location timeline is a breadcrumb trail that never gets swept away.

So the forward test is not whether location can be eliminated, or whether technology can be made pure. The test is smaller and sharper: when a service asks to know where you are, is it being invited into a single moment, or into the long memory of your life?

Chapter 11
Data Brokers And Marketing

On 18 December 2013, in Washington, D.C., the United States Senate Committee on Commerce, Science, and Transportation released a report with the unglamorous title *A Review of the Data Broker Industry*. It described a business that most people had never knowingly used, yet almost everyone had fed. The language was bureaucratic, the findings quietly unsettling: companies collecting, packaging, and selling fragments of ordinary life at scale, often without a direct relationship to the people being described. A fact-checker can pull the document in seconds. The harder task is recognising its subject in daily life. A supermarket receipt, creased in a pocket; an online "exclusive offer"; a form that asks for a phone number it does not actually need. The paper trail is familiar. The *shadow receipt* is not.

Privacy conversations tend to cling to what can be seen: a browser tab, a camera lens, a location dot sliding across a map. Data broking is different. It is privacy's backstage economy, where visibility is a cost rather than a feature. If a social network wants attention, it builds a feed. If a data broker wants profit, it builds a dossier that rarely needs to face the person it describes. The result is a peculiar modern feeling: being addressed by systems that seem to know you without having ever met you. Not because you are uniquely interesting, but because your life resembles patterns that can be priced.

A useful way to enter this chapter is to think about the difference between being watched and being *accounted for*. Surveillance implies an observer. Accounting implies a ledger: a set of entries that can be compared, merged, and sold without anyone caring who you are. The ledger model fits marketing better than the spy model. It also clarifies why so many privacy choices feel strangely moralised. People are told to "be careful online" as if the problem were indiscretion. Much of the problem is simply participation in modern commerce. Buying things, travelling, having a phone number, moving house, joining a gym, signing up for a newsletter—these are not sins. They are inputs.

Show: a person buys a train ticket, pays with a card, checks an email confirmation, then receives an advert for luggage the next day. Name: attribution. Explain: marketing works by linking actions across contexts, attempting to infer that one event caused another and that a particular person is likely to buy a particular thing. Implication: the privacy stakes are not confined to one website or one app; they extend to the market's ability to connect dots that feel, subjectively, unconnected.

This chapter arrives after a sequence of practical, device-level disciplines: permissions, passwords, browsing habits, networks, and the way location turns into a story. Those chapters sharpen control at the edges of personal technology. Data brokers shift the angle again. The question becomes less "what does my phone reveal?" and more "what is being said about me when I am not in the room?" That question can sound melodramatic until you notice how many decisions are mediated by profile data: which offers appear, which identity checks are triggered, which accounts are flagged as risky, which marketing lists you land on, which people-finder pages are able to stitch together a household. The world does not need to know your inner life to shape your outer life.

To avoid helplessness, it helps to name the cast. There are the services you knowingly use: retailers, banks, airlines, apps, utilities. There are advertisers: brands paying to place messages in front of likely buyers. There are platforms: the machinery that auctions attention and measures outcomes. Data brokers sit alongside and between these groups, buying and selling information derived from public records, commercial activity, and online signals, then packaging it into "audiences", "segments", or more direct products—lists, risk scores, identity verification feeds. Not all brokers look the same. Some sell marketing categories. Some support fraud prevention. Some specialise in identity matching. Some operate in legal grey zones that vary by jurisdiction. The ecosystem is not monolithic; that is part of its power. It is harder to argue with a cloud than with a person.

Show: a person is offered credit at checkout, then later receives credit offers from unrelated companies. Name: secondary use. Explain: data gathered for one transaction can be reused, resold, or combined with other sources, depending on contracts, consent language, and local law. Implication: the "reason" you gave data is rarely the full story of where it may travel.

There is a temptation, when faced with this machinery, to collapse into fatalism. People shrug and say the equivalent of: "They already know everything." It feels sophisticated. It is usually wrong. Data about individuals is often incomplete, stale, contradictory, and probabilistic. It is not a perfect mirror; it is a model. Models can be surprisingly effective even when they are imperfect, because they do not need to be right about you as a person. They need to be right enough about you as a consumer, or right enough to make a guess that pays off more often than it fails. That is cold comfort, but it is also an opening: imperfect models are easier to disrupt than omniscient ones.

Still, disruption is not the same as disappearance. This chapter is not a fantasy about becoming unfindable. It is about practical leverage in a market that prefers you uncurious. It begins with a sober look at how the trade works, not to inflame outrage but to make the machinery legible. Once you can see the gears, you can stop wasting energy on symbolic gestures and focus on changes that actually reduce what gets collected, how long it persists, and how widely it spreads.

One way to make the broker economy feel real is to follow a single, mundane act and watch it develop a second life. Consider the loyalty card: a small piece of plastic, a barcode on a keyring, a "member" account in an app. The point-of-sale screen frames it as kindness—prices lowered, points earned. The ledger frames it differently. A loyalty programme ties purchases to an identity across time. It turns shopping into a behavioural record. That record can be used internally to predict what you might buy next, to time promotions, to decide which coupons are worth offering. Depending on the programme and the jurisdiction, it may also be shared or sold in aggregated or more targeted forms. The individual does not need to read any fine print to feel the bargain. The bargain is designed to feel like a bargain.

Show: a person uses a loyalty card for a small discount on coffee and, months later, finds their inbox crowded with offers that seem oddly well-timed. Name: behavioural continuity. Explain: linking purchases across time creates a predictive stream; the value lies in repetition. Implication: the decision is not "do I like discounts?" but "is this particular discount worth turning my shopping into a persistent identity record?"

The same logic appears in online forms, where optional fields are rarely treated as optional in practice. A website asks for a date of birth to "verify age", then uses it to categorise households. It asks for a phone number for "account security", then uses it as an identity anchor for marketing and matching. It asks for a home address for a digital service because it is convenient to have on file, then that address becomes a key for linking records elsewhere. In each case, the person is not being tricked by malice; they are being nudged by design. Defaults matter because they become the path of least resistance for busy people.

Against that background, the most powerful privacy move is almost boring: reduce the data you hand over. Not as a performance, not as a crusade, but as a routine choice—like declining a bag at the checkout when you already have one. The effect compounds over years because the broker economy feeds on accumulation. A single missing detail may not matter. Many missing details, consistently, change what can be stitched together. A ledger with gaps is less marketable.

This is where the chapter's tone needs discipline. It is easy to scold people for "oversharing", as if the individual were the problem. The truth is that many systems are built to solicit more information than they need because more information makes matching easier and advertising more profitable. The privacy skill is not virtue. It is discernment: noticing what is genuinely required to deliver a service and what is requested because it is useful *to them*.

The next shift is from prevention to repair: opting out where possible. Opt-outs can feel like shouting into fog. Sometimes they are. Sometimes, however, they work well enough to be worth the effort, particularly with high-risk categories such as people-finder databases and marketing lists that expose address histories or family connections. "Opt-out" rarely means erasure from the universe; it often means removal from a particular product or suppression of a record from public display. It can be time-limited. It can be jurisdiction-limited. It can be imperfect. But imperfect relief is still relief when the alternative is indefinite exposure.

There is also a moral nuance here that is too often ignored. Some data uses are socially valuable: detecting fraud, verifying identity, preventing account takeover, stopping stolen cards being used. A world with zero data sharing is not obviously a better world; it is a world where certain harms become easier. The real issue is proportionality and transparency. People can accept that some data flows are necessary if those flows are bounded and accountable. What corrodes trust is the sense of being traded as an object without meaningful notice or control.

That leads naturally to identity documents—the heaviest entries in the ledger. A passport number, a national insurance number, a driving licence, proof of address: these are not mere contact details. They are keys. In modern systems, they often function as the bridge between a physical person and a digital profile, between "someone who clicked an advert" and "someone who can open an account". When such identifiers leak, or when they are requested casually, the consequences are out of proportion to the moment of disclosure. This is why identity documents sit in the same chapter as marketing. The broker economy does not always deal in passport numbers directly, but it thrives on identity resolution: matching records confidently enough to say that one person is the same person across contexts. Strong identifiers make matching cheap.

Show: an organisation asks for a copy of an ID document for a service that feels low-risk. Name: identifier inflation. Explain: institutions often normalise high-proof identity checks for convenience, compliance theatre, or to reduce their own risk, even when lower-proof methods would suffice. Implication: the individual's burden rises quietly; the ledger becomes easier to complete.

The deeper significance of this chapter is not merely technical. It is philosophical. Data broking reveals a shift in how society assigns meaning to personal information. In older models of privacy, information was private because it was hard to gather. You had to follow someone, ask around, keep notes. In the ledger model, information is private because it is yours—because control is a civic idea, not a logistical accident. The broker economy exploits the collapse of logistical friction. It turns scattered facts into a commodity. The response, therefore, is not nostalgia for a vanished past. It is deliberate modern citizenship: choosing when to be knowable, by whom, for what purpose, and at what cost.

The *shadow receipt* returns here because it captures the chapter's mood. A receipt is evidence of a transaction. It shows what changed hands. In everyday life, you see one receipt: the one you are given. The shadow receipt is what the system keeps—what it infers, stores, shares, and uses later. Marketing is full of shadow receipts. So are identity checks. So is the steady, quiet work of data brokers. The goal is not to burn every receipt. The goal is to notice that two receipts exist, and to begin caring about the one you never see.

The closing tension is practical and personal. Modern life offers countless small bargains: a discount for joining, a faster checkout for saving details, a smoother login for linking accounts, an "improved experience" for allowing tracking, a cheaper insurance quote for sharing driving behaviour, a convenience feature for syncing contacts to a car. Each bargain is plausible. None is obviously evil. The question, then, is not whether you accept bargains—everyone does—but whether you accept them by default, or only after a quiet internal audit: *what exactly am I paying with, and who else will be able to cash it later?*

How Data Brokers Operate

On 18 December 2013, in Washington, D.C., the United States Senate Committee on Commerce, Science, and Transportation released a report titled *A Review of the Data Broker Industry*. It was not a bestseller, nor was it meant to be. It read like a filing cabinet: methodical, grey, almost shy. Yet it described an industry whose most successful products are precisely the ones ordinary people never notice. A Senate report is a blunt instrument, but it has one advantage over the usual privacy folklore: it is checkable. The existence of data brokers is not a rumour; it is a matter of record. A photocopier hums in the background of this scene, papers sliding out with a dry rasp, as if the building itself is producing evidence that something large has been happening quietly.

The report's significance was not merely that it named the trade, but that it described a particular kind of commerce: firms that collect information about individuals, combine it with other sources, and sell it onwards—often without a direct relationship to the people being described. That last detail is the pivot. Most people can imagine a retailer keeping purchase history. Many people can tolerate a social platform showing adverts based on posts. The broker model is stranger. It moves personal data into a wholesale market, where the "customer" is another company, the "product" is a person's inferred traits, and the individual is neither buyer nor seller. They are the raw material.

Consider a common scene that feels almost too small to matter: an email arrives offering a "pre-approved" credit card, or a glossy letter lands on the mat promising a balance transfer. There is a postcode window, a surname, and the faint smell of ink. It feels personal, yet it was produced at scale. It is a commercial message shaped by a profile, not a conversation. The question is not whether marketing exists. It is how the sender decided you were worth the postage.

Show: a marketing list produces a letter addressed to a specific person at a specific address. Name: data brokerage. Explain: brokers assemble and sell audience segments and identity-linked lists to brands, lenders, insurers, and platforms. Implication: personal data can influence what comes to you long before you realise a decision has been made.

The first task, if the machinery is to feel comprehensible rather than supernatural, is to separate three roles that are often blurred in casual talk: the services you directly use, the advertisers who want to persuade you, and the brokers who trade in your describability. The service is the supermarket, the airline, the streaming provider, the bank, the estate agent, the fitness app—the organisations you recognise because you have handed them money, time, or attention. The advertiser is the brand paying to put a message in front of someone likely to buy. The broker is the middle actor who may never appear in your life as a brand at all, yet can influence which offers reach you, which categories you land in, and how easily you can be matched across datasets.

A broker's basic business model is simple enough to say in a single sentence: buy data, clean it, combine it, then sell it. The complexity lies in the details, because "data" is not a single substance. It is a bucket of different materials with different origins and rules. Some comes from public records: electoral rolls, property records, company directorships, court filings, planning applications—depending on jurisdiction and access. Some comes from commercial transactions: loyalty schemes, catalogue orders, subscription services, warranty registrations, and the endless administrative moments when a form asks for a date of birth or a phone number. Some comes from the online advertising world: cookies, device identifiers, inferred interests, and behavioural signals collected through tracking technology. Some comes from surveys and competitions: "Win a hamper" forms that quietly request far more than a hamper requires. Some comes from data cooperatives and partnerships that sound, in legal language, like "sharing with trusted partners".

Show: a person registers a new appliance to get an extended warranty, typing an address and email into a cheerful web form. Name: secondary collection. Explain: information gathered for one purpose can be repurposed for marketing, analytics, or data sharing under broad terms. Implication: the moment feels like customer service; the downstream value may be customer classification.

After collection comes cleaning, the unromantic work that turns messy human life into something a spreadsheet can tolerate. Names are misspelt. Addresses change formats. People move. Two people share a name. Someone uses a nickname. Someone divorces and changes a surname. A broker's advantage is not omniscience; it is persistence. They continuously reconcile records to increase confidence that "this entry" and "that entry" refer to the same individual or household. This is called identity resolution. The phrase sounds abstract until you translate it into an everyday consequence: the system decides whether you are you across contexts.

Identity resolution uses anchors. Some anchors are explicit identifiers: email addresses, phone numbers, postal addresses. Some are device-related: advertising IDs on mobile phones, cookies in browsers, device fingerprints created from combinations of settings.

Some are probabilistic: "same Wi-Fi network at night", "same IP address", "same pattern of purchases", "same household composition inferred from shared address". Brokers and related firms do not need certainty in every case. They need enough confidence to sell a segment that performs. Marketing is not a courtroom. It is a bet.

This is why the broker economy can feel like a fog with teeth. The individual sees disconnected events—a supermarket purchase, a website visit, a change-of-address form—and later receives a string of "coincidences". The mind reaches for a storyteller. It imagines a watcher. Often the reality is more banal and more powerful: a ledger in which small entries have been linked, multiplied, and priced.

A quiet motif helps keep this legible: the ledger. A ledger is not a spyglass; it is an accounting device. It does not care about your inner life. It cares about classification. Brokers sell classifications because classifications can be used. A lender wants to reduce default risk. An insurer wants to price risk. A retailer wants to target likely buyers. An advertiser wants to avoid wasting money on people unlikely to respond. The ledger serves all of them by making people measurable.

Show: an online advert follows someone from a flight search to a hotel offer. Name: retargeting. Explain: platforms and their partners tag browsing activity and use it to deliver adverts to the same or similar devices later. Implication: the person experiences "being followed"; the market experiences "reducing wasted impressions".

It matters, though, not to turn every tracking phenomenon into "data brokers did it". Some data use happens entirely within a single platform. A large platform can track and target using its own data and infrastructure, without buying from an external broker. A retailer with millions of customers can build its own segments. An app company can use data collected within its ecosystem. That distinction is not hair-splitting; it affects what is possible and what is realistic. The broker industry is large, but it is not the only engine of profiling. The broader truth is that brokerage sits inside a wider market for data and inference, alongside platforms, analytics companies, and fraud-prevention providers. The ledger has many bookkeepers.

Here is a named, checkable example that shows both the reach and the limits of public understanding. In 2017, the UK Information Commissioner's Office (ICO) produced a report on the use of data analytics for political campaigning, including the scandal associated with Cambridge Analytica and Facebook. The key point for our purposes is not the politics; it is the demonstration of how personal data, behavioural targeting, and opaque intermediaries can intersect, and how difficult it can be for outsiders to trace precisely who received what data and under what terms. Investigations can reveal enough to prove harm and illegibility in the same breath. The ledger is real. The ledger is also hard to audit from the outside.

Show: regulators investigate a complex chain of data use and find gaps in accountability. Name: opacity. Explain: data flows are mediated by contracts, technical integrations, and shifting corporate structures that resist simple tracing. Implication: the feeling of "faceless surveillance" is sometimes accurate, not because there is a single puppet-master, but because the market has grown faster than scrutiny.

A broker's products generally fall into a few families, even if marketing language disguises them. One family is audiences: "people likely to be moving house", "new parents", "high-income households", "sports enthusiasts", "frequent travellers". These segments are sold so advertisers can aim messages with fewer wasted impressions. Another family is identity data: name-address pairs, email lists, phone lists, sometimes called "contact data" or "identity graph" services. Another family is enrichment: adding inferred attributes to an existing customer list—age range, likely interests, household composition, purchasing power bands. Another family is risk-related services: identity verification, fraud detection, credit referencing and related scoring—sometimes handled by firms that are not marketed as brokers yet operate on similar principles of combining datasets to make a judgement.

It is tempting, at this point, to collapse everything into a single moral category. But there is a credible limitation worth stating plainly: some data sharing serves protective purposes, and not all broker-like activity is aimed at selling you more things. Fraud prevention often relies on pattern recognition across many accounts, devices, and transactions. Credit referencing, regulated and culturally normalised in many places, underpins lending decisions and can help prevent reckless lending, even as it raises serious privacy questions. Identity checks can stop account takeovers. These uses do not nullify privacy concerns. They complicate them. The question becomes: what is proportionate, what is transparent, and what is governed?

And yet, even protective uses have a marketing shadow. A system built to reduce fraud can become a system that quietly categorises and excludes. A score built to predict repayment can become a proxy for socio-economic sorting. A dataset built for one purpose can, through "partnerships", begin to serve another. The ledger does not stay in one drawer.

Show: a risk score affects whether a transaction is allowed or a verification is triggered. Name: automated decisioning. Explain: firms use statistical models trained on data histories to decide when to trust and when to challenge. Implication: privacy is not only about adverts; it can shape friction, access, and suspicion.

To make this less theoretical, consider the mechanics of a targeted advert and why brokers matter even when you never visit a broker's website. A brand wants to sell running shoes. It tells an advertising platform it wants people "interested in running" within certain postcodes. The platform can build that audience from its own signals—searches, likes, watched videos, app usage. Or it can accept a list from a broker: email addresses hashed into a format the platform can match, perhaps labelled "recent gym joiners" or "sports apparel buyers". If the platform finds matches between the broker list and its users, the brand can target those accounts. The person sees an advert and assumes the brand is psychic. The brand is merely renting a category.

Show: a list of hashed emails is uploaded for ad targeting. Name: list matching. Explain: platforms compare hashed identifiers to their own records to find overlapping users without revealing plain text emails to the advertiser. Implication: the individual can be targeted without a "direct" data exchange that feels obvious.

Now consider a credit offer. A lender wants new customers who are likely to qualify. It buys a marketing list, or it uses an intermediary that combines public records, credit-related data sources, and behavioural indicators to build a set of prospects. The offer is then mailed or served online. The person experiences a judgement before any application: "we think you are the kind of person worth courting". The judgement may be wrong. It may be based on household rather than individual. It may be based on stale address history. But it can still influence behaviour—what you consider, what you ignore, what you assume is available to you.

This is where the ledger metaphor pays off. The broker industry is not primarily an industry of secrets. It is an industry of *linking.* Linking is its skill, its value proposition, and its risk. When data is linked, it gains power. A single shopping transaction is trivial. A decade of shopping linked to a stable identifier is not. A single location ping is noise. A year of location history is a map of habits. A single web visit is fleeting. A web profile that travels across sites, devices, and logins is a portrait. Brokers specialise in selling the *linked version.*

It also helps to keep hold of a second truth that prevents despair: broker data is often imperfect. It is frequently probabilistic and sometimes laughably wrong. People find themselves categorised as pet owners when they are not, as homeowners when they rent, as parents when they are not. Errors are not an accident; they are a feature of modelling. The market tolerates a level of wrongness because it sells in aggregates. If a segment performs slightly better than random, it pays. That is not reassuring. But it is a reminder that the industry is not omnipotent. It is powerful in a statistical way, not a mystical one.

Show: an individual checks a profile category and finds it inaccurate. Name: inference. Explain: systems infer traits from patterns and proxies, not from a confession. Implication: the story being sold about you may not be "truth", yet it can still be acted upon.

The emotional core of this topic is control. People often feel that brokered data turns them into an object. That feeling is rational. A market that trades in descriptions of people without a relationship to them is a market that treats people as inventory. But the response that works is not panic. It is clarity. Once you understand who is who—service, advertiser, platform, broker—you can ask better questions about a given interaction. You can also stop wasting energy on the wrong target. Complaining to a retailer about an advert auction may miss the real mechanism. Complaining to a platform about a marketing letter may miss the source of the list. Clarity does not solve the market. It stops the market from feeling like a ghost.

A final point matters for continuity with the book's broader approach: privacy here is not asceticism. It is not the fantasy of never being known. Brokers operate because modern life rewards frictionless identity. Businesses want to know who is buying. Regulators want systems to prevent fraud. People want deliveries to arrive. The ledger grows because convenience is genuinely useful. The question is where the ledger's edge should be—what should remain unlinked, unshared, or time-limited.

The forward test, then, is not whether data brokers exist. They do. The test is quieter and more practical: when a form, a loyalty scheme, an "exclusive" sign-up, or an innocently phrased permission request appears, can you see the ledger entry it would create, and can you decide—deliberately—whether that entry is worth what you are being offered?

Reducing Data Collection

On 25 May 2018, the General Data Protection Regulation began to apply across the European Union, and the internet briefly developed a nervous tic. In London that morning, the ordinary act of reading the news acquired a new sound: the hollow click of consent banners being dismissed, again and again, as though the web had turned into a corridor of polite doormen. The law's language was formal, but its implications were intimate. It insisted—on paper—that organisations should collect only what they need. It gave a name to something most people recognise instinctively when a form asks for a mobile number "just in case": data minimisation (European Union, GDPR, Article 5(1)(c), 2018). The blank box matters.

That blank box is the real battlefield. Not the cinematic one of hackers and hoodies, but the daily one of optional fields, loyalty schemes, newsletter pop-ups, "complete your profile" nudges, and apps that behave as if your address book were a public resource. Most of the data that becomes brokered, bundled, and resold does not begin as a secret. It begins as a convenience. It begins as a small yes.

A five-word sentence fits here. Small habits scale into dossiers.

The most reliable way to limit data broking is not to win an arms race against the market's cleverness, but to reduce the raw material available to trade. That sounds moralistic until it is framed properly. This is not about purity. It is about arithmetic. Every extra identifier you hand over—an email used everywhere, a phone number given to shops, a birthday typed because the form asked nicely—acts like a staple in the ledger described earlier, binding separate moments into a single, more valuable record. Brokers profit from linkage. Linkage depends on identifiers. If the staples are fewer, the ledger becomes harder to assemble.

Show: a checkout screen asks for a postcode "to find your nearest store" even though the store is already chosen. Name: scope creep.

Explain: organisations often request extra data because it might be useful later—analytics, marketing, segmentation—rather than because the service cannot function without it. Implication: the default direction of travel is towards more collection unless someone, somewhere, says no.

The cultural trick is that collection is usually presented as a compliment. "Personalise your experience." "Save time next time." "Unlock offers." The vocabulary is soft. The mechanics are not. Personalisation requires memory; memory requires data; data requires capture; capture requires a moment of agreement. The market has become exquisitely skilled at making that moment feel trivial. It is a tick-box, a swipe, a pre-ticked checkbox, a field that turns red if left empty. The form does not mention that a postcode can imply affluence bands, that a date of birth can distinguish you from others with the same name, that a phone number can become a cross-service identifier, that an email address can be hashed and matched inside advertising platforms. None of this is magic. It is bookkeeping.

If the blank box is the battlefield, then the loyalty card is the most familiar uniform in it. In February 1995, Tesco launched Clubcard in the United Kingdom, an event that retail historians and business journalists still cite as a turning point in customer analytics. The scheme did not invent loyalty programmes, but it normalised a particular bargain at national scale: trade purchase history for rewards. The immediate outcome was measurable. Retailers gained a way to link baskets to households, day after day, building behavioural patterns that could inform stock, pricing, and marketing. Shoppers gained vouchers and tailored discounts. Neither side was foolish. It was a rational exchange. It was also a template, replicated across sectors that are not "retail" in any cosy sense—pharmacies, petrol stations, travel, even charities.

Show: a shopper scans a loyalty card to save a few pounds. Name: transaction linkage. Explain: the scan converts an anonymous purchase into an identifiable one, turning what would have been a one-off event into part of a continuous record. Implication: repeated small savings can buy a remarkably detailed portrait.

This is where "reducing data collection" becomes intellectually interesting rather than merely frugal. The goal is not to eliminate all sharing. The goal is to decide, with adult seriousness, what kind of trade is being made. A loyalty scheme is a trade of identity for discount. A newsletter sign-up is a trade of contactability for updates. A "complete your profile" prompt is a trade of self-description for smoother onboarding. When these trades are explicit, people can consent meaningfully. When they are disguised as defaults, consent becomes theatre.

Many people discover, slightly too late, that optional fields are not decorative. They are an invitation to self-enrichment. A registration form asks for title, gender, date of birth, postcode, job role, company size, interests. The service might only require an email and a password. The rest is "optional", yet the form is designed to make optional feel expected. The psychology is subtle: a sense of being cooperative, of "doing it properly". Organisations benefit from that politeness. The individual gains nothing concrete, except perhaps the relief of completing the form without resistance.

Show: a conference registration page requests dietary preferences, role seniority, and LinkedIn URL for "networking". Name: voluntary profiling. Explain: optional fields collect segmentation data that can be used for marketing and sponsorship value, even if the attendee never asked for tailored adverts. Implication: the person's professional identity becomes legible to third parties in ways that outlast the event.

The same mechanism operates in the small theatre of online accounts. Services that do not need a real name ask for one anyway. Apps that do not need a phone number claim it is for "security". A shop offers a receipt by email and turns it into a marketing channel. A delivery service asks for permission to access contacts, not because it must, but because it is building growth loops. A "birthday treat" becomes a date-of-birth database. The ledger thickens by hospitality.

At this point, a credible counter-argument deserves room. Data minimisation is not always a personal choice, and it is not always desirable in the simple way people imagine. Some organisations genuinely must collect data to comply with law or manage risk. Banks and financial institutions operate under "know your customer" obligations in many jurisdictions; employers must collect payroll data; airlines must collect passport details; schools must keep safeguarding records; medical providers must keep accurate contact information. Fraud prevention often requires identifiers precisely because identity fraud exists. Even a seemingly innocent refusal—declining to provide a phone number—can lead to account lockouts, delivery failures, or extra verification. The blank box can cost time.

Still, that limitation clarifies rather than defeats the principle. It separates *necessary* collection from *opportunistic* collection. Necessary collection tends to have a clear explanation tied to a function: "We need this to ship your order," "We need this to verify your identity," "We need this to comply with regulation." Opportunistic collection tends to be vague: "for a better experience," "for marketing purposes," "to help us improve." The first category may be unavoidable. The second is negotiable. The trick is to treat negotiable data as negotiable, even when the interface performs certainty.

Show: a bank asks for proof of identity and address. Name: mandated collection. Explain: regulated sectors often require verified identifiers to prevent fraud and comply with anti–money laundering rules. Implication: privacy is not refusal; it is proportion, and proportion depends on context.

A second named example illuminates how "small" data can produce outsized consequences. In 2012, *The New York Times* reported a case involving Target in Minneapolis, where marketing based on purchase patterns led to pregnancy-related coupons being sent to a teenage girl's home, revealing information to her family before she had disclosed it. Whatever one thinks of the story's later retellings, the core point is robust: predictive marketing can infer sensitive life events from apparently mundane shopping data, and those inferences can escape the intended channel. The data did not need to be sold to a third-party broker to cause harm. The harm arose from linkage and inference.

Show: a retailer infers a life event from shopping patterns and mails targeted offers to a household. Name: inference spillover. Explain: analytics can transform ordinary transactions into sensitive conclusions, which then travel through mail, notifications, or shared accounts. Implication: the cost of oversharing is not always what you share; it is what can be deduced.

This is why reducing collection is best framed as reducing *predictability* available to strangers, not hoarding secrets. Each additional data point is a piece of scaffolding for inference. A postcode can stand in for income. A shopping pattern can stand in for health status. A set of apps installed can stand in for beliefs. A cluster of late-night location pings can suggest relationship status. The ledger is not only about what you have said. It is about what can be computed.

The modern friction is that many services push for a single, stable identity across contexts. It is efficient for them. It is expensive for you. A single email address used for everything becomes a master key: it links retail receipts to subscription services, job applications to dating apps, newsletters to bank alerts. A single phone number does the same, with the added problem that phone numbers are frequently used as recovery channels. When a broker tries to unify records, stable identifiers are the easiest glue. Remove the glue, and the portrait becomes harder to paint with confidence.

The book's tone has no patience for purity theatre, so it is worth stating plainly: most people will not—and need not—build an elaborate persona-management system. The point is not to become unfindable. The point is to avoid making linkage effortless. A person who uses one contact point for high-value accounts and another for low-value sign-ups is not "hiding"; they are practising basic compartmentalisation, the same principle that underpins separate keys for separate doors. The blank box returns here, not as stubbornness but as design: leaving some fields empty keeps some doors unlabelled.

Show: a sign-up form asks for phone number and date of birth "optional". Name: identifier overreach. Explain: platforms seek durable identifiers because they persist across devices and sessions, improving tracking and recovery systems. Implication: the individual can reduce future linkage by declining durable identifiers when the service can function without them.

There is a social dimension too. Many data collection moments are framed as relationship-building: "Create your profile," "Tell us about yourself," "Add your family members." These features often make the product nicer. They also create permanent records that outlast the relationship with the product. People do not merely share data; they deposit it. Deposits sit somewhere. Deposits accrue interest for someone else.

This is where the GDPR's data minimisation principle becomes more than regulatory wallpaper. It articulates a norm: collect what is adequate, relevant, and limited. When individuals adopt that norm as a personal filter, they begin to notice how often it is violated. The moment you see it, you cannot unsee it: the insurance quote form that asks for marital status when it has no obvious bearing; the app that requests access to contacts for "finding friends"; the platform that insists on a real name for "safety" while selling behavioural adverts; the shop that makes email compulsory for a digital receipt. Each is a small attempt to thicken the ledger.

A limitation persists, and it matters to speak it aloud: individual restraint does not dismantle the market. Brokers will still trade public records. Platforms will still infer. Employers will still collect. The ledger will still exist. And yet, personal minimisation changes the shape of what can be linked with confidence. It reduces the number of stable staples. It reduces the ease of matching. It reduces the accuracy of inferences. It is not heroic. It is incremental. Incremental is how most real change happens.

To keep this grounded, pair the abstractions with visible behaviours and decisions that occur in ordinary work and family life. A researcher downloads a white paper and is asked for job title and budget range. A parent signs a child up for a club and is asked for "emergency contact" plus marketing consent. A professional joins a webinar and is asked to tick boxes about purchasing authority. A tenant completes a utility switch and is asked to "verify identity" through a third-party service. These are not rare edge cases. They are the grammar of modern services. Each extra field is a bid for future influence: segmentation, sales, or retargeting.

Show: a webinar registration form asks for "purchasing timeline". Name: lead scoring. Explain: businesses collect qualifiers to rank prospects and direct sales effort efficiently. Implication: professional attention becomes a commodity; the price is disclosure.

The quiet motif of the blank box can do more work here. The blank box is not empty in a moral sense; it is full of possibility. It is the space where a person decides what they owe this interaction. It is also the space where power shifts, slightly, away from default extraction and towards deliberate exchange. When enough blank boxes remain blank, the ledger becomes thinner. Thin ledgers are harder to resell.

So the forward test is not whether one can stop data brokers from existing. The test is smaller and sharper: when the next form appears—at a checkout, in an app, in a professional sign-up—can you tell which fields are truly required for the service you want, and which fields exist to make you legible to someone else later? And when you notice the difference, what will you choose to leave blank?

Opting Out Where Possible

On 13 May 2014, in Luxembourg, the Court of Justice of the European Union delivered a judgment that made a new kind of request imaginable: an ordinary person could ask for certain search results about them to stop appearing under their name. The case—Google Spain SL and Google Inc. v Agencia Española de Protección de Datos (AEPD) and Mario Costeja González—turned on a small, stubborn fact: an old notice about a debt, lawful at the time, had become a permanent shadow once indexed and endlessly resurfaced. In the court's language, the public's right to know had to be weighed against an individual's interests, particularly where information had become "inadequate, irrelevant or no longer relevant". Outside the courtroom, the outcome sounded almost like an *eraser* had been placed on the desk of modern life. A clean slate. A second chance. Five words: The eraser leaves smudges.

That smudge is the beginning of realism. "Opting out" is not a magic trick; it is a set of legal and procedural levers that vary by place, by industry, and by the type of data involved. It can mean deletion, suppression, delisting, "do not sell", "do not share", objection to processing, restriction, or simply being moved into a "do not contact" file that remains, ironically, another file about you. The phrase is tidy. The practice is not.

Show: a person searches their own name and finds their address, relatives, and age on a people-finder page. Name: exposure surface. Explain: certain databases and index sites package identifying details into a form designed to be browsed, copied, and re-sold; the harm is less about a single fact than about ease of access. Implication: opting out, where it exists, is often worth attempting first where the data is most *usable* by strangers.

The attraction of opting out is understandable. Earlier we watched how ledgers thicken when identifiers accumulate. Opt-out seems to offer the inverse: thin the ledger after the fact. The difficulty is that data brokerage is not a single library with a helpful receptionist. It is a market of duplicates, re-sellers, compilers, and enrichment firms, each with their own intake sources and their own definitions of "removal". Some work with public records; some with commercial feeds; some with inferred attributes; many with a mixture. When you request deletion from one repository, you are not draining a lake; you are bailing a boat. It can still matter. You just need to know what kind of water you are dealing with.

A useful starting distinction is between data that is primarily *published* and data that is primarily *processed*. People-finder sites and certain marketing lists are published: their value comes from making personal details easy to retrieve. In contrast, many brokers operate in the background, selling segments and scores—"new parent", "likely homeowner", "frequent traveller"—rather than a page with your address. Opting out of published exposure tends to feel satisfying because you can check whether the page is gone. Opting out of background processing often feels anticlimactic because you cannot see the output you have influenced. Both can reduce risk; only one gives instant feedback.

Show: a marketing email arrives addressed to a name you never use socially. Name: data provenance clue. Explain: small anomalies—an old surname, a misspelt first name, an obsolete address—often reveal which historical record or supplier is feeding a system. Implication: the most efficient opt-out efforts usually begin where provenance is easiest to infer.

The law matters here, and it matters in a strictly practical sense. In the European Union and the United Kingdom, the GDPR framework (and the UK GDPR after Brexit) formalised rights that include access, erasure in certain circumstances, restriction, and objection, alongside duties such as data minimisation and purpose limitation (EU GDPR, 2018). Those rights do not guarantee deletion on demand; they are conditional. A company can refuse erasure where processing is necessary for legal obligations, public interest tasks, or the establishment of legal claims, among other grounds.

The *eraser* exists, but it is not yours alone; it is shared with other interests, and sometimes it is locked away.

In California, legislation commonly referred to as the CCPA, effective from 1 January 2020, created consumer rights including the right to request deletion of personal information held by a business (with exceptions) and the right to opt out of the "sale" of personal information (California Consumer Privacy Act, 2018; operative 2020). Later amendments expanded and refined these concepts. The key conceptual difference is instructive: one lever is framed as deletion, another as "do not sell/share". Deletion implies the record is removed. "Do not sell" implies the record may remain but cannot be trafficked in particular ways. Each changes incentives differently.

Show: a website footer displays a "Do Not Sell or Share My Personal Information" link. Name: statutory interface. Explain: some laws force businesses to expose a specific mechanism because otherwise opt-out would be effectively invisible. Implication: when opt-out is easy to find, it is usually because regulation compelled clarity.

The phrase "where possible" is doing heavy lifting. Opt-out exists because someone made it exist—often after harm, scandal, or sustained advocacy. Where it does not exist, the individual is left with indirect strategies: reducing future collection, limiting identifiers, and controlling sharing. Even where opt-out exists, enforcement and compliance vary. Data can persist through backups, legal holds, or required retention periods. In some regimes, companies can keep certain information to prevent fraud or to maintain "suppression lists" so that marketing does not resume. That is an uncomfortable irony: to stop contacting you, a firm may need to remember that you asked them to stop.

This is the moment to be honest about what "removal" usually means in practice. For many commercial databases, an opt-out request leads to one of three outcomes. The first is deletion: the record is removed from active systems and will no longer be processed, except perhaps in backups until they roll off. The second is suppression: the record remains but is flagged so it is not displayed or sold in certain contexts. The third is delisting: the record still exists, but a particular public-facing page is hidden, or a particular index (often a search engine) no longer links it to your name. All three can reduce exposure. They are not equivalent. Calling them all "deletion" encourages disappointment.

Show: a search engine no longer shows a result for a person's name, yet the underlying webpage still exists. Name: delisting. Explain: removal from one index changes discoverability without changing the underlying source. Implication: a reduction in casual exposure may coexist with persistence in deeper channels.

The most persuasive argument for selective opt-out is not moral, but economical. Time is finite. The effort is not evenly rewarded. A realistic strategy prioritises high-risk categories first: sources that expose addresses, phone numbers, household composition, and other details that can enable stalking, harassment, impersonation, or targeted scams. A list of "interests" used for advertising is annoying; an address tied to family names is actionable. This is not a claim about what is more "private" in an abstract sense; it is about what is more *dangerous* when misused.

Show: a scammer quotes an address and a relative's name to sound legitimate. Name: credibility laundering. Explain: attackers use accurate personal details to bypass scepticism; the truthiness of small facts makes the lie easier to swallow. Implication: removing publicly retrievable household details can reduce a scammer's easiest props.

This connects to the earlier discussion of threat modelling without repeating it. Opting out is best understood as a risk-reduction tactic aimed at specific threat pathways. People-finder exposure maps onto stalking and harassment risks, and also to social engineering. Certain marketing lists map onto nuisance and mild reputational risks. Credit and identity databases map onto financial risks, but they are typically regulated differently and often cannot be "opted out" in the straightforward sense because they serve functions like fraud prevention and creditworthiness assessment. The question becomes not "Can I remove myself?" but "Which surfaces make my life materially easier to intrude upon?"

A second checkable example shows how a jurisdiction can attempt to impose order on a market that thrives on being hard to see. In 2018, Vermont's Act 171 required certain data brokers to register with the state and disclose basic information about their practices, creating a publicly accessible registry administered by the Vermont Secretary of State. Montpelier is not usually imagined as a centre of information warfare, yet the idea was quietly radical: name the brokers, make the market legible, and thereby make oversight imaginable. This did not abolish brokerage. It did not erase records. But it illuminated a sector that depends on people not knowing who is holding their data.

Show: a public registry lists broker names and contact details. Name: market legibility. Explain: when actors must identify themselves, individuals and regulators can direct requests and scrutiny more effectively. Implication: opt-out becomes less like shouting into fog and more like addressing a letter—still imperfect, but aimed.

Now, the counter-example—the limitation with teeth—is that much of the most valuable data is not a static file of facts but a dynamic product of inference. An "opt-out" request can remove a raw record yet leave intact the model's conclusions, at least until the model is rebuilt. A broker can agree not to sell data directly identifying you, yet still sell segments that include you, especially where the segment is defined statistically. A platform can suppress a people-finder page, yet the same source data can reappear through another reseller or through refreshed public records. The *eraser* scrapes one layer, and another shows through.

The honest reconciliation is that opting out is not a one-time cleanse; it is a choice about diminishing returns. Some opt-outs are "sticky": once removed, the exposure rarely returns unless you actively publish it again. Others are "leaky": the record reconstitutes through upstream feeds, public updates, or subsequent purchases. The effort is still rational when the stakes are high enough. It is also rational to stop once the cost outweighs the marginal benefit. The goal is not to win; it is to make certain kinds of harm harder.

This is where language does a quiet service. "Opt-out" can tempt people into thinking of themselves as a single entry in a master database. In reality, a person appears as many partial reflections: sometimes as a name and an address, sometimes as a hashed email, sometimes as a device identifier, sometimes as a cluster of behaviours, sometimes as a household. Removal from one reflection does not remove the others. But each successful removal can reduce the ease with which reflections are reconciled. That is the same linkage logic, inverted. Thin the staples. Disrupt the joins.

Show: a broker's record contains two addresses and an outdated phone number. Name: record drift. Explain: broker data is often stale, stitched together from historical sources; this drift both reduces accuracy and creates multiple "you"s. Implication: opt-out can prevent stale, misleading data from being treated as current, which matters for safety as much as for privacy.

A further complication is that opt-out sometimes requires identification. That is not a moral failing; it is a structural problem. A broker claims to hold your data and asks you to prove you are you before it will remove anything. The request can be sensible—otherwise anyone could delete anyone else's record. Yet it can also feel like a trap: to remove data, you must supply more data. The situation resembles being asked to write your name on a box labelled "names". The reader's time-conscious scepticism is justified. Verification is necessary, but it should be proportionate. The ideal is a process that confirms identity without demanding excessive new identifiers. The reality varies widely.

It is also worth noting that opt-out often changes what strangers can find, not what institutions can know. Credit reporting, electoral registers (in some jurisdictions), professional licensing, land registries, company directorship records—these systems exist for reasons that include transparency, accountability, and commerce. Many allow some forms of suppression for safety reasons, but none are designed around the idea that an individual can simply withdraw from public life while continuing to enjoy all its benefits. A mature privacy posture accepts this. Privacy is not the abolition of civic records. It is the reduction of unnecessary exposure and opportunistic trade.

Show: a property ownership record remains accessible while a marketing list entry disappears. Name: civic persistence. Explain: some databases serve public or legal functions and therefore resist deletion; others are purely commercial and more negotiable. Implication: expecting the same outcome everywhere leads to frustration; differentiating categories preserves energy.

For professionals, researchers, and students—the audience that lives by calendars and deliverables—the question becomes how to evaluate whether opt-out is "worth it" without turning life into a compliance hobby. The sensible metrics are not spiritual; they are pragmatic. Can a stranger find an address in under a minute? Can a phone number be matched to relatives? Can a profile be scraped at scale? Can an old identity be dredged up easily in a professional context? Opting out is most valuable where it changes those answers.

The *eraser* motif returns because it captures the right emotional posture: hopeful, but not gullible. When a system lets you request removal, it is offering a small admission that perpetual memory has costs. When it refuses, it is admitting something else: that its incentives are aligned with retention, not with your comfort. Either way, the interaction reveals the shape of the system you are living in. Seeing that shape is power.

Opt-out efforts also create a secondary benefit that is easy to miss: they force clarity about what you are dealing with. The moment you try to remove a record and discover that it is mirrored across multiple sites, you learn something concrete about how brokerage flows. The moment a company offers suppression rather than deletion, you learn how it thinks about your data—as a product it can shelve rather than destroy. Even a refusal teaches you which relationships are not voluntary.

The forward test, then, is not whether opt-out can deliver purity. It cannot. The test is subtler and more adult: when you encounter a database that makes your address, family links, or identity details easily retrievable, do you treat that exposure as an acceptable cost of living in public, or as a negotiable risk worth the friction of pushing back against? And, having decided, how much smudge are you willing to live with when the eraser meets the paper?

Handling Identity Documents

In September 2017, at an Equifax office in Atlanta, a failure that began in ordinary software maintenance rippled into something more intimate: names, dates of birth, addresses, and—in the United States—Social Security numbers were exposed in a breach the company later said affected about 147 million people. A reader does not need to enjoy corporate melodrama to grasp the concrete outcome. When identity numbers leak, they do not leak like a photograph or a password. They leak like a *key cut to a lock you cannot change*, and the sound is not a cinematic alarm so much as the quiet clack of forms being filled in by someone else, somewhere else, with details that resemble yours closely enough to open doors.

That is why identity documents deserve their own mental category. A passport number, a National Insurance number, a driving licence, a birth certificate, a tax reference—these are not just "personal data". They are institutional handles. They let organisations index you, reconcile you with other databases, and decide what you can access. They are, in the plainest sense, powerful. A phone number can be swapped. An email address can be replaced. An identity document sits closer to the skeleton of your public life.

This is not an argument for paranoia, and it is certainly not a demand for invisibility. It is an argument for precision. Most of us treat identity documents as items to be produced when asked, like showing a ticket at a barrier. The barrier opens. We move on. The problem is that the barrier is often not a single gatekeeper. It is a chain of subcontractors, verification vendors, scanning tools, cloud storage, and internal systems built by people with deadlines and budgets. The moment a document is photographed, scanned, uploaded, or emailed, it stops being an object in your hand and becomes a record that can be copied, forwarded, archived, and queried. The document's power does not diminish when it becomes digital. It usually increases.

Show: a receptionist asks for a passport scan "for the file" and offers an email address. Name: casual capture. Explain: organisations often default to collecting more than they strictly need because it feels tidy, because it reduces future admin, or because "this is how we've always done it". Implication: small moments of convenience create durable risk, because copies outlive the reason they were requested.

To handle identity documents well, it helps to distinguish between *verification* and *collection*. Verification is the act of confirming that a person is who they claim to be, or that a particular attribute is true: age, address, right to work, eligibility for a service. Collection is the act of keeping a copy, storing the identifier, and making it part of a record. The two are often conflated. They should not be. Many contexts genuinely require verification; fewer contexts genuinely require indefinite retention of full document images.

Consider how much of identity checking is actually attribute checking. A venue needs to know someone is over a certain age. A bank needs to satisfy "know your customer" obligations and reduce fraud. An employer needs to verify right to work. A landlord may need enough information to run referencing checks. Each of these has a rationale that can be described without mysticism. Yet the routine response is frequently to ask for the richest possible artefact:

a full scan, a full photo, the entire document front and back, sent through whatever channel is easiest. That richness is seductive. It makes the organisation feel "covered". It also creates a concentrated prize.

Show: a form requests a passport number, a National Insurance number, and a full scan. Name: over-collection. Explain: when a process is designed around worst-case exceptions, it becomes normal to demand everything from everyone. Implication: the default shifts from "prove this one thing" to "hand over a portable identity package".

A second, subtler distinction matters as well: *identifier* versus *evidence*. An identifier is a number or reference used to look you up: passport number, NI number, tax file number, national ID number in other jurisdictions. Evidence is supporting documentation that demonstrates something about you: proof of address, proof of qualification, proof of name change. Organisations often treat identifiers as evidence because they look official. Yet an identifier by itself is rarely evidence of anything beyond its own existence; it is a pointer into a system you do not control. Treating it as a universal proof encourages it to be used in contexts it was never designed for.

This is where identity documents differ from passwords in a way worth stating cleanly. A password is a secret shared between you and a service. If it leaks, you can rotate it. A document number is not a shared secret in the same way; it is an administrative anchor. When it leaks, you cannot simply "change" your historical identity. The human cost is not only financial. It is time. It is anxiety. It is the slow accumulation of "prove it's really you" moments.

Five words, early and exact: Copies outlive the appointment.

The modern identity economy also includes a growing class of verification intermediaries. A bank, an employer, or a rental platform may not want to build identity checking from scratch, so they outsource it to a specialist provider that asks for photos of documents and sometimes a video selfie. That can reduce certain kinds of fraud. It also widens the circle of organisations that hold copies, logs, and metadata about the verification. A reader can hold both thoughts without contradiction. Outsourcing can improve security in one dimension and expand exposure in another.

Show: a user is asked to upload a driving licence to an app they have never heard of. Name: delegated verification. Explain: identity checks are increasingly mediated by third parties, creating additional repositories beyond the service you actually want. Implication: a decision that feels like "I trust my bank" may quietly become "I trust my bank's vendors".

The key question, then, is not whether identity documents should ever be shared. They must be, sometimes. The question is *under what conditions* sharing is appropriate, and what friction is justified to keep the sharing bounded. The answer begins with an unglamorous habit: ask what specific purpose the document serves in that moment. Purpose is not a slogan; it is a test. If the organisation cannot name the purpose clearly, it is often collecting out of habit, or for future convenience, or because the form was copied from somewhere else. Purpose also helps distinguish legitimate need from opportunism. A mobile phone provider may need proof of identity to open an account. A newsletter does not. A gym offering a free trial does not need a passport scan. A solicitor handling a property transaction may have regulatory obligations that change the calculus. The same artefact can be reasonable in one context and absurd in another.

Show: a hotel asks for a passport at check-in and takes a photocopy. Name: frictionless retention. Explain: hospitality practices vary; some jurisdictions require guest registration and identity details, but copying entire passports is not always legally required and may be done "for speed". Implication: when retention is framed as convenience, the risk is being traded for someone else's administrative comfort.

Still, there is uncertainty. Practices differ by country, industry, and even individual branch. The point is not to win every negotiation; it is to notice which requests are routine and which are genuinely necessary. The more automatic the request, the more valuable it is to pause. Not dramatically. Simply enough to observe the shape of the system.

Two named, checkable examples help ground this. The Equifax breach (2017, United States) demonstrated how central identifiers—particularly Social Security numbers—become toxic when exposed, because they are used widely for authentication and credit processes. In the United Kingdom, the National Audit Office has repeatedly examined identity and fraud risks in public systems; its reports on fraud and error in public spending underscore a related truth: identity is not a private matter in the narrow sense, it is a governance matter, and the costs of weak handling are social as well as personal (National Audit Office, various years). The details of each system differ, but the logic rhymes: identity data is valuable, widely replicated, and hard to reclaim once it escapes.

Now the limitation: some organisations genuinely cannot proceed without collecting certain details, and refusing may mean losing access. Banks, employers, and regulated industries often have statutory or compliance obligations. The reconciliation is not to pretend those obligations vanish, but to separate what is unavoidable from what is optional. Much harm comes not from the unavoidable core, but from the optional fringe: the extra scan sent by email because it was easiest; the unencrypted attachment left in an inbox; the photocopy placed in a drawer; the staff member who keeps a "handy" folder of IDs "just in case".

This is the quiet motif worth threading: *keys and copies*. Identity documents are keys, and copies multiply. Keys are meant to be controlled. Copies are meant to be convenient. Convenience is not a vice. It is merely expensive when it is paid for with long-lived exposure.

The channels used to share documents matter as much as the decision to share. A document handed over in person for inspection is not the same as a high-resolution scan sent through email. A secure upload portal with access controls is not the same as an unstructured WhatsApp chat. Even within the same channel, format matters. A full-colour scan with machine-readable zones intact is richer than a redacted image. Richness can be useful for verification; it also increases the value to a criminal and the harm of leakage. Organisations often default to the richest possible version because it is easier for them. The individual's task is to recognise that default and weigh whether it is justified.

Show: a staff member requests "a clear photo, please—make sure everything is readable". Name: maximal capture. Explain: readability is framed as necessity, but it can be an overcorrection that collects more than needed for the stated purpose. Implication: insisting on maximal clarity can unintentionally insist on maximal risk.

A practical way to think about redaction, without turning it into a hobby, is to treat each document as a bundle of attributes. A passport contains a photograph, name, nationality, date of birth, place of birth, passport number, issuing authority, issue and expiry dates, and a machine-readable zone. Many requests only need a subset: for example, a venue might need date of birth and photo; a hiring process might need name and right-to-work evidence. A document copy that exposes the entire bundle when only one attribute is required is a classic case of over-collection. The concept has a name: data minimisation (EU GDPR, 2018). The behaviour is visible: sharing less within the same artefact.

This connects directly to breach fallout. When a database holding email addresses leaks, the downstream harm is often increased spam and phishing. When a database holding identity documents leaks, the downstream harm can include fraud attempts that are harder to distinguish from legitimate processes. It also enables more credible impersonation. A fraudster who can quote a passport number or a scanned image can exploit institutional scripts: "We just need to confirm…" The harm is not only that someone might apply for something in your name; it is that you may be forced into repetitive proof.

There is also a social dimension that professionals sometimes underestimate. Identity documents are routinely exchanged in housing, education, travel, and employment. These are life transitions, and life transitions already generate stress. In that state, people comply quickly. They want the process to end. That is the moment when poor practices become normal. A rushed move, a new job, a last-minute travel booking: the email is sent, the attachment is attached, the copy is made. A month later, no one can remember who has it. The paper trail becomes literal.

Show: during a house move, a tenant sends multiple ID scans to different agents. Name: transition exposure. Explain: transitional periods multiply requests, and people prioritise speed over control. Implication: the riskiest identity sharing often happens when life is already busy.

A further modern twist is that identity documents are increasingly used not only to verify, but to *train* systems. Images of documents may be used to improve document-reading software. Face images may be used to improve liveness detection. Organisations should, under many regimes, disclose such secondary uses and obtain an appropriate legal basis. The individual rarely reads the fine print. The result is that a document shared for one purpose can become raw material for another. This is not science fiction; it is the natural consequence of digitising processes and treating data as a reusable asset. When you feel the faint itch of discomfort, that is the itch of purpose drift.

What does "handling" look like at the level of everyday judgement? It is a posture, not a checklist. It is the habit of asking, quietly, three things: what is being asked for, what purpose it serves, and what channel is being used. It is also the habit of noticing when an organisation is asking for a document when an attribute would do, or asking to keep a copy when viewing might suffice. Some will accommodate. Some will not. Either way, the question itself produces clarity, and clarity is a form of control.

The conversation about photocopying is especially revealing. Photocopies feel old-fashioned, and therefore safe. They are neither. Paper copies can be misfiled, copied again, photographed, or disposed of badly. They also have a strange permanence: a paper copy in a drawer can survive staff turnover and office moves. The digital equivalent, at least, leaves logs and access controls when handled well. The danger of paper is not that it is inherently worse; it is that it is often handled casually.

Show: an office keeps a folder of photocopied IDs "for emergencies". Name: informal archive. Explain: informal archives exist outside governed systems, escaping retention policies and access logging. Implication: the most sensitive identity data often leaks from the places that never considered themselves "systems" at all.

This returns us to the wider ecosystem of breaches and brokers. Identity documents and numbers are the easiest data to monetise indirectly because they enable account takeovers, fraudulent applications, and convincing social engineering. They are also the data that, once leaked, pushes people towards more invasive verification in future. That is the vicious circle: breaches lead to stricter checks; stricter checks lead to more collection; more collection creates bigger prizes; bigger prizes lead to more breaches. Breaking the circle requires restraint—not only by individuals, but by institutions. Individuals, however, can at least avoid feeding the optional parts of the loop.

A final, forward-facing tension sits at the heart of modern identity handling. Digital life demands frictionless proof, yet safety often demands friction. The more we automate verification, the more we commoditise the proofs. The more we commoditise the proofs, the more we incentivise their capture and trade. The reader's task is not to reject verification, but to decide where to place friction deliberately: where to insist on purpose, where to prefer inspection over retention, where to prefer bounded channels over casual ones, and where to accept that a transaction is not worth the identity package it demands.

Keys want to be controlled. Copies want to multiply. The unresolved question is not whether you will ever share identity documents—you will. The question is whether, the next time someone asks for a "quick scan", you can tell the difference between a lock that genuinely needs your key and a door that simply enjoys collecting keys because it has never been taught to do otherwise.

Chapter 12
When Breaches And Scams Hit

On 15 July 2020, Twitter's public square briefly became a trapdoor. High-profile accounts—politicians, entrepreneurs, brands—began posting the same implausible promise: send Bitcoin, receive more back. The messages looked official because, in a narrow technical sense, they were. They came from the real accounts. In offices and kitchens far from Twitter's headquarters in San Francisco, phones chimed and screens lit up with the kind of authority people are trained to trust. The scam was not new. The theatre was.

Most people hear a story like that and instinctively reach for a technical explanation, as though the danger lives in code alone. Yet the unsettling part is how ordinary the human mechanism is. The attackers did not need to persuade the world; they only needed to persuade the right person, at the right moment, to take the wrong action. That is the modern pattern, repeated with variations: a breach makes private information available, and a scam turns that information into leverage. The machinery is complex. The pressure point is simple. *Stress makes people click fast.*

It helps to name this without melodrama, because calm naming is how panic is replaced with choice. A breach is not a moral failure. A scam is not proof of stupidity. They are predictable outcomes of systems that are built for speed, delegation, and convenience. Our tools move money, memories, contracts, health records, and reputation with astonishing ease; the cost of that ease is that a mistake can travel just as quickly. The honest question is not whether something will ever go wrong, but how a person behaves when it does.

The first truth worth holding is that scammers tend to be better psychologists than engineers. The vocabulary changes—phishing email, fake delivery text, investment pitch, impersonated helpline—but the emotional grammar stays stubbornly familiar. Urgency is the favourite verb. Authority is the costume. Secrecy is the lighting. A message tells someone that a parcel is stuck, a bank account is frozen, a colleague is waiting, a child is in trouble, a romance is "special", a deadline is minutes away. The details are often bland; the timing is sharp. A mind that has been jolted into haste will accept contradictions it would normally laugh at.

Watch how these hooks behave in the wild and they become almost embarrassingly repetitive. An email that announces an "unusual sign-in" is not simply providing information; it is manufacturing a small internal emergency. A text about a missed delivery is not trying to explain logistics; it is trying to summon the itch of unfinished business. A caller who claims to be from an institution is not merely making a claim; they are inviting someone to step into a script where obedience feels like competence. Once a person is inside the script, each next step feels smaller than the last, until the final step—handing over a code, resetting an account, sending a payment—feels like tidying up.

The second truth is that breaches and scams are now intertwined. Data spills do not always lead directly to fraud, but they widen the stage. A criminal who knows an address, a recent purchase, the last four digits of a card, or a family connection does not need perfect information; they need *enough* to sound plausible for long enough. That is why some of the most effective scams feel oddly personal while still being mass-produced. A message can be sent to thousands, yet each recipient experiences it as a one-to-one problem. The deeper the data trail, the more convincing the lie.

That is also why "common sense" is an unreliable shield. Common sense works best against unfamiliar dangers, where a person has time to think. The modern scam aims to remove thinking time. It works by collapsing the space between message and action. A seasoned professional can be caught on a Tuesday afternoon when a meeting has overrun, a child needs collecting, and a phone buzzes with "security alert". A thoughtful student can be caught at 1 a.m. when fatigue makes the brain treat any decision as a burden to be cleared. The scammer is not looking for ignorance. They are looking for conditions.

A breach notification arriving in an inbox has its own psychological trick. It compresses uncertainty into a single sentence: "We experienced unauthorised access." A mind that dislikes uncertainty will try to do something immediately—anything—to escape the discomfort. That is why the worst response to a breach is often a frantic one: rushing into resets, replies, and new sign-ups while still shaken. It is not that action is wrong. It is that action without sequence is expensive. A good response has an order, because order reduces the chance that an attacker's next move is faster than yours.

Sequence matters because accounts are not isolated; they are linked like rooms in a building. Email is often the master corridor, because it resets other passwords and receives security notices. A phone number is often the spare key, because it receives codes and recovery messages. Financial accounts are the obvious prize, but social accounts are the useful disguise, because they can be used to trick other people. A compromised social profile is not merely embarrassing; it is a distribution system. A compromised email address is not merely inconvenient; it is a command centre. Understanding those roles changes what "recovery" means. The goal is not only to regain access, but to stop the incident from widening.

This is where a reader's attention shifts from the dramatic to the procedural. When a breach hits, the question is not "How bad is it?"—that question often cannot be answered immediately. The better question is "What does this message allow someone else to do next?" If a leaked password could be used elsewhere, the risk is lateral movement across services. If a leaked email address and phone number could be used for convincing impersonation, the risk is social engineering. If a leaked address and family relationship could be used for intimidation or stalking, the risk is personal safety and unwanted contact. Different breaches leak different ingredients. The response is shaped by ingredients, not headlines.

A quiet but useful analogy sits underneath all of this: treat breaches as fire alarms rather than prophecies. A fire alarm does not tell you that a building will burn down; it tells you to move through a known routine, quickly and without improvisation. The routine is not exciting. That is its strength. When a breach notice arrives, a prepared person does not need brilliance. They need a drill they can run while tired, busy, or upset. The drill is the opposite of panic: it is action with an internal map.

And yet it would be dishonest to pretend drills are effortless. Recovery often involves friction, especially when support teams require proof, when automated systems lock accounts to "protect" them, or when a service's process was designed for a neat world where people have one device and perfect records. The hard part is not the password change. The hard part is the administrative limbo: waiting, verifying, re-verifying, and discovering which accounts were quietly using an old email address you forgot you had. That friction tempts people to settle for partial fixes. Partial fixes are how incidents recur.

There is a particular kind of cruelty in how compromised accounts behave. An attacker rarely announces themselves. They alter a recovery email here, a forwarding rule there, a secondary phone number somewhere else. The victim continues using the account while a second person quietly holds the strings. This is why regaining control is less like changing a lock and more like checking the whole doorframe: the hinges, the spare keys, the hidden latch. Even highly technical people can miss the small settings because the mind wants a single decisive act. The reality is a chain of small acts, done in the right order, until the chain becomes a barrier.

The moral centre of this chapter, though, is not suspicion. It is dignity. People do not deserve to be punished for being trusting, busy, lonely, or helpful. Scams exploit those ordinary human states, which is why shame is such a common aftertaste. Shame also helps criminals, because ashamed people keep quiet. They do not warn friends. They do not report. They do not ask for help. A culture that mocks victims is, unintentionally, a culture that subsidises scammers.

That culture reaches beyond the self. Many readers are not only protecting their own accounts, but also acting as informal guardians for relatives, colleagues, or friends who are more vulnerable: an elderly parent who answers unknown calls, a teenager whose online social life moves faster than adult comprehension, a partner who handles household bills, a colleague who processes invoices. The point is not to turn family life into compliance training. It is to recognise that a single person's compromised account can become a pathway into a wider network of people who trust them. That is why scam literacy is a form of care, not a hobby.

There is also a delicate boundary worth stating. Some people respond to the reality of scams by retreating into a fantasy of perfect safety: never click, never trust, never connect. That fantasy is rarely lived, and when it is, it tends to shrink a life rather than protect it. The aim here is not a bunker. It is resilience. Resilience means expecting occasional shocks and building habits that absorb them. It means measuring risk in terms of time, money, emotional cost, and disruption—not in terms of fear. It means accepting that technology is a tool and a theatre at once: useful, persuasive, and sometimes predatory, all in the same interface.

The final movement of the book depends on this shift from one-off fixes to lived practice. A person can harden a phone, tidy a browser, and reduce data trails, and still be caught by a well-timed, well-targeted lie. That is not failure; it is the price of participating in systems where identity and access are constantly negotiated. The practical question is whether the reader's habits create slack—small buffers of time and attention—so that a sudden message does not dictate the next move. The human brain is not a fraud-detection appliance. It is a meaning-making machine. Scammers are good at feeding it meaning. The countermeasure is not constant vigilance, which is exhausting, but repeatable procedure, which is survivable.

The most important payoff of this chapter is not the ability to spot a single trick. It is the ability to hold one's nerve when the trick is customised, when the caller is charming, when the email looks plausible, when the account really does show a warning, when the stakes feel high. The difference between being safe and being trapped is often one pause, one decision not to be hurried, one refusal to treat someone else's urgency as your responsibility.

A reader turning the page should carry a single forward test, as plain as it is uncomfortable. When a message arrives that claims authority and demands speed, what is the one action that would make the situation worse—and can you notice that action before you take it?

Spotting Common Scams

On 18 September 2023, MGM Resorts International disclosed that a cyberattack had disrupted hotel and casino operations across the United States. Guests reported long queues; keycards failed; staff reverted to paper; slot machines went quiet. The technical story mattered, but the human entry point was the tell: the company later indicated the incident involved social engineering, the kind of attack that does not begin with a firewall but with a voice and a moment of persuasion. In Las Vegas, where the carpet is thick underfoot and the air always smells faintly of cooling systems and perfume, it is easy to forget that modern fraud rarely needs a crowbar. It needs a conversation.

That is the first uncomfortable fact about scams worth facing squarely. The stereotype of the scammer as a hoodie-wearing genius tapping furiously in a dark room is convenient, because it suggests an enemy that only specialists can understand. Real scams are often better described as applied behavioural science with a small technical wrapper. The criminal is not trying to out-compute anyone; they are trying to out-time them. They aim for the minutes when a person is hungry, rushed, pleased, worried, lonely, flattered, or tired. Security systems do not have moods. Humans do.

It is easy to miss.

Once that is admitted, the subject becomes less spooky and more legible. A scam is a structured attempt to steer behaviour using predictable psychological levers: urgency, authority, secrecy, and emotional hooks. The exact wording changes, but the levers repeat with eerie discipline. A person who learns to recognise the levers is not becoming paranoid; they are becoming literate. Literacy does not mean never being fooled. It means noticing when a message is trying to shrink the space for judgement.

Start with urgency, the scammer's favourite instrument because it is cheap and reliable. A phishing email does not merely ask for a password; it manufactures a small emergency. "Your account will be suspended in 24 hours." "Payment failed, action required." "Unusual login detected." The goal is not information but acceleration: click now, decide later. The urgency often carries a timebox because timeboxes trigger compliance. That impulse is ancient and useful in real emergencies; scams counterfeit it. When a bank genuinely flags fraud, speed can protect money. When a stranger demands speed, speed protects the stranger.

The lever has a recognisable shape. In a typical phishing email, the recipient is offered a narrow corridor: there is one problem, one official route, one button. The email may look professionally formatted, with a familiar logo and a tone of calm competence. That competence is not decoration; it is a behavioural cue. The message is trying to evoke what psychologists call *authority bias*—the tendency to comply with perceived authority figures even when details are unclear. Stanley Milgram's obedience experiments at Yale University in the early 1960s are often invoked for their moral drama, but the mechanism is mundane: people use cues of legitimacy to decide quickly who deserves obedience. Scammers decorate their messages with the cues because cues are faster than reasoning.

Authority has siblings: familiarity and routine. The most successful scams often imitate a process the victim already performs. A "document share" email arrives because a person already receives shared documents at work. A "missed delivery" text lands because parcels are genuinely common. A "security alert" appears because modern services do send security alerts. The scam is parasitic on normal life. It does not need to invent a new habit; it needs to attach itself to an old one.

A delivery scam is a perfect example of this parasitism because it uses an object that is both physical and vague. A parcel might be delayed for dozens of reasons, and the recipient cannot easily falsify the claim in their head. The scammer's message exploits that ambiguity: a link to "rebook", a small "customs fee", a request to "confirm address". Notice how the sum is often modest. That is not generosity; it is strategy. A small fee is easier to pay without reflection. It also sets a precedent: once a person has complied once, they are more likely to comply again, because the mind prefers consistency. This is not mystical. It is a well-described tendency in behavioural research: after an initial small commitment, people are more susceptible to escalating requests.

Secrecy is the lever that makes this escalation easier. Many scams include a line that isolates the victim: "Do not share this code." "Keep this confidential." "This matter is sensitive." In legitimate contexts, secrecy can be reasonable—two-factor codes should not be shared casually, and employers may handle investigations discreetly. Scams counterfeit the language of discretion to prevent outside correction. A person who reads a message aloud to a friend often hears its absurdity immediately. The scammer wants the victim alone with the message, because social reality-checking is the enemy.

There is a cruel elegance to how these levers combine. Urgency reduces thinking time. Authority supplies a reason to obey. Secrecy prevents consultation. Emotional hooks supply energy. The victim is not being asked to "be gullible"; they are being guided through a corridor where each step feels smaller than the last. A link click becomes a login. A login becomes a code. A code becomes access. A small payment becomes a larger one. Each step is framed as the last tidy action needed to resolve a problem.

This corridor appears in one form or another across the main families of scams, and seeing it clearly is the beginning of competence. Consider the phishing email that imitates a popular service. The "Show" is familiar: an inbox, a subject line that looks routine, a body that uses the service's colours and typography. The "Name" is impersonation. The "Explain" is that email is not a proof-of-identity system; anyone can send a message that looks plausible, and many people only check the surface cues. The "Implication" is that visual professionalism is not evidence. It is marketing for theft.

The same corridor appears in what might be called "support scams", where the criminal pretends to be a helpdesk agent. The first contact might be a phone call, a pop-up, or a message that says "We detected suspicious activity". The victim is invited into a relationship: the scammer plays the role of a calm fixer, the victim plays the role of the grateful client. Relationship itself becomes the hook. Humans do not like to be unkind to helpers. Scammers know this, and they cultivate politeness as a weapon. The "Name" here is social engineering in its purest form: manipulating people into doing what systems cannot extract on their own. The "Explain" is that modern life is full of legitimate support interactions, and people have been trained to hand over details to fix problems quickly. The "Implication" is that a person's helpfulness, not their ignorance, becomes the exploited resource.

Romance scams add a different emotional fuel: attachment. They are not primarily about money at the start; they are about connection. The pattern is recognisable in hindsight and invisible in the moment, which is why it is important to treat it with seriousness rather than mockery. A romance scam often begins with ordinary conversation on a platform where strangers meet. The scammer invests time. They message frequently. They mirror interests. They create a sense of specialness. Then comes an engineered obstacle—distance, bureaucracy, a sudden crisis—and the victim is invited to prove loyalty by solving it. Money is often the later stage, but the earlier stage is something more intimate: the manufacture of emotional dependence.

The "Name" here is grooming, not in the sensational sense the internet sometimes uses for clicks, but in the behavioural sense: building trust and commitment over time to increase compliance later. The "Explain" is that the scammer is not selling a story; they are selling a role for the victim to occupy, often the role of saviour or confidant. The "Implication" is that the victim is not merely losing funds; they are losing a relationship they believed was real. That pain can be profound, and it is precisely why the scam can persist even when doubts appear. A mind will fight to preserve the meaning it has invested in.

Still, not every suspicious message is a scam.

That concession matters, because the world contains genuine mishaps, clumsy legitimate communications, and real emergencies. Overzealous scam awareness can mutate into cynicism, which is its own kind of vulnerability. Cynical people can be trapped too, often by being given a story that flatters their scepticism: "You are the only one who understands this." The point is not to treat every interaction as hostile; it is to notice the combination of levers, especially when they are deployed to compress time and isolate decision-making.

A useful way to remain honest is to acknowledge the counter-example that proves the rule: some fraud warnings are real, and taking them seriously is sensible. Banks do freeze cards. Online services do send password reset notices. Courier services do contact customers. Even friends do sometimes message in urgent tones. The difference is rarely the mere existence of urgency; it is the shape of the requested action and the channel used to request it. Legitimate processes tend to tolerate verification: they allow a person to pause, to call back via a known number, to log in via a saved bookmark, to check within an official app rather than through a random link. Scams tend to punish verification: they pressure, they flatter, they get irritated, they try to keep the victim inside the corridor.

This is where modern relevance becomes sharply practical. The scams most people encounter now are increasingly "hybrid": they combine small bits of real data with broad messaging. A delivery text might include a postcode fragment. A phishing email might include a real full name. A caller might reference a recent purchase. That is not magic; it is the downstream effect of leaked data, purchased marketing lists, and the ordinary exhaust of online life. The sophistication is less about technical trickery and more about the realism of the stage props. When the props improve, relying on instinctive "that looks fake" judgements becomes less reliable. The better habit is to notice the levers rather than the cosmetics.

A quiet motif can help here: the corridor. Many scams are corridors designed to keep a person moving forward. The corridor has a beginning (a ping), a narrowing (a threat or promise), and a door at the end (a link, a code, a payment). When a message tries to herd someone down a corridor, the most valuable act is to step sideways, back into open space. In open space, verification is possible. In open space, a second opinion can exist. In open space, the body calms, and a calmer body produces a better brain.

The corridor is especially dangerous when it is made social. "Your colleague needs this invoice paid." "Your boss asked you to buy gift cards." These scams are common because workplaces are built on delegated trust. A junior employee is trained to respond quickly to senior requests. A helpful colleague is trained to keep projects moving. The scammer uses organisational culture as a lever. The "Show" might be an email that appears to come from a manager, with a plausible tone and a plausible task. The "Name" is business email compromise, often abbreviated as BEC. The "Explain" is that compromising or spoofing email accounts allows criminals to imitate internal authority, and humans are more likely to comply with internal authority than external advertising. The "Implication" is that scams thrive where politeness and responsiveness are prized. Good cultures must learn to make verification socially acceptable.

For families, the same social lever appears in a different costume: fear for loved ones. Messages that claim a relative is stranded, in trouble, or needs urgent money aim straight for protective instincts. The request is often framed to bypass discussion: "Don't tell Mum, she'll worry." Secrecy appears again, now wrapped as kindness. The victim is asked to act alone, quickly, in order to be a good carer. The scam is not only stealing money; it is borrowing the victim's love as fuel.

That is why spotting scams is not a selfish skill. It is a protective habit that can be shared without turning into a lecture. Vulnerable relatives are often not vulnerable because they are unintelligent; they are vulnerable because they have different social norms. Many older adults were trained to trust institutions and to respond politely to official-sounding requests. Many teenagers are trained to respond quickly to peer pressure and to interpret social cues at high speed. Scammers tailor corridors to the norms of the audience. A household that understands the pattern can talk about the pattern rather than the shame of individual mistakes.

Evidence matters here, not to prove that scams exist—any inbox does that—but to ground the scale. The FBI's Internet Crime Complaint Center (IC3) has for years published annual reports showing large reported losses to internet-enabled crime, including phishing and confidence schemes, while also noting the likelihood of under-reporting because many victims never file complaints (FBI IC3, 2023). Numbers fluctuate and categories change, but the trend is stable: scams are not fringe. They are a regular tax on attention. They succeed not because every target is naïve, but because enough targets are human.

The human part is the point. If a scam were merely a puzzle of technical detection, then smarter people would be safe. Yet many of the victims of high-impact scams are competent professionals. Competence can even increase risk in specific ways. Competent people are used to solving problems quickly. They are used to being relied upon. They may feel responsible for preventing disruption. Scams exploit that sense of responsibility. The corridor becomes a test of competence: "Fix this now." A person who wants to be useful is tempted to comply in order to restore order. The scam is a counterfeit emergency that recruits the victim's identity as a fixer.

The deepest learning, then, is not a catalogue of tricks but a recognition of incentives. Scammers aim for high volume and low effort. They recycle scripts that work. They do not need to win every time; they need to win often enough. This is why the same words appear across years and countries, why the same fake delivery phrasing returns, why the same "security alert" style persists. The message is a tool, and tools are iterated. When a tool stops working, scammers adjust. When it works, they keep it.

So what does "spotting" mean in a rigorous sense? It means noticing when the message is structured to deprive the recipient of verification. It means noticing when the sender is asking for an unusual action through a convenient channel. It means noticing when an emotional state is being deliberately triggered. It means measuring the mismatch between the claimed identity and the requested behaviour. A bank that asks for a password via email is behaving oddly. A delivery company that demands immediate payment via a shortened link is behaving oddly. A new romantic interest who quickly asks for money, secrets, or isolation from friends is behaving oddly. Oddness is not proof, but it is a reason to slow down.

The chapter's larger arc depends on this slowing down, because later recovery steps are only useful if the next corridor is recognised early enough to avoid walking to the end. The reader does not need to become a detective. They need to become a tempo-setter. Scams are tempo games: the attacker sets a fast tempo, and the victim is meant to follow. A safe person sets their own tempo and refuses to outsource it to a stranger.

The corridor returns one last time as a forward test. The next message that arrives and demands speed will not announce itself as a scam. It will arrive dressed as normal life: a parcel, a password, a colleague, a lover, a warning. The diagnostic question is simple enough to remember when tired, and sharp enough to matter: is this message trying to keep the decision inside its corridor, or does it tolerate being checked from the outside?

What To Do After Breaches

On 6 September 2018, British Airways announced that customer data had been stolen through its website and mobile app, and that the incident affected personal and financial details during a defined period. In London, where so much of life is conducted between stations and meetings, the breach arrived for many people not as a headline but as an email glimpsed on a phone screen: a corporate logo, a clipped apology, a promise to investigate. The message sat among newsletters and receipts, another small rectangle asking for attention. For some, the first sensation was heat in the face, the quickened pulse that comes when a private life is abruptly made public in someone else's systems. Panic makes small mistakes multiply.

A breach notification is an odd kind of document. It is both mundane and intimate. It is written in a legalistic tone, but it speaks about you: your account, your details, your exposure. It often arrives late, after the event has already happened, and it rarely tells you what you most want to know. That gap—between the crispness of the email and the fuzziness of the reality—creates the perfect conditions for bad decisions. The mind hates uncertainty. It tries to close it fast.

The first discipline after a breach is not technical at all. It is tempo. Breaches create a trapdoor into urgency, and urgency is where secondary mistakes flourish: logging in through a fake link, resetting the wrong account, reusing the same "new" password everywhere, or trusting a convincing follow-up call. A good response begins by widening the corridor. The simplest move is to treat every inbound message about the breach as potentially related to the breach *and* potentially opportunistic. That sounds paranoid until one remembers how criminals operate: they read the news too, and they know that a freshly worried population is a profitable one.

A breach notification, when legitimate, is best read as a triage note rather than a full diagnosis. The most valuable information is usually buried in the plainest sentences. The "Show" is a familiar pattern: the notice states the organisation, the approximate time window, and the categories of data involved. The "Name" for this step is scope. The "Explain" is simple: different data types create different downstream risks. Names and email addresses are not the same as passwords; passwords are not the same as payment card numbers; and none of these is identical to identity documents. The "Implication" is that the response should match what was exposed, not the general dread the word "breach" produces.

A practical reading asks three quiet questions. What exactly was taken? How long does it remain useful to an attacker? Where else has the same information been used? The first question is about the breach itself. The second is about time: some stolen data expires in value quickly, while other data remains reusable for years. The third question is about reuse, which is where individual choices meet systemic failure. An organisation's security may have been the root cause, but the blast radius is often determined by whether the same credentials or recovery details sit across multiple services.

The most common hard outcome of a breach is not immediate theft from a bank account. It is account takeover via credential reuse and follow-on scams using leaked contact details. That is why the "routine" response so often begins with credentials, even when the breach did not clearly include passwords. The "Show" is the ordinary life of passwords: many people reuse them, or reuse the structure, or reuse the recovery email and security questions in ways that link accounts together. The "Name" is credential stuffing, the practice of trying known username–password pairs on many services because it works often enough to be worth automating. The "Explain" is that attackers do not need to crack a new password if they can borrow an old one from somewhere else. The "Implication" is that the response to a breach can be partly preventative even when the notification sounds vague, because the leak may still fuel targeted attempts elsewhere.

Equifax is the canonical example of how long the shadow can be. In September 2017, Equifax disclosed a breach that exposed sensitive personal information in the United States, with consequences that unfolded not in hours but over years. The "Show" was not just inconvenience; it was a change in how people thought about identity itself—something that could be copied, traded, and replayed. The "Name" is durable identifiers: data points that do not expire in the way a card number can be replaced. The "Explain" is that when durable identifiers escape, they become raw material for impersonation and persuasive fraud, even if no single victim sees an immediate loss. The "Implication" is that a calm response plan matters precisely because the harm can be delayed and indirect, arriving later as a strange phone call, a convincing letter, or a login attempt that "should not be possible".

So what does a plan actually look like, when it is stripped of drama and inflated promises? It looks like a drill—something practiced enough to be executed without improvisation. The word "drill" matters because drills are not performed in the middle of the fire; they are rehearsed so that the mind has a script when adrenaline arrives. In breach response, the drill begins by securing the accounts that control other accounts. Email is usually at the centre of that web because password resets flow through it, and because many services treat email access as proof of identity. When a person's email is compromised, everything else becomes harder. This is not ideology. It is mechanics.

From there, the plan becomes an exercise in ordering. The "Show" is a familiar post-breach behaviour: someone changes a few passwords at random, then stops, exhausted and unsure whether it mattered. The "Name" is incomplete remediation. The "Explain" is that partial fixes can create a false sense of safety while leaving the real choke points untouched. The "Implication" is that the response should be sequenced around leverage points—places where one change reduces multiple risks—rather than scattered across dozens of low-value accounts.

A useful plan distinguishes between accounts that hold money, accounts that hold identity, and accounts that hold social reach. A bank login is not the same as a music streaming login. An email inbox is not just messages; it is a control panel. A social account is not merely photos; it is an identity that can be used to manipulate others. When a breach occurs, the decision is less about "fix everything" and more about "protect the systems that can be used to pivot". The plan, done well, is boring. Boring is good.

The next discipline is verification. Breach notifications often contain links to "learn more" or "secure your account". Some are legitimate. Some are not. Criminals imitate breach notices because they know people will click. The "Show" is the plausible email: correct brand colours, familiar phrasing, an urgent suggestion to act. The "Name" is secondary phishing. The "Explain" is that a widely reported breach creates a temporary fog in which imitation is easier; people expect strange messages, so they lower their guard. The "Implication" is that a careful response treats links as untrusted by default, preferring known routes such as typing the organisation's address manually, using a bookmarked login page, or going through an official app rather than a message.

There is also a quiet emotional hazard: shame. Many people feel that being caught in a breach reflects a personal failure. It does not. A breach is primarily an organisational failure, often the result of neglected systems, flawed processes, or an adversary with time. Shame is useful only to criminals because it keeps victims silent and isolated. A plan that includes other people—family members, colleagues, anyone who might also be exposed—turns the response into shared hygiene rather than solitary embarrassment. That matters not for moral reasons, but for practical ones: attackers often move through social graphs. A compromised account is a launching pad for convincing messages to friends and colleagues.

The second named example worth holding in mind is the Marriott/Starwood incident, disclosed in November 2018, which involved guest reservation data connected to a global hospitality chain. The "Show" was not just stolen records; it was the unsettling idea that travel histories and contact details could be exposed as a by-product of ordinary life. The "Name" is aggregation risk: the fact that one service can hold a surprisingly complete portrait because it sits at a junction of identity, payment, and movement. The "Explain" is that the modern consumer relationship is not a single transaction; it is a long-running dossier. The "Implication" is that breach response is not merely about the breached company; it is about recognising which kinds of companies act as data hubs and treating them as high-stakes accounts even if they feel mundane.

A credible limitation deserves honesty here: sometimes the rational response is smaller than the fear suggests. Not every breach includes usable credentials. Sometimes data is encrypted well enough to be effectively useless without additional keys. Sometimes the "breach notice" is legally required disclosure for a narrow incident with limited impact. And sometimes the most damaging thing a person can do is to churn passwords impulsively, locking themselves out of accounts or weakening security by choosing memorable but predictable replacements under stress. The plan must therefore include restraint. Restraint is not inaction. It is targeted action, matched to credible exposure, executed deliberately.

That is where monitoring becomes part of the drill—without turning into obsession. Monitoring is simply the practice of noticing signals that something has changed: a login alert you did not trigger, an unexpected password reset email, a new device listed in an account's security page, a message in a sent folder you do not recognise. These are behavioural indicators, not theoretical risks. They can be checked quickly and periodically, the way one checks that a door is locked without spending all day staring at it. When organisations such as the UK National Cyber Security Centre publish guidance on responding to cyber incidents, the underlying logic is consistent: focus on account control, verify communications, and reduce opportunities for attackers to reuse stolen data. The point is not to become a security analyst. It is to keep ownership of one's identity and access.

The drill metaphor returns because it captures the emotional truth. During a real fire drill, people do not invent new routes while smoke rises; they follow a rehearsed path. After a breach, the rehearsed path is: slow down, verify the message, identify what was exposed, secure the accounts that can reset other accounts, and then work outward to the services most likely to be abused for impersonation or financial harm. Each step has a purpose. Each step reduces a specific risk. The order matters.

There is an additional, easily missed payoff to having a drill. It changes how a person experiences breach headlines. Without a plan, a headline feels like a personal threat—another wave in a sea of uncontrollable surveillance. With a plan, the headline becomes information: relevant, sometimes annoying, but not spiritually destabilising. The reader is no longer stuck choosing between panic and denial. There is a third option: method.

The unresolved tension that remains—because it is real—is that no individual can prevent breaches from happening. Systems fail. Organisations make trade-offs. Attackers adapt. The forward test, then, is not whether technology can be made perfect, but whether a person's response can be made reliable: when the next notification arrives, will it pull you into its urgency, or will you recognise it as the starting gun for a drill you already know how to run?

Recovering Compromised Accounts

On 7 January 2020, Twitter confirmed that attackers had used social engineering to gain access to internal systems, later enabling account takeovers of prominent users. The episode is remembered for public tweets, but the more instructive detail was quieter: the intrusion did not begin with exotic code, it began with a conversation, a change of hands, a door opened from the inside. In San Francisco, where many of those systems were administered, the incident became a lesson in modern fragility. A single compromised pathway can turn identity into a puppet. A phone vibrates. A notification lands. Something that feels like "you" is suddenly acting without you.

Account compromise rarely arrives with cinematic clarity. It is more often discovered in the margins: a password reset email you did not request, a security alert about a login from a city you have never visited, a friend asking why you sent them a strange link, an unfamiliar forwarding rule in your inbox, a new recovery number you do not recognise. The sensory experience is peculiar. The room is the same, the kettle whistles, the laptop keycaps feel unchanged under your fingers, and yet there is a new presence in the digital house—someone else moving through corridors that used to be yours.

The first task is not revenge, nor cleverness. It is containment. A five-word sentence matters here: *Stop the bleeding, then think.* That is not bravado; it is the recognition that compromised accounts behave like falling dominoes. Each account that controls another becomes a lever. If the lever remains in the wrong hands, every later fix becomes reversible.

The most important concept to name early is the control plane. Email, and sometimes a primary phone number, sits at the centre of most people's account ecosystems because password resets, verification codes, and security alerts funnel through them. If an attacker has your email, they may not need your bank password; they can request a reset. If they have your phone number, they may be able to intercept some forms of verification. The "Show" is the common pattern: a person races to change the password on a social account, only to see it taken again hours later. The "Name" is compromised recovery channel. The "Explain" is that recovery channels are effectively master keys. The "Implication" is that the first recovery work should target the master keys, not the most emotionally upsetting symptoms.

A calm approach begins by deciding which device to trust. That decision is more practical than philosophical. If the device you are using is itself compromised, it can steal new passwords as fast as you type them. If you have access to a second device you use less often—perhaps a work laptop with managed security, or a tablet that has not been used for casual downloads—this becomes valuable. The motif worth carrying through the recovery is a simple one: a keyring. Accounts are keys; email is the keyring; a compromised keyring makes replacing one key meaningless because the thief can simply take the replacements.

Once the trusted device is chosen, the next move is to secure the email account that anchors everything. The "Show" is the inbox as control room: it contains password reset links, archived statements, and years of identity traces that make impersonation easier. The "Name" is account takeover recovery. The "Explain" is that email providers typically offer a specific set of security pages: recent activity, signed-in devices, connected apps, forwarding rules, and recovery details. The "Implication" is that recovery is as much about removing hidden access as it is about changing a password.

Hidden access is where people lose. An attacker who has been inside an email account may create a forwarding rule that quietly sends copies of messages to another address, or may add an app with permission to read mail, or may change recovery options. Those changes are designed to persist after the victim performs the obvious fix. The recovery mindset therefore treats password changes as necessary but insufficient. It searches for persistence mechanisms—ways to remain present after the door has been locked. Persistence is the right word because it matches how attackers think: not "one-off theft", but "ongoing foothold".

A second named, checkable incident makes the point from another angle. In 2016, journalists and researchers reported on SIM-swap attacks being used against individuals to capture SMS-based authentication codes, with cases documented in the United States and elsewhere. The "Show" is the sudden loss of phone service, or unexpected messages from a mobile provider, followed by account reset notifications. The "Name" is SIM swapping (or SIM hijacking). The "Explain" is that if a phone number is treated as identity proof, whoever controls that number can receive verification codes. The "Implication" is not that phones are futile, but that the recovery path must consider whether an attacker controls the number, not merely the accounts behind it.

This is why the ordered approach is so powerful. Email first. Then phone number if it is used widely for verification. Then the accounts that can cause the greatest harm quickly: financial accounts, services that store payment methods, and then social accounts that can be used to scam friends and colleagues. The order is not moral; it is economic. Financial systems can leak money and create debt. Social systems can leak trust and create secondary victims.

Talking to support teams is often the least glamorous part of this. It is also where recovery either succeeds cleanly or turns into weeks of frustration. The "Show" is the familiar support loop: an automated chatbot, a form, a response that feels as if it came from a different planet. The "Name" is identity verification. The "Explain" is that providers must avoid handing accounts to impostors, so they require evidence that can feel invasive or arbitrary. The "Implication" is that recovery is smoother when a person can supply consistent, verifiable details quickly—without improvising under stress.

Evidence tends to fall into a few practical categories: proof of previous access (old passwords, approximate creation date, last successful login), proof of billing relationship (last four digits of a card used, transaction IDs, invoice numbers), proof of identity (for some services), and proof of device continuity (recognised devices, browser fingerprints, recovery codes). The crucial behaviour is not collecting every possible piece of evidence, but keeping the story coherent. Support staff—human or automated—are trying to match the claimant to the account history. Coherence is a metric. Contradictions trigger delays.

A limitation deserves to be stated plainly: sometimes recovery is not possible. Accounts created with throwaway details, or services that offer minimal support, can be effectively unrecoverable once an attacker has changed recovery channels. Some providers are excellent; some are brittle. And sometimes the most rational option is to treat the account as lost, mitigate damage, and move on—particularly if it is low value and high friction. Still, even this limitation can be reconciled with the ordered mindset: if the keyring is secured early, the number of unrecoverable accounts that matter shrinks dramatically.

Understanding how the incident happened is not a forensic hobby; it is the difference between recovery and recurrence. The "Show" is a common tragedy: a person regains an account, then loses it again because the original pathway remains open. The "Name" is root cause analysis, borrowed from engineering. The "Explain" is that without an explanation of the breach pathway—phishing link, reused password, compromised device, support-team manipulation—the fix is guesswork. The "Implication" is that a short, honest reconstruction of events is part of regaining control, not an optional extra.

Reconstruction can be mundane. A browser extension installed in haste. A document opened from an email that mimicked a delivery company. A password reused from an old forum breach. A public computer used to check email while travelling. Each is a small act. Each is a crack in the wall. The recovery mindset does not moralise these acts. It measures them. It treats them as data points in a timeline.

The timeline matters because compromise often involves a sequence, not a single moment. An attacker may first gain access to a newsletter account, then use that to search for other services associated with the email address, then attempt password resets, then use the inbox contents to answer security questions or to craft convincing messages to a bank. The "Show" is the attacker reading your life like a manual. The "Name" is account chaining. The "Explain" is that accounts are not isolated; they are connected by email, phone numbers, shared passwords, and stored payment tokens. The "Implication" is that the recovery plan must break chains, not merely replace one link.

When the recovery reaches social accounts, the problem shifts from money to reputation. Social accounts are identity amplifiers. If an attacker controls a social profile, they can use it to ask friends for "urgent help", to distribute malicious links, or to impersonate the victim in ways that cause real-world consequences. The recovery "Show" is a friend receiving a message that sounds almost right, with just enough wrongness to be unsettling. The "Name" is trusted-channel exploitation. The "Explain" is that people believe messages from known accounts more readily than messages from strangers. The "Implication" is that swift, clear communication—through alternative channels—can reduce harm to others even while the victim is still regaining control.

There is a subtle psychological trap here. Many people feel they must act alone, quietly, until everything is fixed. Silence can be costly. A short message to close contacts through a different channel—"My account may be compromised; ignore unusual messages"—can stop a cascade. It is also a reminder that privacy and security are social phenomena. They are not merely settings. They are relationships.

The keyring motif returns at this stage because it keeps the mind focused on what matters. During recovery, it is tempting to obsess over the most vivid symptom: the hijacked profile photo, the spam posts, the altered bio. Those are humiliating. They are also superficial compared to the keyring. If the keyring is safe, cosmetic damage can be repaired. If the keyring is not safe, cosmetic repairs are a theatre.

Another limitation worth naming is time. Providers may take days to respond. Some recovery processes are intentionally slow because speed helps attackers too. This creates an uncomfortable interval where the victim is neither fully locked out nor fully in control. The practical implication is that recovery includes patience as a security measure. Rushing often produces the very errors attackers rely on: sharing codes over the phone, clicking links from messages, trusting inbound "support" calls that are in fact predators circling a wounded account.

This is why a disciplined approach contains a small set of recurring checks: confirm which devices are signed in, confirm whether recovery options changed, confirm whether new apps have access, confirm whether forwarding rules exist, confirm whether any accounts are linked through single sign-on. Each check is a simple act of verification. Together, they create confidence that is earned rather than wished for.

Underneath all of this is a deeper point about identity. Digital identity is not a single credential. It is an accumulation of claims: an email address used for years, a phone number that appears on forms, a set of devices that regularly sign in, payment methods attached to subscriptions, and patterns of behaviour that providers treat as normal. When an account is compromised, the attacker is not merely stealing access; they are borrowing your normal. Recovery is the process of reclaiming normality, piece by piece, and then tightening the system so that the attacker cannot borrow it again.

The forward tension at the end of recovery is not whether you can secure every account perfectly. It is whether you can answer one diagnostic question honestly: after control is restored, will the next change be to the locks, or to the keyring itself? If the keyring remains sprawling—too many accounts, too many recovery channels, too much reuse—then the next compromise is not a thunderbolt. It is a probability waiting for a moment.

Building Lasting Privacy Habits

On 1 October 2016, in London, the UK's National Cyber Security Centre opened its doors and began publishing public guidance aimed not at spies or banks, but at ordinary households and ordinary working lives. That institutional shift was quietly radical. It treated digital safety less as a specialist discipline and more as public hygiene: the sort of thing you do because you live among other people. The same week, across thousands of kitchens and commute routes, nothing visibly changed. Phones still buzzed. Laptops still slept and woke. Yet the underlying claim had altered: security was no longer a once-a-year panic after a bad headline, but a set of habits that could be learned, repeated, and made boring.

Boring is underrated. Boring is durable. Boring survives stress. A privacy practice that only works when you feel motivated is not a practice; it is a mood. The trouble is that digital life constantly invites moods—fear, urgency, curiosity, convenience—and each mood has an "accept" button attached. If privacy is to become a way of living rather than a series of heroic weekends, it must sit below the mood layer. It must live where teeth brushing lives. No one wakes up thrilled to floss. People floss anyway.

A five-word sentence matters here: *Habits beat intentions, every time.* That is not a slogan; it is an observation about attention. Modern systems are designed to consume attention precisely because attention is the throttle controlling data. If you decide, each time, whether to grant access, whether to share, whether to log in, whether to keep an app, you will lose—not because you are foolish, but because you are human and busy. The practical question is therefore not "What is the perfect setting?" but "What is the smallest repeatable behaviour that keeps me roughly pointed in the right direction?"

Behavioural science offers a useful anchor. In a widely cited study at University College London, Lally and colleagues followed participants forming everyday habits and reported that automaticity—behaviour becoming more effortless—took, on average, about 66 days, with wide variation depending on the person and the behaviour (Lally et al., 2010). The number is not magical. The implication is. If habit formation takes weeks, then privacy routines should be designed like training plans: small, consistent, and forgiving of missed sessions. If you try to "fix everything" on a Saturday, you will likely create an impressive spreadsheet and an exhausted future self who avoids looking at it again.

The first move in making privacy last is to choose reliable triggers—existing moments in life that already happen. The visible behaviour might be mundane: paying a bill, filing tax documents, switching the clocks, doing the annual boiler service, packing for travel, replacing smoke-alarm batteries. The name for this strategy is *habit stacking*, popularised in modern form by writers such as James Clear, but older than the phrase itself: you attach a new behaviour to an old one so the old one carries the new one into the calendar. The explanation is that the brain is better at recognising an existing routine than at remembering a novel obligation. The implication is that privacy becomes less dependent on willpower and more dependent on the passage of time.

Time, in this context, is not a vague concept. It is a schedule with texture. Consider tax time: in the UK, the self-assessment deadline on 31 January is an annual rhythm that forces many people to gather documents, check accounts, and reconcile information. That is an ideal moment to do a quick audit of what matters most: your primary email account's recovery options, the presence of two-factor authentication on accounts with payment methods, and whether old cloud links are still public. The behaviour is checking a small set of things at a moment you are already handling sensitive material. The name is a *privacy checkpoint*. The explanation is that you are already in a "serious paperwork" mode, which makes the friction feel lower. The implication is a routine that piggybacks on an unavoidable deadline rather than competing with it.

Now bring in a second named example that illustrates how defaults change beneath our feet, making routines necessary even for competent people. In September 2017, the US National Institute of Standards and Technology (NIST) updated its digital identity guidance, including advice that pushed against old folklore—such as mandatory periodic password changes without evidence of compromise—and emphasised screening against commonly used or breached passwords (NIST SP 800-63B, 2017). The show is the professional world revising what it considers sensible. The name is standards evolution. The explanation is that threats and evidence change, and so do best practices. The implication is that a privacy habit cannot be "set and forget" because the ground moves: platforms update, defaults shift, products age, and yesterday's sensible compromise becomes tomorrow's soft target.

That shifting ground is why lasting habits should focus less on specific tools and more on stable principles expressed as visible decisions. "Reduce exposure" becomes "decline permissions you do not need". "Limit persistence" becomes "delete accounts you no longer use". "Control recovery" becomes "keep recovery channels current and protected". "Contain damage" becomes "separate high-value accounts from casual sign-ups". Each principle translates into a decision you can actually perform in minutes. If a principle cannot be performed, it is not yet a habit; it is a philosophy seminar.

A recurring motif helps unify this without turning it into moral theatre. The motif I recommend is *housekeeping*. Not the glamorous kind—no white-gloved inspectors—but the everyday kind: emptying a bin, checking the lock, filing a receipt, putting a spare key somewhere sensible. Housekeeping is what stops small messes becoming infestations. Digital housekeeping does the same. A single unchecked permission here, a forgotten account there, a cloud folder shared "temporarily" three years ago: tiny neglects accumulate. You have already seen that logic throughout this book. The finishing move is to make housekeeping periodic, not emotional.

Periodicity also solves a problem professionals often underestimate: decision fatigue. Each privacy decision has an opportunity cost. Every minute spent reviewing settings is a minute not spent doing work, parenting, resting, or simply living. A sustainable system acknowledges that cost openly. It does not pretend you will become a monastic auditor of your own metadata. Instead, it limits the number of decisions by batching them into short sessions. One session might be fifteen minutes at the start of each season. Another might be five minutes on the first working day of each month. The exact rhythm matters less than the existence of one.

Imperfection is not merely tolerable; it is structural. People travel. People get ill. People take on new jobs. Teenagers install apps at speed. Elderly relatives click things. A privacy system that collapses when life becomes messy was never designed for real life. The credible counter-example here is the perfectionist approach: the person who decides to replace every service, migrate every password, remove every photo from the cloud, and reconfigure every device at once. Sometimes it works, particularly for those who enjoy technical projects. More often, it produces a week of intense effort followed by months of avoidance because the standard set was too high to maintain. The reconciliation is simple: aim for *resilience*, not purity.

Resilience means the system keeps working when you miss a step. Purity means the system only works when you behave flawlessly. Choose resilience.

Resilience is also social. Privacy habits endure when they are shareable in a household or team without becoming oppressive. The behaviour might be as small as a shared rule: "We do not post children's photos without asking," or "We do not share passwords by message," or "We do not connect unknown devices to the main Wi-Fi." The name is *norm-setting*. The explanation is that norms reduce negotiation; they turn repeated debates into defaults. The implication is fewer arguments and fewer rushed exceptions. Importantly, norms can be gentle. They do not require surveillance. They require clarity.

One of the most overlooked parts of lasting privacy is ritualising the boring maintenance that prevents panic later. Backups are the obvious example, but the deeper category is *recovery readiness*. That includes keeping a small, accurate record of which email address is the recovery address for which account, whether recovery codes exist, and where they are stored. The decision is whether you want to treat recovery as a future emergency or as present housekeeping. The implication is stark: emergencies are expensive. Housekeeping is cheap.

Another durable habit is learning to notice "creep". Creep is what happens when a system quietly expands: another account tied to the main email, another payment method stored for convenience, another device signed in "just for a moment", another app granted location access because it nagged you twice. Creep is not villainy; it is drift. The behaviour is periodic drift correction. The name is *baseline reset*. The explanation is that you periodically return to a known-good configuration: a main browser with sensible defaults, a clean separation between high-value and casual accounts, and devices that are updated and locked. The implication is that privacy becomes a maintained posture rather than a fading memory of what you once configured.

This is also where kindness to your future self becomes part of the ethic. The future self is the one who inherits your rushed decisions, your messy folders, your abandoned accounts, and your half-configured settings. You can either burden that person with archaeology, or you can leave them a tidy map. The difference is not intelligence. It is habit.

Of course, some friction is unavoidable. Stronger privacy often costs something: time, convenience, or money. The lasting habit is not eliminating trade-offs. It is making them deliberate. A concrete example: choosing to use a "clean" browser for sensitive tasks costs you the mild annoyance of switching apps; in exchange, it reduces cross-site tracking and accidental login persistence. Another example: declining a loyalty scheme costs you a few pence of discount; in exchange, it reduces the data trail attached to your shopping habits. These are not moral commandments. They are micro-economics. Measure the cost. Choose the value.

A final thread worth pulling is identity as narrative. Privacy habits are easier to maintain when they match the person you believe yourself to be. If you see yourself as someone who keeps a tidy desk, digital housekeeping fits. If you see yourself as someone who protects their family, asking before sharing fits. If you see yourself as someone who values autonomy, reducing unnecessary data sharing fits. This is not sentimental. It is behavioural. People consistently act to preserve their self-concept. The implication is that framing privacy as "paranoia" makes it brittle, but framing it as "autonomy" makes it durable.

The book's last message, then, is not that you will finish privacy. You will not. New services will appear. Old ones will decay. Devices will be replaced. Relationships will change. Work will shift. There is no stable end-state, and pretending otherwise creates shame when reality intrudes. The better aim is a life in which your technology obeys you more often than it obeys other people's incentives, and where the maintenance required to keep it that way is small enough to repeat.

The forward test is this: when you look at your next month—not an imaginary month, the real one with deadlines and interruptions—what is the smallest piece of digital housekeeping you can attach to something you already do, so that your privacy improves even when you are tired?

About the Author

Omar Valen cares about helping ordinary people feel at home in a digital world that often treats them as raw material. For years he has sat at kitchen tables and in crowded living rooms, untangling privacy settings and explaining jargon to friends, relatives, and neighbours who want to stay connected without feeling exposed. His work grows from those conversations rather than from laboratories or boardrooms.

Raised in a noisy city where doors were often left on the latch but serious topics were discussed in low voices, Omar learnt early that privacy is not about hiding; it is about choosing who needs to know what. That childhood mix of openness and discretion shapes his approach to technology today.

He writes and teaches in plain language, preferring examples drawn from school runs, family group chats, and shared laptops rather than abstract theory. Omar's aim is not to turn readers into security experts, but to give them the confidence to make small, steady changes that add up. Private, Not Hidden reflects his belief that good privacy is a normal life skill, like locking your front door or closing the curtains at night: simple, human, and entirely compatible with joy.

9 789376 558667

Printed at Repro India Ltd.